7/09

THEATERS

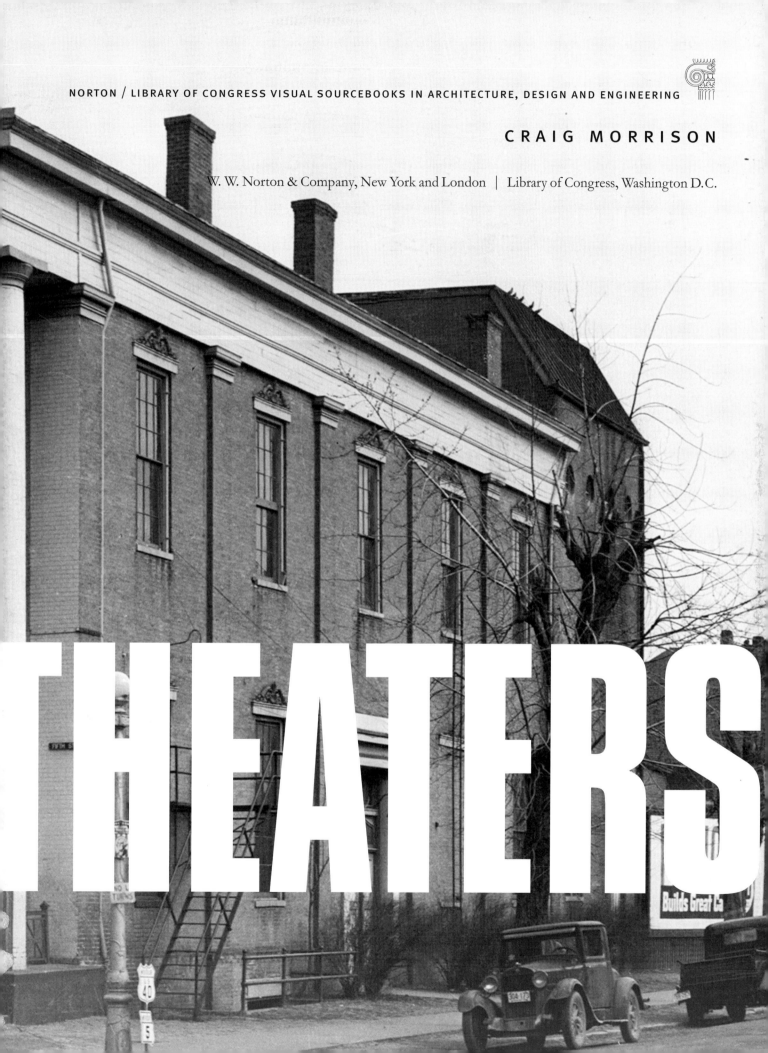

NORTON / LIBRARY OF CONGRESS VISUAL SOURCEBOOKS IN ARCHITECTURE, DESIGN AND ENGINEERING

CRAIG MORRISON

W. W. Norton & Company, New York and London | Library of Congress, Washington D.C.

THEATERS

TO DEBBIE KINZER

For information about permission to reproduce selections from this book, write to
Permissions, W. W. Norton & Company, Inc., 500 Fifth Avenue, New York, NY 10110

Manufacturing by Courier-Westford
Book design by Kristina Kachele Design LLC
Composition and paging by Ken Gross
Production manager: Leeann Graham
Indexing by Bob Elwood

Library of Congress Cataloging-in-Publication Data
Morrison, Andrew Craig
  Theaters / Craig Morrison.
    p. cm. — (Norton/Library of Congress visual sourcebooks in architecture, design, and engineering)
  Includes bibliographical references and index.
  ISBN 0-393-73108-1
    1. Theater architecture—United States. 2. Theater and society—United States. I. Title. II. Series.

NA6830.M67 2005
725'.822'0973—dc22   2005048839

W. W. Norton & Company, Inc.   W. W. Norton & Company Ltd.
500 Fifth Avenue   Castle House, 75/76 Wells St.
New York, N.Y. 10110   London W1T 3QT

0 9 8 7 6 5 4 3 2 1

CONTENTS

The Center for Architecture, Design and Engineering and the Publishing Office of the Library of Congress are pleased to join with W. W. Norton & Company to publish the pioneering series of the Norton / Library of Congress Visual Sourcebooks in Architecture, Design and Engineering.

Based on the unparalleled collections of the Library of Congress, this series of handsomely illustrated books draws from the collections of the nation's oldest federal cultural institution and the largest library in the world, with more than 130 million items on approximately 530 miles of bookshelves. The collections include more than 19 million books, 2.7 million recordings, 12 million photographs, 4.8 million maps, and 58 million manuscripts.

The subjects of architecture, design, and engineering are threaded throughout the rich fabric of this vast archive, and the books in this new series will serve not only to introduce researchers to the illustrations selected by their authors, but also to build pathways to adjacent and related materials, and even entire archives — to millions of photographs, drawings, prints, views, maps, rare publications, and written information in the general and special collections of the Library of Congress, much of it unavailable elsewhere.

Each volume serves as an entry to the collections, providing a treasury of select visual material, much of it in the public domain, for students, scholars, teachers, researchers, historians of art, architecture, design, technology, and practicing architects, engineers, and designers of all kinds.

A CD-ROM accompanying each volume contains high-quality, downloadable versions of all the illustrations. It offers a direct link to the Library's online, searchable catalogs and image files, including the hundreds of thousands of high-resolution photographs, measured drawings, and data files in the Historic American Buildings Survey, Historic American Engineering Record, and, eventually, the recently inaugurated Historic American Landscape Survey. The Library's Web site has rapidly become one of the most popular and valuable locations on the Internet, experiencing over three billion hits a year and serving audiences ranging from school children to the most advanced scholars throughout the world, with a potential usefulness that has only begun to be explored.

Among the subjects to be covered in this series are building types, building materials and details; historical periods and movements; landscape architecture and garden design; interior and ornamental design and furnishings; and industrial design. *Theaters* is an excellent exemplar of the goals and possibilities on which its series is based.

JAMES H. BILLINGTON
THE LIBRARIAN OF CONGRESS

The introduction to this book provides an overview of the development of theaters in the United States. It is a view that is broad and inspired by the depth and quality of the resources of the Library of Congress. The balance of the book, containing 1,132 images, which can be found on the CD at the back of the book, is organized into nine sections and two "interludes." Figure-number prefixes designate the section; the abbreviations "Art" and "Lens" designate the interludes.

Captions give the essential identifying information: subject, location, opening date, architect(s), creator(s) of the image, date, and Library of Congress call number, which can be used to find the image online. Note that a link to the Library of Congress Web site may be found on the CD.

DPCC	Detroit Publishing Company Collection
FSA	Farm Security Administration
Gen. Coll.	General Collection
HABS	Historic American Building Survey
LC	Library of Congress
P&P	Prints and Photographs Division

THEATERS IN AMERICA

THEATERS AS A BUILDING TYPE

Theaters are special places. Large or small, lavish or Spartan, they are steeped in good memories and good associations. People have gathered in them to laugh, to cry, to learn, sometimes to love. In them children have giggled, teens have had their first dates, young adults have courted, families have bonded, and elders have reminisced. Through careful design, theaters have been places of comfort and welcome. As buildings, they have received widespread popular admiration. They have been looked upon as urban monuments, often the largest and most richly embellished of a community's buildings.

A theater is expected to have a pretty face, but behind its facade it is a complex building that must satisfy multiple demands. To an audience member it is an environment of comfort and often lavish beauty. To a performer it is a highly specialized workplace. To its operator it is a rough-and-tumble business venue, where entertainment is a commodity to be sold. It is a place where people of varied sorts and kinds, even some who might otherwise avoid one another, feel welcome and at ease. To fulfill the expectations of this functional and social mix is a formidable design challenge. To meet its specialized needs, a live-performance theater usually must be a windowless box with one end rising awkwardly above the rest. A movie theater, which requires only a rudimentary stage, may be more comfortably rectilinear, but it remains a solid shell, its bulk relieved only by an assortment of blank doors arrayed at odd levels and connected by the spidery lines of code-mandated steel fire escapes. A theater's often diminutive street facade is expected to be an essay in design that exemplifies good taste even as it may throw it to the winds. It is an architectural advertisement, sometimes calmly distinguished, sometimes as gaudily dramatic as the performances that are given within. Often its most distinctive features are the great marquee and soaring electric sign that override and sometimes conceal the architect's best efforts and shape the theater's primary public identity.

Within, a theater is historically a sequence of sizable, highly decorated rooms. But inside as out, function precludes the balance and symmetry that architects seek to achieve. An auditorium's focus is at one end, with all lines fanning outward and upward from the great maw of the proscenium. By necessity its floor is bowled with a tilt that places it at variance with the plumb and level lines of the walls. Its spatial volume is interrupted by the stepped wedges of one or more balconies. The equipment that provides brilliantly controlled lighting and powerfully effective sound intrudes upon the decorative elegance. Spotlights and movie-projectors' beams must be unobstructed on their path to the stage or screen. Yet, through all the technological clutter, an audience expects to find itself in the comfortable splendor of an elegant salon.

America's most noted architects rarely designed theaters. Most were done by architects who specialized in theater design and whose names are not generally known. Although Louis Sullivan—strongly girded by the technological expertise of his partner, Dankmar Adler—briefly made them a specialty, those who defined and perfected the theater's form generally were far removed from the architectural pantheon. Earliest among America's theater specialists was John M. Trimble, who worked from New York in the decades before the Civil War. His thirty-two-plus theaters rose as far afield as North Carolina and Ohio (see 1-029). After the war, several theater specialists developed busy regional and national practices. Leon H. Lempert worked in the vicinity of Rochester, New York; Oscar Cobb's influence radiated from Chicago. The entrepreneurial J. M. Wood, who always called himself "Colonel," designed, and sometimes operated, theaters across the Midwest and in California. Most prolific of the specialists was the canny and sometimes irascible J. B. McElfatrick. Working from St. Louis and New York, he and his two sons designed hundreds of theaters from coast to coast. Like all architects of the day, these men learned their trade through apprenticeship. Their designs were pragmatic, the fruits of experience. In an era before photographs were published, they used printed sketches as guides to emulate European prototypes that they never had actually visited. McElfatrick is said to have attended his first theatrical performance at the opening of a theater of his own design!

The twentieth century fostered a new generation of architects who far outpaced their predecessors in education, travel, and design sophistication. Thomas White Lamb, a Scot transplanted to New York, assumed McElfatrick's mantle as America's most prolific theater designer. First for vaudeville entrepreneurs, then for their moving-picture counterparts, he worked in the delicately elegant neoclassical style popularized by the Adam brothers in eighteenth-century England (see 4-066). Although it became Lamb's trademark, the Adam style was frequently borrowed by others. C. Howard Crane used it often, first in his home city, Detroit, then across the country. The Midwest produced two prominent teams of brothers. Cornelius W. (C. W.) and George L. Rapp, of Chicago, defined the movie-palace form. The florid richness of their baroque style was never surpassed (see 6-117). Farther west, Kansas City's Boller Brothers brought a high level of theater design to Missouri, Kansas, and Oklahoma. The West Coast produced its own roster—G. Albert Lansburgh, of San Francisco, and B. Marcus Priteca, of Seattle, whose work strongly recalled that of Lamb and the Rapps. Unique in the confraternity was John Eberson, of Chicago and New York, who brought to movie theater design the exoticism that became its ultimate defining quality (see 6-158).

AN AUDIENCE

A theater's two users—those who entertain and those who are entertained—diverge widely in their needs, habits, and expectations, considerations that must be balanced by the theater's operator as they are translated into building form. An American theater operator is an entrepreneur, driven by the laws of the marketplace. Working without the royal subsidies that enabled Europe's great opera halls, operators seek always to satisfy the most people at the least cost and in the least amount of space.

Performers, although exalted in the public perception and essential to attracting business, are to operators no more than employees, whose temperamental nature must be tolerated. Actors arrive early and leave late, usually through a stage door removed from the public eye, and are generally provided only the most utilitarian accommodations. To a performer, physical comfort is a scarce and welcome treat. To the audience, comfort and elegance are essential and integral to the theatrical experience. These qualities are relative, though, and expectations have increased over time. America's early theatergoers tended to come and go during a performance; they moved about the building but did not congregate outside the auditorium. America's early theater operators, therefore, were frugal with circulation space. Today, the audience arrives in a trickle but leaves en masse. They gather during formal intermissions to eat, drink, and socialize, a practice that requires a large and attractive lobby and commodious amenities. Demands vary among performance types: The standards of appearance, comfort, service, and courtesy expected by an opera audience are different from those usually found at a rock music concert.

By tradition, ticket holders are seated on the basis of admission price and, once seated, are discouraged from moving to other, more expensive areas of the auditorium. The balance of firmness and subtlety by which this separation is enforced has evolved over time. Box seats, provided with individual chairs, traditionally have been looked upon as places of special status. Although once available only by prior arrangement and with their privacy protected by lockable doors, they now usually are open to anyone who purchases a seat in them. Low-priced seating always has been located at a theater's least desirable level, a place that has shifted in time from the auditorium's bottom to its top. For more than a century cheap seats were unassigned, undivided, unupholstered wooden benches that would be unacceptable today.

Safety has been a concern through most of America's theater history. Fires, which were frighteningly common during the nineteenth century, caused many people to feel anxious while attending a show and others to avoid the theater entirely. When the benches moved from the main floor to the upper gallery, their former location was filled with dangerously crowded loose chairs with no formal aisles or passages. The upper levels often were served by a single stairway, even in gaslit wooden buildings; smoking was a common practice. The adoption of ever more stringent design and safety regulations, beginning early in the twentieth century, made theaters at last safe and secure.

From every seat, the audience expects to see and hear without interference. The box partitions and support columns that characterized America's early playhouses disappeared as engineering technology and steel construction permitted the wide-spanning cantilevered balconies that have become universal today.

A critical aspect of theater design has been the evolving control of interaction between actors and audience and between various groups within the audience itself. Although the degree and means of control have changed, the separation between actors and audiences has become progressively firmer even as audiences, once strictly divided by race and social class, have become more homogeneous. Although experimental dramatists have relaxed audience/actor separation through such devices as theater "in the round," mainstream presenters have maintained the concept of the proscenium as a fourth wall dividing the stage from the seats.

EARLY THEATERS

America acquired cultural unity by fits and starts. For a century and a half after its first settlement, the nascent nation was a set of disparate and fiercely independent colonies that often seemed to share little other than language. Thrown together by circumstances into uneasy union, the former colonists labored for another three-quarters of a century to build a new society. By declaration it was to be unified, democratic, and founded upon personal equality; in reality it remained rigidly stratified. In its early years, when gentry, merchants, artisans, and laborers constituted classes that interacted only hesitantly and with an element of discomfort, a theater was one of the few places where they could gather with ease and commonality. To create that meeting ground was a tall order.

Prerevolutionary America provided little opportunity for innovative theater design. Indeed, there was little theater design at all. Protestant asceticism, widespread in the new nation, held that moral strength could be derived only through hard work and hard worship. Within that ethic, theater was considered an instrument of the devil, sometimes legally proscribed as a moral offense and a conspicuous waste. Nevertheless, theatrical activity persisted. By the end of the eighteenth century, especially in the developing cities, the climate began to change.

Theater almost always has been an urban phenomenon. To flourish, it requires audiences that are sizable and sophisticated. In Charleston, Williamsburg, Boston, Philadelphia, and New York, purpose-built theaters began to appear shortly after the Revolution, though for a number of years America's greatest metropolis, Philadelphia, banned theater entirely within its corporate limits. When George Washington and his compatriots sought entertainment, they were compelled to cross South Street, the city's boundary. They did so often enough that the Southwark Theater became a cultural monument.

Serious theater building began some twenty years after independence. Because it was a land of former British colonies, it is not surprising that America's earliest theater forms derived from memories of England. To understand them, we must look back to the place that the colonists had left behind.

The most notable of Elizabethan England's theaters was the Globe, William Shakespeare's professional home, built in 1599 and reconstructed after a 1614 fire. Its form originated in the show wagon, a curtain-enclosed mobile stage that could be pulled into a place of public gathering. From it, shows, generally of a religious nature, were presented to spectators who stood on the pavement around the wagon or watched from nearby balconies and windows. The permanent theaters that evolved from this arrangement were roughly cylindrical buildings, hollow, with thatched roofs. Inside, three tiers of roofed seating galleries overlooked an open yard into which the stage projected. Above the stage, supported by two ornamental columns, was an operating loft from which scenic pieces could be lowered. Called the "heavens," its soffit was painted to resemble the sky. The stage was open on three sides, but enclosed at the rear. Its back wall contained a curtained opening, the proscenium of an inner stage. Doors on each

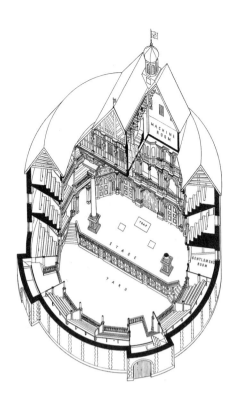

IN-001. The Globe Theater. America's first permanent playhouses were built in the 1760s. Their general form was an enclosed version of Shakespeare's Globe Theatre. Gen. Coll., NA 6840.67L4.

side of the opening permitted performers to enter and exit, while above, a small gallery provided seating for distinguished guests. While design evolution has rendered these elements unfamiliar, all have remained integral to American theaters (see IN-001).

In the Elizabethan playhouse, a basic admission fee allowed access to the unroofed yard, which patrons entered through narrow corridors under the first seating tier, then through low doors near the stage. An additional fee allowed entry to the upper galleries, where seating took the form of wide, backless planks. Although creature comfort was lacking, the dense, cheering crowd must have enjoyed a spirit of unity and excitement akin to that of the spectators at a parade or a college football game today.

During Oliver Cromwell's humorless and iconoclastic Commonwealth (1649–60) English theater building ceased. The Globe had been demolished in 1644; its contemporaries met a similar fate. Theater went underground, presenting only in temporary facilities.

Architect and theater designer Inigo Jones, while traveling in Italy in 1613, had visited Andrea Palladio's impressive Teatro Olimpico, at Vicenza, an enclosed adaptation of the Greco-Roman theater form, with steeply raked circular seating and a permanent stage set of radial street vistas rendered in forced perspective. Upon returning to England, Jones sketched designs based upon Vicenza, but none was put into a permanent form. The Restoration favored Jones's son-in-law and protegé, John Webb, and the well-known Christopher Wren. Webb's Cockpit-in-Court (1660) and Wren's Theatre Royal, Drury Lane (1672–74) introduced the polish of Renaissance and baroque classicism to London's theater scene.

America's earliest theaters adhered more closely to Restoration precedent than did their London contemporaries. The reasons were several. The colonies were far from the cultural wellspring and their enterprises were commercial, not subject to royal patronage. An American theater was designed not by a sophisticated architect but by a practical master builder tutored in the skills of sturdy construction. The New World's relatively harsh climate dictated that a theater be an interior space. Outside, the building looked simple and substantial, not unlike a church or meeting hall (see 1-001). Inside, like its antecedents, it was carefully planned to accommodate, and separate, the elements of a socially diverse population. Robert Frost one day would write, "Good fences make good neighbors." America's earliest theater designers knew the principle well (see 1-002).

In American practice, the yard's equivalent, called the pit, remained a low-class area. Its occupants, the city's cobblers and coopers, carpenters and craftsmen, crowded together, enjoying the show with a lusty, demonstrative spirit. Like the old yard, the pit was reached through doors on either side of the stage, with access corridors that bypassed the main lobby and opened directly to the street. Seating took the form of long, backless benches arranged without aisles. Three seating tiers surrounded the pit. The lower two were partitioned into boxes. Their supporting columns rose in a direct line with the balcony railings to create a visual closure to the auditorium's volume. The wealthiest patrons, the city's merchants and politicians, occupied these boxes, from which they enjoyed the show in semi-seclusion. It often was observed that they devoted more attention to their finery, their friends, and their conversation than to the performance on stage. These members of the city's upper crust were oblivious to the noisy occupants of the pit immediately in front of them, and firmly separated from them by the box railing. The third tier, or gallery, where seating was open, accommodated a still respectable but less affluent crowd made up largely of single men. A corps of prostitutes worked actively and openly there through the evening.

The stage evolved more markedly than the auditorium from its English precedent. With its curtained proscenium, it was an enlarged version of the Globe's inner stage. Its apron still extended far forward into the pit, bringing the performers well into the audience space. Above the apron, on each side of the proscenium, was a door surmounted by a simulated window. These vestiges of the old onstage gallery now served not as seating for select patrons but as places from which actors could make their entrance. They would continue to evolve, first into the showy proscenium box seats that housed Victorian plutocrats in grandeur, then into the organ grilles of the great movie palaces.

These early halls abysmally lacked the comforts that we now expect in a theater. They were crowded and noisy, heavily used, and often in need of decorative repair. The sight lines were imperfect, the seating uncomfortable. The air was dense with the odors of unwashed patrons and tobacco smoke and the sounds of snuffing, sneezing, and spitting. During the program, which typically lasted several hours, people came and went at will, often to patronize the adjoining bar room, a significant audience amenity. The constant presence of prostitutes deterred attendance by those women and families who did not have entrée to the sheltering seclusion of the box seats.

EVOLUTION OF THEATER FORM

As the nineteenth century approached its midpoint, theaters became more highly decorated, more spacious, and more egalitarian. At a glance, it might seem that the building form was simply following a natural course of improvement, that American taste was becoming more refined and audiences more demanding. Actually, the evolution derived from social changes and the concomitant aesthetic maturation. Ever responsive to their customers' desires, theater owners and their designers were keeping pace with America's transformation into an urban nation.

By the 1820s, America's productivity had begun to shift from field to factory. Young people, farmers' sons and daughters, abandoned the land for the mill towns of New England. There they lived in company housing, where their activities were closely supervised by factory managers. Church and theater were the only refuge from the fatigue and boredom of long working hours. Towns like Lowell, Massachusetts and Manchester, New Hampshire came to boast opera houses that rivaled those in far more established metropolises.

Industrialization reorganized American society. At the top sat the mill owner, his investors, and their families. At the bottom were the mill hands, young, impecunious, generally single. And there were outsiders to the social order—homeless youngsters, compelled by circumstance to seek their own fortunes as newsboys or beggars. They were unwelcome wherever they went.

Most significant to the evolving order was the growing cadre of employees who kept the company's books, processed its paperwork, hired its laborers, and made up its sales force. They occupied the management office, a level below the boardroom but well above the factory floor. Situated socially and professionally between capitalists and mill hands, they constituted a new group, a middle class. These administrators distanced themselves from the machine operators, whom they perceived as inferior, even as they were distanced by top management, whose respect they envied and whose life style they aspired to attain. They wore white shirts and kept their hands washed. They sought cleanliness of mind and morals. They went to church and listened to their preachers. They eschewed profane language and abstained from alcoholic drink. They included their wives and children in their leisure activities. And they assiduously avoided the theater. Disdaining the rough-cut denizens of the pit as much as they abhorred the riffraff in the gallery above, middle-class families walked briskly past the box office. Theater managers were perplexed.

Showman, master marketer, and proprietor of a commercial museum, Phineas T. Barnum was the first to understand the new ethos. His solution, characteristically brilliant, was to embed within his museum a theater, which he called a lecture hall (see 1-023). By cloaking entertainment in the guise of education, he transformed his theater from a place of perceived immorality to one of uplift. Important to the process was a reworking of the auditorium's form. Its overall appearance remained comfortably familiar, but, with the columns set well back from the balcony fascias, it had a newly open, hospitable look, one that was distinctively American (see 3-025).

In the midcentury auditorium the pit was given a stylish new name, the parquet. Its rude benches were replaced with cushioned "opera seats" comfortable enough for the most delicate of managerial wives and daughters. A vestige of the old lower box tier remained. Now called the parquet circle, it no longer was partitioned into cubicles and was distinguished from the gentrified parquet only by a brass railing and its distinctive seating arrangement, a tight curve that aligned with the balconies above and acted as a visual counterpoint to the parquet's relatively straight rows. In a direct appeal to corporate spouses and children, the second tier was renamed the family circle. Egalitarian in arrangement, its box partitions were removed and its seating was arranged in open rows. The rowdies who had occupied the pit were moved to the uppermost tier, the gallery or amphitheater, where they sat on straight-backed wooden benches and remained out of genteel sight, if not earshot. A separate, direct entrance from the street kept them safely isolated from the respectable folk below. In the new arrangement, the stage apron still projected well into the audience, but the old doors and windows beside the proscenium became elaborately decorated seating boxes. More elegant, but far fewer in number than the boxes that once had surrounded the main floor, these were prominent architectural elements, vying in importance with the stage itself. Situated directly over the ends of the stage apron, they were perfect spots for the wealthiest of townspeople to display themselves before the rest of the crowd and to interact with the cast, easily presenting flowers, or barbs, to the performers (IN-002).

As a critical step in attracting the middle-class audience, managers were forced to gain control over their theaters. The practice of in-house liquor service was discontinued, the

IN-002. A theatre party. Harper Pennington, artist; from *Harper's Bazaar*, June 23, 1888. P&P, CAI-Pennington, no. 1 (B size). As the century entered its last decade America's theaters were set to enter a period of unprecedented elegance. The raffishness of earlier decades, if not completely repressed, had been swept away from direct contact. Box seats, once places of refuge, became places from which people of society aspiration could display themselves and their finery.

prostitutes evicted, the riffraff shunted aside. The movement toward managerial control had a defining moment. May 10, 1849, promised to be a rowdy night at New York's Astor Place Opera House, a theater built to serve New York's upper crust, but which in practice entertained the usual diverse mix of patrons. On that night the British actor William Macready portrayed Macbeth while American Edwin Forrest played the same role at the nearby Bowery Theatre. Disguising class rivalry as patriotism, a tough crowd cheered Forrest and an equally tough crowd (only seven women were said to have been present) jeered Macready, pelting him and his defenders with eggs and insults. Although such behavior was not uncommon, the Astor Place management took the unprecedented step of calling the militia to quell the disturbance. At that point the fight became one less of nationalism than of audience rights. By evening's end thirty-one rioters had been killed and a hundred and fifty wounded. The Astor Place survived only a few more months, but management's right to control audience behavior had been firmly established (see 1-027).

Women constituted a new and potentially important audience segment. The availability of industrially produced clothing had relieved many of them of the time-consuming drudgery of spinning, weaving, and sewing even as affordable domestic help freed them from heavy housework and cooking. Enjoying a newfound level of leisure, middle-class women were able to look toward beautifying their homes and their minds through cultural enrichment. In 1869, when eminent tragedian Edwin Booth opened his magnificent theater in New York City (see 3-009), he located just outside the established theater district on Broadway near Union Square, in a growing area of department stores and specialty shops called the "Ladies' Mile." In that context, Booth's Theatre introduced the matinee, a performance timed to attract women who had come to the neighborhood to shop while their husbands were at work and their children were in school. The influence of the family audience would be long lasting.

A NATIONAL STYLE

In the decades following the Civil War, theater design was influenced less by social class than by performers' requirements. As railroads spanned the continent, swift, reliable, and relatively easy coast-to-coast travel spawned new towns across the great West. As they prospered, each community developed its own gentry, businessmen who took pride in the places they had created. Each wanted the town that had rewarded him with wealth and success to be world class, and a world-class city needed an opera house. Although opera rarely was on the bill, the Grand Opera House, often situated above the owner's hardware store, was both his monument and the community's pride (see 3-038).

America's theatrical performers always had been itinerant. Before the Civil War, thespians traveled by horse and wagon over difficult roads. Upon arriving in town, they sought out a venue to present their acts, played until audience interest waned, then moved on. After the war, the railroads that facilitated the rise of new towns across the land enabled performers to travel in an organized, scheduled fashion. They could book dates in advance, enjoy a predetermined stay, then proceed to the next engagement. With travel schedules tight, actors had little time to set up their productions and none to learn the idiosyncrasies of the theater in each town. At every stop they had to know what to expect and be assured that their scenery and props would fit the stage. As de facto parts of a national network, the new opera houses of the West had to incorporate technical provisions equal to those found in the established and carefully designed theaters of New York City.

In the early years of the nineteenth century New York began to eclipse Philadelphia as America's theatrical capital. Although not yet the nation's largest city, it was big, bustling, cosmopolitan, and lacking in the prudish qualities that hampered theatrical growth in Philadelphia, its closest rival. The Park Theatre, opened in 1798, was almost twice the size of Philadelphia's Chestnut Street Theatre. When, in 1826, the Park was joined by the vast Bowery Theater (see 1-015 and 1-016) and the several smaller playhouses that dotted lower Manhattan, New York achieved a primacy that would never wane. The abundance of its audiences and halls made the city a logical home for performers and hence for the professionals who supported their work. When a string of new theaters developed in the 1860s near Union Square, the neighborhood quickly became home to costumers, scenic artists, stage mechanics, playwrights, producers, songwriters, music publishers, makeup dealers, and others related to the business of the stage. Broadway, whose length hosted an ever moving and expanding concentration of theaters, became as synonymous with the American stage as Wall Street did with American finance.

As much as they eased the travel experience, the railroads complicated the process of travel planning. Each year, toward summer's end, theater managers converged on New York to make themselves available to performers. Together they would arrange mutually workable schedules. The process was haphazard. Meetings took place in hotel rooms, restaurants, even on the benches of Union Square, the hub of the theater district. This distraction, drawing managers away from their theaters and performers from their rehearsals, provided an opportunity for a new professional service. Around Union Square, entrepreneurs hung out their shingles as theatrical agents, dedicated coordinators of the booking and travel processes. Agents armed themselves with master lists of theaters and performers as well as railroad maps and schedules (IN-003). They provided theater clients with a full calendar of acts, performer clients with an itinerary of efficient train connections, a maximum number of first-class theaters, and a minimum number of idle nights.

Not surprisingly, this profession snowballed from usefulness toward monopoly. Expanding their purview from service to control, agents began to demand exclusive contracts that enabled them to rule over both theaters and acts. Nonsubmissive performers were blacklisted and recalcitrant theater managers were denied good talent. Control progressed to ownership and the creation of theater conglomerates. F. F. Proctor's vaudeville circuit came to prominence in the 1880s. By 1906, former theater owner B. F. Keith and his partner, Edward F. Albee, had incorporated the United Booking Office. Steamrollering Proctor, it took firm control of vaudeville in the East. Similarly, Martin Beck's Orpheum Circuit lorded over the West.

Keith and Albee may have modeled their methods on the syndicate founded by Marc Klaw and Abe Erlanger in 1896, which already had gripped the dramatic stage. Stakes were high and the organizations corporate, building strength through boycotts and mergers. Newcomers Marcus Loew, in 1904, and the Shubert brothers—Sam S., Lee, and Jake (J. J.)—in 1905, entered the field as self-styled reformers but quickly built monopolies of their own. Such strong local independents as S. Z. Poli in Connecticut and the first Oscar Hammerstein in New York were able to play political cards, allying themselves as expedient with one or another of the major players. In the same decade burlesque operators formed their own competing circuits, or "wheels"—Empire, Mutual, Columbia. Theater had become show business, as cutthroat a business as there ever had been.

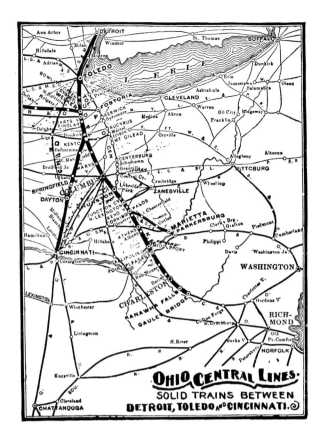

To the audience these machinations were little in evidence. Shows on the vaudeville circuits had become branded commodities. They were first-rate and customers were happy. Continuing in their effort to attract middle-class families, circuit managers advertised a dedication to entertainment that was firmly controlled and squeaky clean. B. F. Keith blacklisted performers for off-color language and content. F. F. Proctor advertised his theaters as safe and wholesome enough for children to attend during the day, offering a de-facto babysitting service for the price of a ticket.

Coincident with theater's business consolidation was a significant refinement in theatrical mechanics. Nineteenth-century America was proud of its technological prowess. In theater, new technology was directed toward ever more spectacular scenic effects. The post–Civil War years added the need for portability, as scenery had to travel with performers from one city and one theater to another. Previously, scenery had been painted on large rigid boards, loosely held at top and bottom in wooden grooves and mechanically linked so that they could be set into motion at once, sliding in and out of view quickly to effect scenic transformations that recalled the visual magic of a kaleidoscope.

From these large, awkward sliding "flats," scenic designers turned to the concept of raising, or "flying," scenery upward into a high stage loft, where it could be stored and from which it could be lowered as needed into audience view. By eliminating the need for rigidity, they could paint the scenes on canvas that could be rolled for storage and easy transport.

Theater designers also turned their attention to regularizing stage dimensions, developing a standard proscenium size (32 feet square) and a standard depth (about 35 feet)—dimensions that prevail on Broadway to this day—as well as standard rigging provisions that were incorporated into new theaters across the land.

Continuing improvements in gas and then electric lighting and in stage machinery enabled show designers to achieve ever-greater scenic realism, a trend that worked hand in hand with the owners' growing penchant for control. Enhanced effects could most successfully be achieved in the environment of an enclosed stage. Likewise, show content and presentation were more readily controlled if performers remained within the stage's confines, where they could be held to a predetermined script with diminishing spontaneous interaction with the audience. The projecting stage apron began to become an anachronism. From the mid-1880s on, designers ended the stage at a proscenium that was seen as a fourth wall, an impenetrable window into a simulated reality. Showman David Belasco became a leading proponent of the "box set," a stage setting enclosed by side walls and a ceiling. Actors who once had performed in front of a backdrop, in the audience's midst, now could work in their own world without acknowledging the audience's presence. Removal of the stage apron reoriented the box seats. Although still elaborate in appearance, and still next to the stage, they no longer were part of it. Their occupants had become one with the audience.

A SHOW BUSINESS NEWCOMER

The turn of the twentieth century found American theater in a golden era. Its performances were artful, its settings luxurious, and its buildings as expertly designed as they were numerous. But this all was about to be disrupted by a mechanical device, a peep-show box within which illuminated images flickered into simulated motion. On April 14, 1894, on lower Broadway, Thomas Edison presented to the public his newest invention, the Kinetoscope (IN-004; see 8-170 and 8-171). The filmed vignettes that moved within the tall wooden cabinets were short and their content meager, but the public found the devices captivating. Technology soon enabled moving pictures to be shown on a large screen to a theater audience and on April 23, 1896, at Koster & Bial's Music Hall in New York City, a new kind of entertainment experience was born.

Could the movies really be called theater? They had neither live performer nor plot. Their attraction was their novelty. The earliest movies were shown in established theaters as a brief bit of amazement between traditional live variety acts. The first purpose-built movie showplaces generally were remodeled storefronts outfitted simply with loose

IN-004. Mutoscope. From David Robinson's *From Peep Show to Palace: The Birth of American Film*, p. 57. Gen. Coll. PN 1993.5.U6R59.

A mutoscope was similar to a kinetoscope in that it served a single viewer. A kinetoscope was wooden and displayed a loop of film. A mutoscope was cast iron and displayed flip cards.

chairs, a projector, a screen, and a piano to provide a musical background. Presenting a movie show was cheap—there were only the projectionist and pianist to pay. The theater's operator owned the film, so there was no additional cost for repeat performances, and since a film was available in multiple copies, it could be shown in many locations at once. The opportunity for profit was enticing. Starting in the spring of 1905, tiny screening rooms began to pop up in downtowns and working-class neighborhoods across the country (see 6-010). With a five-cent admission fee, they came to be called nickelodeons.

A nickelodeon's customers were well familiar with the amusement parks that had drawn summer visitors since the early 1890s. Nickelodeon facades were modeled on the parks' shooting galleries and sideshow booths. Most featured a wide-spanning arch framed with elaborately modeled architectural elements, geometric patterns, and three-dimensional lettering, all outlined with a multitude of electric bulbs. Within the arch, a central ticket booth was flanked by two doors. Above, there might be a tinkling piano or a blaring phonograph to call the attention of passersby. Nickelodeons clustered in entertainment districts that much resembled the amusement park midways made popular in 1893 by the World's Columbian Exposition in Chicago (see 5-033). Customers could go from one theater to another, stopping along the way at the confectionaries and soda shops that were interspersed among them. Inside, the picture show, as it then was called, was a disjointed potpourri of short, plotless vignettes—a man rowing a boat or sneezing, a crowd of workers leaving a factory, a swirling vaudeville dancer—always accompanied by the tinkling piano. Although the establishments called themselves theaters, their names suggested their nature more accurately. It was definitely not a desire for

IN-005

IN-005. Sheldon Theater, 1416 West Madison Street, Chicago, Illinois. Decorators' Supply Corporation, photographer, ca. 1909. P&P, LC-USZ62-92105.

intellectually stimulating drama that attracted customers to the Pastime, the Onlysho, the Amuse U, the Kum-C, the Happy Hour, or the Fairyland. It was no more than the chance to spend a bit of time in a pleasantly mindless diversion.

The nickelodeon's business model was based on four factors: a low admission price, a small seating capacity, a short show, and a morning-to-night schedule. The system worked until films became able to command an audience's extended attention. When longer, story-telling films—photoplays—first became available in 1911, they were shown in legitimate theaters at a full theater admission price. By 1915, when D. W. Griffith's *The Birth of a Nation* played for forty-four weeks at New York's Liberty Theatre, the feature-length film had become the accepted standard (IN-005–IN-008).

For an exhibitor, when a twenty-minute show became a two-hour show, either the admission price or the audience size had to increase dramatically. Prices rose a bit, but

IN-006. On New York's East Side, melodrama flaunts its eternal lure. George Hand Wright, artist; from Harrison Rhodes's "Majestic Movies" in *Harper's Magazine,* January, 1919. P&P, CAI-Wright, no. 56.

IN-007. The matinee line is a study in democracy. George Hand Wright, artist; from Harrison Rhodes's "Majestic Movies" in *Harper's Magazine,* January, 1919. P&P, CAI-Wright, no. 54.

IN-008. The picture palace has become part of the life of the American people. George Hand Wright, artist; from Philip Gibbs's "Things I Like in the United States" in *Harper's Magazine,* October, 1919. P&P, CAI-Wright, no. 65.

IN-006

IN-007

IN-008

IN-009

IN-010

IN-009. Three men standing outside an unidentified motion picture theater, possibly in Denver, Colorado. Unidentified photographer, 1910–1930. P&P, LC-USZ62-92108.

IN-010. The Clinch, movie theater. Mabel Dwight, artist, 1928. P&P, Ben and Beatrice Goldstein Foundation Collection, unprocessed item in D-022, no. 1425.

the 99-seat nickelodeons quickly gave way to larger new theaters seating six hundred or more. The silently moving image, once an adjunct to a variety show, became a primary entertainment form. If live acts were included on the bill, they were not of the first quality and always were secondary to the film in the mix of the evening's entertainment.

In the decades preceding World War I, cities underwent phenomenal growth. As to the New England mill towns a century earlier, young people flocked from rural America to the massive industrial plants of Cleveland, Detroit, Chicago, and other great cities of the North. The unattached newcomers enjoyed the opportunity to get out and have fun in the exciting city, and movies were the perfect outlet (IN-009; see LENS-007, LENS-008, and LENS-045). Purpose-built movie theaters became larger and more substantial. As they gained a permanent place in the urban scene, even their names acquired an impressive ring—Majestic, Capitol, Regent. Carefully designed and skillfully managed, they became places of elaborate architectural embellishment and impeccable service.

In 1913, the 2,460-seat Regent Theater opened in New York City's tony Harlem district. When it faltered, its owners hired a new manager, Samuel "Roxy" Rothafel, a showman with experience in several cities. Rothafel operated the Regent with elegance and precision. Customers were treated royally by a staff that had been drilled in courtesy. The Regent came to be looked upon as the operational model of high-class film presentation. By war's end in 1918, the country's aging Grand Opera Houses were being eclipsed by vast and gilded cinemas.

Auditoriums built for the movies took on a distinct form, derived partially from function, partially from the nature of their audiences. Designers working for the vaudeville circuits and dramatic realists already had effected the separation of actor from audience, stage from seating. Movie house architects now began actually to isolate audience members from one another by means of a simple seating realignment. In theaters from Shakespeare's time to Keith's, audience members could view one another clearly. From curved galleries and parquet circles theatergoers could look out over the assembled crowd and feel part of it. In a purpose-designed movie house, all seats faced the screen. Even patrons in the balcony could see their fellows only from behind (IN-010; see 6-071). The audience became an anonymous mass. The boxes where local swells once had presided lost their seats. Although they looked more elegant than ever, they were no more than elaborate screens that concealed the workings of the theater's pipe organ (see 6-176 and 6-183). Stages changed too. Although often equipped with an elaborate complement of turntables and elevating floor sections, they were shallow, designed to accommodate at most a small vaudeville act or a kick line. Catering to the tastes of audiences and movie moguls alike, architects frosted their auditoriums with more and more ornament. The public was mesmerized.

The movie palace could have developed only in the heady cultural climate of 1920s America. After World War I, it seemed that peace and prosperity would reign forever. Cities continued to fill with young people. Active, single, and often far from home, they had a voracious appetite for fun on a modest budget (IN-011 and LENS-069). On January 16, 1920, Prohibition was thrown into the mix. At a stroke the tavern was eradicated as a place of popular recreation; the fashionable speakeasies were much too expensive to attract a young clientele. Legitimate drama remained available, but many looked upon it as too racy or sophisticated, and far too pricey. For young working folk, a few hours at the movies surrounded by gilt, brocade, and crystal was the perfect evening out. In words that could not have been surpassed even by a Hollywood press agent, architect George Rapp summed up the spirit:

> Watch the eyes of a child as it enters the portals of our great theatres and treads the pathway into fairyland. Watch the bright light in the eyes of the tired shop-girl who hurries noiselessly over carpets and sighs with satisfaction as she walks amid furnishings that once delighted the hearts of queens. See the toil-worn father whose dreams have never come true, and look inside his heart as he finds strength and rest within the theatre. There you have the answer to why motion picture theatres are so palatial.*

Long the center of American theater, New York became the country's first film capital. Utilizing the city's ample supply of actors, stagehands, and support personnel, such early studios as Edison and Biograph shot films on the rooftops of Fourteenth Street

* George L. Rapp, 1926, quoted in Ben M. Hall, *The Best Remaining Seats*. New York: Bramhall House, 1961, p. 136.

and in large studios in the Bronx, while cowboys chased Indians across the hills of Fort Lee, New Jersey. The industry's formative figures—Marcus Loew, William Fox, and Adolph Zukor—shared the immigrant experience of growing up in the teeming streets of Manhattan's Lower East Side. Each emerged from the garment trade to use the nickelodeon business as a springboard to success. In 1906, Zukor and Loew opened a Fourteenth Street nickelodeon. Quickly parting ways with Loew, whom he did not trust, Zukor founded the Famous Players Film Company, which, in 1916, he merged into Paramount Pictures. Loew, in the meantime, prospered as a vaudeville operator and booking agent. By 1919 he controlled fifty-six theaters. William Fox, another nickelodeon and small-time vaudeville operator, made his first film in 1914. Like the others, his operation grew. America's studio/exhibition industry was born.

After World War I, the maturing filmmakers abandoned New York's changeable weather and expensive labor for the sunny skies of California, where they lodged in the tiny town of Hollywood, on the outskirts of Los Angeles. Like the earlier vaudeville monopolists, they worked to expand their spheres of influence. Consolidating the fledgling studios with theater chains, they became moguls of nationwide empires. In 1924 Marcus Loew attained control of Metro Pictures, merging it with the operations of Samuel Goldfish (later Goldwyn) to form Loew-Metro-Goldwyn, later Metro-Goldwyn-Mayer. MGM supplied product to over a hundred and fifty Loew-owned theaters and many more subsidiaries across the country. William Fox, who formed his Fox Theater Corporation in 1925, eventually controlled over five hundred theaters, including New York's Roxy. In 1926 Adolph Zukor combined his Paramount Pictures with Balaban & Katz, of Chicago, to form a third massive combine, Publix Theatres. In 1928, Joseph Kennedy facilitated the takeover of the declining Keith–Albee and Orpheum vaudeville circuits to create RKO, initials that would bespangle America's marquees for a generation. Latecomers to movie production, the Warner Brothers, who had opened their first nickelodeon, the Cascade, in New Castle, Pennsylvania, in 1906 became major players in the era of sound.

By the mid-1920s, just as it seemed that movie palaces had reached an unsurpassable peak of size and opulence, they entered their final stage of development. After more than a decade of emulating regal grandeur, their designs leaped into the realm of exotic fantasy. Again, the names are revealing. Next to the Capitol, Majestic, and Grand now stood the Oriental, the Avalon, the Chinese, the Egyptian. Theater architects had become showmen. Working for William Fox, C. Howard Crane abandoned his elegantly detailed Adamesque salons in favor of vast auditoriums where up to five thousand patrons could surround themselves with Indo-Persian or Sino-Venetian splendor as they watched well-crafted, but still silent, cinematic dramas accompanied by a symphony orchestra or the oozing, visceral sound of a mighty Wurlitzer organ. Thomas Lamb, who had maintained a consistently dignified Adamesque elegance, plunged into the exotic for Marcus Loew. For Paramount–Publix, Rapp & Rapp adapted the design vocabulary of Versailles into soaring vaulted lobbies and auditoriums.

Unique among the designers was John Eberson, who introduced exoticism as the ultimate defining quality of the picture palace and who produced his trademark designs for all of the major exhibition concerns. Austrian by birth, Eberson trained in Dresden and Vienna before moving to the United States in 1901. Here, he apprenticed with Midwestern opera house builder George Johnson before beginning his own practice in 1908. A born salesman, Eberson quickly obtained sizable commissions. His first designs were much in the mode of his peers, though with a chromatic richness that reflected a mastery of color and a personal affection for earthy tile and delicate ironcraft (see 6-157). On January 29, 1923, at Houston's Majestic Theatre, he unveiled what would become his trademark. The idea was not really new. Palladio's 1585 Teatro Olimpico, in Vicenza, Italy, had pretended to be out-of-doors and Shakespeare's Globe had actually been so. In 1794, the ceiling of Philadelphia's Chestnut Street Theatre had been painted to resemble the sky. Any number of nineteenth-century opera houses had sky-colored domes embellished with painted clouds, stars, or flying muses. Some even incorporated hidden windows to give dramatic lighting to their ersatz heavens, or gas jets in their stars to make them twinkle. In 1910, architect J. E. O. Pridmore ornamented Chicago's Cort Theater with what looked like a nighttime sky seen through a trellis. Eberson even had tried his idea a few months earlier at the Orpheum Theater in Wichita, Kansas. But the Majestic was different. While its predecessors were more or less conventional auditoriums whose ceilings seemed to have openings to the sky, the Majestic united architecture with the set designer's art to create a realistic outdoor effect. The setting emulated an Italian piazza. The auditorium walls were asymmetrical, representing varied building facades, with iron balconies and windows lighted from within. As they met the ceiling, they were capped with eaves of simulated tile. Atop the facades, vine-draped caryatid porticos and temple-like pergolas were softened with artificial vines and trees, and feathered papier-mâché doves were suspended as if in flight. To one side a fountain trickled as recordings softly played nighttime sounds. The ceiling was plain and painted dark blue. Around its edges, powerful blue lights gave it a daytime glow. As they dimmed for the show to begin, a bank of orange lamps momentarily rose and fell to simulate sunset. Twinkling constellations dotted the darkened sky as projected images of clouds floated by. The moon rose, an airplane passed; the experience was magical (see 6-165).

CHANGING PATTERNS

October 28, 1927, marked the premiere of a Warner Brothers film, *The Jazz Singer,* in which Al Jolson sang a song whose recorded sound was synchronized with the moving image by linking the projector with a phonograph. This had been done before. But after the song something new happened. Jolson spoke: "Wait a minute. You ain't heard nothin' yet!" Audiences hadn't, but from then on they would.

Ironically, the "talkies" arrived on the scene in the same year that theater operators became wholehearted in their flight into fantasy. Old theaters were being refurbished and refitted to compete with new ones of unprecedented size and elaboration. Many theaters installed new Wurlitzers even as they were being wired for sound. It was a pinnacle and an end. Before long the stage spectacles would be discontinued and the great organs gradually silenced. Sound pictures offered multisensory realism and a new level of audience absorption. Exhibitors could see that it was more appropriate to show them in an atmosphere that was quietly attractive but that did not intrude upon the audience's attention. The architectural press was filled with a new, simplified design fashion called "modernism," and with John Eberson and Thomas Lamb in the vanguard, theater architects quickly adopted the new style (see 7-027–7-029, 7-047). Gilt ornament, classical moldings, antique statuary, and exoticism were replaced by simple surfaces, often gently and evocatively curved. Hidden lighting superseded crystal chandeliers. The grandly simple International Music Hall at Radio City heralded the new era (see 7-020).

The movies' popularity affected both the nature of American drama and the design of the theaters built for it. When they were the sole source of urban entertainment, playhouses were designed to serve an audience that crossed class lines, with accommodations appropriate for rich and poor alike. But the nickelodeons drew the working-class customers away. To please the more affluent and educated audience that remained, the repertoire's long-standing staples, popular melodrama and slapstick comedy, were joined with "legitimate" drama, which flowered as a high literary art in the hands of such playwrights as Eugene O'Neill and, later, Tennessee Williams. Each theater type, live and movie, developed its own homogeneous audience. The movies were popular, but their audiences were a world apart from the elegant crowd that populated the "legitimate" theaters. New playhouses looked like smaller, more sophisticated versions of their cinematic counterparts, varying from their nineteenth-century predecessors in that their seats were aligned to face directly toward the stage, and their second balcony with its separate entrance had disappeared. Its occupants had gone to the movies.

The end of World War II ushered in a new way of life. Even with Prohibition over, more than a decade of Depression and war had rendered Americans sobered, settled, and sedate. Unimaginably, the nation's great cities slid into decline. Returning veterans married and moved with their new families into loosely populated areas on the urban edge. The automobile became their main mode of transportation. Living at a distance from the transit lines that had served an older and denser urban population, and constrained by the needs of their small children, they found it easier to drive to nearby neighborhood theaters than to travel to entertainment downtown. Exhibitors responded to the baby boom by developing the drive-in theater, where children could play, eat, and sleep while their parents enjoyed the show from their car (see 8-147–8-152). Neighborhood theaters acquired a distinctly come-as-you-are atmosphere. Returning to an early nineteenth-century etiquette, customers arrived, left, and moved about during the course of the show. Popcorn and candy, introduced grudgingly in the depth of the Depression to generate needed extra income, became integral with the movie experience and made the refreshment counter a magnet for peripatetic customers (see 9-016–9-018). The downtown movie palaces remained grand, but their audiences were declining.

A generation old, these one-time Xanadus showed their age. Their drapes were tattered, their chandeliers dusty. The wide screens and new neon marquees intended to upgrade their appearance were tawdry (see 4-064 and 4-065). Their auditoriums smelled of stale popcorn; their carpets squished with spilled soda; they needed new air-conditioning, new roofs. By the end of the 1960s they had lived out their economic lives.

As its popularity boomed in the 1950s and 1960s, television changed the theater business yet again. In the same way that movies had lured populist, working-class audiences from playhouses, television lured them from the movie theaters. The cowboys and detectives, the teenage genre flicks and kiddie shows that had long been studio staples moved from the big screen to the home tube. In production quality and exhibition technique, movies were better than ever. But they were far fewer in number. B-grade films and twice-a-week changes of double features were things of the past. Teenagers with wheels augmented the movies with the drive-in restaurant and the shopping mall, leaving their parents at home with the television set. Like the theater when it became legitimate, the movies gentrified. Their adult audiences selected their shows more carefully, often guided by the comments of professional reviewers. They arrived on time, without children. They sought an undistracted one-to-one experience with the actors on screen.

Live theater was somewhat less affected than the movies by the pervasive spread of in-home entertainment. Upper-class audiences remained strong and were joined by a middle class educated and sophisticated in its entertainment taste. As movie theaters became smaller and simpler, live theaters came fully into the purview of architecture's modernist innovators. The proscenium stage that isolated performer from audiences came strongly into question. The thrust stage, a throwback to Shakespearean times, was tried, as was theater "in the round," in which the stage was an island surrounded by the audiences and actors made their entrances by running down the aisles. Some auditoriums, particularly in university theaters, were highly mechanized to enable seating and stage sections to be elevated, rotated, and slid into a variety of configurations. In the end, ironically, the proscenium configuration, perhaps with a slight extension of the apron, proved to be as good a setting as any. It continues to dominate theater construction to this day.

Theaters designed solely for orchestra use have continued to be showcases of combined innovation and splendor. More than ever in history they are constructed according to principles of scientific acoustical design. The prime innovator was Philharmonic (now Avery Fisher) Hall in New York's Lincoln Center for the Performing Arts. Designed to be capable of acoustical adjustment and fine tuning, its initial design was a failure, but the sort of failure that prodded acousticians and architects to seek ever better solutions. The most innovative of the new halls have placed the orchestra in the midst of multiple audience tiers and have provided for day-by-day acoustical adjustment to meet the requirements of varied musical genres even as many halls have adapted configurations reminiscent of the classic theaters and opera houses of a century past.

As surprising as it may seem, it took a century to devise an ideal setting for the movies. Since Edison first astonished an audience with a projected moving image, architects and exhibitors alike had persisted in thinking of movie houses as theaters rather than as

IN-012. Couple wearing 3D glasses, kissing in a movie theater. Weegee, photographer, ca. 1960. P&P, USZ62-112822.

environments uniquely suited to a new presentation mode. The great picture palaces, the pride of an earlier generation but inflated playhouses at best, were dinosaurs bound for extinction. By the 1970s the old traditions began to give way. Sidewalk ticket kiosks, remnants of the nineteenth-century amusement parks, were eliminated, as were the uniformed ushers who once had marched smartly through palatial lobbies. Cineplexes, in which several auditoriums shared a single lobby, gave exhibitors flexibility in programming as new film and digital technologies eliminated the need for projection-room staff. Consolidated and vastly expanded refreshment services provided an important income source. The new cinema auditorium was an entirely neutral presence, designed to immerse the patron in the picture without the distraction of decor or exotic effects (see 7-066). Stadium seating, introduced to American movie theaters in the twenty-first century, provided rows so steeply raked that the filmgoers' view of the screen was unobstructed, even by the heads of the people immediately in front of them. Distraction was gone; isolation was complete. But was it something new or just the culmination of a trend that began in the 1880s? Was a row of auditoriums along a corridor and a central refreshment counter really that different from the nickelodeon and soda-shop clusters of a century gone by? Had a unique building form that had grown, developed, and achieved greatness been irretrievably lost?

The National Register of Historic Places was created in 1966. As the survivors of the golden age of the movie palace reached eligibility (at age fifty), many became the object of ardent historic preservation activity. The early years saw Rapp & Rapp's Loew's Penn Theatre, in Pittsburgh, and their St. Louis Theatre, in St. Louis, become Heinz and

Powell Halls, respectively; John Eberson's Loew's Richmond Theatre became the Carpenter Center for the Performing Arts. Indeed, centers for the performing arts became the twentieth- and twenty-first-century equivalent of the nineteenth-century Grand Opera House, a theater that presented popular entertainment in a building that was perceived as a civic monument. Through this upgrading, many of the finest theaters of bygone eras have found new audiences and new purpose.

A NOTE ABOUT ORGANIZATION

The images in this book are arranged, generally, in chronological groupings. Through them we can watch the form of the pioneering playhouse evolve into the opera house, the vaudeville theater, the movie palace, and the modern theater, which has continued to evolve in the twenty-first century. We can see the spread of theaters on the American frontier and the way in which amusement parks profoundly influenced the form of the developing movie theater. We can visit specialty theaters that occupied niches outside the mainstream.

As a convention, following American usage, the building type is called the *theater* here. Because exhibitors almost invariably preferred the Franco/British precedent, however, individual theater names are spelled *theatre,* a compromise that defers equally to Noah Webster and Roxy.

Each image is captioned, when the information is available, with the theater's name, address, opening date, architect, and seating capacity, followed by the name of the creator of the image, the date of creation, and the source of the image. The notation "(color)" following a caption indicates that the image is shown in color on the accompanying CD. A theater that was renamed is listed by its original name with subsequent names given within parentheses, unless otherwise stated. Because everyone knew where major theaters were located, published sources often provide imprecise addresses, and in many cities street names and numbering systems have been altered. As fully as possible, the illustrations are provided with present-day addresses. Sources often conflict with regard to opening dates and seating capacities. Sometimes we know only a projected opening date or a dedication date that may have been a private preview rather than a public opening. Often, exhibitors inflated seating capacity. While some of the dates and capacities presented here may vary from actuality, they are sufficient to place each theater into historical context and to give an idea of its physical magnitude.

THEATERS FOR A NEW NATION

AMERICA'S FIRST DECADES were a time of profound change. The nation was new. The very premise of its national ethic—leadership from within rather than from above—was new. Dissent, ever present, would be tolerated and made open. But how would it be managed? Into this philosophical stew were added radical new technologies. The industries that they spawned had in themselves the power to bring about societal change. All of this had its effect on America's theaters, buildings that above all others acted as barometers of social organization.

The era began with theaters that had seen little basic change in two centuries. But forms relocated intact from London's Bankside to Philadelpia's Chestnut Street or St. Charles Street in New Orleans could not suffice in a democratic land. Theaters somehow had to lose their aura of social stratification. As much as America's political theorists proclaimed it a land of equality, inequalities remained. The wealthy flaunted the frills of etiquette and finery. They looked down on, even feared, the workers, who reacted in a rougher, noisier, more natural way to an entertaining presence. The theater manager and his architect had to devise a means of accommodating both audiences in the same room at the same time.

By the time the Revolution ended, the youthful nation was set toward a new era of expansion, and theaters had taken on a new look. They were designed to accommodate a growing middle class. Balconies became open and private cubicles were removed as their silk-clad occupants disappeared. Alcohol, too, disappeared and those who found their joy in noisy interaction with one another and the actors were moved high up out of sight. As the Civil War approached, some of America's greatest auditoriums were built. Some serve us today, still relevant as truly American theaters.

1-001

1-002

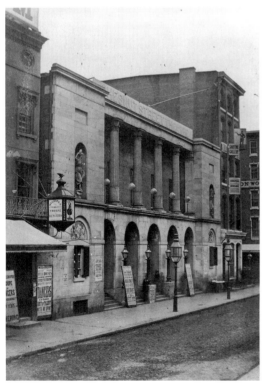

1-003

1-001. Chestnut Street Theatre, 615 Chestnut Street, Philadelphia, Pennsylvania. Opened February 17, 1794; 1,155 seats; John Inigo Richards, architect. William Russell Birch, engraver, 1804. P&P, LC-USZ62-80587.

1-002. Chestnut Street Theatre, 615 Chestnut Street, Philadelphia, Pennsylvania. Opened February 17, 1794; 1,155 seats; John Inigo Richards, architect. W. Ralph, engraver; from W. S. Lewis's drawing in *New York Magazine*, April, 1794. Gen. Coll., AP2 .A2N5.

The Chestnut Street was built for the Wignell and Reinagle repertory company and was designed by Thomas Wignell's brother-in-law, an English scene painter. Its gray interior was made colorful with pink wallpaper and gilded columns. The ceiling was painted to imitate the open sky that would have been visible in an Elizabethan theater. The Chestnut illustrates the interior configuration, adapted from the Elizabethan model, which evolved throughout the pre–Civil War period. The stage projected well beyond the proscenium, with side doors and window-like boxes framing it. Seats were backless benches and there were no aisles. The pit was entered through small doors at either side of the stage. Circling the pit were two tiers of private boxes and an open upper gallery.

1-003. New (Chestnut Street, Old Drury) Theatre, 615 Chestnut Street, Philadelphia, Pennsylvania. Opened December 2, 1822; William Strickland, architect. Unidentified photographer, 1855. P&P, LC-USZ62-11636.

The Chestnut Street burned in 1820. Its replacement was designed by the talented young Philadelphia architect William Strickland, whose monumental Second Bank of the United States was rising within sight of the new playhouse. William Rush's wooden statues of Comedy and Tragedy, salvaged from the previous theater, were placed in niches on the new facade. While the three-tiered interior arrangement was retained, the columns were drawn inward to improve sight lines.

1-004. Front (bottom) and rear (top) elevations, theater, Richmond, Virginia. Projected 1798; Benjamin Henry Latrobe, architect. P&P, LC-USZ62-22886; LC-USZC4-99 (color).

Had it been built, Latrobe's Richmond theater would have been the most elegant and well conceived in the new nation. His facades were of traditional Virginia red brick, updated with the blind arches that had been made a vogue by London architect John Soane. The elegant curve of the entry arcade was a master touch.

1-005. Theater, Richmond, Virginia. Projected 1798; Benjamin Henry Latrobe, architect. P&P, LC-USZ62-22883; LC-USZC4-96 (color).

Elegant but deceptive, the entry arcade would not welcome all: Latrobe maintained rigid separation between class-defined audience areas. The central door led directly to the main floor, an undesirable seating level. A door at either end of the arcade gave access to the upper tiers. The column grid in the upper portion of this ground-floor plan would have supported the stage.

1-006. Theater, Richmond, Virginia. Projected 1798; Benjamin Henry Latrobe, architect. P&P, LC-USZ62-22884; LC-USZC4-97 (color).

Elegant curved stairways were to lead up to the box tier, the projected domain of Richmond's elite; a two-story reception room is shown in the upper left. As the concept of changing scenery by raising and lowering sets had yet to be developed, Latrobe showed a European staging technique: tall, narrow scenic segments arranged along angled lines to create a perspective effect.

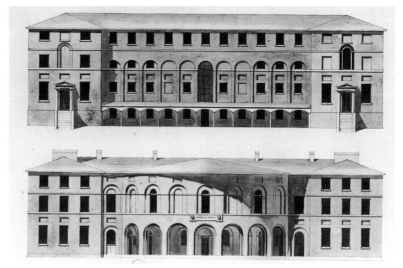

1-004

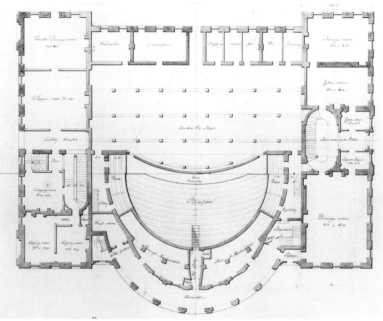

1-005

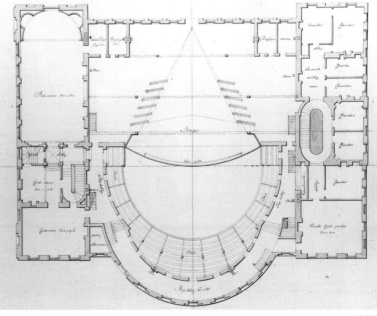

1-006

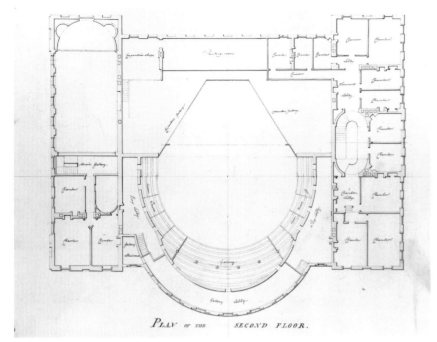

1-007

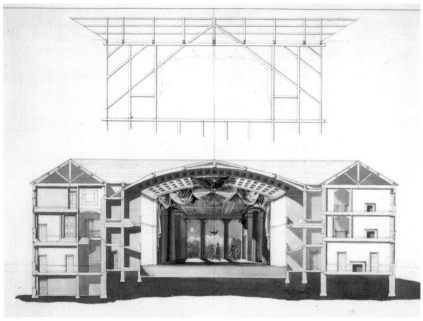

1-008

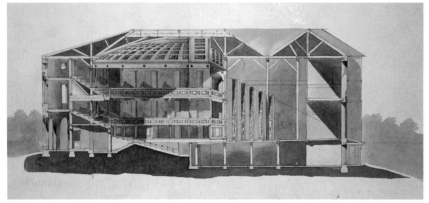

1-009

1-007. Theater, Richmond, Virginia. Projected 1798; Benjamin Henry Latrobe, architect. P&P, LC-USZ62-22885; LC-USZC4-98 (color).

The upper tier was to be divided between side boxes and a central open seating area.

1-008. Theater, Richmond, Virginia. Projected 1798; Benjamin Henry Latrobe, architect. P&P, LC-USZC4-102 (color).

The perspective effect of the scenery was extended into the auditorium by a gently flaring sounding board over the stage. A large, centrally positioned eagle provided a patriotic touch.

1-009. Theater, Richmond, Virginia. Projected 1798; Benjamin Henry Latrobe, architect. P&P, LC-USZ62-2521; LC-USCZ4-101 (color).

Latrobe's longitudinal section shows the low-ceilinged stage, the perspective scenery, the steeply raked pit, and the two upper seating tiers. The scenic perspective continues beyond the stage into the sloping railings of the proscenium boxes.

1-010. Theater, Richmond, Virginia. Projected 1798; Benjamin Henry Latrobe, architect. P&P, LC-USZ62-1221; LC-USZC4-4553 (color).

The shallow-domed ceiling with its tapering rows of simple coffers would have been more at home in Soane's London than in Latrobe's Richmond. In this whimsical actor's view, workers are seen applying the final touches of gilt and upholstery to the box-tier colonnades.

1-011. Theater, Richmond, Virginia. Projected 1798; Benjamin Henry Latrobe, architect. P&P, LC-USZ62-1222; LC-USZCN4-36 (color).

The entry sequence to the first box tier included a grandly designed reception room in the Anglo-Roman style. Similar ball-rooms would be seen in great theaters throughout the pre–Civil War era.

1-012. Walnut Street Theatre (The Circus, The Olympic), 825 Walnut Street, Philadelphia, Pennsylvania. Opened February 2, 1809; 1,539 seats; reconstruction 1828, John Haviland, architect. Fenner, Sears & Co., engravers, after Charles Burton, artist, 1831. P&P, LC-USZ62-47365.

Inaugurated in 1809 as The Circus, the venerable Walnut took almost twenty years to settle into life as a theater. When a stage was added in 1811, the theater was renamed The Olympic. On November 11, 1820, it became the Walnut Street Theatre but reverted to its original circus use, and again The Olympic name, from 1822 until 1827. Permanent theatrical status, and John Haviland's elegant marble and stucco facade, finally came about in 1828. Since then there have been several reconstructions, but while little remains of its earliest form, the Walnut is generally acknowledged to be America's oldest continuously operating entertainment venue.

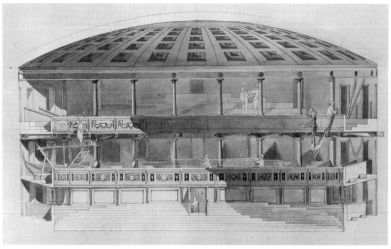

1-010

1-011

1-012

1-013

1-014

1-015

1-013. Lafayette Theatre, 308–310 West Broadway, New York, New York. Opened July 4, 1825; Peter Grain, architect. James Eddy, engraver; from *New York Mirror*, 1827. P&P, LC-USZ62-32485.

A theater's ability to attract patrons generally is due more to location than design. In appearance, no New York theater could surpass the handsome Lafayette, but its outlying location at the time precluded lasting success. The Lafayette was just over four years old when it burned on July 22, 1829.

1-014. Italian Opera House (National Theatre), 240 Church Street, New York, New York. Opened November 18, 1833. R. Bengouch, artist; S. Hollyer, engraver, 1839. P&P, U.S. Building Types File-Theaters.

A blocky Greek Revival portico distinguished the facade of the Italian Opera House, but its specialized fare and overly aristocratic proprietors' boxes deprived it of popular success. After three years of operatic production it was sold to the decidedly non-Italian theater manager, James W. Hackett. Successive fires in 1839 and 1841 ended its existence.

1-015. Bowery (New York, American, Thalia) Theatre, 46–48 Bowery, New York, New York. Opened August 28, 1828; 3,000 seats; Joseph Sera, architect. P&P, LC-USZ62-47363.

The Bowery (its longest-lasting name) survived six fires and five rebuildings as it provided over a century of service. Located a bit northeast of New York's gritty and crime-infested Five Points neighborhood, it was intended as a counterpoint to the old and elite Park Theatre in the heart of downtown. The first Bowery Theatre, opened on October 23, 1826, was designed by Ithiel Town, the finest of America's Greek Revival architects. It featured a pedimented facade with a recessed portico supported by two massive Doric columns. On May 26, 1828, it burned. The third and fourth incarnations both burned to the ground as well. On August 4, 1845, the fifth version of the theater opened, this one designed by theater specialist John M. Trimble. There would be another fire in 1923 before a final blaze felled the house for good on June 5, 1929. The Bowery always was a theater for mass audiences. Over the years it served successive waves of German- and Yiddish-speaking immigrants who populated its neighborhood. When it closed it was presenting in the language of its surrounding Chinatown.

1-016. Bowery (Thalia) Theatre, 46–48 Bowery, New York, New York. Opened August 4, 1845; 1,288 seats; John M. Trimble, architect. From *Frank Leslie's Illustrated Newspaper*, September 13, 1856. P&P, LC-USZ62-2519.

Trimble's interior for the 1845 Bowery was among the great auditoriums of the period, with four balconies hugging its side and rear walls. By this time the balcony boxes had been eliminated and the columns pulled back to give the auditorium an open, egalitarian appearance.

1-017. St. Charles Theatre, 426 St. Charles Street, New Orleans, Louisiana. Opened January 18, 1843; 1,625 seats; Dr. George King Pratt, architect. G. Tolti, artist and lithographer; D. Theuret, engraver. P&P, LC-USZ62-37475.

The second St. Charles Theatre was built on the site of its predecessor, which had opened on November 30, 1835, and burned in 1842. Its floridly decorated interior, with a complicated series of balconies and mezzanines that retained an old-fashioned sense of enclosure, reflected the French culture of its city. The pattern of class distinction was especially pronounced in the sparsely occupied uppermost gallery, where the central section was rigidly walled from the sides. It is likely that one portion was reserved for working-class white patrons while the other was restricted to African Americans who accompanied their owners. This theater burned in 1899.

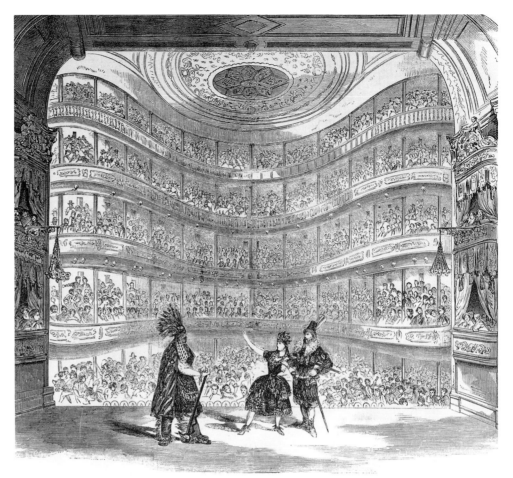

1-016

1-017

1-018

1-018. Arch Street Theatre, 609–615 Arch Street, Philadelphia, Pennsylvania. Opened October 1, 1828; 1,911 seats; William Strickland, architect. F. De B. Richards, photographer, 1853–1861. P&P, LC-USZ62-122391.

More conservative in style, and less discriminating in clientele than his earlier Chestnut Street Theatre (1-003), Strickland's Arch Street incorporated similar design elements. Here the colonnaded portico and arched gallery entries were mounted against a front whose simplicity recalled the Quaker meeting houses that dotted old Philadelphia.

1-019. Arch Street Theatre, 609–615 Arch Street, Philadelphia, Pennsylvania. Opened October 1, 1828; refaced 1861. Philip B. Wallace, photographer, June, 1936. P&P, LC-USZ62-111512.

When John Drew acquired the Arch Street in 1861, he removed Strickland's classical portico and extended the building to the sidewalk line. The monumental statue from the original pediment was reset atop the new facade, at the center of the third floor (obscured by the fire escape). The Arch Street wavered between classical and ethnic presentations, and live shows and movies before closing in 1936.

1-019

1-020. National Theatre, 312 Sycamore Street, Cincinnati, Ohio. Opened July 3, 1837. Jacob Brethauer, delineator, February 20, 1934. P&P, HABS,OH-23-7, sheet no. 3.

In 1856 a business block was constructed in front of Cincinnati's twenty-year-old National Theatre. A large central portal provided access to the theater behind.

1-021. National Theatre, 312 Sycamore Street, Cincinnati, Ohio. Opened July 3, 1837. Edgar D. Tyler, photographer, February 26, 1934. P&P, HABS,OHIO,31-CINT,4-2.

Constructed of mustard-toned Berea Ohio sandstone, the National's new facade combined monumentality with delicacy. An unusual Palladian motif above the arched portal and graceful angels highlighted the theater's alleyway entry.

1-020

1-021

1-022

1-023

1-024

1-022. Barnum's American Museum, 218 Broadway, New York, New York. Opened December 27, 1841. Thomas Benecke, lithographer, 1855. P&P, LC-USZ62-2501; LC-USZC4-2722 (color).

Phineas T. Barnum got it right. In an era when male-dominated audiences had given theaters a shady reputation, he sought to attract an audience of women who would bring with them their husbands and children. His vehicle was a prominently located museum (and later an auditorium) that displayed natural-history specimens. Some were genuine, most were fabricated. Many were examples of human deformity, or "freaks." Most famous were the Feejee Mermaid, concocted by sewing together a fish and a monkey, and longtime stars Tom Thumb and "Zip, the What-is It," who appeared in Barnum's theater, or "lecture room." Barnum's marketing concept, entertainment cloaked in the guise of education, works to this day.

1-023. Barnum's American Museum, 218 Broadway, New York, New York. Opened December 27, 1841. From *Gleason's Pictorial Drawing-Room Companion*, January 29, 1853. P&P, LC-USZ62-2641.

In 1855 the American Museum added its impressive auditorium. Barnum euphemized its theatrical function by calling it a lecture room and emphasizing the "moral" nature of its presentations. The characterization was actually fairly accurate. Its longest-running presentation was Uncle Tom's Cabin. How could any clergyman object?

1-024. Barnum's American Museum, 218 Broadway, New York, New York. Opened December 27, 1841. From *Harper's Weekly*, July 29, 1865. Gen. Coll., E461.H3.

Barnum's Museum burned on July 13, 1865. Although there were no casualties among either attendees or performers, the loss of many animals was poignant. Many thought that the rascally Barnum had received his just deserts.

1-025

1-025. Barnum's New American Museum, 539–541 Broadway, New York, New York. Opened September 6, 1865. From *Frank Leslie's Illustrated Newspaper*, September 30, 1865. P&P, LC-USZ62-72719.

After Barnum's museum burned, he rebuilt it several blocks up Broadway in the growing theater district. It incorporated its own highly ornamental auditorium. When this museum burned on March 3, 1868, again with extensive loss of animal life, Barnum left the museum business for good to concentrate his energies on traveling circus shows.

1-026. Barnum's New American Museum, 539–541 Broadway, New York, New York. Opened September 6, 1865. From *Frank Leslie's Illustrated Newspaper*, September 30, 1865. P&P, LC-USZ62-72719.

1-027. Astor Place Opera House, 5 Astor Place, New York, New York. Opened November 22, 1847; 1,800 seats; Isaiah Rogers, architect. Nathaniel Currier, lithographer, ca. 1849. P&P, KC-USZ62-42326; LC-USZC2-2532 (color).

The site of the infamous riot that established managerial control over theaters, the Astor Place Opera House, an elegant structure, survived for only a short time.

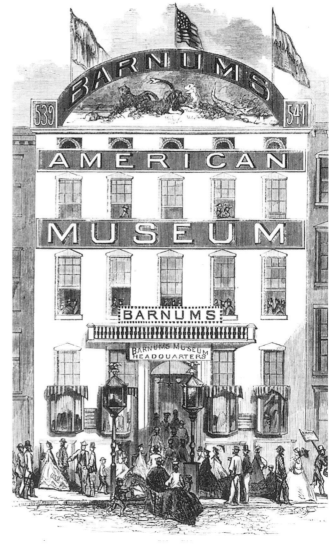

1-026

1-027

1-028

1-028. Broadway Theatre, 326–328 Broadway, New York, New York. Opened September 27, 1847; 4,500 seats; John M. Trimble, architect. Sarony, Major & Knapp, lithographers; from D. T. Valentine's *Manual for the Corporation of the City of New York*, 1911. P&P, LC-USZ62-15691.

Although its promoters intended that the Broadway, New York's largest theater to date, would replace the venerable Park Theatre as the city's preeminent performance facility, their endeavor was unsuccessful. The Park maintained its reputation until it burned in 1848. The Broadway lasted only until 1859.

1-029. Tripler Hall (Metropolitan, Burton's Theatre, Winter Garden), 682–684 Broadway, New York, New York. Opened October 17, 1850. Risdon & Conger, engravers; from *Frank Leslie's Illustrated Newspaper*, January 5, 1856. P&P, LC-USZ62-79813.

After refurbishment by architect John M. Trimble, this theater opened as Laura Keene's Varieties. Keene lost the lease after only one season, but soon thereafter opened a theater of her own, one of the grandest of prewar New York (1-030).

1-029

1-030. Laura Keene's (Jane English's, Mrs. John Wood's Olympic) Theatre, 624 Broadway, New York, New York. Opened November 18, 1856; 2,500 seats; John M. Trimble, architect. From *Frank Leslie's Illustrated Newspaper*, December 13, 1856. P&P, LC-USZ62-2522.

Beautiful, strong, and resilient, Laura Keene was one of the most remarkable personalities in American theater history. An abused wife, she left England with two small daughters to pursue a theatrical career in America. Within three years she opened her first theater (1-029). Losing it to a hostile landlord, she opened her own venue the following season. Having succeeded as a presenter she turned to acting, where she became noted for her grace and natural ease. She appeared in over 150 plays, the most noted of which was *Our American Cousin*. President Lincoln attended this show at Ford's Theatre on the night of his assassination (1-048–1-050). At the fateful moment, Laura Keene was on stage.

1-031. Niblo's Garden Theatre, 568–576 Broadway, New York, New York. Opened July 30, 1849. Wood, engraver; from *Ballou's Pictorial Drawing-Room Companion*, February 24, 1855. P&P, LC-USZ61-368.

When William Niblo established his first theater, the Sans Souci, in a private park on the edge of New York, he founded an institution that would survive fires and rebuildings to become a theatrical legend. The elegant auditorium illustrated here was the result of a rebuilding in 1854. Niblo attracted a family audience to presentations by the Ravels, a family of acrobats. His most famous offering, *The Black Crook*, opened in 1866. It was America's first musical play, featuring America's first chorus line and incorporating America's first simulation of near nudity.

1-030

1-031

1-032

1-033

1-034

1-032. Masonic Opera House, 516 Hancock Street, New Bern, North Carolina. Dedicated June 10, 1809; 450 seats. P&P, HABS,NC,25-NEBER,22-1.

The new St. John's Masonic Lodge, of which the Opera House was a part, was considered to be the grandest building in North Carolina. A versatile facility, its uses ranged from fraternal meetings to the town jail. Even before its completion, it hosted traveling theatrical companies. In 1905, the auditorium was renovated to become a full-time theater. Until 1974, when it closed, St. John's Lodge claimed to be America's oldest continuously operating theater.

1-033. Eagle Lodge (King Street Opera House), 142 West King Street, Hillsborough, North Carolina. Built 1823; Captain William Nichols, architect. Jack E. Boucher, photographer, February, 1965. P&P, HABS,NC,68-HILBO,6-2.

The Eagle Lodge, a Masonic institution, served its community for decades as lecture hall, concert hall, Civil War hospital, opera house, observatory, and general meeting facility. The purity of its classical form, a 20-foot cube with a carefully proportioned Ionic portico, reflects the architectural grounding of freemasonry as well as the designer's careful study of ancient and Renaissance architectural models.

1-034. Odd Fellows Hall (Henry Street Opera House, Troubadour Theatre), North Main Street at Henry Street, Lexington, Virginia. Built 1853; 750 seats. Unidentified photographer, July, 1968. P&P, HABS,VA,872-LEX,14-1.

Built for the Independent Order of Odd Fellows, this building doubled for many years as a lodge hall and Lexington's opera house. In 1925 it was purchased by Washington and Lee University, which opened it ten years later as the Troubadour Theatre.

1-035. Odd Fellows Hall (New American Theatre), 17 South Royal Street, Mobile, Alabama. Built ca. 1840. W. N. Manning, photographer, February 27, 1934. P&P, HABS,ALA,49-MOBI,17-1.

1-036. Thespian Hall (Thespian Opera House, Stephen's New Opera House, Lyric Theatre), Fifth and Vine Streets, Boonville, Missouri. Built 1855; 500 seats. Piaget-van Ravenswaay Survey, photographer, 1936. P&P, HABS,MO,27-BOONV,1-5.

The serenity of Thespian Hall's columned facade belies the complexity of its history. In 1855, the new hall held five hundred spectators, a capacity that by the end of the century had grown to 850 through the addition of a balcony. In the twentieth century a new stage gave the theater up-to-date technology and 197 new seats on the site of the original stage. The electric sign hanging between the columns adds an irreverently lively touch to the venerable facade.

1-037. Wallack's (Germania, Star) Theatre, 842–846 Broadway, New York, New York. Opened September 25, 1861; Thomas R. Jackson, architect. P&P, LC-USZ62-55037.

In the pre–Civil War period a theater typically was operated by an actor/manager who appeared in his own productions with his own repertory company—a group of actors who played in varied roles, much like a modern opera troupe. Of these companies, none was more consistent in quality and dedication than Lester Wallack's players. Their work and their theater became legendary. In Wallack's Theatre an elaborate front building, seen to the left, masked an auditorium that was entirely devoid of pretension. When Wallack built a new theater uptown (see 3-035), this one became devoted to German productions. Its demolition in 1901 was recorded in an early stop-motion film (see 9-051).

1-035

1-036

1-037

1-038

1-039

1-038. McVicker's Theatre, 25 West Madison Street, Chicago, Illinois. Opened November 5, 1857; 2,500 seats. Louis Kurz, artist; from James W. Sheahan, *Chicago Illustrated*, 1866. P&P, LC-USZ62-2515.

A Chicago mainstay for generations, McVicker's Theatre had a tumultuous history. John H. McVicker opened his first theater, illustrated here, in 1857. In 1871, faced with competition from newer venues, he worked with architect Otis L. Wheelock to completely modernize and upgrade the building. Six weeks after its opening, the new McVicker's, along with the rest of central Chicago, burned. Its successor, opened on August 15, 1872, on the same site and designed by Wheelock & Thomas, was the first public building to go up after the Great Fire. In 1885, McVicker worked with architects Adler & Sullivan on a thorough update. When that theater burned, in 1891, he worked again with Adler & Sullivan to build its replacement. Opened on March 31, 1892, it was demolished in 1921 to be replaced by yet another McVicker's, a large cinema by architects Newhouse & Bernham that opened on September 26, 1922.

1-039. Academy of Music, 2 Irving Place, New York, New York. Opened October 2, 1854; 2,100 seats; Alexander Saeltzer, architect. Thomas Nast, artist; from *Harper's Weekly*, March 27, 1867, p. 232. Gen. Coll., E461.H3.

The first of the great auditoriums to climax America's pre–Civil War theater construction, New York's Academy of Music was the city's unchallenged home of high culture. For a generation the cream of New York's society filled its white-and-gold auditorium with glamour and finery. Rivaled in later years by the Metropolitan Opera House (see 8-039–8-049), the Academy eventually turned to vaudeville presentations. When it was demolished in 1926, its name was transferred to a new movie palace directly across Fourteenth Street (see 6-075 and 6-076).

1-040. American Academy of Music, 236–242 South Broad Street, Philadelphia, Pennsylvania. Opened January 26, 1857; 2,838 seats; Napoleon LeBrun & Gustave Runge, architects. DPCC, photographers, ca. 1905. P&P, LC-D4-18593.

Movement toward an opera house in Philadelphia began in 1852, contemporary with similar efforts in New York and Boston. By century's end the Academy had hosted Tchaikovsky, Strauss, Saint-Saens, Rachmaninoff, Stravinsky, and Victor Herbert conducting their own works. It presented the American premiere of Wagner's *The Flying Dutchman*, and it became home to the newly formed Philadelphia Orchestra. The Academy of Music remains one of America's oldest continuously operating theaters, almost unaltered and arguably the finest of its era.

1-041. American Academy of Music, 236–242 South Broad Street, Philadelphia, Pennsylvania. Opened January 26, 1857; 2,838 seats; Napoleon LeBrun & Gustave Runge, architects. Cortland V. D. Hubbard, photographer, November, 1967. P&P, HABS,PA,51-PHILA,294-6.

The Academy's lobby was more spacious than most in its day. Its chandelier and newel torchières, products of Philadelphia's Cornelius & Sons, remain masterpieces of American Victorian decorative art.

1-042

1-043

1-044

1-045

1-042. American Academy of Music, 236–242 South Broad Street, Philadelphia, Pennsylvania. Opened January 26, 1857; 2,838 seats; Napoleon LeBrun & Gustave Runge, architects. Cortland V. D. Hubbard, photographer, November, 1967. P&P, HABS,PA,51-PHILA,294-7.

Located immediately above the lobby, with high arched windows overlooking Broad Street, the Academy's Grand Foyer or Ballroom has hosted Philadelphia's elite for a century and a half.

1-043. American Academy of Music, 236–242 South Broad Street, Philadelphia, Pennsylvania. Opened January 26, 1857; 2,838 seats; Napoleon LeBrun & Gustave Runge, architects. Cortland V. D. Hubbard, photographer, November, 1967. P&P, HABS,PA,51-PHILA,294-9.

Architect Gustave Runge brought to the Academy a firsthand acquaintance with the theaters of his native Germany. While its balconies possess an openness that had become exclusive to American auditorium design, the Academy's scale and grandeur vividly recall the great opera houses of the Continent.

1-044. American Academy of Music, 236–242 South Broad Street, Philadelphia, Pennsylvania. Opened January 26, 1857; 2,838 seats; Napoleon LeBrun & Gustave Runge, architects. Cortland V. D. Hubbard, photographer, November, 1967. P&P, HABS,PA,51-PHILA,294-14.

Conservatism is in Philadelphia's nature. The Academy retained gas lighting well into the twentieth century and its original seating layout is still intact. It displays the wonderfully intimate quality of even a very large Victorian theater, where the surrounding balconies confine the open volume.

1-045. American Academy of Music, 236–242 South Broad Street, Philadelphia, Pennsylvania. Opened January 26, 1857; 2,838 seats; Napoleon LeBrun & Gustave Runge, architects. Cortland V. D. Hubbard, photographer, November, 1967. P&P, HABS,PA,51-PHILA,294-8.

Curving ambulatories provided access to all levels of the Academy's horseshoe-shaped auditorium. The original, elaborate decorative scheme of marbling, graining, and trompe-l'oeil painting has recently been restored.

1-046. Academy of Music, 176–178 Montague Street, Brooklyn, New York. Opened January 15, 1861; 2,300 seats; Leopold Eidlitz, architect. From *Harper's Weekly*, February 2, 1861, p. 77. Gen Coll., E461.H3.

The pre–Civil War era would see the opening of another major Academy of Music, a great music hall that ended the perception that Brooklyn was a cultural backwater. The *New York Times* recognized the transformation, as did Brooklyn's own Walt Whitman who praised the Academy as "beautiful outside and in, and on a scale commensurate with similar buildings, even in some of the largest and most polished capitals of Europe." This first Brooklyn Academy of Music burned in 1903.

1-047. Academy of Music, 176–178 Montague Street, Brooklyn, New York. Opened January 15, 1861; 2,300 seats; Leopold Eidlitz, architect. From *Harper's Weekly*, February 2, 1861, p. 77. Gen Coll., E461.H3.

The Brooklyn Academy's auditorium continued the design vocabulary of the exterior. In front of the ornate proscenium, the timber structure was exposed. Observers perceived it as both Gothic and Moorish, especially in its vivid coloration. To a *New York Times* reviewer it conveyed a "certain barbaric splendor" that was at once "unique and pleasing."

1-046

1-047

1-048

1-049

1-050

1-048. Ford's Theatre, 511 Tenth Street NW, Washington, D.C. Opened August 27, 1863; 1,624 seats; James J. Gifford, architect. Unidentified photographer, April, 1865. P&P, LC-B817-7765.

Ford's Theatre, so new that its metal cornice had not yet been installed, typified popular theater building of the day. A venture of Baltimore entrepreneur John T. Ford, it was built on the remains of the First Baptist Church, which had burned nine months earlier. Painting the lower facade white to recall marble gave its no-nonsense facade a bit of monumentality. Three large roof ventilators provided air circulation to the windowless interior. The front doors led to distinctly separate seating areas: The door at far left was a dummy; the second door opened to the dress circle stairs; the next two to the lobby and main floor; and the door to the far right opened to the family circle, the theater's uppermost gallery.

1-049. Ford's Theatre, 511 Tenth Street NW, Washington, D.C. Opened August 27, 1863; 1,624 seats; James J. Gifford, architect. Currier & Ives, lithographers, 1865. P&P, LC-USZ62-2073.

The pre–Civil War period ended with sudden finality on Good Friday, April 14, 1865, as a shot rang out in a crowded theater. As he laughed at Laura Keene in the popular comedy *Our American Cousin*, Abraham Lincoln suddenly was gone.

1-050. Ford's Theatre, 511 Tenth Street NW, Washington, D.C. Opened August 27, 1863; 1,624 seats; James J. Gifford, architect. Unidentified photographer, April, 1865. P&P, LC-B811-3403.

To have the president in attendance was a distinct honor for Ford. In preparation, he removed the partition between the stage-left boxes and added Lincoln's favorite rocking chair to the box's miscellaneous furnishings. The rail was draped with American and Treasury Guard flags and a portrait of George Washington.

1-051. Ford's Theatre, 511 Tenth Street NW, Washington, D.C. Opened August 27, 1863; 1,624 seats; James J. Gifford, architect. Underwood & Underwood, photographer, ca. 1932. P&P, LC-USZ62-126702.

Although Lincoln's assassination did nothing to change Ford's intent to operate his theater, public sentiment did. In the face of popular opposition to its being used as a theater again, the building was acquired by the government. The auditorium was removed and office floors were inserted. That the new interior collapsed, with loss of life, caused some to think the building was cursed, profaned by its location within the shell of a church. The interior was quickly rebuilt, again as offices. A Museum of Lincolniana, shown here, occupied the ground floor.

1-051

1-052. Ford's Theatre, 511 Tenth Street NW, Washington, D.C. Opened August 27, 1863; 1,624 seats; James J. Gifford, architect. Jack E. Boucher, photographer, May, 1968. P&P, HABS,DC,WASH,421-2.

Opened on the building's centennial, the reconstructed Ford's Theatre superbly illustrates pre–Civil War theater design. The stage extends far into the auditorium. The box seats are actually on stage and place their occupants very much in the action. Lower-floor patrons occupy wooden chairs that were originally tightly packed, precluding clearly defined aisles and raising seating capacity. The cast-iron columns that support the upper tiers make their presence felt in the view of rear seat occupants.

1-052

1-053. Ford's Theatre, 511 Tenth Street NW, Washington, D.C. Opened August 27, 1863; 1,624 seats; James J. Gifford, architect. Jack E. Boucher, photographer, May, 1968. P&P, HABS,DC,WASH,421-4.

Ford's lower floor was divided into two sections defined only by differing styles of loose chairs. The first nine rows were the orchestra, the last seven were the parquet. The first tier, with chairs that matched those of the parquet, was the dress circle. Its predominantly male occupants looked down on a family audience below. Despite its name, the steeply sloped family circle in the second tier was occupied not by families but by tightly packed, often rowdy young men who had purchased a 25-cent general admission to sit on its hard wooden benches.

1-053

THEATERS AT THE NATION'S EDGE

As he built John Sutter's sawmill, in Coloma, California, gold was the last thing on James Marshall's mind. But on January 24, 1848, as he worked on the new millrace, Marshall noticed a few shiny flakes. Sutter tried to keep the discovery secret, but by late spring word was out. By August the nearby hills held four thousand prospectors' camps and within a year some forty thousand "forty-niners" were working the territory. By the 1880s they were gone, and only a few golden dregs dotted the despoiled land.

The story of California's mother lode was not unique. Across the West newfound deposits of gold, silver, and copper became immediate magnets for fortune seekers. The riches were there in quantity, but only briefly. Once the ore was gone, the miners were gone. A thriving community could be abandoned within a day.

Prospectors' communities were thrown up quickly for populations whose growth was explosive. Money was no object—the hills held more than could be imagined. The towns were overwhelmingly male. Young prospectors sought their fortunes alone. At least temporarily, their wives and girlfriends stayed back East.

Inevitably, followers came—prostitutes and troublous men fleeing old reputations and identities to make problems anew. Money lust and money availability combined, but had no outlet. Lacking structured government, the towns were lawless, rife with gambling and violent crime. The atmosphere came to be portrayed in fiction and drama for a century.

If the roistering townsmen had a vulnerability, it was the emptiness of isolation and loneliness. Surrounded by riches, they were homesick and starved for entertainment, and the new frontier theaters filled that void. Predictably, their preference was for pretty girls. It was said that on stage a woman had no need to sing or act; merely to present herself before a male audience would win applause and lavish payment; as prominent actors made the arduous prairie trek to appear in the frontier theaters, homegrown talents such as Lola Montez and Lotta Crabtree grew to enjoy national recognition. Bret Harte and Mark Twain visited to lecture and to chronicle the scene. Levi Strauss came to manufacture sturdy garments made of tent canvas with riveted pockets.

A prairie theater was built hurriedly. Neither time nor construction technology existed to emulate the eastern model. The building was simple and shedlike, masked by the "false front" that was characteristic of boomtown architecture. The facade could look quite grand, ornamented with classical cornices, window trim, pilasters, and quoins carved from wood and painted to look like cut stone, but the interior often did double duty, housing a fraternity or a miners' union as well. To accommodate gambling, meetings, and dances its floor generally was flat. The balcony, proscenium, and boxes were showy but flimsy constructions of painted canvas. Built on an instant fortune, sometimes even on a whim to please a favored showgirl, even the greatest opera house always smelled of the mining camp.

2-001

2-001. Union Theater ("First Theater in California"), Scott and Pacific Streets, Monterey, California. Opened 1847. P&P, HABS, CAL,27-MONT,12-1.

Monterey was founded in 1770 as a mission and a military outpost. By 1820 a few families had settled outside its adobe walls, and by 1840 it had been laid out as a town. In 1843 Jack Swan built a saloon and apartment house there. His building's use was flexible. Rising partitions allowed its four rooms to be combined into a single space. In the fall of 1847, four army volunteers joined with three locals to present minstrel performances in the unused dining room. Encouraged by their success, Swan remodeled the building, adding a pit and stage and renaming it the Union Theater. Performances continued until 1851. After years of increasing dilapidation, the theater was restored in the 1930s.

2-002. Old Theatre, San Andreas, California. Built 1850s. Unidentified photographer, 1925. P&P, HABS,CAL,5-SAND,5-1.

San Andreas was established in 1848 as a Mexican gold mining camp, but by 1850 the native Mexicans had been crowded out by American prospectors. In 1854, when large gold deposits were discovered, the population burgeoned. San Andreas did not follow the boom-and-bust cycle of many such towns. By 1866 it had become the county seat of Calaveras County. Edwin Booth was among the famous actors who appeared in this modest performance hall.

2-003. Miners' Union Hall (left), Main Street, Bodie, California. Opened June 26, 1878. Unidentified photographer, 1962. P&P, HABS,CAL,26-BODI,2-1.

Waterman S. Body discovered gold in the high Sierras in 1859, but it was not until 1874 that a mine cave-in revealed the richness of his find, the vast Comstock Lode. Word got out—in five years Bodie's population grew to 12,000. By 1890, eleven years later, the boom was over. Although gold extraction continued until 1932, successive fires had leveled most of the town. Besides serving its members, the Miners' Union Hall was a church, a meeting hall, and an entertainment center.

2-004. Miners' Union Hall, Main Street, Bodie, California. Opened June 26, 1878. Tony E. Smith, delineator. P&P, HABS CA-1919, sheet no. 4, detail.

2-002

2-003

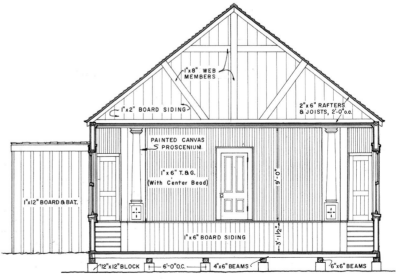

2-004

2-005

2-005. Central City Opera House, 200 Eureka Street, Central City, Colorado. Opened March 4, 1878; 750 seats; Robert S. Roeschlaub, architect. Bernal Wells, photographer, January 24, 1934. P&P, HABS,COLO,24-CENCI,1-1

When Colorado's gold was discovered in 1859, Central City quickly became an important regional center. After a major fire in 1874, the community rebuilt on a scale consistent with its reputation as the richest square mile in America. The new opera house was a rarity, a permanent, professionally designed theater that could have stood proudly on any Main Street in America. Central City's varied dramatic interests necessitated two grand openings, a concert the first night and a dramatic performance the second. By 1890 the gold had dwindled and Central City's population had dropped from ten thousand to four hundred.

2-006. Proscenium, Central City Opera House, 200 Eureka Street, Central City, Colorado. Opened March 4, 1878; 750 seats; Robert S. Roeschlaub, architect. Bernal Wells, photographer, January 24, 1934. P&P, HABS,COLO,24-CENCI,1-5.

In 1932 a thorough restoration revived the long-ignored opera house. New art deco wall murals and a new chandelier complemented artist John C. Massman's original, elaborately painted ceiling. Today Central City Opera House is a nationally acclaimed summer opera venue.

2-006

2-007. Uray (Ouray) Theatre, 472 Main Street, Ouray, Colorado. Opened 1889; 230 seats; George & Ed White, architects. Russell Lee, photographer, September, 1940. P&P, LC-USF34-037651-D.

Named after a Ute chief, Ouray sat at the center of Colorado's gold and silver territory. Within a decade of its founding in 1876, the town's population had grown to twelve hundred. As it was a shipping center rather than a mining town, Ouray had more families and more stability than most of its neighboring towns. In addition, Ouray's natural beauty made it a sought-after destination, one of several places called the "Switzerland of America." Substantially built and well maintained, many of Ouray's early buildings remain. The old opera house still serves as the town's theater.

2-008. Miners' Union Hall (American Legion Building), 1069 Greene Street, Silverton, Colorado. Built 1901. Lee Russell, photographer, September, 1940. P&P, LC-USF34-037743-D.

Gold was discovered in Silverton in 1860, the town was platted in 1874, and the population had doubled by 1875. When the railroad arrived in 1882, the town became the metropolis of a widespread gold and silver mining area. It is said that the Western Federation of Miners completed construction of their hall themselves to avoid the high price of professional bricklayers. After generations of use as a lodge and community meeting hall, the building became the Miners Union Theatre in 1991.

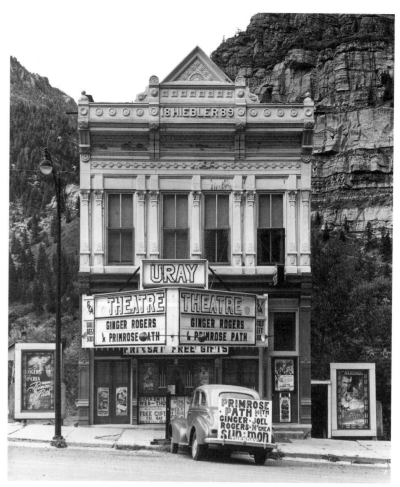

2-007

2-008

2-009

2-009. Piper's Opera House, 1 North B Street, Virginia City, Nevada. Opened March 6, 1885. Robert W. Kerrigan, photographer, March, 1937. P&P, HABS, NEV,15-VIRG,17-3.

Virginia City's gold deposits, which came to light in 1859, proved difficult to extract from the muddy soil. The sticky earth turned out to be silver ore, part of the Comstock Lode. America's richest silver deposit, it fueled the nearby Carson City Mint, built San Francisco, and financed the Civil War. The prospectors called the place Virginny Town, a name later solemnized as Virginia City. At its peak, the population neared thirty thousand. By 1878, the mines had become depleted. Operations ceased in October, 1886.

In 1862 John Piper purchased a business building in the town's booming center. A year later he ventured into the theater business by acquiring Maguire's Opera House. When it burned in 1875, Piper built a new auditorium behind his business block. The second theater burned in 1883 and once again Piper rebuilt, opening the opera house shown here in 1885.

2-010. Longitudinal (top) and transverse (bottom) sections, Piper's Opera House, 1 North B Street, Virginia City, Nevada. Opened March 6, 1885. Robert P. Mizell, delineator, 1973. P&P, HABS NV-15-7, sheet nos. 6 and 7, details.

Piper's architect had the dual challenge of incorporating an existing structure—the old business building—and building the new auditorium into a steep hill. In the finished opera house, patrons ascended from the lobby entrance to the second-floor auditorium whose floor was still at grade. The stage was at an even higher ground level. The third Piper Opera House had a balcony, elegant boxes, and a stage with technical provisions far superior to any in the vicinity. Its flat, spring-mounted floor enabled it to double as a ballroom and arena.

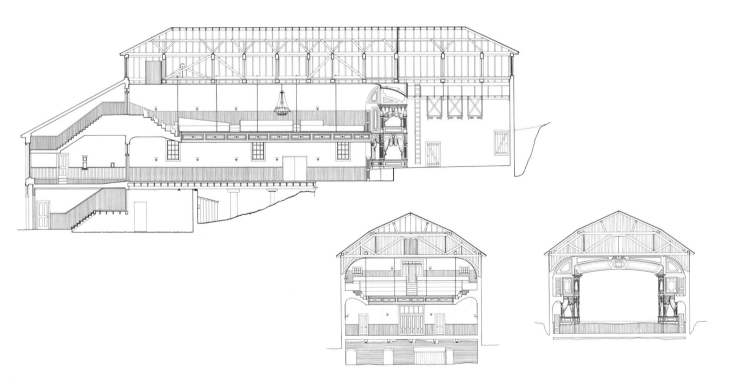

2-010

2-011. Miners' Union Hall, B Street, Virginia City, Nevada. Built 1876. Robert W. Kerrigan, photographer, March, 1937. P&P, HABS,NEV,15-VIRG,19-1.

Like its counterparts in other communities, Virginia City's Miners' Union Hall served the business needs of its members as well as the entertainment needs of the town. When Piper's Opera House was rebuilding from fire, it was the bustling city's only theater.

2-012. Miners' Union Hall, B Street, Gold Hill, Nevada. Unidentified photographer, May, 1940. P&P, HABS,NEV,15-GOLD,2-1

A satellite community of Virginia City, Gold Hill's rise and fall reflected the activity of the Comstock Lode mine. Its 1873 population of eight thousand had dropped to fewer than fifty by the end of the century. Like similar buildings in other communities, the Miners' Union Hall served a mixture of business and pleasure needs. Although the building was simple, its facade pretended to be grand. Using wood to imitate masonry, its designer gave it the solidly monumental look of a bank or a civic hall.

2-011

2-012

SHEET METAL FACIA

COMMON BRICK FRONT.
HEADER BOND EVERY
8ᵗʰ COURSE – WOOD
CASING FOR WINDOWS

GRANITE

SHEET METAL FACIA

COLORED GLASS IN
SMALL SQUARES

CAST IRON COLUMN
COVERS. SEE
SHEET 9 FOR
DETAILS

WOOD PANELS

1890

MINERS UNION
HALL

THIRD FLOOR

SEE SHEET
NO. 4
DETAIL A

SECOND FLOOR

¼" PLATE
GLASS

FIRST FLOOR

5'-4"

11'-9"

12'-9"

44'-8"

14'-10"

NORTH ELEVATION

2-013

2-014

2-013. Elevation, Miners Union Hall, Main Street, Granite, Montana. Opened December 31, 1890; J. R. Roberts, architect. U. James Blackburn, delineator. P&P, HABS MT-15, sheet no. 5, detail.

2-014. Miners Union Hall, Main Street, Granite, Montana. Opened December 31, 1890; J. R. Roberts, architect. P&P, HABS,MONT,20-GRANI,1-4

Granite's history typified the Western boomtown story. In 1872, while following a wounded deer, a hunter found a piece of ruby silver. Five years later a capitalist opened a mine. Within eleven years Granite was in full operation as one of the richest silver areas in the United States, with a population of over three thousand. In 1893, when Congress repealed the Sherman Act and the bottom fell out of silver prices, the town emptied in a single day. By year's end only 140 people remained.

Granite's Miners Union Hall stood tall above the wooden structures around it. Above a first-floor pool hall and club were a library, dance hall, and auditorium. Built for permanence, it presided over a ghost town within three years. Now the building is a ruin, its theatrical origin visible only in the lyre decorations cast into its iron columns.

2-015. Bird Cage (Elite) Theatre, East Allen Street at Sixth Street, Tombstone, Arizona. Opened September 23, 1881; 185 seats; William J. Hutchison, designer/builder. Russell Lee, photographer, April, 1940. P&P, LC-USF34-036248-D.

Founded by Ed Schieffelin, who concocted the town's name, Tombstone was laid out on March 5, 1879. Within a year the population had risen from one hundred to three thousand; by 1881 it had reached seven thousand; by the 1890s, fifteen thousand. Locked in a rich silver mining area, Tombstone was as rough and ready as a town could get (its newspaper is still called the *Epitaph*). It was home to Wyatt Earp, Doc Holliday, the Clanton Clan, and the O. K. Corral. The Bird Cage was one of the more formal of the town's entertainment spots. Its facade had a simple elegance that would have been as much at home in New Orleans as in the Arizona desert.

2-016. Bird Cage (Elite) Theatre, East Allen Street at Sixth Street, Tombstone, Arizona. Opened September 23, 1881; 185 seats; William J. Hutchison, designer/builder. Russell Lee, photographer, May, 1940. P&P, LC-USF34-036387-D.

The Bird Cage's level main floor accommodated gaming tables as easily as theater seats. The simple stage and proscenium boxes, constructed of painted canvas and thin wood, hosted performances by the likes of Lola Montez, her protegée Lotta Crabtree, Eddie Foy, and Lillie Langtry.

2-017. Bird Cage (Elite) Theatre, East Allen Street at Sixth Street, Tombstone, Arizona. Opened September 23, 1881; 185 seats; William J. Hutchison, designer/builder. Russell Lee, photographer, April, 1940. P&P, LC-USF34-036304-D.

The Bird Cage derived its name from the fourteen canvas-constructed boxes suspended along both sides of the auditorium. An interesting throwback to America's earliest theaters, these provided a modicum of privacy even as they allowed house prostitutes to appeal to the tough crowd assembled below. The Bird Cage's around-the-clock operation was based on ample money, hard drink, homesickness, and boredom. The many scores settled there have left dozens of bullet holes in the theater's walls.

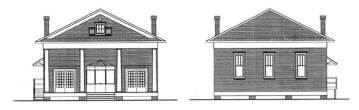

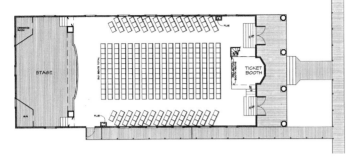

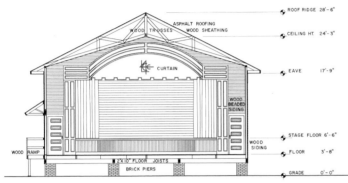

2-018

2-019

2-018. Fisher Opera House, U.S. Highway 171, Fisher, Louisiana. Built ca. 1910. D. Friedman and C. Boatright, delineators, 1995. P&P, HABS LA-1251-C, sheet nos. 1 and 4, details.

The frontier spirit was limited neither to the American West nor to the nineteenth century. Young men living in isolation, whether in the gold field or the lumber camp, did not require elaborate settings in which to enjoy their entertainment. Fisher, in far western Louisiana, was incorporated on July 15, 1899, by the Louisiana Long Leaf Lumber (4L) Company. More substantial than most such communities, it looked more like an independent town than the company-owned enclave that it was. Fisher's tiny hall, like its counterparts in the Western mountains, hardly merited the name Opera House. But people from the countryside flocked there because it was the only picture show around. In 1972, the successor logging company transferred the entire town to the Fisher Heritage Foundation to ensure its preservation.

2-019. Star Theatre, 13939 River Road, Locke, California. Built 1915–19. Jet Lowe, photographer, 1979. P&P, HABS,CAL,34-LOCKE,1/4-5.

Straddling Locke's two principal streets, the Star could be entered either directly from Main Street or by twin flanking stairs leading up from River Road. The theater's faded name remains above the simple arches, whose lightbulbs recalled the nickelodeon facades of nearby San Francisco.

2-020. Star Theatre, 13939 River Road, Locke, California. Built 1915–19. Jet Lowe, photographer, 1979. P&P, HABS,CAL,34-LOCKE,1/4-1.

Although the American frontier came to an end in about 1890, its pioneering spirit continued into the new century. When the Chinese district of Walnut Grove burned in 1915, its residents decided to build completely anew. Prohibited by race and nationality from owning real estate, they leased land from George Locke upon which to build a new town, Lockeport, later Locke. As it evolved into a gathering spot for Chinese workers from local asparagus farms, Locke's population grew to over six hundred. With neither government nor police, its streets roistered with activity both legal and shady. Like other cities that were built to serve a specialized need, Locke as an ethnic community has declined disastrously. It is now home to less than one hundred, fewer than ten of whom are Chinese.

2-020

2-021. Theater, 13923 Main Street, Locke, California. Built 1915. Jet Lowe, photographer, April, 1984. P&P, HABS,CAL,34-LOCKE,1/16-1

Locke's second theater has long since been used as a municipal warehouse.

2-022. Academy of Music, Pine Street below Montgomery Street, San Francisco, California. Built ca. 1860. Unidentified photographer, ca. 1868. P&P, HABS,CAL,38-SANFRA,43-1.

Four sidewalk lanterns and a balcony (just beyond the projecting bay windows) over its entrance marked the Academy of Music, built by Tom Maguire, a theatrical entrepreneur whose enterprises dotted the Western territories (2-009). Unsuccessful as a home for grand opera, the Academy eventually became a furniture warehouse.

2-023. Metropolitan Theatre, Montgomery Street south of Jackson Street, San Francisco, California. Opened July 1, 1861. Unidentified photographer, 1868. P&P, HABS,CAL,38-SANFRA,57-1.

As the West's early metropolis, San Francisco was home to several important theaters. The Metropolitan's distinguished facade could have fronted an eastern financial or civic building equally well. David Belasco made his stage debut here on March 18, 1873, in the role of Emperor Norton, a character who became locally renowned as the self-proclaimed emperor of the United States. Later in the same year the Metropolitan was demolished to provide space for a new street right-of-way.

2-021

2-022

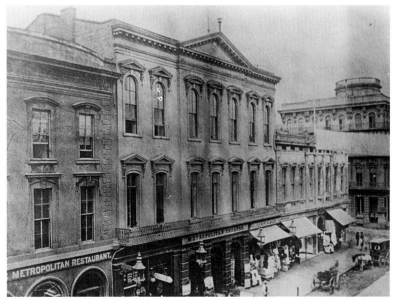

2-023

2-024

2-024. Merced Theatre, 418 North Main Street, California. Opened December 31, 1870; 400 seats; E. F. Kysor, architect. Henry F. Withey, photographer, June, 1936. P&P, HABS, CAL,19-LOSAN,8-1.

The Merced was both the first theater in Los Angeles and the city's tallest building. Its stucco facade was carefully detailed to look like cut sandstone. The second-floor auditorium interconnected with the elegant Hotel Pico next door, while owners William and Merced Abbott lived above. Both theater and hotel remain landmarks of the city's historic Pueblo district.

2-025. Elevation, Merced Theatre, 418 North Main Street, Los Angeles, California. Opened December 31, 1870; 400 seats; E. F. Kysor, architect. George Hodgkinson, delineator. P&P, HABS CA-327, sheet no. 2

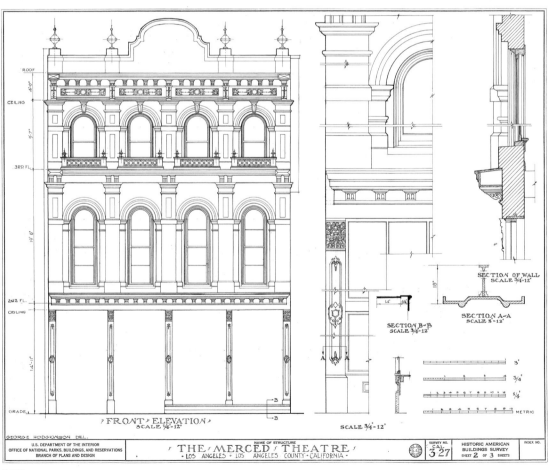

2-025

2-026. New Market and Theater, SW Second Avenue at Ankeny Street, Portland, Oregon. Opened March 24, 1875; 1,200 seats; W. W. Piper, architect. P&P, HABS,ORE,26-PORT,1-1.

Portland's first public market was a local architectural wonder. Its twenty-eight market stalls were arrayed between marbleized columns that supported a vaulted ceiling. Above were offices, a gymnasium, and a popular theater. The elegance was short-lived. Within ten years demographic changes had made the neighborhood a commercial backwater, and both market and theater were converted to other uses.

2-027. Tabor Grand Opera House, 1535 Curtis Street, Denver, Colorado. Opened September 5, 1881; 1,510 seats; Willoughby J. Edbrooke & Franklin P. Burnham, architects. Louis C. McClure, photographer, 1908. P&P, LC-USZ62-116142.

Less on the frontier than of the frontier, Denver's self-image instantly changed from outpost to great city with the construction of the Tabor Grand. In 1869, Horace and Augusta Tabor made the six-week trek from Vermont to Colorado. Stopping briefly at the future site of Denver, they moved on to set up general stores in other mining towns. Investments in the silver mines of Leadville made Tabor an overnight millionaire. He was propelled into politics and returned to Denver as lieutenant governor, and he purchased an entire city block. Building his great opera house on half, he donated the rest to the federal government as the site of a post office. Damaged by his divorce from Augusta and his subsequent marriage to Baby Doe McCourt, Tabor's political career waned just as Leadville's mines became exhausted. Within ten years he was working as a common laborer. Shortly before Tabor's death, President McKinley appointed him Denver's postmaster, stationing him in the post office next to his opera house. Closed in October 1964, the theater was demolished shortly thereafter.

2-026

2-027

2-028

2-029. Broadway Theatre, 1756 Broadway, Denver, Colorado. Opened August 18, 1890; 1,624 seats; J. M. Wood, architect. Unidentified photographer, ca. 1892. P&P, HABS,COLO,16-DENV,12-, data p. 15.

The Broadway, Denver's second great theater, had no street presence. In this distant view its auditorium can be seen behind the Metropole Hotel, through which the Broadway was entered.

2-029. Broadway Theatre, 1756 Broadway, Denver, Colorado. Opened August 18, 1890; 1,624 seats; J. M. Wood, architect. Louis C. McClure, photographer, ca. 1892. P&P, HABS,COLO,16-DENV,12-, data p. 18.

What it lacked in street presence, the Broadway made up for within. No theater anywhere could surpass the exotic visual display that veteran theater architect J. M. Wood incorporated into its vast auditorium, and few could equal it. "A Glimpse of India," the scene painted on the asbestos safety curtain, was extended into the third tier for the Broadway's audiences, who found themselves engulfed in an Indo-Moorish fantasy that surpassed even New York's extravagant Casino (see 4-001 and 4-002). The Broadway was demolished in 1955.

2-029

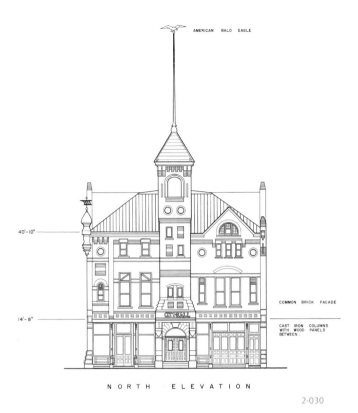

2-030

2-031

2-032

2-030. Elevation, City Hall and Opera House, East Main Street and Rouse Avenue, Bozeman, Montana. Opened September 14, 1890; 800 seats; Bryan S. Vreeland & George Hancock, architects. U. James Blackburn, delineator, 1965. P&P, HABS MT-18, sheet no. 7, detail.

Bozeman borrowed a New England tradition by combining city offices, a fire department, and a theater into a single building. Opened with a concert by the Queen City Band, the opera house was lauded as the finest between St. Paul and Portland.

2-031. City Hall and Opera House, East Main Street and Rouse Avenue, Bozeman, Montana. Opened September 14, 1890; 800 seats; Bryan S. Vreeland & George Hancock, architects. P&P, HABS,MONT,16-BOZ,1-6.

In stone and stained glass the entry clearly stated its dual purpose.

2-032. City Hall and Opera House, East Main Street and Rouse Avenue, Bozeman, Montana. Opened September 14, 1890; 800 seats; Bryan S. Vreeland & George Hancock, architects. Al Huntsman, photographer, 1965. P&P, HABS,MONT,16-BOZ,1-10.

For many years the derelict auditorium served as a storage facility for the city offices that shared its building. Although this use was inappropriate, it was not damaging. The space retained its original form and decoration until it was demolished in 1965.

THEATERS ACROSS THE CONTINENT

ON MAY 10, 1869, as a hammer drove home a golden spike at Promontory Point, Utah, the transcontinental railroad become a reality.

Since 1862 homesteaders had been driving their wagons into the solitude of the prairie, leaving their Eastern homes to begin anew in the West. But the land was so vast that the flow of newcomers had no more impact than a trickle. Now, with the Civil War over, united by the railroad, the nation was set to grow. If fortune had placed them near the railroad, small trading towns were primed to become great shipping centers. As they came for the raw materials of the West, the trains brought products from the East—fashionable clothing, furnishings, books. The gandy dancer's blow on the golden spike was a signal to dancers of other sorts—singers, Shakespeareans, tragedians, and comedians—that they had a new territory to serve.

The new theaters resulted from private enterprise. Well-to-do entrepreneurs had become paragons of local society. They owned the largest businesses in town—the grain elevator, the hardware store—and had taken their turns as aldermen, mayors, and judges. Now was the time for them to build a monument, a building that would proclaim the Western community's newfound strength and sophistication. Just like Philadelphia or New York, London or Paris, the new city on the prairie would have an opera house, a place where its bourgeois could congregate. It probably would be designed by a specialist in theater architecture. Practitioners like Leon Lempert, Oscar Cobb, Col. J. M. Wood, and J. B. McElfatrick honed their skills as they designed theaters across the land.

The buildings developed a distinct form. A business establishment was usually located on the ground floor. Upstairs, the auditorium had a main floor, a parquet circle, two balconies, and three tiers of elaborate proscenium boxes. The parquet was comfortable, even luxurious, with velvet upholstered seats. The gallery's wooden benches held the young and rowdy. The stage provided well for the visiting performers, with equipment and dimensions that matched the playhouses of the East. Dressing rooms were spartan but convenient. With luck, they even had running water.

Opera houses in name only, these theaters presented more melodrama than high art. As points of civic pride they were incomparable. Standards of architecture and performance were high. A level of quality once unique to New York was available across the land.

3-001. Concordia, 8–12 South Eutaw Street, Baltimore, Maryland. From *Frank Leslie's Illustrated Newspaper*, November 4, 1865. P&P, LC-USZ62-1752.

3-001

3-003

3-002. Crosby's Opera House, 12–30 West Washington Street, Chicago, Illinois. Opened April 20, 1865; W. W. Boyington, architect. John Carbutt, photographer, 1865–1870. P&P, LC-USZ62-106688.

Opened to an audience still stunned by Lincoln's assassination, Uranus Crosby's Opera House instantly became Chicago's cultural center. W. W. Boyington's restrained facade concealed a large and lavish auditorium. The opera house survived for only five years. Along with most of the city, it burned on October 9, 1871. (Boyington's nearby Water Tower survived to become a beloved Chicago landmark.)

3-003. Lincoln Hall, 401 Ninth Street NW, Washington, D.C. Opened 1867; Starkweather & Plowman, architects. Unidentified photographer, ca. 1870. P&P, LC-USZ62-114926.

Lincoln Hall contained a business college, several shops, and Washington's YMCA as well as an attractive auditorium on its third floor. When this hall burned in 1886, a new Lincoln Music Hall was built on its site.

3-004. Lincoln Hall, 401 Ninth Street NW, Washington, D.C. Opened 1867; Starkweather & Plowman, architects. Unidentified photographer, ca. 1870. P&P, LC-USZ62-113935.

Without a proscenium, fly loft, or backstage, Lincoln Hall was more a meeting and concert hall than a true theater. Its seating was divided between a steeply sloping parquet and a squared parquet circle. The patented I. P. Frink chandelier and extensive trompe-l'oeil decorations were hallmarks of theaters in the post–Civil War period.

3-004

3-005

3-006

3-007

3-005. Tammany Hall, 141–147 East Fourteenth Street, New York, New York. Opened May 18, 1868; 1,000 seats; Thomas R. Jackson, architect. Irving Underhill, photographer, ca. 1914. P&P, LC-USZ62-101734.

Tammany's meeting hall, located in the heart of the Fourteenth Street theatrical district, next door to the prestigious Academy of Music (see 1-039), served as a public theater well into the twentieth century.

3-006. Tammany Hall, 141–147 East Fourteenth Street, New York, New York. Opened May 18, 1868; 1,000 seats; Thomas R. Jackson, architect. P&P, LC-USZ62-2064; LC-USZC4-1222 (color).

Tammany Hall was elaborately decorated for the Democratic Nominating Convention of 1868. As a theater it was home to Dan Bryant's famous minstrel company and later to pioneering vaudeville manager Tony Pastor.

3-007. Tammany Hall, 141–147 East Fourteenth Street, New York, New York. Opened May 18, 1868; 1,000 seats; Thomas R. Jackson, architect. Strobridge & Company, lithographers, ca. 1896. P&P, LC-USZ6-424; LC-USZC4-10303 (color).

Founded in 1788 as an association of artisans, the Society of St. Tammany evolved into an infamous political machine that controlled New York's government for nearly a century by catering, through public service and overt bribery, to its large and shifting immigrant community, bringing to power such characters as the infamous Boss Tweed. While it might have struck fear into the hearts of opposing politicians, the Tammany Tiger was made light of by New York sophisticates. On this colorful sheet-music cover the society's hall serves as a backdrop as a member of the upper crust and a working-class upstart cavort with the evil beast.

3-008. Grand Duke's Opera House, Baxter and Park Streets, New York, New York. 50 seats. Joseph Becker, illustrator; from *Frank Leslie's Illustrated Newspaper*, January 17, 1874. P&P, LC-USZ62-122657.

When Russian Grand Duke Alexis visited New York in 1871, he was feted at the tony Academy of Music but made time to visit the Five Points, a stronghold of the Tammany organization. There he stopped for a performance at a tiny theater in the basement of a tenement owned, built, operated, and attended by neighborhood boys. Forever after it would be called the Grand Duke's Opera House. Horatio Alger featured it in his 1904 novel, *Julius the Street Boy*.

3-009. Booth's Theatre, 70–74 West Twenty-third Street, New York, New York. Opened February 3, 1869; 1,700 seats; James Renwick, architect. From *Harper's Weekly*, February 27, 1869. Gen. Coll., E461, H3.

Veteran repertory actor Edwin Booth built New York's most lavish theater. Located in "Ladies' Mile"—the city's department-store district—it attracted an audience of women by presenting afternoon "matinee" performances.

3-010. Arch Street Opera House (Park, Continental, Gaiety, Casino, Palace, Trocadero, Troc Theatre), 1003–1005 Arch Street, Philadelphia, Pennsylvania. Opened August 20, 1870; 1,000 seats; Edwin F. Durang, architect. Unidentified photographer, October 11, 1916. P&P, HABS,PA,51-PHILA,470-2.

Built for Simmons & Slocum's minstrel company, this delightful theater has been home to a wide variety of entertainment types. For many years, as the Trocadero, it was Philadelphia's principal burlesque theater. Upon the death of live burlesque, it was restored as a showcase for Chinese moving pictures, interrupted occasionally by live operatic performances by the Philadelphia Opera Theatre. More recently it has served as a cabaret and music venue. After serving for 133 years, it arguably holds an American record for continuous commercial operation.

3-008

3-009

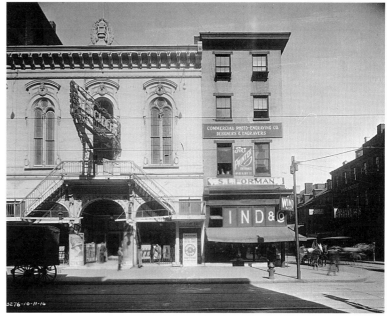

3-010

3-011

3-012

3-013

3-011. Jack Harris (J. J. Kehler, Jim White, Garden) Theatre, South Lehigh Avenue, Frackville, Pennsylvania. Built ca. 1870; 700 seats. P&P, Subject File-Theaters.

3-012. Union Square (Acme) Theatre, 54–58 East Fourteenth Street, New York, New York. Opened September 11, 1871; 1,200 seats. Illustration from a photograph by Hill Brothers; from *Harper's Weekly*, March 10, 1888. Gen. Coll., E461. H3.

Built by businessman Sheridan Shook, the Union Square operated for a year as a variety theater before becoming home to Albert M. Palmer's repertory company. Almost adjacent to Wallack's Theater (see 1-037), the Union Square rivaled its older neighbor as a home of finely produced drama. In comparison with Wallack's unassuming interior, the Union Square's auditorium was considered to be one of New York's prettiest. A devastating fire on March 24, 1888, provided *Harper's Weekly*'s artist the opportunity for this evocative image. The theater was rebuilt and stood until the mid-1990s.

3-013. Ford's Grand Opera House, 320 West Fayette Street, Baltimore, Maryland. Opened October 2, 1871; 2,250 seats; James J. Gifford, architect. P&P, LC-USZ62-15672; LC-USZC4-4614 (color).

Baltimore entrepreneur John T. Ford maintained a multiplicity of theaters. In Washington, D.C., he owned Ford's Opera House (Ninth and C Streets, rebuilt in 1869 and later called Bijou and Majestic) and the ill-starred Ford's Theatre (see 1-048–1-053). In his home city he owned the Holliday Street Theater (in the 100 block of North Holliday Street, built in 1795) and his flagship, Ford's Grand Opera House. The opera house had an especially long life. It operated for over ninety years as Baltimore's principal home of legitimate drama.

3-014. Springer Opera House, 105 Tenth Street, Columbus, Georgia. Opened February 21, 1871; 1,363 seats; Daniel M. Foley, architect. Unidentified photographer, 1980. P&P, HABS,GA,108-COLM,31-1.

Francis Joseph Springer moved to Columbus from his native Alsace before the Civil War. Successful in the grocery business, he developed the theater as much to express civic pride as to garner personal profit.

3-015. Springer Opera House, 105 Tenth Street, Columbus, Georgia. Opened February 21, 1871; 1,363 seats; Daniel M. Foley, architect. Unidentified photographer, 1980. P&P, HABS,GA,108-COLM,31-2.

In 1901, the Springer acquired a new auditorium. J. B. McElfatrick & Sons updated its twin horseshoe balconies and numerous box seats. Unseen, but even more important to the theater's success, an enlarged stage fitted with the latest technology brought the theater into state-of-the art condition as it entered the twentieth century.

3-014

3-015

3-016

3-018

3-017

3-016. Elevation, Union Hall, 110–112 West Market Street, Mount Carroll, Illinois. Dan Erdman, delineator. P&P, HABS IL-114, sheet no. 9, detail.

Even without an ostentatious front, a theater proclaimed itself by its sheer bulk as well as by the tall windows that illuminated its upper-floor auditorium. Such was the case with Mount Carroll's handsome Union Hall .

3-017. Grand Opera House (Masonic Hall), 818 North Market Street, Wilmington, Delaware. Opened December 22, 1871; 1,330 seats; Dixon & Carson, architects. David Ames, photographer. P&P, HABS,DEL,2-WILM,51-1.

Like many of its counterparts across the country, Wilmington's opera house was built by the city's Freemasons as a combined fraternal meeting hall and public theater. It presented a wide variety of entertainment types before settling into decades of use as a cinema. Restored, it is now used for live presentations. Its white cast-iron facade is the jewel of Market Street.

3-018. Opera House, 19 Touro Street, Newport, Rhode Island. Opened 1867; 1,217 seats; Benjamin Coit, architect. DPCC, photographer, ca. 1905. P&P, LC-D4-18336.

Newport's Opera House was built just after the Civil War and upgraded in 1902. An electric light suspended over the new entrance may have made it the brightest spot in town, even as its old signs remained over the original central doorway. Hidden for years behind a screen of aluminum and plastic, the original facade reemerged in the summer of 2003, once again to ornament Washington Square. The interior remained divided into small cinemas.

3-019. Macauley's Theatre, 329 West Walnut Street, Louisville, Kentucky. Opened October 13, 1873; 1,900 seats; J. B. McElfatrick & Sons, architects. C. Fischer, photographer, August 29, 1925. P&P, LC-USZ62-52343.

Macauley's was Louisville's principal theater for half a century. When it closed, its name was transferred to a new downtown theater. This photograph was taken on the old theater's last night.

3-020. Academy of Music, 516 North Howard Street, Baltimore, Maryland. Opened January 5, 1875; 1,800 seats. Walter Goater, artist; from *Frank Leslie's Illustrated Newspaper*, April 24, 1880. P&P, LC-UZ62-75200.

The Academy supplanted aging Concordia Hall (3-001) as one of Baltimore's great perform-ance halls. Later an important cinema, it was demolished in 1927. The level floor, pictured here, was built over the Academy's parquet seats for a charity ball held in 1880.

3-021. Marquette Opera House (Delft Theatre), 128 West Washington Street, Marquette, Michigan. 900 seats. DPCC, photographer, 1900–1910. P&P, LC-D4-68410.

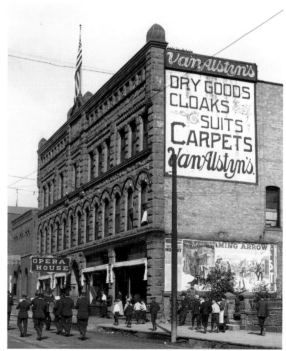

Marquette, on the Lake Superior shore of Michigan's Upper Peninsula, was once a great iron-ore and timber shipping center. Incorporated into the town's Masonic Temple, the Opera House provided entertainment to a town that was wealthy but isolated, especially in winter. Its rusticated sandstone facade was typical of the region. The Opera House burned in 1938.

3-022

3-025

3-023

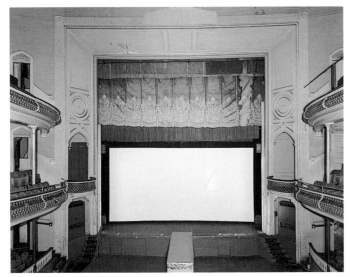

3-024

3-022. Academy of Music, 68–114 South Main Street, Fall River, Massachusetts. Opened January 6, 1876; 2,050 seats; Hartwell & Swasey, architects. William W. Owens, photographer, September, 1979. P&P, HABS MASS,3-FALL,9-1.

Covering an entire block in central Fall River, the Academy of Music with its surrounding commercial block was an imposing presence. The Academy's diminutive entrance, near the far end of the facade, was marked by projecting piers that rose to the building's roof.

3-023. Academy of Music, 68–114 South Main Street, Fall River, Massachusetts. Opened January 6, 1876; 2,050 seats; Hartwell & Swasey, architects. William W. Owens, photographer, September, 1979. P&P, HABS MASS,3-FALL,9-5.

With tall windows that revealed the mass of the auditorium within, the Academy's rear elevation looked more theatrical than its front. Paired openings below the windows were part of the building's ventilation system as was the small peaked penthouse on the roof.

3-024. Academy of Music, 68–114 South Main Street, Fall River, Massachusetts. Opened January 6, 1876; 2,050 seats; Hartwell & Swasey, architects. William W. Owens, photographer, September, 1979. P&P, HABS MASS,3-FALL,9-15.

The Academy's 35-square-foot proscenium, filled here with a movie screen, and 48-foot-high rigging loft were in every way comparable to their counterparts in New York.

3-025. Academy of Music, 68–114 South Main Street, Fall River, Massachusetts. Opened January 6, 1876; 2,050 seats; Hartwell & Swasey, architects. William W. Owens, photographer, September, 1979. P&P, HABS MASS,3-FALL,9-17.

The Academy's stage originally extended to the outer line of the box seats but was cut back to the proscenium line as part of an early modernization. The original, front-facing parquet, with its distinctly separated parquet circle, remained, as did the horseshoe balcony and the gallery with wooden bench seating. The stageward slant of the balconies was a touch of distinctly American pragmatism. The diminutive box seats signal the Academy's early date.

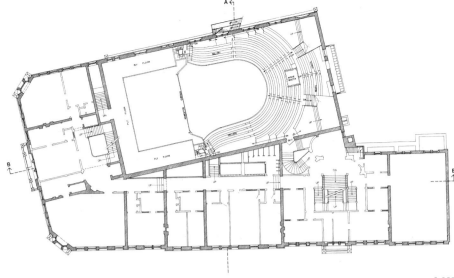

3-026

3-027

3-026. Academy of Music, 68–114 South Main Street, Fall River, Massachusetts. Opened January 6, 1876; 2,050 seats; Hartwell & Swasey, architects. William W. Owens, photographer, September, 1979. P&P, HABS MASS,3-FALL,9-18.

The great chandelier that ornamented the Academy until the end had a dual function. As its gas jets lit the auditorium, their heat created a column of air that rose through a ceiling vent. Fresh air drawn in near the floor displaced the heated air to ventilate the space.

3-027. Academy of Music, 68–114 South Main Street, Fall River, Massachusetts. Opened January 6, 1876; 2,050 seats; Hartwell & Swasey, architects. Chia-Ming Sze, delineator, 1976. P&P, HABS MA-1000, sheet no. 5, detail.

Theatrical architects became adept at fitting their complex and demanding building forms onto oddly shaped sites. Fall River's angled streets gave the Academy building a safety pin-shaped configuration with the auditorium at the rear. Offices at the front surrounded the lobby and its system of stairways.

3-028. Academy of Music, 68–114 South Main Street, Fall River, Massachusetts. Opened January 6, 1876; 2,050 seats; Hartwell & Swasey, architects. William W. Owens, photographer, September, 1979. P&P, HABS MASS,3-FALL,9-7.

The small balcony over the Academy's entrance became obscured by a later marquee. Almost universal in late nineteenth-century theaters, the entrance balcony had been pioneered by P. T. Barnum as a place from which a band could play to attract audiences.

3-028

3-029

3-030

3-031

3-029. Cincinnati Music Hall, 1243 Elm Street, Cincinnati, Ohio. Opened May 14, 1878; 3,634 seats; Hannaford & Proctor, architects. C. H. Muhrman, photographer, ca. 1881. P&P, LC-USZ62-116141.

Located in the heart of a large German district known as Over the Rhine, Cincinnati's Music Hall replaced the old Saengerfest Hall as home to an annual May Festival of choral singing. The vast structure's central auditorium was flanked by two large exhibit halls. Its bulk is ornamented by an array of gables, turrets, and pinnacles (a model is shown here).

3-030. Cincinnati Music Hall, 1243 Elm Street, Cincinnati, Ohio. Opened May 14, 1878; 3,634 seats; Hannaford & Proctor, architects. DPCC, 1900–1910. P&P, LC-D4-34315.

3-031. Cincinnati Music Hall, 1243 Elm Street, Cincinnati, Ohio. Opened May 14, 1878; 3,634 seats; Hannaford & Proctor, architects. Joseph Boggs Beale, illustrator; from *Frank Leslie's Illustrated Newspaper*, July 3, 1880. P&P, LC-USZ62-99005.

At the heart of the Music Hall was Springer Auditorium, a large rectilinear concert hall with a single horseshoe balcony and an open choral stage. Its pipe organ, by Hook & Hastings of Boston, was the largest in America at the time. In 1895 a fully equipped stage and proscenium were added to the hall. The Music Hall continues to be Cincinnati's primary cultural venue.

3-032. The Playhouse (Belknap Playhouse), Third Street and West Cardinal Boulevard, Louisville, Kentucky. Built 1874; 533 seats; C. J. Clark, architect. P&P, Subject file-Theaters.

When the University of Louisville established its present campus in 1925, this chapel, built for the Louisville House of Refuge, was claimed by the drama department as the university's theater. In 1977, when it stood in the way of a new library, it was disassembled, stored for three years, and reerected on its present site.

3-033. Opera House in unidentified city. P&P, LC-USZ62-58912.

An unusual clock tower gave a landmark presence to this second-floor opera house, which shared space with the town's fire department.

3-032

3-033

3-034

3-034. Academy of Music (Music Hall), Washington and Dover Streets, Easton, Maryland. Opened July 1879; 480 seats; Frank Davis, architect. P&P, Subject file-Theaters.

Set in the central square of this picturesque Chesapeake Bay town, the Academy bore an uncanny resemblance to the New York State Capitol Building. Within were offices and a second-floor theater that had become a cinema by the time of this photograph. Long concealed by renovations, the auditorium was rediscovered in 2003.

3-035. Wallack's Theatre, 1220 Broadway, New York, New York. Opened January 4, 1882; 1,274 seats; William B. Pettit, architect. Graham & Thulstrup, artists; from *Harper's Magazine*, January 7, 1882. Gen. Coll., E461.H3.

In 1882, Lester Wallack moved his repertory company from Thirteenth Street (see 1-037) to Thirtieth Street as New York's theatrical district edged up Broadway toward Times Square. The new theater's fine design befitted Wallack's reputation, but the theater, especially after Wallack's retirement, never was truly successful. It was demolished in 1915.

3-035

3-036. Pensacola Opera House, 304 Jefferson Street, Plaza Ferdinand VII, Pensacola, Florida. Opened January 4, 1883; 1,400 seats; Daniel F. Sullivan, architect. DPCC, photographer, 1900–1906. P&P, LC-D4-16275.

The Opera House's delicately detailed mansard roof made it the ornamental highlight of Pensacola's Plaza Ferdinand VII. Destroyed by a hurricane on September 28, 1917, its ruins lingered for over ten years. During this time some of its bricks and ornamental features, including the main balcony rail, were removed and incorporated into the new Saenger Theatre, which was being built nearby.

3-037. Academy of Music, Washington Avenue at William Street, East Saginaw, Michigan. Opened December 16, 1884; 1,200 seats; J. M. Wood, architect. DPCC, photographer, 1900–1910. P&P, LC-D4-70275.

In selecting an architect, owner Samuel G. Clay considered J. B. McElfatrick and J. M. Wood. Wood won. Towering above its neighbors, the new building became an instant landmark and an important symbol of Saginaw's transformation from village to emerging city. The Academy burned in 1917.

3-036

3-037

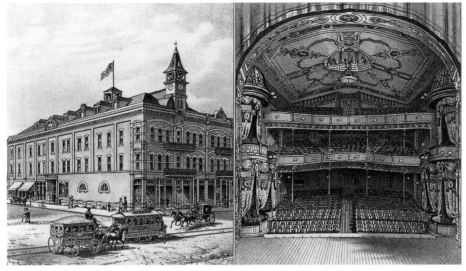

3-038

3-039

3-040

3-038. Ragsdale (Knoepker) Opera House, Main Street at Broadway, Newton, Kansas. Opened December 8, 1885; 850 seats. From *Kansas Atlas*, 1887, p. 215. P&P, LC-USZ62-31969.

Newton's main street was crowded with carriages and even horse-drawn trolleys, and it boasted a massive, up-to-date opera house that James and Thaddeus Ragsdale, successful in the diverse businesses of groceries, real estate, lumber, cattle, and banking, built as an expression of community pride. The auditorium displayed changes that occurred quite suddenly in theatrical design in 1885. The stage projects only slightly beyond the proscenium; the box seats have attained an extraordinary level of elaboration. These features would remain consistent through the next half-century of theater design.

3-039. Grand Opera House (Lyceum Theatre), 1008 Randolph Street, Detroit, Michigan. Opened September 13, 1886; 2,605 seats; John Scott (building), J. B. McElfatrick & Sons (theater), architects. DPCC, photographer, 1900–1906. P&P, LC-D4-17261.

Detroit's plethora of opera houses included two called Detroit Opera House (3-060 and 3-061), two called Whitney Grand Opera House (3-041), and one called Grand Opera House. Destined to become a glittering theater row, Detroit's Monroe Street was anchored to the west by the Detroit Opera House and to the east by the Grand Opera House. Unassuming on the exterior, the Grand contained the city's most elaborate auditorium.

3-040. Grand Opera House (Lyceum Theatre), 1008 Randolph Street, Detroit, Michigan. Opened September 13, 1886; 2,605 seats; John Scott (building), J. B. McElfatrick & Sons (theater), architects. DPCC, photographer, 1900–1906. P&P, LC-D4-42951.

The Grand's interior was elaborately painted in a Moorish style. Its pride was the Thompson drop curtain. As was typical in the period, it imitated elaborate velour drapery but was painted on stiff canvas—even the flower vase that appeared to stand on the stage.

3-041. Whitney Grand Opera House (Garrick Theatre), 1122 Griswold Street, Detroit, Michigan. Opened October 31, 1887; 1,409 seats; J. M. Wood, architect. DPCC, photographer, 1900–1906. P&P, LC-D4-17260.

In Detroit's second Whitney Grand, a monumental office building concealed an intimate auditorium. In its days as the Garrick Theatre, it housed Jesse Bonstelle's noted repertory company and drama school. In 1926 magician Harry Houdini appeared, giving an uncharacteristically poor performance. Afterward he was taken to Grace Hospital, where he died early the next morning. By freakish coincidence, both the Whitney Grand's opening and Houdini's death occurred on October 31, Halloween.

3-042. Mansfield Opera House, Mansfield, Pennsylvania. 800 seats. P&P, Subject file-Theaters.

Shallow blind arches, a tall central gable, and an entrance balcony distinguished the facade of this well-designed small-town opera house.

3-041

3-042

3-043

3-044

3-043. Hollis Street Theatre, 10–14 Hollis Street, Boston, Massachusetts. Opened November 9, 1885; 1,632 seats; John R. Hall, architect. P&P, HABS MASS,13-BOST,48-2.

The Hollis Street Church dated from 1810 but entered a new phase of its life in 1885. In its conversion to a theater, the tower and vestibule gave way to a new entry and lobby, while the main body of the church remained intact as the new auditorium was installed within. The house pictured across the street to the right would one day be the site of the giant Metropolitan Theatre.

3-044. Hollis Street Theatre, 10–14 Hollis Street, Boston, Massachusetts. Opened November 9, 1885; 1,632 seats; John R. Hall, architect. P&P, HABS MASS,13-BOST,49-1.

The old church walls remain recognizable beyond the Hollis Street's new entrance marquee.

3-045. Hollis Street Theatre, 10–14 Hollis Street, Boston, Massachusetts. Opened November 9, 1885; 1,632 seats; John R. Hall, architect. P&P, HABS MASS,13-BOST,49-5.

The elaborate box tiers were integral to the proscenium decoration, but entirely separate from the stage. The two added boxes that visually extended the uppermost balcony provided an extra opportunity to sell high-priced tickets.

3-046. Hollis Street Theatre, 10–14 Hollis Street, Boston, Massachusetts. Opened November 9, 1885; 1,632 seats; John R. Hall, architect. Arthur C. Haskell, photographer, 1935. P&P, HABS MASS,13-BOST,49-3.

The postwar theater typically had a tall, rectangular proscenium. The Hollis Street's was 4 feet wider and 8 feet higher than the usual 32-foot square.

3-045

3-046

3-047. Section, Hollis Street Theatre, 10–14 Hollis Street, Boston, Massachusetts. Opened November 9, 1885; 1,632 seats; John R. Hall, architect. Lester E. Wilson, delineator. P&P, HABS MA-157, sheet no. 5, detail.

3-048. Hollis Street Theatre, 10–14 Hollis Street, Boston, Massachusetts. Opened November 9, 1885; 1,632 seats; remodeled 1885, John R. Hall, architect. Lester E. Wilson, delineator, 1935. P&P, HABS MA-157, sheet no. 1.

As a theater, the Hollis Street was of a typical post–Civil War form. Its lobby was small and its other audience amenities limited. Built in the latter part of the period, its stage was fully contained within the proscenium and its orchestra pit was small. The main floor, which contained 616 of the theater's 1,632 seats, was arranged without a parquet circle. The stairs in the rear corner of the auditorium provided access only to the first balcony. Stairs shown at the lower right corner, entered from a door on Holley Square, provided the only original access to the upper balcony.

3-049. Hollis Street Theatre, 10–14 Hollis Street, Boston, Massachusetts. Opened November 9, 1885; 1,632 seats; remodeled 1885, John R. Hall, architect. Lester E. Wilson, delineator, 1935. P&P, HABS MA-157, sheet no. 3.

The Hollis Street's balcony retained the horseshoe shape of earlier days but was much extended toward the rear as its architect sought to direct the sight lines more toward the stage than toward the audience. The first balcony held 550 customers, almost as many as the main floor.

3-050. Hollis Street Theatre, 10–14 Hollis Street, Boston, Massachusetts. Opened November 9, 1885; 1,632 seats; remodeled 1885, John R. Hall, architect. Lester E. Wilson, delineator, 1935. P&P, HABS MA-157, sheet no 4.

The uppermost balcony, with continuous wooden benches rather than individual seats, often was the largest of a theater's tiers. At the Hollis Street, though, this level held only 361 seats. Designed for occupancy by low-paying rowdies, this level was carefully isolated from the rest of the auditorium. It had its own meager toilet facilities, and its patrons entered without passing through the main lobby. Connecting stairs with the first balcony were added in later days.

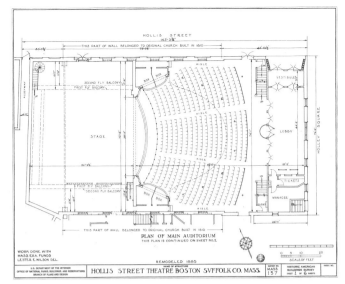

3-048

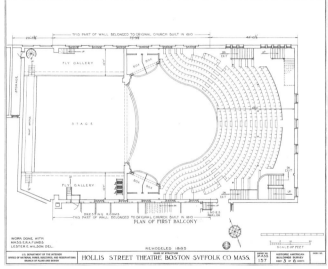

3-049

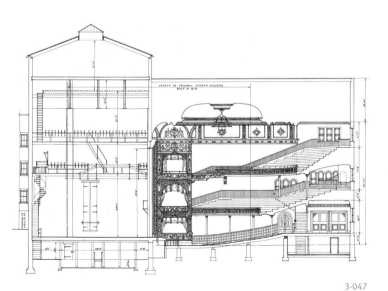

3-047

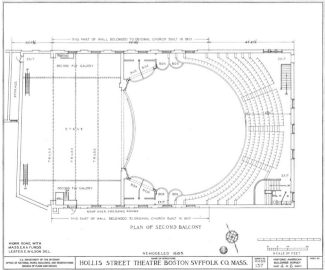

3-050

3-051

3-051. Schiller (Dearborn, Garrick) Theatre, 64 West Randolph Street, Chicago, Illinois. Opened September 29, 1892; 1,270 seats; Adler & Sullivan, architects. P&P, HABS,ILL,16-CHIG,60-7.

Its towering facade has brought the Schiller Building universal praise as a pioneering skyscraper design, but the theater within has generally been overshadowed by Louis Sullivan's larger Chicago Auditorium (8-050–8-062). Built for a German-American opera company, the building combined commercial offices with club rooms and a delightful theater.

3-052. Schiller (Dearborn, Garrick) Theatre, 64 West Randolph Street, Chicago, Illinois. Opened September 29, 1892; 1,270 seats; Adler & Sullivan, architects. Janis J. Erins, delineator, 1964. P&P, HABS,ILL,16-CHIG,60-2, sheets 2 and 7, details.

The Schiller's auditorium displays the marriage between the romanticism of Louis Sullivan's ornament and the rationality of Dankmar Adler's volumetric design. The flare of the ceiling arches, progressively widening from the stage, was scientifically determined to provide optimal acoustical properties.

3-053. Plan, Schiller (Dearborn, Garrick) Theatre, 64 West Randolph Street, Chicago, Illinois. Opened September 29, 1892; 1,270 seats; Adler & Sullivan, architects. P&P, HABS ILL-1058, sheet no. 2.

The Schiller Theatre's auditorium, a geometrically rigorous circular form, had no internal supporting columns.

3-054. Section, Schiller (Dearborn, Garrick) Theatre, 64 West Randolph Street, Chicago, Illinois. Opened September 29, 1892; 1,270 seats; Adler & Sullivan, architects. P&P, HABS ILL-1058, sheet no. 7.

The auditorium was skillfully and audaciously tucked into the first six stories of Sullivan's tallest building. Extensive club rooms and an additional performance space were located on the thirteenth floor.

3-052

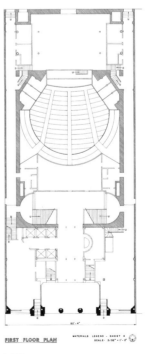

FIRST FLOOR PLAN

3-053

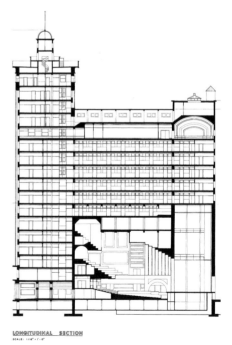

LONGITUDINAL SECTION

3-054

3-055. Court Square Theatre, 11–25 Elm Street, Springfield, Massachusetts. Opened September 5, 1892; 1,865 seats; J. B. McElfatrick & Sons, architects. DPCC, 1900–1910. P&P, LC-D4-34907.

As America's large cities acquired truly great theaters, an established cadre of experienced specialist architects provided smaller towns with auditoriums that were elaborate and superbly functional, albeit less venturesome in design.

3-056. Empire (Lafayette) Theatre, 125 West Lafayette Avenue, Detroit, Michigan. Opened December 25, 1893; 1,664 seats. DPCC, 1900–1906. P&P, LC-D4-17262.

3-057

3-058

3-057. Littleton Opera House (Grand Opera House, Town Hall), 2 Union Street, Littleton, New Hampshire. Opened 1895; 463 seats; Fred T. Austin, architect. DPCC, photographer, 1900–1910. P&P, LC-D4-34984.

Although found throughout the country, incorporating a theater into a community's town hall is a practice most closely associated with New England, where the tradition of town meetings remains strong. For over a century the Opera House has anchored a delightful main street and drawn crowds to a wide variety of activities.

3-058. Claremont Opera House, Tremont Square, Claremont, New Hampshire. Opened June 22, 1897; 783 seats; Charles A. Rich, architect. Jet Lowe, photographer, 1978. P&P, HAER,NH,10-CLAR,18-1.

3-059. Metropolitan (Lyceum, Strand, Park, Capitol) Theatre, 148 West Washington Street, Indianapolis, Indiana. DPCC, 1900–1905. P&P, LC-D4-17322.

A long-standing entertainment center in downtown Indianapolis, the Metropolitan Theatre first opened in 1858. The building illustrated here shows it rebuilt after a fire in early 1897. Although it represented the finest design practice of its day, when the Indiana Theatre opened next door, the Metropolitan was quickly overshadowed and closed in 1935 (see 6-102–6-115).

3-060. Detroit Opera House, 5–15 Campus Martius, Detroit, Michigan. Opened September 12, 1898; 1,757 seats; Mason & Rice, architects. DPCC, photographer, ca. 1906. P&P, LC-D4-19601.

For almost a century, Detroit's architectural centerpiece was the Detroit Opera House, which opened on March 29, 1869, (Sheldon and Mortimer L. Smith, architects) and was located on the second floor, above a retail space tenanted by clothier J. L. Hudson, whose massive department store would one day rise immediately behind the old theater. When the opera house burned, in 1897, it was replaced with the grandly classical building shown here. The Merrill Fountain (Carrère & Hastings, architects) was added to the scene in 1901.

3-061

3-062

3-063

3-061. Detroit Opera House, 5–15 Campus Martius, Detroit, Michigan. Opened September 12, 1898; 1,757 seats; Mason & Rice, architects. DPCC, photographer, 1904. P&P, LC-D43-46104.

The Detroit Opera House's interior, designed by Alpheus W. Chittenden, represented an important step in the evolution of auditorium design. It retained the customary two balconies of earlier halls, and the social hierarchy that they supported, but eliminated their horseshoe form. The result was a monumentally large spatial volume in which all seats faced the stage. A few box seats remained.

3-062. Litchfield Opera House, 126 North Marshall Avenue, Litchfield, Minnesota. Built 1900; 590 seats; William T. Towner, architect. P&P, Subject file-Theaters.

The Litchfield Opera House conveyed an aura of architectural solidity and distinction. After a generation of serving traveling dramatic companies, it became a community center in 1935.

3-063. May's Opera House (Miami Theatre), 207–209 North Wayne Street, Piqua, Ohio. Opened February 10, 1903; 1,360 seats. P&P, Subject file-Theaters.

Fences became de facto billboards for theater advertising. The billboards next to Piqua's handsome opera house spelled out a tempting array of entertainment possibilities for the weeks ahead.

3-064. Majestic (Hippodrome) Theatre, North Street, Corbin, Kentucky. Built ca. 1906; 750 seats. P&P, Subject file-Theaters.

3-065. Traer Opera House, 414 Second Street, Traer, Iowa. Opened February 17, 1905; 800 seats. P&P, Subject file-Theaters.

3-066. Michel Opera House, 216 Main Street, Marble Falls, Texas. Built 1905; 300 seats. P&P, Subject file-Theaters.

In 1891, German immigrant Ernst Gustav Michel opened a drugstore in this central Texas community. Rebuilding after a fire in 1905, he incorporated a second-floor opera house and a third-floor residence for himself and his family. When the newer building burned in 1927, it was rebuilt without the theater. The drugstore remains in the Michel family more than a century later.

3-067. Bradford Theatre (Opera House), 125 Main Street, Bradford, Pennsylvania. Built ca. 1905; 1,544 seats. P&P, Subject file-Theaters.

3-065

3-066

3-064

3-067

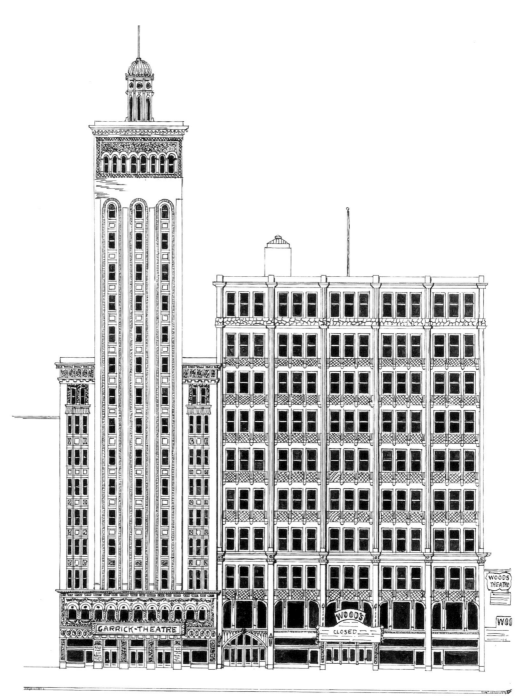

~ GARRICK THEATRE ~ ·AFD·1932 ~ WOOD'S THEATRE ~

FORMERLY SCHILLER

E. RANDOLPH & N. DEARBORN STS.
CHICAGO ILL.

THEATERS IN AN ARTIST'S EYE

Railroad stations, hotels, and department stores all have their aficionados, but it would be safe to bet that theaters attract far more than their rivals. Some of these fans collect programs, others index theater architects and opening dates; some are community activists, fighting for historic preservation; some tour the countryside looking for old marquees to photograph. Still others make sketches. In that respect, few could match Anthony F. Dumas.

About Dumas we know little. He seems to have grown up in Connecticut and lived in New York City, where he is said to have worked at restoring paintings for the city's museums. That several of his drawings were made on the reverse of United States Patent Office forms hints that he may have produced drawings for patent applicants. We can say with certainty that he loved theaters, and he spent many hours with pen in hand drawing them.

While Dumas may have traveled, sketching in the field, that can account for only part of his output. As many of his subjects had been demolished long before he drew them, it is clear that he often worked from photographs. What was his basis for selection and how many theaters did he illustrate in all? We do not know.

Dumas inserted himself into his drawings. He could be highly original in his manner of indicating a theater's hidden parts—the stages that rose above and behind their facades. His marginalia often included whimsical figures of flappers or character actors. He was not averse to modifying his subjects, stretching them in one dimension or another. Tall buildings sometimes lack a few of their floors, and at least one facade is drawn with fewer window bays than a photograph would have shown. Even a name lettered directly on a building cannot always be counted upon for accuracy.

Collectively, Dumas's sketches provide a remarkably encyclopedic view of America's theaters as they existed during the 1930s. For this we must thank him. We must be particularly thankful that he never saw a burlesque theatre that he didn't like. His images—most originals of which measure 10" x 15"—are a rare and valuable record in detail and character of American theater building.

These images represent the entirety of Dumas's American theater drawings in the Library of Congress; more are in other repositories. Although multiple images sometimes appear on a single sheet, here they are separated and grouped by state, taking us on a thoroughly fascinating, albeit imaginary, tour.

CALIFORNIA

ART-001. State Theatre, 703 South Broadway, Los Angeles, California. Opened November 12, 1921; 2,422 seats; Weeks & Day, architects. Anthony F. Dumas, artist, 1939. P&P, ADE 11-Dumas No. 1.

ART-002. Warfield Theatre, 982 Market Street, San Francisco, California. Opened May 13, 1922; 2,655 seats; G. Albert Lansburgh, architect. Anthony F. Dumas, artist, 1938. P&P, ADE 11-Dumas No. 2.

ART-003. Orpheum (Palace) Theatre, 630 South Broadway, Los Angeles, California. Opened June 6, 1911; 2,200 seats; G. Albert Lansburgh, architect. Anthony F. Dumas, artist, 1935. P&P, ADE 11-Dumas No. 3A (A size).

ART-004. Child's Grand Opera House (Orpheum Theatre), 108–112 South Main Street, Los Angeles, California. Built 1884; 775 seats. Anthony F. Dumas, artist, 1935. P&P, ADE 11-Dumas No. 3B.

ART-005. Columbia (Wilkes, Geary) Theatre, 415–431 Geary Street, San Francisco, California. Opened January 10, 1910; 1,450 seats; Bliss & Faville, architects. Anthony F. Dumas, artist, 1933. P&P, ADE 11-Dumas No. 4.

ART-006. Curran Theatre, 455 Geary Street, San Francisco, California. Opened September 10, 1922; 1,758 seats; Alfred Henry Jacobs, architect. Anthony F. Dumas, artist, 1935. P&P, ADE 11-Dumas No. 5.

ART-007. Orpheum (Columbia) Theatre, 147 O'Farrell Street, San Francisco, California. Opened April 19, 1909; 2,500 seats; G. Albert Lansburgh, architect. Anthony F. Dumas, artist, 1916. P&P, ADE 11-Dumas No. 6.

COLORADO

ART-008. Orpheum Theatre, 1537 Welton Street, Denver, Colorado. Opened 1903. Anthony F. Dumas, artist, 1935. P&P, ADE 11-Dumas No. 7.

LOEW'S STATE THEATRE

ART-002

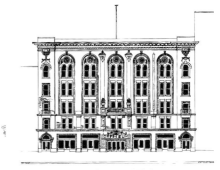

NEW ORPHEUM THEATRE

ART-003

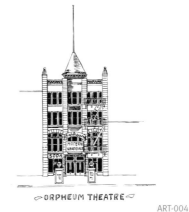

ORPHEUM THEATRE

ART-004

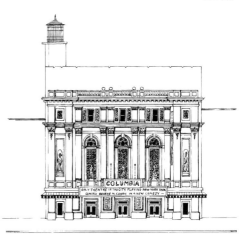

A. L. ERLANGER NEW COLUMBIA THEATRE

ART-005

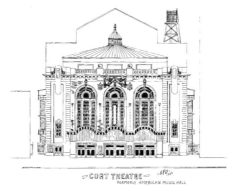

CORT THEATRE
FORMERLY AMERICAN MUSIC HALL

ART-006

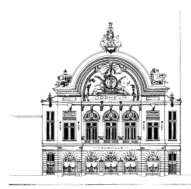

ART-007

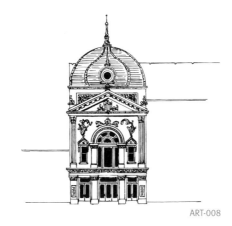

ART-008

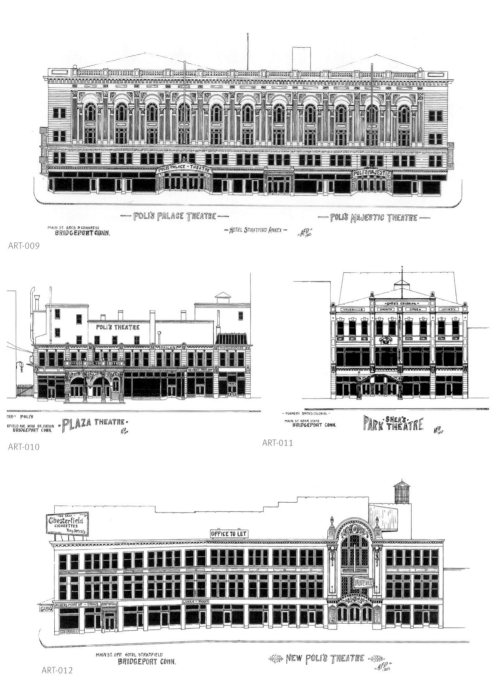

ART-009

MAIN ST. ARCH & CONGRESS
BRIDGEPORT CONN.
— POLI'S PALACE THEATRE —
— HOTEL STRATFORD ANNEX —
— POLI'S MAJESTIC THEATRE —

ART-010

POLI'S THEATRE
MERY POLI'S
RFIELD AVE. NEAR BR. STATION
BRIDGEPORT CONN.
— PLAZA THEATRE —

ART-011

SHEA'S COLONIAL
VAUDEVILLE DRAMA OPERA COMEDY
FORMERLY SMITH'S COLONIAL
MAIN ST. NEAR STATE
BRIDGEPORT CONN.
PARK SHEA'S THEATRE

ART-012

THE GREAT
Chesterfield
CIGARETTES
They Satisfy
OFFICE TO LET
ACTOR'S MAKE UP · DRESS ·
LADIES · ROOM
VAUDEVILLE
GARAGE
MAIN ST. OPP. HOTEL STRATFIELD
BRIDGEPORT CONN.
NEW POLI'S THEATRE

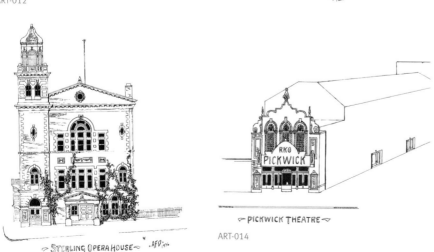

ART-013

— STERLING OPERA HOUSE —
CITY HALL

ART-014

RKO
PICKWICK

— PICKWICK THEATRE —

ART-009. Palace (Poli) Theatre (left), 1325 Main Street, Bridgeport, Connecticut. Opened September 14, 1922; 3,642 seats. Majestic Theatre (right), 1347 Main Street, Bridgeport, Connecticut. Opened November 4, 1922; 2,246 seats; Thomas W. Lamb, architect. Anthony F. Dumas, artist, 1923. P&P, ADE 11-Dumas No. 8.

ART-010. Hawe's Opera House (Bunnell, Park City, Poli's, Plaza) Theatre, 35 Fairfield Avenue, Bridgeport, Connecticut. Opened 1876; 1,670 seats. Anthony F. Dumas, artist, 1920. P&P, ADE 11-Dumas No. 9.

ART-011. Smith's Colonial (Jackson, Park) Theatre, 847 Main Street, Bridgeport, Connecticut. Opened August 23, 1902; 2,392 seats; J. B. McElfatrick & Sons, architects. Anthony F. Dumas, artist, 1920. P&P, ADE 11-Dumas No. 10.

ART-012. Poli's (Globe) Theatre, 1270–1280 Main Street, Bridgeport, Connecticut. Opened December 23, 1912; 2,792 seats; James C. Van Buren, architect. Anthony F. Dumas, artist, 1923. P&P, ADE 11-Dumas No. 11.

ART-013. Sterling Opera House, City Hall, Elizabeth and Fourth Streets, Derby, Connecticut. Opened April 2, 1889; 1,250 seats; H. E. Ficken, architect. Anthony F. Dumas, artist, 1936. P&P, ADE 11-Dumas No. 12.

Dumas saw his first moving picture here in 1906.

ART-014. Pickwick Theatre, 36–42 West Putnam Avenue, Greenwich, Connecticut. Opened November 21, 1929; 1,925 seats; W. J. MacEvoy, architect. Anthony F. Dumas, artist, 1937. P&P, LC-USZ62-105506.

ART-015. Parsons Theatre, 66 Prospect Street, Hartford, Connecticut. Opened April 1, 1896; 1,817 seats; J. B. McElfatrick & Sons, architects. Anthony F. Dumas, artist, 1921. P&P, ADE 11-Dumas No. 14.

ART-016. Majestic (E. M. Loew's) Theatre, 174 Asylum Street, Hartford, Connecticut. Opened February 8, 1915; 1,217 seats. Anthony F. Dumas, artist, 1921. P&P, ADE 11-Dumas No. 15.

ART-017. Grand (Cameo, Proven, Center, New Parsons) Theatre, 1087 Main Street, Hartford, Connecticut. Opened September 7, 1914; 1,147 seats; Fred C. Walz, architect. Anthony F. Dumas, artist, 1921. P&P, ADE 11-Dumas No. 16.

ART-018. Capitol (Poli's) Theatre, 591 Main Street, Hartford, Connecticut. Opened August 28, 1920; 3,014 seats; Thomas W. Lamb, architect. Anthony F. Dumas, artist, 1926. P&P, ADE 11-Dumas No. 17.

ART-019. Poli Palace Theatre, 645 Main Street, Hartford, Connecticut. Opened May 25, 1914; 1,639 seats; Thomas W. Lamb, architect. Anthony F. Dumas, artist, 1931. P&P, ADE 11-Dumas No. 18.

ART-020. Poli's Wonderland (Bijou and Bijou Dream Theatres), 24–28 Church Street, New Haven, Connecticut. Built 1894; J. B. McElfatrick & Son, architects. Anthony F. Dumas, artist, 1925. P&P, ADE 11-Dumas No. 19A.

This was E. Z. Poli's first vaudeville theater.

ART-021. Bijou Theatre, 26–28 Church Street, New Haven, Connecticut. Opened 1912; 1,429 seats; Thomas W. Lamb, architect. Anthony F. Dumas, artist, 1925. P&P, ADE 11-Dumas No. 19B.

This theater replaced the earlier Bijou (originally Poli's Wonderland), on the same site, that burned in 1909 (ART-020).

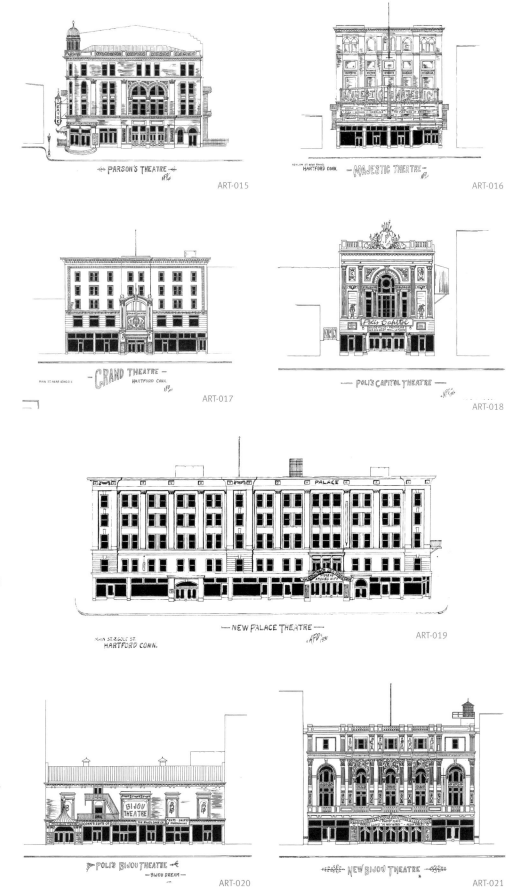

ART-015

ART-016

ART-017

ART-018

ART-019

ART-020

ART-021

ART-022

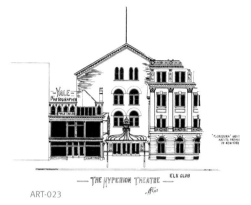

ART-023

ART-024

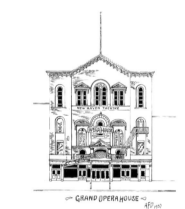

ART-025

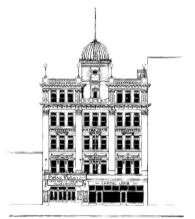

ART-026

ART-027

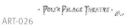

ART-028

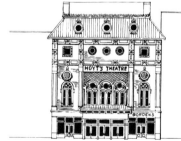
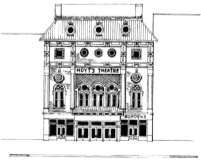

ART-029

ART-022. Sam S. Shubert Theatre, 81 College Street, New Haven, Connecticut. Opened December 11, 1914; 1,657 seats; William Albert Swasey, architect. Anthony F. Dumas, artist, 1923. P&P, ADE 11-Dumas No. 20.

ART-023. Carll's Opera House (Hyperion, College Theatre), 1030–1032 Chapel Street, New Haven, Connecticut. Opened September 20, 1880; 2,128 seats. Anthony F. Dumas, artist, 1923. P&P, ADE 11-Dumas No. 21.

ART-024. Gordon (Olympia, Paramount) Theatre, 140–144 Temple Street, New Haven, Connecticut. Opened September 13, 1915; 2,373 seats. Anthony F. Dumas, artist, 1924. P&P, ADE 11-Dumas No. 22.

ART-025. Music Hall (Grand Opera House, New Haven Theatre), 182 Crown Street, New Haven, Connecticut. Opened 1860; 2,200 seats. Anthony F. Dumas, artist, 1937. P&P, ADE 11-Dumas No. 23.

ART-026. Poli's New (Palace) Theatre, 23 Church Street, New Haven, Connecticut. Opened 1905; 2,800 seats. Anthony F. Dumas, artist, 1920. P&P, ADE 11-Dumas No. 24.

ART-027. Capitol Theatre, 39 Bank Street, New London, Connecticut. Opened November 21, 1921; 1,730 seats; W. H. Lane, architect. Anthony F. Dumas, artist, 1931. P&P, ADE 11-Dumas No. 25.

ART-028. Garde Theatre, 325 State Street, New London, Connecticut. Opened September 22, 1926; 1,603 seats; Arland W. Johnson, architect. Anthony F. Dumas, artist, 1931. P&P, ADE 11-Dumas No. 26.

ART-029. Hoyt's (Rialto) Theatre, 128 Washington Street, South Norwalk, Connecticut. Opened 1893; 929 seats. Anthony F. Dumas, artist, 1932. P&P, ADE 11-Dumas No. 27.

ART-030. Jacques Opera House, Abbott Street, Waterbury, Connecticut. Opened November 1, 1886; D. H. Meloy, architect. Anthony F. Dumas, artist, 1930. P&P, ADE 11-Dumas No. 28.

DELAWARE

ART-031. Aldine Theatre, 808 Market Street, Wilmington, Delaware. Opened 1920; 1,783 seats; Thomas W. Lamb, architect. Anthony F. Dumas, artist, 1936. P&P, ADE 11-Dumas No. 29.

ART-032. Arcadia Theatre, 510 Market Street, Wilmington, Delaware. 1,305 seats. Anthony F. Dumas, artist, 1934. P&P, ADE 11-Dumas No. 30.

ART-033. Garrick Theatre, 832 Market Street, Wilmington, Delaware. 1,300 seats. Anthony F. Dumas, artist, 1929. P&P, ADE 11-Dumas No. 31.

ART-034. Playhouse Theatre, Market Street, Wilmington, Delaware. Opened 1913; 1,238 seats; Charles A. Rich, architect. Anthony F. Dumas, artist, 1931. P&P, ADE 11-Dumas No 33.

DISTRICT OF COLUMBIA

ART-035. Lafayette Square Opera House (Belasco Theatre), 17 Madison Place NW, Washington, D.C. Opened September 30, 1895; 1,467 seats; Wood & Lovell, architects. Anthony F. Dumas, artist, 1930. P&P, ADE 11-Dumas No. 146.

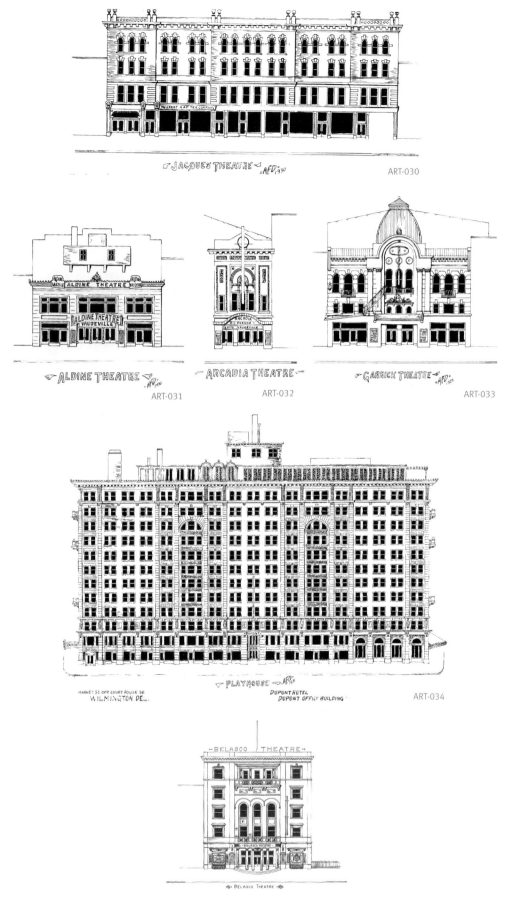

JACQUES THEATRE — AFD, 1930
ART-030

ALDINE THEATRE
ART-031

ARCADIA THEATRE
ART-032

GARRICK THEATRE — AFD, 1929
ART-033

MARKET ST OPP COURT HOUSE SQ
WILMINGTON DE

PLAYHOUSE — AFD, 1931
DUPONT HOTEL
DUPONT OFFICE BUILDING
ART-034

BELASCO THEATRE
Belasco Theatre
ART-035

New National Theatre

ART-036

New National Theatre

ART-037

Poli's Theatre

ART-038

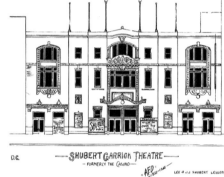

D.C.   SHUBERT GARRICK THEATRE
FORMERLY THE CASINO
LEE & J.J. SHUBERT LESSEES

ART-039

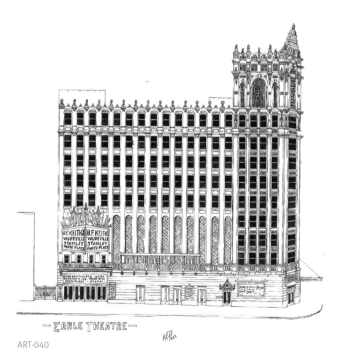

EARLE THEATRE

ART-040

ART-036. National Theatre, 1317–1325 E Street NW, Washington, D.C. Opened October 5, 1885; 1,759 seats; Alfred B. Mullett (building), J. B. McElfatrick & Sons (theater), architects. Anthony F. Dumas, artist, 1930. P&P, LC-USZ62-86645.

ART-037. National Theatre, 1317–1325 E Street NW, Washington, D.C. Facade and internal renovation, Warren & Wetmore, architects, 1922. Anthony F. Dumas, artist, 1930. P&P, ADE 11-Dumas No. 146.

ART-038. Grand Opera House (Albaugh's, Chase's, Poli's Theatre), 1424 Pennsylvania Avenue NW, Washington, D.C. Opened November 10, 1884; 1,851 seats; W. B. Gray, Harvey L. Page, architects. Anthony F. Dumas, artist, 1930. P&P, ADE 11-Dumas No. 146.

ART-039. Casino (Shubert-Garrick) Theatre, 632 F Street NW, Washington, D.C. Opened January 30, 1910; 1,250 seats; B. Stanley Simmons, architect. Anthony F. Dumas, artist, 1930. P&P, ADE 11-Dumas No. 146.

ART-040. Earle (Warner) Theatre, 505 Thirteenth Street NW, Washington, D.C. Opened December 27, 1924; 2,154 seats; C. Howard Crane, architect. Anthony F. Dumas, artist, 1930. P&P, ADE 11-Dumas No. 146.

ART-041. Lincoln Music Hall (Academy of Music, Orpheum, Strand Theatre), 401 Ninth Street NW, Washington, DC. Opened 1889; 1,148 seats; Appleton P. Clark Jr., architect. Anthony F. Dumas, artist, 1930. P&P, ADE 11-Dumas No. 146.

ART-042. Gayety (Shubert) Theatre, 513 Ninth Street NW, Washington, D.C. Opened August 26, 1907; 2,150 seats; William H. McElfatrick, architect. Anthony F. Dumas, artist, 1930. P&P, LC-USZ62-114081.

ART-043. Lyceum (American, Capitol, President) Theatre, 1014 Pennsylvania Avenue NW, Washington, D.C. Opened 1891; 1,929 seats; W. B. Gray, architect. Anthony F. Dumas, artist, 1930. P&P, LC-USZ62-114081.

The Lyceum was modeled after the Washington Assembly Rooms, built in 1822.

ART-044. Fox (Capitol) Theatre, 1328 F Street NW, Washington, D.C. Opened September 19, 1927; 3,434 seats; C. W. & George L. Rapp, architects. Anthony F. Dumas, artist, 1930. P&P, ADE 11-Dumas No. 146.

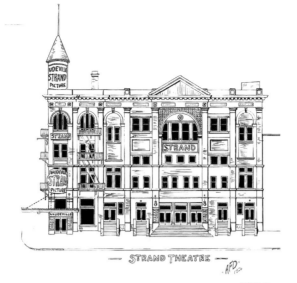

ART-041

ART-042

ART-043

ART-044

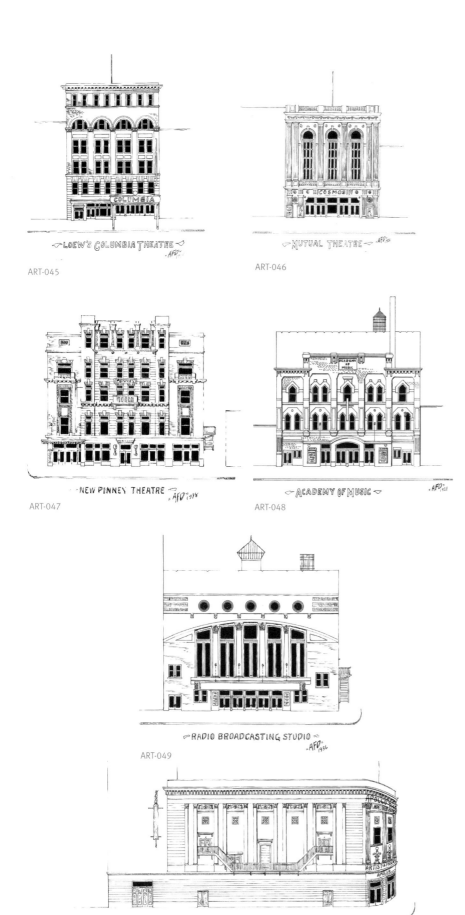

ART-045

⌐LOEW'S COLUMBIA THEATRE⌐
AFD

⌐MUTUAL THEATRE⌐ *AFD* 1931

ART-046

⌐NEW PINNEY THEATRE⌐ *AFD* 1938

ART-047

⌐ACADEMY OF MUSIC⌐ *AFD* 1938

ART-048

⌐RADIO BROADCASTING STUDIO⌐ *AFD* 1936

ART-049

⌐AL. H. WOOD'S APOLLO THEATRE⌐ *AFD* DIRECTION OF AL. H. WOOD

ART-050

ART-045. Columbia Theatre, 1112 F Street NW, Washington, D.C. Opened November 9, 1896; 1,174 seats; Appleton P. Clark Jr., architect. Anthony F. Dumas, artist, 1930. P&P, ADE 11-Dumas No. 146.

The Columbia was remodeled from the earlier Metzerott Music Hall.

ART-046. Cosmos (Mutual) Theatre, 919–921 Pennsylvania Avenue, NW, Washington, D.C. Opened 1909; 830 seats; Harding & Upman, architects. Anthony F. Dumas, artist, 1930. P&P, ADE 11-Dumas No. 146.

IDAHO

ART-047. Pinney Theatre, 809 West Jefferson Street, Boise, Idaho. Opened 1908; 924 seats; Tourtelotte & Hummel, architects. Anthony F. Dumas, artist, 1938. P&P, ADE 11-Dumas No. 46.

ILLINOIS

ART-048. Academy of Music, 16 South Halsted Street, Chicago, Illinois. Opened 1878; 2,450 seats; Oscar Cobb, architect. Anthony F. Dumas, artist, 1938. P&P, ADE 11-Dumas No. 47A.

ART-049. American Music Hall, 741 South Wabash Avenue, Chicago, Illinois. Opened 1912; 1,226 seats; A. N. Mahler, architect. Anthony F. Dumas, artist, 1931. P&P, ADE 11-Dumas No. 69.

ART-050. Apollo (United Artists) Theatre, 45 West Randolph Street, Chicago, Illinois. Opened May 30, 1921; 1,704 seats; Holabird & Roche, architects. Anthony F. Dumas, artist, 1924. P&P, ADE 11-Dumas No. 48.

The Apollo's interior was replaced in 1927 by architect C. Howard Crane. It reopened as the United Artists Theatre on October 26th of that year.

ART-051. Blackstone Theatre, 60 East Balbo Street, Chicago, Illinois. Opened January 1, 1911; 1,400 seats; Marshall & Fox, architects. Anthony F. Dumas, artist, 1934. P&P, ADE 11-Dumas No. 50.

ART-052. Central Park Theatre, 3535 West Roosevelt Street, Chicago, Illinois. Opened October 27, 1917; 1,746 seats; C. W. & George L. Rapp, architects. Anthony F. Dumas, artist, 1928. P&P, ADE 11-Dumas No. 51.

ART-053. Chicago Auditorium, 58 East Congress Street, Chicago, Illinois. Opened December 9, 1889; 4,237 seats; Adler & Sullivan, architects. Anthony F. Dumas, artist, 1931. P&P, ADE 11-Dumas No. 71.

ART-054. Chicago Musical College (Capri, Punch 'N' Judy Theatre), 64 West Van Buren Street, Chicago, Illinois. Opened 1896; Dwight Perkins, architect. Anthony F. Dumas, artist, 1928. P&P, ADE 11-Dumas No. 49.

ART-055. Columbia (Clark, Adelphi) Theatre, 19 North Clark Street, Chicago, Illinois. Opened 1913; 867 seats; J. E. O. Pridmore, architect. Anthony F. Dumas, artist, 1936. P&P, ADE 11-Dumas No. 73.

ART-056. Cort Theatre, 132 North Dearborn Street, Chicago, Illinois. Opened October 25, 1909; 949 seats; J. E. O. Pridmore, architect. Anthony F. Dumas, artist, 1929. P&P, ADE 11-Dumas No. 52.

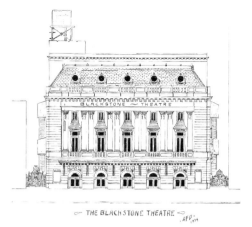

THE BLACKSTONE THEATRE

ART-051

CENTRAL PARK THEATRE

ART-052

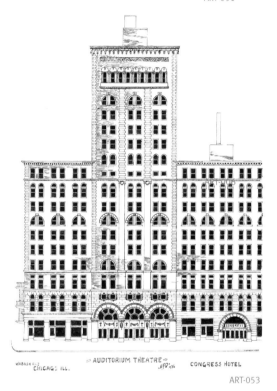

AUDITORIUM THEATRE — CONGRESS HOTEL

WABASH AVE. CHICAGO ILL.

ART-053

GARRITT CENTRAL THEATRE

ART-054

ADELPHIA THEATRE

ART-055

CORT THEATRE

ART-056

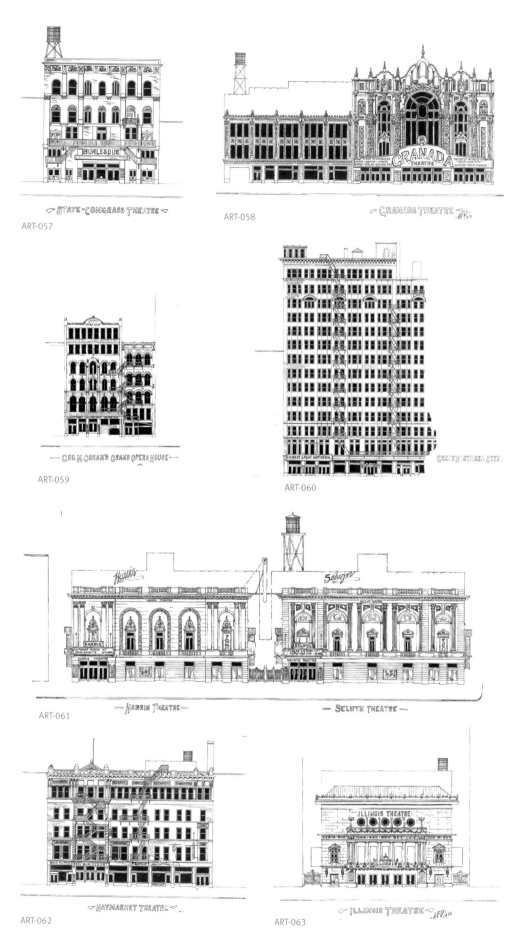

ART-057. Folly (State-Congress) Theatre, 531 South State Street, Chicago, Illinois. Built 1884; 1,600 seats. Anthony F. Dumas, artist, 1929. P&P, ADE 11-Dumas No. 61.

ART-058. Granada Theatre, 6427 North Sheridan Road, Chicago, Illinois. Opened September 18, 1926; 3433 seats; Levy & Klein, architects. Anthony F. Dumas, artist, 1933. P&P, ADE 11-Dumas No. 75.

ART-059. Grand Opera House, 119 North Clark Street, Chicago, Illinois. Opened September 6, 1880; 1,750 seats; Dankmar Adler, architect. Anthony F. Dumas, artist, 1918. P&P, ADE 11-Dumas No. 76.

ART-060. Great Northern (Lyric, Hippodrome) Theatre, 21 West Quincy Street, Chicago, Illinois. Opened November 9, 1896; 1,385 seats; Burnham & Root, architects. Anthony F. Dumas, artist, 1928. P&P, ADE 11-Dumas No. 60.

ART-061. Harris (Michael Todd, Goodman) and Selwyn (Cinestage, Goodman) Theatres, 170–186 North Dearborn Street, Chicago, Illinois. 1,058 seats; C. Howard Crane, architect. Anthony F. Dumas, artist, 1924. P&P, ADE 11-Dumas No. 74.

Called the twin theatres, the Selwyn opened on September 18, 1922 and the Harris on October 2. They later were combined as the Goodman Theatre.

ART-062. Haymarket Theatre, 722 West Madison Street, Chicago, Illinois. Opened December 24, 1887; 2,196 seats; John S. Flanders, architect. Anthony F. Dumas, artist, 1928. P&P, ADE 11-Dumas No. 54.

ART-063. Illinois Theatre, 65 East Jackson Street, Chicago, Illinois. Opened October 5, 1900; 1,304 seats; Wilson & Marshall, architects. Anthony F. Dumas, artist, 1930. P&P, ADE 11-Dumas No. 66.

ART-064. Kingsbury Music Hall (Olympic, Apollo Theatre), 169 North Clark Street, Chicago, Illinois. Opened October 6, 1873; 1,600 seats; Burling & Adler, architects. Anthony F. Dumas, artist, 1927. P&P, ADE 11-Dumas No. 57.

The Kingsbury Music Hall was the first theater to open in Chicago after the great fire of 1871. Its entry corridor passed through a succession of street-front buildings, one of which is depicted here.

ART-065. McVicker's Theatre, 25 West Madison Street, Chicago, Illinois. Opened September 26, 1922; 1,975 seats; Newhouse & Bernham, architects. Anthony F. Dumas, artist, 1926. P&P, ADE 11-Dumas No. 56.

The McVicker's was the fourth theatre of that name to occupy the site. The first, designed by Otis L. Wheelock, opened on November 5, 1857 and burned in the great fire of 1871. Wheelock & Thomas designed its rebuilding, which opened on August 15, 1872 (see 1-038). This, too, burned, in 1891, and was replaced on March 31, 1892 by an Adler & Sullivan design that, in turn, was replaced with the theater illustrated here.

ART-066. Masonic Temple, 165 North State Street, Chicago, Illinois. Opened 1892; Burnham & Root, architects. Anthony F. Dumas, artist, 1935. P&P, ADE 11-Dumas No. 67.

ART-067. Oriental Theatre, 20 West Randolph Street, Chicago, Illinois. Opened May 8, 1926; 3,164 seats; C. W. & George L. Rapp, architects. Anthony F. Dumas, artist, 1928. P&P, ADE 11-Dumas No. 55.

ART-068. Palace Music Hall (Erlanger Theatre), 127 North Clark Street, Chicago, Illinois. Opened April 1, 1912; 1,500 seats. Anthony F. Dumas, artist, 1927. P&P, ADE 11-Dumas No. 53.

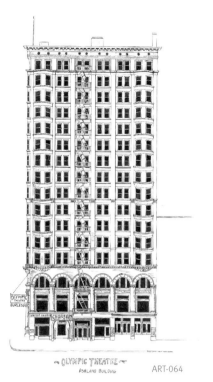

OLYMPIC THEATRE
ASHLAND BUILDING

ART-064

McVICKER'S THEATRE

ART-065

MASONIC TEMPLE
MASONIC TEMPLE THEATRE

ART-066

NEW UNITED MASONIC TEMPLE
BUILT ON SITE OF THE COLONIAL THEATRE

ART-067

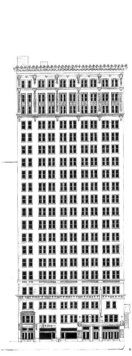

ERLANGER THEATRE
FORMERLY
PALACE MUSIC HALL
N. CLARK & CITY HALL
CHICAGO, ILL.

ART-068

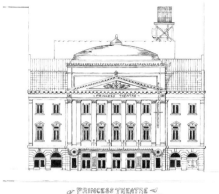

ART-069

ART-070

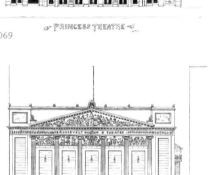

ART-071

ART-072

ART-073

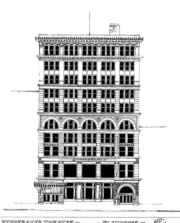

ART-074

ART-075

ART-069. Princess Theatre, 319 South Clark Street, Chicago, Illinois. Opened 1908; 900 seats; Kirchoff & Rose, architects. Anthony F. Dumas, artist. P&P, ADE 11-Dumas No. 58.

ART-070. Rialto Theatre, 336 South State Street, Chicago, Illinois. Opened 1920; 1,500 seats; Marshall & Fox, architects. Anthony F. Dumas, artist, 1936. P&P, ADE 11-Dumas No. 72.

ART-071. Roosevelt Theatre, 110 North State Street, Chicago, Illinois. Opened April 23, 1921; 1,535 seats; C. Howard Crane, architect. Anthony F. Dumas, artist, 1926. P&P, ADE 11-Dumas No. 59.

ART-072. Schiller (Garrick) Theatre, 64 West Randolph Street. Opened September 29, 1982; 1,286 seats; Adler & Sullivan, architects. Woods Theatre, 50 West Randolph Street, Chicago, Illinois. Opened March 11, 1918; 1,200 seats; Marshall & Fox, architects. Anthony F. Dumas, artist, 1932. P&P, ADE 11-Dumas No. 65.

ART-073. Star & Garter Theatre, 815 West Madison Street, Chicago, Illinois. Opened January 19, 1908; 2,000 seats. Anthony F. Dumas, artist, 1938. P&P, ADE 11-Dumas No. 47B.

ART-074. Studebaker and Playhouse Theatres, 203 South Michigan Avenue, Chicago, Illinois. Opened October 29, 1898; Solon S. Beman, architect. Anthony F. Dumas, artist, 1929. P&P, ADE 11-Dumas No. 62.

ART-075. State-Lake Theatre, 190 North State Street, Chicago, Illinois. Opened March 17, 1919; 2,626 seats; C. W. & George L. Rapp (office building), G. Albert Lansburgh (theater), architects. Anthony F. Dumas, artist, 1932. P&P, ADE 11-Dumas No. 64.

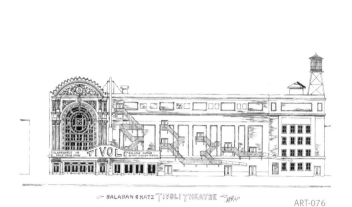

ART-076

NEW VICTORIA THEATRE

ART-077

ART-076. Tivoli Theatre, 6329 South Cottage Grove Avenue, Chicago, Illinois. Opened February 16, 1921; 3,414 seats; C. W. & George L. Rapp, architects. Anthony F. Dumas, artist, 1933. P&P, ADE 11-Dumas No. 63.

ART-077. Victoria (Vic, German, Old Vic) Theatre, 3143 North Sheffield Street, Chicago, Illinois. Opened 1912; 1,414 seats; J. E. O. Pridmore, architect. Anthony F. Dumas, artist, 1935. P&P, ADE 11-Dumas No. 68.

ART-078. West Englewood Theatre, 1806 West Sixty-third Street, Chicago, Illinois. Opened 1920; 2,065 seats. Anthony F. Dumas, artist, 1938. P&P, ADE 11-Dumas No. 70.

INDIANA

ART-079. Indiana Theatre, 136 West Washington Street, Indianapolis, Indiana. Opened June 19, 1927; 3,133 seats; Rubush & Hunter, architects. Anthony F. Dumas, artist, 1937. P&P, ADE 11-Dumas No. 77.

ART-080. Palace Theatre, 215–217 North Michigan Street, South Bend, Indiana. Opened November 21, 1922; 2,665 seats; J. S. Aroner, architect. Anthony F. Dumas, artist, 1934. P&P, ADE 11-Dumas No. 78.

IOWA

ART-081. Capitol Theatre, 326 West Third Street, Davenport, Iowa. Opened December 25, 1920; 2,500 seats; C. W. & George L. Rapp, architects. Anthony F. Dumas, artist. P&P, ADE 11-Dumas No. 79.

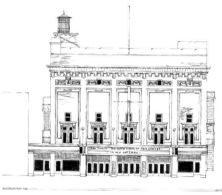

ASCHER'S WEST ENGLEWOOD THEATRE

ART-078

INDIANA THEATRE

ART-079

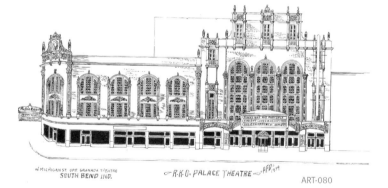

W. MICHIGAN ST. OPP. GRANADA THEATRE
SOUTH BEND IND.

R.K.O. PALACE THEATRE

ART-080

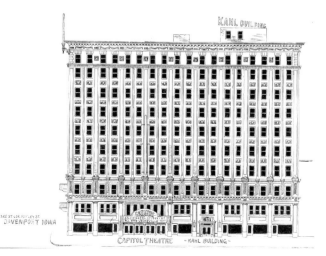

CAPITOL THEATRE — KAHL BUILDING —

ART-081

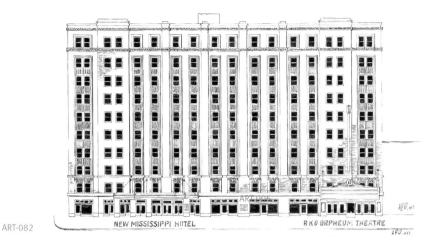

NEW MISSISSIPPI HOTEL   RKO ORPHEUM THEATRE

ART-082

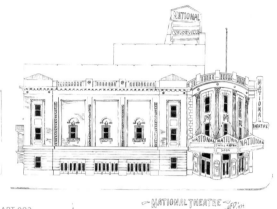

NATIONAL THEATRE

ART-083

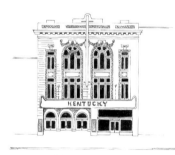

KENTUCKY THEATRE

ART-084

WALNUT THEATRE

ART-085

ORPHEUM THEATRE
NEW ORLEANS LA.

ART-086

SINGER ORPHEUM THEATRE

ART-087

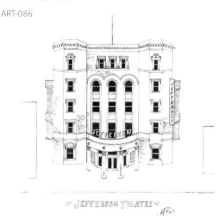

JEFFERSON THEATRE

ART-088

ART-082. Orpheum (Adler) Theatre, 136 East Third Street, Davenport, Iowa. Opened November 25, 1931; 2,708 seats; C. W. & George L. Rapp, architects. Anthony F. Dumas, artist, 1933. P&P, ADE 11-Dumas No. 80.

KENTUCKY

ART-083. National Theatre, 500 West Walnut Street, Louisville, Kentucky. Opened 1914; 2,507 seats; Albert Kahn, architect. Anthony F. Dumas, artist, 1934. P&P, ADE 11-Dumas No. 32.

ART-084. Kentucky Theatre, 208 East Main Street, Lexington, Kentucky. Opened October 1, 1922; 1,276 seats; Joseph & Joseph, architects. Anthony F. Dumas, artist. P&P, ADE 11-Dumas No. 81.

ART-085. Walnut (Scoop) Theatre, 416 West Walnut Street, Louisville, Kentucky. Opened 1912; 700 seats. Anthony F. Dumas, artist, 1934. P&P, ADE 11-Dumas No. 82.

LOUISIANA

ART-086. Orpheum (St. Charles) Theatre, 426 St. Charles Street, New Orleans, Louisiana. Opened 1902; 1,625 seats; Favrot & Livaudais, architects. Anthony F. Dumas, artist, 1936. P&P, ADE 11-Dumas No. 83.

ART-087. Orpheum Theatre, 129 University Place, New Orleans, Louisiana. Opened February 7, 1921; 1,660 seats; G. Albert Lansburgh, architect. Anthony F. Dumas, artist, 1936. P&P, ADE 11-Dumas No. 84.

MAINE

ART-088. Jefferson Theatre, 112 Free Street, Portland, Maine. Opened September 1897; 1,661 seats; Wood & Lovell, architects. Anthony F. Dumas, artist, 1929. P&P, ADE 11-Dumas No. 85.

ART-089. Keith's (Civic) Theatre, 477 Congress Street, Portland, Maine. Opened 1908; 1,800 seats. Anthony F. Dumas, artist, 1928. P&P, ADE 11-Dumas No. 86.

ART-090. State Theatre, 609 Congress Street, Portland, Maine. Opened November 8, 1929; 2,058 seats; Herbert W. Rhodes, architect. Anthony F. Dumas, artist, 1930. P&P, ADE 11-Dumas No. 87.

MARYLAND

ART-091. Kernan's Auditorium (Mayfair Theatre), 508 North Howard Street, Baltimore, Maryland. Opened September 4, 1905; 1,760 seats; John D. Allen, architect. Academy of Music, 516 North Howard Street, Baltimore, Maryland. Opened January 5, 1875; 1,832 seats; J. Crawford Neilson, architect. Anthony F. Dumas, artist, 1921. P&P, ADE 11-Dumas No. 88.

ART-092. Washington Hall (Olympic, Kernan's Monumental, Folly Theatre), East Baltimore Street, Baltimore, Maryland. Built 1837; 2,004 seats. Anthony F. Dumas, artist, 1924. P&P, ADE 11-Dumas No. 89.

ART-093. Ford's Grand Opera House, 320 West Fayette Street, Baltimore, Maryland. Opened October 2, 1871; 2,250 seats; James J. Gifford, architect. Anthony F. Dumas, artist, 1921. P&P, ADE 11-Dumas No. 90.

ART-094. Gayety Theatre, 405 East Baltimore Street, Baltimore, Maryland. Opened February 5, 1906; 1,500 seats; J. B. McElfatrick & Sons, architects. Anthony F. Dumas, artist, 1929. P&P, ADE 11-Dumas No. 91.

ART-095. Hippodrome Theatre, 12 North Eutaw Street, Baltimore, Maryland. Opened November 23, 1914; 2,100 seats; Thomas W. Lamb, architect. Anthony F. Dumas, artist, 1935. P&P, ADE 11-Dumas No. 92.

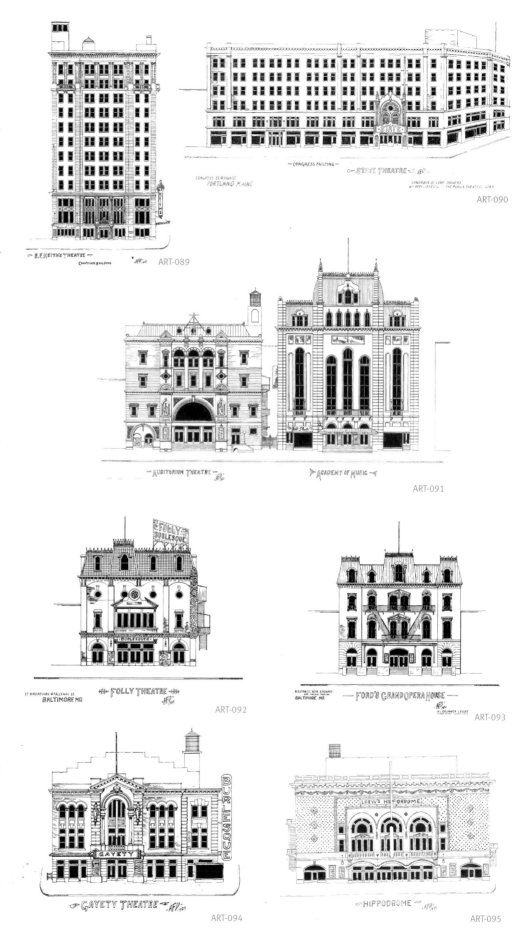

ART-096

~ MARYLAND THEATRE ~

ART-097

NEW LYCEUM THEATRE
FORMERLY ALBAUGH'S THEATRE

ART-096. Maryland Theatre, 320–322 West Franklin Street, Baltimore, Maryland. Opened October 19, 1903; 1,972 seats; John D. Allen, architect. Anthony F. Dumas, artist, 1921. P&P, ADE 11-Dumas No. 93.

ART-097. New Lyceum (Albaugh) Theatre, 1309 North Charles Street, Baltimore, Maryland. Opened 1892; 1,314 seats; W. B. Gray, architect. Anthony F. Dumas, artist, 1926. P&P, ADE 11-Dumas No. 94.

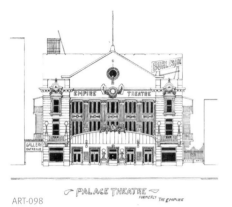

ART-098

~ PALACE THEATRE ~
FORMERLY THE EMPIRE

ART-099

~ ARLINGTON THEATRE ~

ART-098. Empire (Palace, Town) Theatre, 315 West Fayette Street, Baltimore, Maryland. Opened December 25, 1911; 2,252 seats; Otto Simonson (exterior), William H. McElfatrick (theater), architects. Anthony F. Dumas, artist, 1929. P&P, ADE 11-Dumas No. 95.

MASSACHUSETTS

ART-099. Castle Square (Arlington Square, Arlington) Theatre, 421 Tremont Street, Boston, Massachusetts. Opened November 19, 1894; 2,312 seats; Winslow & Witherell, architects. Anthony F. Dumas, artist, 1928. P&P, ADE 11-Dumas No. 96.

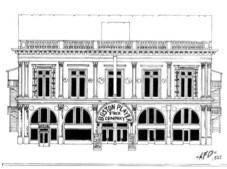

ART-100

~ KEITH-ALBEE ST. JAMES THEATRE ~

ART-101

~ COLONIAL THEATRE ~

ART-100. Chickering Hall, 239 Huntington Avenue, Boston, Massachusetts. Reopened as St. James (Uptown) Theatre, August 30, 1912; 1,636 seats; Peabody & Sterns, architects. Anthony F. Dumas, artist, 1928. P&P, ADE 11-Dumas No. 106.

ART-101. Colonial Theatre, 100–106 Boylston Street, Boston, Massachusetts. Opened December 19, 1900; 1,653 seats; Clarence H. Blackall, architect. Anthony F. Dumas, artist, 1921. P&P, ADE 11-Dumas No. 97.

ART-102

~ COLUMBIA THEATRE ~

ART-102. Columbia Music Hall, 978 Washington Street, Boston, Massachusetts. Opened October 5, 1891; 2,079 seats; Leon H. Lempert, architect. Anthony F. Dumas, artist, 1926. P&P, ADE 11-Dumas No. 98A.

ART-103. Cort (Park Square, Selwyn) Theatre, Park Square at Columbus Avenue,
Boston, Massachusetts. Opened ca. 1913;
1,200 seats; Clarence H. Blackall, architect.
Anthony F. Dumas, artist, 1926. P&P, ADE
11-Dumas No. 113.

ART-104. Fenway Theatre, 136 Massachusetts Avenue, Boston, Massachusetts. Built
ca. 1916; 1,361 seats; Thomas W. Lamb,
architect. Anthony F. Dumas, artist, 1926.
P&P, ADE 11-Dumas No. 98B.

ART-105. Gayety (Publix) Theatre, 661
Washington Street, Boston, Massachusetts.
Opened June 20, 1908; 1,049 seats;
Clarence H. Blackall, architect. Anthony F.
Dumas, artist, 1922. P&P, ADE 11-Dumas
No. 99.

ART-106. Globe (Center, Pagoda) Theatre,
686 Washington Street, Boston, Massachusetts. Opened 1903; 1,655 seats; Arthur H.
Vinal, architect. Anthony F. Dumas, artist,
1931. P&P, ADE 11-Dumas No. 100.

ART-107. Hollis Street Theatre, 10–14 Hollis
Street, Boston, Massachusetts. Opened
November 9, 1885; 1,640 seats; John Roul-
stone Hall, architect. Anthony F. Dumas,
artist, 1921. P&P, ADE 11-Dumas No. 102.

ART-108. Howard Athenaeum, 34 Howard
Street, Boston, Massachusetts. Opened
October 5, 1846; 1,400 seats; Isaiah
Rogers, architect. Anthony F. Dumas, artist,
1921. P&P, ADE 11-Dumas No. 103.

Never a church, the Howard was a purpose-
built theater designed by one of America's
prominent architects. Its gothic design
reflected that of a previous church-turned-
theater on the same site.

ART-109. New York (Keith & Batcheller's)
Museum, 565 Washington Street, Boston,
Massachusetts. Opened January 1883.
Anthony F. Dumas, artist. P&P, ADE 11-
Dumas No. 114B.

As Dumas noted, this tiny museum was the
birthplace of B. F. Keith's vast vaudeville
empire.

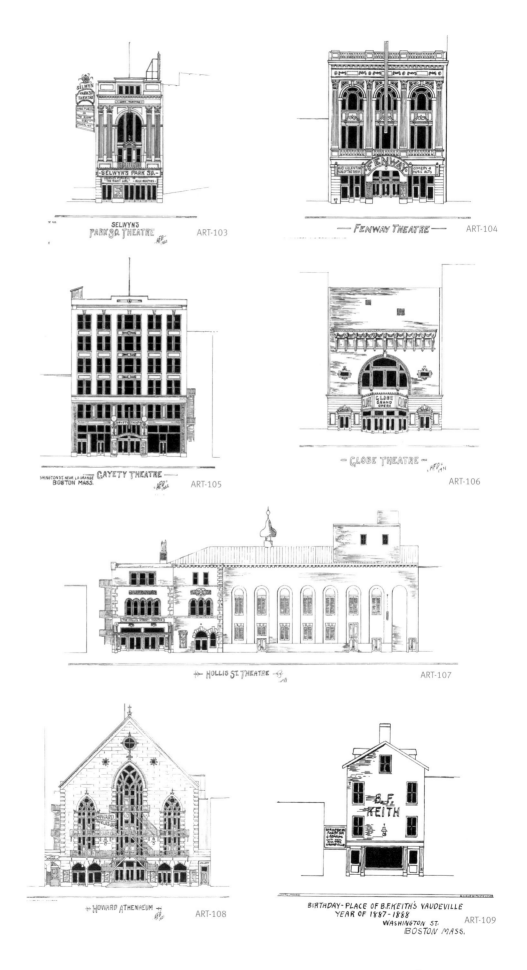

SELWYN'S PARK SQ. THEATRE   ART-103

— FENWAY THEATRE —   ART-104

SHINGTON ST NEAR LA GRANGE GAYETY THEATRE
BOSTON MASS.   ART-105

— GLOBE THEATRE —   ART-106

— HOLLIS ST. THEATRE —   ART-107

— HOWARD ATHENAEUM —   ART-108

BIRTHDAY-PLACE OF B.F.KEITH'S VAUDEVILLE
YEAR OF 1887-1888
WASHINGTON ST.   ART-109
BOSTON MASS.

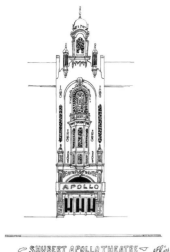

~ SHUBERT APOLLO THEATRE ~

ART-110

~ B.F. KEITH MEMORIAL THEATRE ~

ART-111

~ KEITH-ALBEE NEW BIJOU THEATRE ~

ART-112

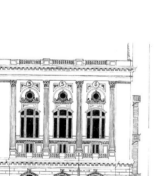

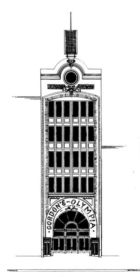

~ MAJESTIC THEATRE ~

ART-113

~ GORDON'S ~
~ SCOLLAY SQ. OLYMPIA THEATRE ~

ART-114

~ GORDON'S OLYMPIA THEATRE ~

ART-115

ART-110. B. F. Keith's New (Shubert Lyric, Apollo, Normandie, Laffmovie) Theatre, 547 Washington Street and 163 Tremont Street, Boston, Massachusetts. Opened March 24, 1894; 1,239 seats; J. B. McElfatrick & Sons, architects. Anthony F. Dumas, artist, 1931. P&P, ADE 11-Dumas No. 114A.

This ornamental building, added in 1897, gave a Tremont-Street presence to B. F. Keith's New Theatre and, later, the B. F. Keith Memorial.

ART-111. B. F. Keith Memorial Theatre (Savoy Theatre, Boston Opera House), 539 Washington Street, Boston, Massachusetts. Opened October 29, 1928; 2,907 seats; Thomas W. Lamb, architect. Anthony F. Dumas, artist, 1929. P&P, ADE 11-Dumas No. 105.

ART-112. Keith-Albee Boston (Keith-Boston) Theatre, 614 Washington Street, Boston, Massachusetts. Opened October 5, 1925; 3,213 seats; Arthur H. Bowditch, architect. Anthony F. Dumas, artist, 1927. P&P, ADE 11-Dumas No. 104.

ART- 113. Majestic (Saxon) Theatre, 219 Tremont Street, Boston, Massachusetts. Opened February 16, 1903; 1,897 seats; John Galen Howard (building) and J. M. Wood (theater), architects. Anthony F. Dumas, artist, 1928. P&P, ADE 11-Dumas No. 109.

ART-114. Scollay Square Olympia Theatre, 56 Scollay Square, Boston, Massachusetts. Built ca. 1915; 2,538 seats; Clarence H. Blackall, architect. Anthony F. Dumas, artist, 1921. P&P, ADE 11-Dumas No. 101B.

ART-115. Olympia (Washington Olympia, Pilgrim) Theatre, 658 Washington Street, Boston, Massachusetts. Opened May 6, 1912; 1,892 seats; Clarence H. Blackall, architect. Anthony F. Dumas, artist, 1921. P&P, ADE 11-Dumas No. 101A.

ART-116. Orpheum Theatre, 413 Washington Street, 6 Music Hall Place, and 1 Hamilton Place (shown), Boston, Massachusetts. Opened January 20, 1916; 2,890 seats; Thomas W. Lamb, architect. Anthony F. Dumas, artist, 1922. P&P, ADE 11-Dumas No. 107.

The Orpheum was a rebuilding of the 1852 Boston Music Hall. The facade shown here dominates and terminates a tiny entry street, off Tremont Street.

ART-117. Park (Trans-Lux) Theatre, 617 Washington Street, Boston, Massachusetts. Opened April 14, 1879; 1,277 seats. Anthony F. Dumas, artist, 1929. P&P, ADE 11-Dumas No. 111.

ART-118. Plymouth (Gary) Theatre, 129 Stuart Street, Boston, Massachusetts. Opened October 16, 1911; 1,500 seats; Clarence H. Blackall, architect. Anthony F. Dumas, artist, 1922. P&P, ADE 11-Dumas No. 112.

ART-119. Shubert Theatre, 265 Tremont Street, Boston, Massachusetts. Opened January 24, 1910; 1,624 seats; Thomas M. James, architect. Anthony F. Dumas, artist, 1929. P&P, ADE 11-Dumas No. 110.

ART-120. State Theatre, 205 Massachusetts Avenue, Boston, Massachusetts; 3,583 seats. Fine Arts Theatre, 70 Norway Street, Boston, Massachusetts; 544 seats. Opened March 13, 1922; Thomas W. Lamb, architect. Anthony F. Dumas, artist, 1926. P&P, ADE 11-Dumas No. 108.

ART-121. Waldron's Casino (Casino), 44 Hanover Street, Boston, Massachusetts. Opened ca. 1920; 1,825 seats. Anthony F. Dumas, artist, 1922. P&P, ADE 11-Dumas No. 116.

ART-122. Ye Wilbur Theatre, 252 Tremont Street, Boston, Massachusetts. Opened 1914; 1,227 seats; Clarence H. Blackall, architect. Metropolitan (Wang) Theatre, 268 Tremont Street, Boston, Massachusetts. Opened October 26, 1925; 4,407 seats; Blackall, Clapp & Whittemore, C. Howard Crane, Kenneth Franzheim, and George Nelson Meserve, architects. Anthony F. Dumas, artist, 1927. P&P, ADE 11-Dumas No. 117.

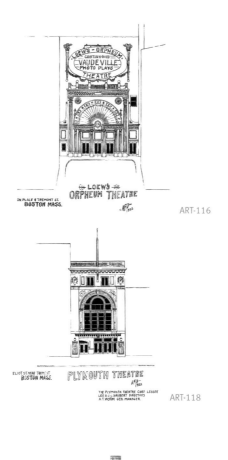

ART-116

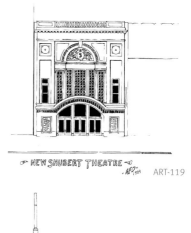

ART-117

ART-118

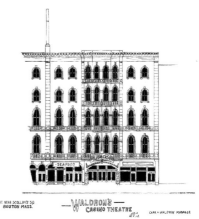

ART-119

ART-120

ART-121

ART-122

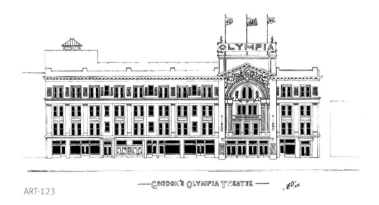

ART-123

MICHIGAN

ART-124

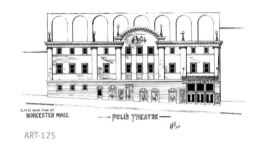

ART-125

ART-126

ART-127

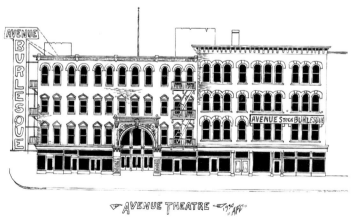

ART-128

ART-129

ART-130. Capitol Theatre (Paramount, Broadway Capitol, Grand Circus, Detroit Opera House), 1526 Broadway, Detroit, Michigan. Opened January 12, 1922; 3,367 seats; C. Howard Crane, architect. Anthony F. Dumas, artist, 1938. P&P, ADE 11-Dumas No. 125.

ART-131. Whitney Grand Opera House (Garrick Theatre), 1122 Griswold Street, Detroit, Michigan. Opened October 31, 1887; 1,409 seats; J. M. Wood, architect. Anthony F. Dumas, artist, 1925. P&P, ADE 11-Dumas No. 126.

ART-132. Gayety Theatre, 100 Cadillac Square, Detroit, Michigan. Opened September 15, 1912; 1,362 seats; Fuller Claflin, architect. Anthony F. Dumas, artist, 1923. P&P, ADE 11-Dumas No. 127.

ART-133. Grand Opera House (Lyceum Theatre, New Detroit Opera House), 1008 Randolph Street, Detroit, Michigan. Opened September 13, 1886; 2,605 seats; John Scott (building) and J. B. McElfatrick & Sons (theater), architects. Anthony F. Dumas, artist, 1924. P&P, ADE 11-Dumas No. 128.

ART-134. Orpheum (Lafayette, Shubert) Theatre, 153 West Lafayette Avenue, Detroit, Michigan. Opened September 7, 1914; 1,489 seats; Smith, Hinchman & Grylls, architects. Anthony F. Dumas, artist, 1924. P&P, ADE 11-Dumas No. 129.

ART-135. Palace Theatre, 130–132 Monroe Street, Detroit, Michigan. Opened February 16, 1914; 1,369 seats; C. Howard Crane, architect. Anthony F. Dumas, artist. P&P, ADE 11-Dumas No. 130A.

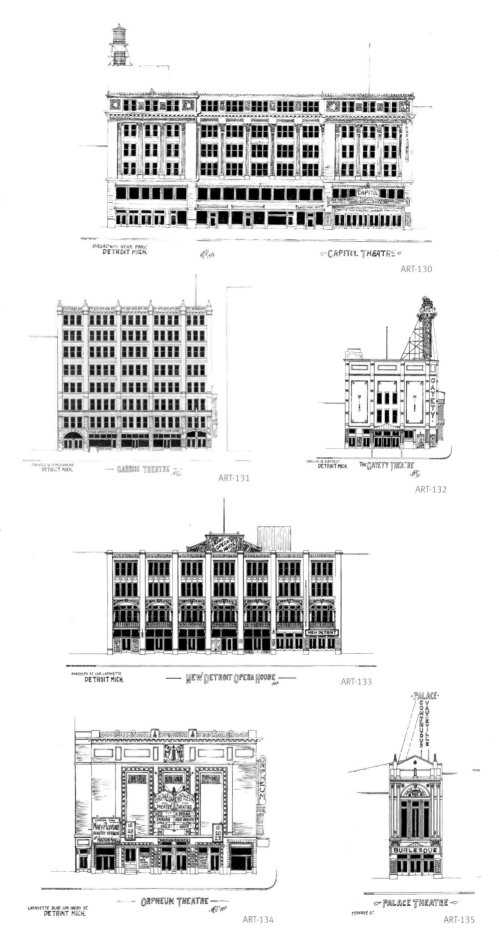

~ NATIONAL THEATRE ~ .AFD.

MONROE ST. NEAR FARMER

ART-136

~ COLUMBIA THEATRE ~

ART-137

DETROIT MICH. ~ SHUBERT MICHIGAN THEATRE ~

ART-138

~ SHUBERT'S DETROIT OPERA HOUSE ~ AFD.

ART-139

MONROE ST. NEAR THE CAMPUS
DETROIT MICH. — TEMPLE THEATRE —

ART-140

~ WILLIAM FOX ~
WASHINGTON THEATRE

ART-141

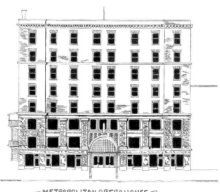

~ METROPOLITAN OPERA HOUSE ~

ART-142

~ ORPHEUM THEATRE ~ AFD

ART-143

ART-136. National Theatre, 118 Monroe Street, Detroit, Michigan. Opened September 16, 1911; 758 seats; Albert Kahn, Ernest Wilby, architects. Anthony F. Dumas, artist. P&P, ADE 11-Dumas No. 130B.

ART-137. Columbia Theatre, 50 Monroe Street, Detroit, Michigan. Opened October 2, 1911; 1,007 seats; C. Howard Crane, architect. Anthony F. Dumas, artist. P&P, ADE 11-Dumas No. 130C.

ART-138. Cadillac (Michigan, Shubert) Theatre, 231 Michigan Avenue, Detroit, Michigan. Opened April 1, 1912; 1,089 seats; Gustave A. Mueller, architect. Anthony F. Dumas, artist, 1923. P&P, ADE 11-Dumas No. 131.

ART-139. Detroit Opera House, 5–15 Campus Martius, Detroit, Michigan. Opened September 12, 1898; 1,757 seats; Mason & Rice, architects. Anthony F. Dumas, artist, 1929. P&P, ADE 11-Dumas No. 132.

ART-140. Wonderland Museum, 17 Campus Martius, and Temple Theatre, 15–19 Monroe Street, Detroit, Michigan. Opened September 1, 1899 (Wonderland), December 23, 1901 (Temple); 1,573 seats; John Scott (building) and James M. Wood (theater), architects. Anthony F. Dumas, artist, 1923. P&P, ADE 11-Dumas No. 133.

ART-141. Washington Theatre, 1505–1513 Washington Boulevard, Detroit, Michigan. Opened July 21, 1913; 1,862 seats; Arland W. Johnson, architect. Anthony F. Dumas, artist, 1926. P&P, ADE 11-Dumas No. 134.

MINNESOTA

ART-142. Metropolitan Opera House, 100 East Sixth Street, St. Paul, Minnesota. Opened September 1, 1890; 1,718 seats; Charles A. Reed, J. B. McElfatrick & Sons, architects. Anthony F. Dumas, artist, 1934. P&P, ADE 11-Dumas No. 135.

ART-143. Orpheum (President) Theatre, 365 St. Peter Street, St. Paul, Minnesota. Opened October 20, 1906; 1,726 seats. Anthony F. Dumas, artist, 1933. P&P, ADE 11-Dumas No. 136.

PARAMOUNT THEATRE
FORMERLY THE CAPITOL

ART-144

NEW ORPHEUM THEATRE

ART-145

ART-144. Capitol (Paramount) Theatre, 22 West Seventh Street, St. Paul, Minnesota. Opened September 8, 1920; 2,362 seats; C. W. & George L. Rapp, architects. Anthony F. Dumas, artist, 1934. P&P, ADE 11-Dumas No. 137.

MISSOURI

ART-145. Orpheum Theatre, 1214 Baltimore Street, Kansas City, Missouri. Opened December 26, 1914; 1,785 seats; G. Albert Lansburgh, architect. Anthony F. Dumas, artist, 1933. P&P, ADE 11-Dumas No. 138.

ART-146. St. Louis Theatre (Powell Hall), 718 North Grand Boulevard, St. Louis, Missouri. Opened November 23, 1925; 3,861 seats; C. W. & George L. Rapp, architects. Anthony F. Dumas, artist, 1939. P&P, ADE 11-Dumas No. 139.

ART-147. Ambassador Theatre, 411 North Seventh Street, St. Louis, Missouri. Opened August 26, 1926; 2,999 seats; C. W. & George L. Rapp, architects. Anthony F. Dumas, artist, 1933. P&P, ADE 11-Dumas No. 140.

MONTANA

ART-148. Orpheum Theatre, Butte, Montana. Anthony F. Dumas, artist, 1938. P&P, ADE 11-Dumas No. 141.

NEBRASKA

ART-149. American Music Hall, Eighteenth and Douglas Streets, Omaha, Nebraska. Anthony F. Dumas, artist, 1935. P&P, ADE 11-Dumas No. 142.

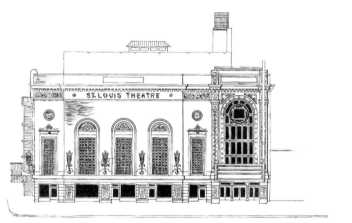

ST. LOUIS THEATRE

ART-146

ORPHEUM THEATRE

ART-148

7TH ST. & LOCUST ST.
ST. LOUIS MO.

SKOURAS BROS AMBASSADOR THEATRE

ART-147

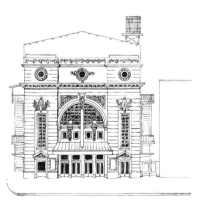

ART-149

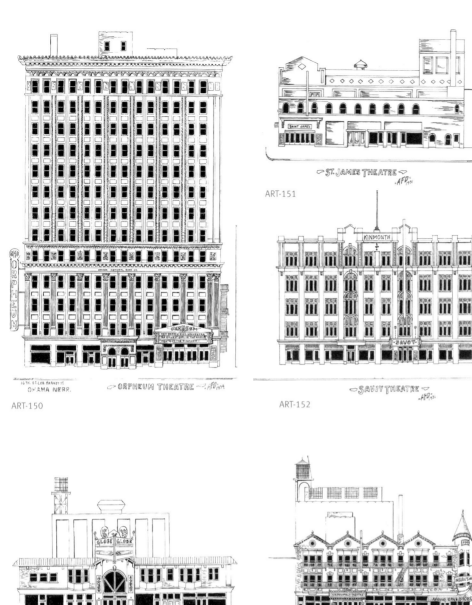

ART-150

ST. JAMES THEATRE

ART-151

SAVOY THEATRE

ART-152

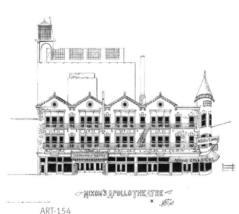

GLOBE THEATRE
FORMERLY NEW NIXON'S THEATRE

ART-153

NIXON'S APOLLO THEATRE

ART-154

SAVOY THEATRE

ART-155

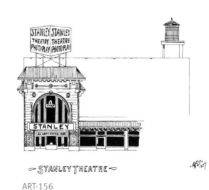

STANLEY THEATRE

ART-156

ART-150. Orpheum Theatre, 409 South Sixteenth Street, Omaha, Nebraska. Opened October 9, 1927; 2,978 seats; Holabird & Roche (building) and C. W. & George L. Rapp (theater), architects. Anthony F. Dumas, artist, 1934. P&P, ADE 11-Dumas No. 143.

NEW JERSEY

ART-151. Saint James Theatre, 300 Cookman Avenue, Asbury Park, New Jersey. Opened August 13, 1917; 1,558 seats; Thomas W. Lamb, architect. Anthony F. Dumas, artist, 1931. P&P, ADE 11-Dumas No. 144.

ART-152. Savoy Theatre, 720 Mattison Avenue, Asbury Park, New Jersey. 873 seats. Anthony F. Dumas, artist, 1931. P&P, ADE 11-Dumas No. 145.

ART-153. Nixon (Globe) Theatre, Boardwalk, Atlantic City, New Jersey. Opened July 14, 1913; 2,227 seats; Magaziner & Potter, architects. Anthony F. Dumas, artist, 1930. P&P, ADE 11-Dumas No. 146.

ART-154. Apollo Theatre, Boardwalk, Atlantic City, New Jersey. Built 1907; 2,200 seats; John D. Allen, architect. Anthony F. Dumas, artist, 1939. P&P, ADE 11-Dumas No. 147.

On March 16, 1926, Anthony Dumas and his bride saw The Student Prince in this theater while on their honeymoon.

ART-155. Woods (Savoy) Theatre, Boardwalk, Atlantic City, New Jersey. Opened 1907; 1,500 seats. Anthony F. Dumas, artist, 1928. P&P, ADE 11-Dumas No. 148.

Dumas and his bride spent their honeymoon in the hotel above the Savoy.

ART-156. Stanley Theatre, 1545 Boardwalk, Atlantic City, New Jersey. Opened July 23, 1925; 2,200 seats; Hoffman & Henon, architects. Anthony F. Dumas, artist, 1937. P&P, ADE 11-Dumas No. 149.

ART-157. Bayonne Opera House (Victory Theatre), 589 Avenue C, Bayonne, New Jersey. Opened 1907; 1,450 seats; E. C. Horn, architect. Anthony F. Dumas, artist, 1935. P&P, ADE 11-Dumas No. 150.

ART-158. Bayonne (Broadway, Bijou, Strand) Theatre, 513 Broadway, Bayonne, New Jersey. Opened October 25, 1906; 1,259 seats; E. C. Horn, architect. Anthony F. Dumas, artist, 1939. P&P, ADE 11-Dumas No. 151.

ART-159. Towers Theatre, 714 Broadway, Camden, New Jersey. Built 1920; 1,420 seats; Hoffman-Henon Company, architects. Anthony F. Dumas, artist, 1939. P&P, ADE 11-Dumas No. 152A.

ART-160. Broadway Theatre, Broadway and Carmen Streets, Camden, New Jersey. 1,022 seats. Anthony F. Dumas, artist, 1939. P&P, ADE 11-Dumas No. 152B.

ART-161. Hippodrome (Liberty) Theatre, 1121 Elizabeth Avenue, Elizabeth, New Jersey. Opened October 6, 1913; 1,521 seats. Anthony F. Dumas, artist, 1919. P&P, ADE 11-Dumas No. 153.

ART-162. Library Hall (Lyceum, Broad Street Theatre), 19–21 South Broad Street, Elizabeth, New Jersey. Opened June 15, 1858; 1,250 seats; renamed Lyceum September 24, 1894, C. Graham, architect; J. B. McElfatrick & Sons, architects. Anthony F. Dumas, artist. P&P, ADE 11-Dumas No. 154.

ART-163. Drake Opera House (People's, Star, Jacobs', Proctor's Theatre), 1146 East Jersey Street, Elizabeth, New Jersey. Opened September 15, 1894; 1,541 seats; Jesse A. Oakley Jr., architect. Anthony F. Dumas, artist, 1919. ADE 11-Dumas No. 155.

- OPERA HOUSE HALL - BAYONNE OPERA HOUSE
26 TH ST. AFD, 1935

ART-157

FORMERLY BAYONNE THEATRE BIJOU THEATRE
S E. 23 RD ST.

ART-158

TOWERS THEATRE

ART-159

BROADWAY THEATRE

ART-160

GORDON'S HIPPODROME
ELIZABETH N.J.
WILLIAM FOX
LIBERTY THEATRE AFD.

ART-161

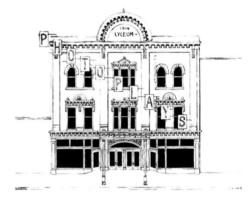

PROCTOR'S BROAD ST THEATRE ART-162

PROCTOR'S E JERSEY ST. THEATRE ART-163

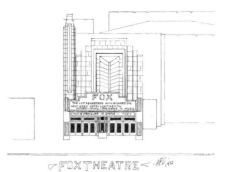

~ FOX THEATRE ~ ·AFD·1932

ART-164

~ ORITANI THEATRE ~ ·AFD·1932

ART-165

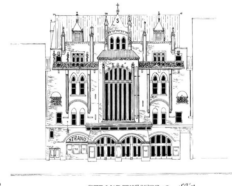

~ FABIAN THEATRE ~ AFD·1928

ART-166

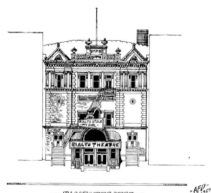

~ RIALTO THEATRE ~   ·AFD·1929

ART-167

~ STRAND THEATRE ~ AFD·1929

ART-168

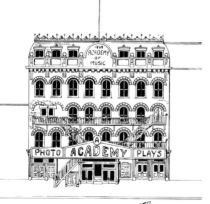

~ ACADEMY OF MUSIC ~ AFD·1936

ART-169

~ BON TON THEATRE ~ ·AFD·1933

ART-170

ART-164. Fox Theatre, 309 Main Street, Hackensack, New Jersey. Opened 1932; 2,230 seats; Thomas W. Lamb, architect. Anthony F. Dumas, artist, 1932. P&P, ADE 11-Dumas No. 156.

ART-165. Oritani Theatre, 300 Main Street, Hackensack, New Jersey. Opened May 6, 1926; 1,967 seats; William E. Lehman, architect. Anthony F. Dumas, artist, 1932. P&P, ADE 11-Dumas No. 157.

ART-166. Fabian Theatre, 69 Newark Street, Hoboken, New Jersey. Opened August 1, 1928; 3,036 seats; Fred W. Wentworth, architect. Anthony F. Dumas, artist, 1928. P&P, ADE 11-Dumas No. 158.

ART-167. Empire (Rialto) Theatre, 118 Hudson Street, Hoboken, New Jersey. Opened September 8, 1902; 1,135 seats; J. B. McElfatrick & Sons, architects. Anthony F. Dumas, artist, 1929. P&P, ADE 11-Dumas No. 159.

ART-168. Gayety (Strand) Theatre, 1013–1019 Washington Street, Hoboken, New Jersey. Opened September 14, 1908; 1,265 seats. Anthony F. Dumas, artist, 1929. P&P, ADE 11-Dumas No. 160.

ART-169. Kepler's Hall (Academy of Music), 4–12 Gregory Street, Jersey City, New Jersey. Opened December 22, 1870; 1,477 seats. Anthony F. Dumas, artist, 1936. P&P, ADE 11-Dumas No. 161A.

ART-170. Opera House (Grand Opera House, Bon Ton, Liberty Theatre), 47 Newark Avenue, Jersey City, New Jersey. Opened September 14, 1891; 1,400 seats; J. B. McElfatrick & Sons, architects. Anthony F. Dumas, artist, 1933. P&P, ADE 11-Dumas No. 162.

ART-171. B. F. Keith's (Palace) Theatre (left), 174 Newark Avenue, Jersey City, New Jersey. Opened November 19, 1906; 1,100 seats. Bijou (Bijou Dream) Theatre (right), 172 Newark Avenue, Jersey City, New Jersey. Opened November 14, 1898; 2,000 seats; J. B. McElfatrick & Sons, architect. Anthony F. Dumas, artist, 1916. P&P, ADE 11-Dumas No. 163A.

ART-172. Majestic Theatre, 275 Grove Street, Jersey City, New Jersey. Opened September 16, 1907; 1,481 seats; William H. McElfatrick, architect. Anthony F. Dumas, artist, 1934. P&P, ADE 11-Dumas No. 164A.

ART-173. Orpheum Theatre, 581 Summit Avenue, Jersey City, New Jersey. Opened October 3, 1910; 1,400 seats; William H. McElfatrick, architect. Anthony F. Dumas, artist, 1919. P&P, ADE 11-Dumas No. 165.

ART-174. Stanley Theatre, 2932 Kennedy Boulevard, Jersey City, New Jersey. Opened March 24, 1928; 4,332 seats; Fred W. Wentworth, architect. Anthony F. Dumas, artist, 1928. P&P, ADE 11-Dumas No. 166.

ART-175. State Theatre, 2854 Kennedy Boulevard, Jersey City, New Jersey. Opened April 24, 1922; 2,226 seats; Percy A. Vivarttas, architect. Anthony F. Dumas, artist, 1931. P&P, ADE 11-Dumas No. 167.

ART-176. Opera House, 20 Liberty Street, New Brunswick, New Jersey. 1,500 seats. Anthony F. Dumas, artist, 1934. P&P, ADE 11-Dumas No. 168A.

ART-177. Branford Theatre, 11 Branford Place, Newark, New Jersey. Opened December 17, 1920; 2,823 seats; Fred W. Wentworth, architect. Anthony F. Dumas, artist, 1936. P&P, ADE 11-Dumas No. 169.

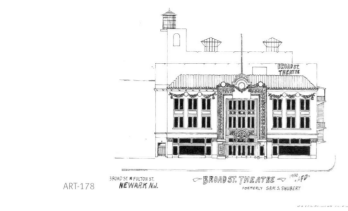

ART-178

3ROAD ST & FULTON ST.
NEWARK N.J.

BROAD ST. THEATRE
FORMERLY SAM S. SHUBERT

ART-178. Shubert (Broad Street) Theatre, 568 Broad Street, Newark, New Jersey. Opened January 8, 1912; 1,383 seats; William H. McElfatrick, architect. Anthony F. Dumas, artist, 1930. P&P, ADE 11-Dumas No. 170.

CAPACITY 2224   JACOB'S COLUMBIA THEATRE

NEW ORPHEUM THEATRE

ART-179

ART-179. Industrial Institute Hall (Grand Opera House, Columbia Theatre, Family Theatre) (left), 401 Washington Street, Newark, New Jersey. Opened October 5, 1876; 2,224 seats. Orpheum Theatre (Newark Opera House) (right), 385 Washington Street, Newark, New Jersey. Opened October 9, 1911; 1,800 seats; William E. Lehman, architect. Anthony F. Dumas, artist, 1936. P&P, ADE 11-Dumas No. 171.

LOEW'S STATE THEATRE

ART-180

ART-180. State Theatre, 635 Broad Street, Newark, New Jersey. Opened December 12, 1921; 2,600 seats; Thomas W. Lamb, architect. Anthony F. Dumas, artist, 1928. P&P, ADE 11-Dumas No. 172.

LYRIC THEATRE

ART-181

ART-181. Lyric Theatre, 211 Market Street, Newark, New Jersey. Opened October 26, 1908; 1,200 seats; Hughes & Backoff, architects. Anthony F. Dumas, artist, 1937. P&P, ADE 11-Dumas No. 173.

ART-182. Mosque Theatre (Salaam Temple, Symphony Hall), 1020 Broad Street, Newark, New Jersey. Opened September 8, 1925; 3,281 seats; Backoff, Grad & Baechlin, architects. Anthony F. Dumas, artist, 1926. P&P, ADE 11-Dumas No. 174.

MOSQUE THEATRE

ART-182

ART-183. Newark Theatre, 195 Market Street, Newark, New Jersey. Opened October 11, 1886; 2,300 seats. Anthony F. Dumas, artist, 1934. P&P, ADE 11-Dumas No. 175.

ART-184. Paramount Newark Theatre, 195 Market Street, Newark, New Jersey. Opened September 1, 1917; 2,003 seats; Thomas W. Lamb, architect. Anthony F. Dumas, artist, 1934. P&P, ADE 11-Dumas No. 175.

The Paramount was a rebuilding of the historic Newark Theatre (ART-183).

ART-185. Payton (Keeney, Shubert, Adams) Theatre, 28 Branford Place, Newark, New Jersey. Opened November 8, 1913; 2,037 seats; William E. Lehman, architect. Anthony F. Dumas, artist, 1935. P&P, ADE 11-Dumas No. 176.

ART-186. Strand (Capitol) Theatre (left), 120 Market Street, Newark, New Jersey. Opened May 1, 1914; 1,027 seats; George M. Keister and William E. Lehman, architects. Proctor's Palace Theatre (right), 116 Market Street, Newark, New Jersey. Opened November 22, 1915; 2,309 seats; John W. Merrow, architect. Anthony F. Dumas, artist, 1916. P&P, ADE 11-Dumas No. 177.

ART-187. Proctor's (Fox, Terminal) Theatre, 86–94 Park Place, Newark, New Jersey. Opened January 6, 1902; 2,026 seats; J. B. McElfatrick & Sons, architects. Anthony F. Dumas, artist, 1935. P&P, ADE 11-Dumas No. 178A.

ART-188. Waller's Opera House (Waldmann's Opera House, Gayety, Ascher's Halsey, Carlton Theatre), 138 Market Street, Newark, New Jersey. Opened 1847; 1,250 seats. Anthony F. Dumas, artist, 1935. P&P, ADE 11-Dumas No. 178B.

ART-189. Regent Theatre, 12 Union Street, Paterson, New Jersey. Opened August 24, 1914; 2,200 seats; Fred W. Wentworth, architect. Anthony F. Dumas, artist, 1926. P&P, ADE 11-Dumas No. 179.

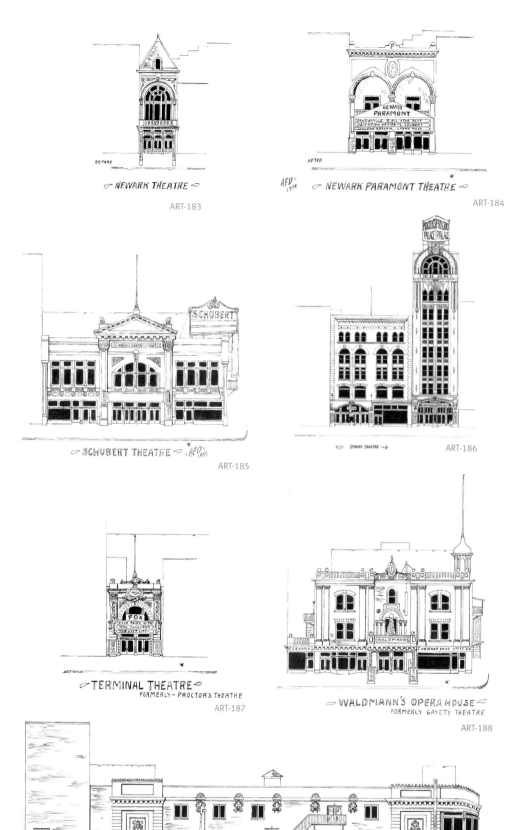

BEFORE

NEWARK THEATRE
ART-183

AFTER

NEWARK PARAMONT THEATRE
ART-184

SCHUBERT THEATRE
ART-185

STRAND THEATRE
ART-186

TERMINAL THEATRE
FORMERLY — PROCTOR'S THEATRE
ART-187

WALDMANN'S OPERA HOUSE
FORMERLY GAYETY THEATRE
ART-188

FABIAN REGENT THEATRE
ART-189

ART-190

— FABIAN THEATRE —

CHURCH ST. NEAR MARKET
PATERSON N.J.

OWNED & OPERATED BY FABIAN ENTERPRISES
DIRECTION STANLEY CO. OF AMERICA

— LYCEUM THEATRE —

ART-191

— GARDEN THEATRE —

ART-192

· MAJESTIC THEATRE ·

ART-193

— ORPHEUM THEATRE —

ART-194

RIVOLI THEATRE

ART-195

· MAJESTIC THEATRE ·

ART-196

ART-190. Fabian Theatre, 45 Church Street, Paterson, New Jersey. Opened December 14, 1925; 3,263 seats; Fred W. Wentworth, architect. Anthony F. Dumas, artist, 1926. P&P, ADE 11-Dumas No. 180.

ART-191. Apollo Hall (Academy of Music, Lyceum Theatre), 123 Van Houten Street, Paterson, New Jersey. Opened ca. 1887; 1,950 seats. Anthony F. Dumas, artist, 1919. P&P, ADE 11-Dumas No. 182.

Apollo opened as a rental hall that was used only occasionally for public presentations. It was refitted and opened as the Academy of Music on September 24, 1888. Rebuilt as the Lyceum, it reopened on December 25, 1905.

ART-192. Garden Theatre, 204 Market Street, Paterson, New Jersey. Opened November 6, 1916; 1,347 seats. Anthony F. Dumas, artist, 1919. P&P, ADE 11-Dumas No. 181.

ART-193. Majestic Theatre, 293 Main Street, Paterson, New Jersey. Opened November 28, 1910; 780 seats; Charles E. Sleight, architect. Anthony F. Dumas, artist, 1920. P&P, ADE 11-Dumas No. 183.

ART-194. Orpheum (State) Theatre, 55 Van Houten Street, Paterson, New Jersey. Opened August 17, 1912; 1,184 seats. Anthony F. Dumas, artist, 1919. P&P, ADE 11-Dumas No. 184.

ART-195. Rivoli Theatre, 130 Main Street, Paterson, New Jersey. Opened November 11, 1925; 1,802 seats; Henry Barrett Crosby, architect. Anthony F. Dumas, artist, 1931. P&P, ADE 11-Dumas No. 185.

ART-196. Majestic Theatre, 273 Madison Avenue, Perth Amboy, New Jersey. Opened 1927; 1,840 seats; Leon Cubberly, architect. Anthony F. Dumas, artist, 1920. P&P, ADE 11-Dumas No. 186.

ART-197. Elkwood Hall (Washington Hall, Amphion, Plainfield, Paramount Theatre), 110–112 West Second Street, Plainfield, New Jersey. Opened as Plainfield Theatre August 24, 1905; 1,353 seats; Fuller Claflin, architect. Anthony F. Dumas, artist, 1922. P&P, ADE 11-Dumas No. 187.

ART-198. Stillman's Music Hall (Red Men's, Masonic Hall, Proctor's, Oxford Theatre), 216 West Front Street, Plainfield, New Jersey. Opened October 16, 1884; 1,630 seats; Eben L. Roberts, architect. Anthony F. Dumas, artist. P&P, ADE 11-Dumas No. 188.

ART-199. Reade's Theatre, 179 South Broad Street, Trenton, New Jersey. 1,318 seats. Anthony F. Dumas, artist, 1931. P&P, ADE 11-Dumas No. 189.

ART-200. Broad Street (Grand, Palace) Theatre, 179–181 South Broad Street, Trenton, New Jersey. Opened February 17, 1912; 1,318 seats. Anthony F. Dumas, artist, 1934. P&P, ADE 11-Dumas No. 190A.

ART-201. Trent Theatre (left), 17 North Warren Street, Trenton, New Jersey. Opened December 7, 1903; 998 seats; J. B. McElfatrick & Sons, architects. Lincoln Theatre (right), 25 North Warren Street, Trenton, New Jersey. Opened 1928; 2,342 seats. Anthony F. Dumas, artist, 1934. P&P, ADE 11-Dumas No. 190.

ART-202. State Street Theatre, 211 East State Street, Trenton, New Jersey. Opened December 9, 1903; 1,500 seats; Albert E. Westover, Angus G. Wade, and William Steele & Co., architects. Anthony F. Dumas, artist, 1919. P&P, ADE 11-Dumas No. 191.

ART-203. Taylor's Opera House (Capitol, International 70 Theatre), 10–18 South Broad Street, Trenton, New Jersey. Opened March 18, 1867; 1,978 seats; Henry E. Finch, architect. Anthony F. Dumas, artist. P&P, ADE 11-Dumas No. 192.

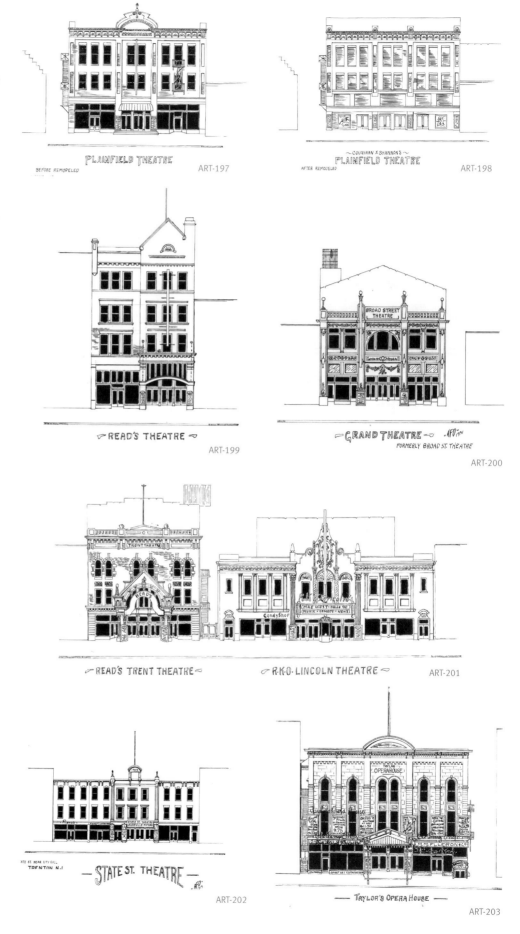

PLAINFIELD THEATRE
BEFORE REMODELED
ART-197

COUNIHAN & SHANNON'S
PLAINFIELD THEATRE
AFTER REMODELED
ART-198

READ'S THEATRE
ART-199

GRAND THEATRE
FORMERLY BROAD ST. THEATRE
ART-200

READ'S TRENT THEATRE
R·K·O· LINCOLN THEATRE
ART-201

STATE ST. THEATRE
ART-202

TAYLOR'S OPERA HOUSE
ART-203

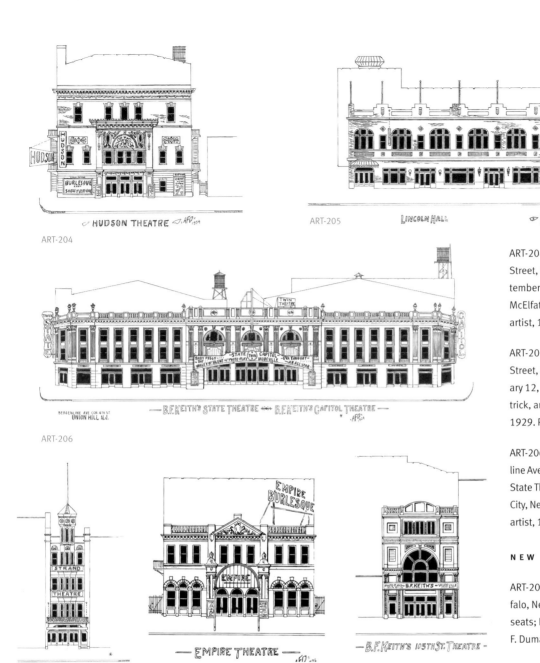

ART-204
HUDSON THEATRE

ART-205
LINCOLN HALL
LINCOLN THEATRE

ART-206
BERGENLINE AVE COR 6TH ST
UNION HILL N.J.
B.F.KEITH'S STATE THEATRE — B.F.KEITH'S CAPITOL THEATRE

ART-207
STRAND THEATRE
TORN DOWN

ART-208
EMPIRE THEATRE

ART-209
B.F.KEITH'S 105TH ST. THEATRE

ART-210
HANNA THEATRE

ART-204. Hudson Theatre, 403 Thirty-eighth Street, Union City, New Jersey. Opened September 14, 1908; 1,350 seats; William H. McElfatrick, architect. Anthony F. Dumas, artist, 1934. P&P, ADE 11-Dumas No. 193.

ART-205. Lincoln Theatre, 518 Thirty-second Street, Union City, New Jersey. Opened February 12, 1916; 1,736 seats; William H. McElfatrick, architect. Anthony F. Dumas, artist, 1929. P&P, ADE 11-Dumas No. 194.

ART-206. Capitol Theatre (right), 4700 Bergenline Avenue, Union City, New Jersey. 2,129 seats. State Theatre (left), 223 Main Street, Union City, New Jersey. 1,794 seats. Anthony F. Dumas, artist, 1924. P&P, ADE 11-Dumas No. 195.

NEW YORK

ART-207. Strand Theatre, 345 Main Street, Buffalo, New York. Opened February 1913; 1,200 seats; Leon H. Lempert Jr., architect. Anthony F. Dumas, artist. P&P, ADE 11-Dumas No. 196.

OHIO

ART-208. Grand (Empire) Theatre, 740–788 Huron Road, Cleveland, Ohio. Opened February 5, 1900; 1,300 seats. Anthony F. Dumas, artist, 1926. P&P, ADE 11-Dumas No. 197A.

ART-209. B. F. Keith's 105th Street Theatre, 10524 Euclid Avenue, Cleveland, Ohio. Opened November 24, 1921; 2,806 seats; A. G. Yost, architect. Anthony F. Dumas, artist, 1926. P&P, ADE 11-Dumas No. 197B.

ART-210. Hanna Theatre, 2065 East Fourteenth Street, Cleveland, Ohio. Opened March 28, 1921; 1,397 seats; Charles A. Platt, architect. Anthony F. Dumas, artist, 1923. P&P, ADE 11-Dumas No. 198.

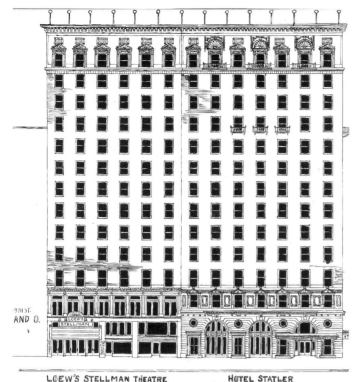

LOEW'S STELLMAN THEATRE   HOTEL STATLER

ART-211

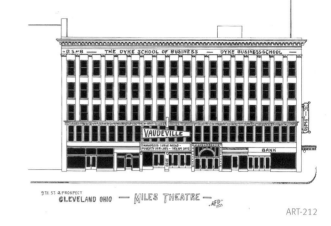

9TH ST. & PROSPECT
GLEVELAND OHIO — MILES THEATRE —

ART-212

ART-211. Stillman Theatre, 1111 Euclid Avenue, Cleveland, Ohio. Opened September 29, 1916; 1,995 seats; George B. Post & Son (building) and Thomas W. Lamb (theater), architects. Anthony F. Dumas, artist, 1940. P&P, ADE 11-Dumas No. 199.

ART-212. Miles (Columbia, Great Lakes, Carter, Federal) Theatre, 915 Huron Road, Cleveland, Ohio. Opened ca. 1911; 998 seats. Anthony F. Dumas, artist, 1923. P&P, ADE 11-Dumas No. 200.

ART-213. Allen Theatre, 1403–1407 Euclid Avenue, Cleveland, Ohio. Opened April 1, 1921; 3,009 seats; C. Howard Crane, architect. Ohio Theatre, 1511–1513 Euclid Avenue. Opened February 14, 1921; 1,338 seats; Thomas W. Lamb, architect. State Theatre, 1515–1519 Euclid Avenue. Opened March 6, 1921; 3,445 seats; Thomas W. Lamb, architect. Palace Theatre, 1621–1631 Euclid Avenue. Opened November 6, 1922; 3,530 seats; C. W. & George L. Rapp, architects. Anthony F. Dumas, artist. P&P, ADE 11-Dumas No. 201.

These theaters, along with the Hanna Theatre across Euclid Avenue (ART-210), collectively constitute Cleveland's Playhouse Square.

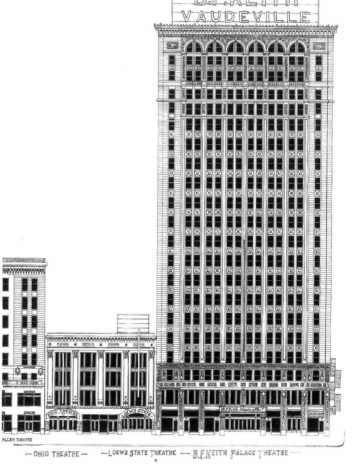

— OHIO THEATRE —   — LOEW'S STATE THEATRE —   B. F. KEITH PALACE THEATRE

ART-213

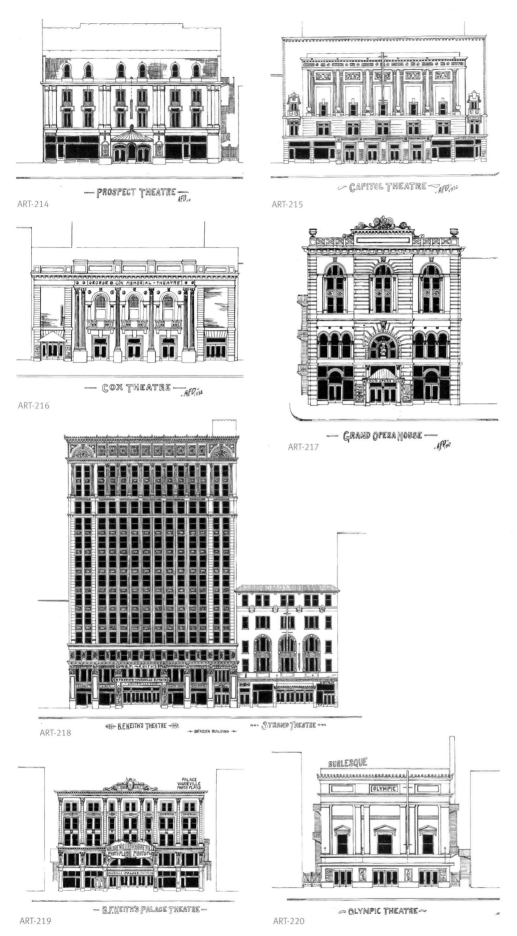

ART-214

PROSPECT THEATRE

ART-215

CAPITOL THEATRE

ART-216

COX THEATRE

ART-217

GRAND OPERA HOUSE

ART-218

B.F. KEITH'S THEATRE — B.F.KEITH BUILDING — STRAND THEATRE

ART-219

B.F. KEITH'S PALACE THEATRE

ART-220

OLYMPIC THEATRE

ART-214. Prospect Theatre, 619 Prospect Avenue, Cleveland, Ohio. Opened April 4, 1904. Anthony F. Dumas, artist, 1924. P&P, ADE 11-Dumas No. 202.

ART-215. Capitol Theatre, Seventh and Vine Streets, Cincinnati, Ohio. Opened April 2, 1921; 1,794 seats; Newhouse & Bernham, architects. Anthony F. Dumas, artist, 1932. P&P, ADE 11-Dumas No. 203.

ART-216. George B. Cox Memorial Theatre, 20 East Seventh Street, Cincinnati, Ohio. Opened 1921; Herbert J. Krapp, architect. Anthony F. Dumas, artist, 1932. P&P, ADE 11-Dumas No. 204.

ART-217. Grand Opera House, 527 Vine Street, Cincinnati, Ohio. Opened September 15, 1902; 1,676 seats; J. B. McElfatrick & Sons, architects. Anthony F. Dumas, artist, 1927. P&P, AE 11-Dumas No. 205.

ART-218. B. F. Keith's Theatre, 517–519 Walnut Street, Cincinnati, Ohio. Opened 1920; 1,521 seats; C. W. & George L. Rapp, architects. Strand (Telenews) Theatre, 531 Walnut Street. Opened 1916; 1,400 seats. Anthony F. Dumas, artist, 1925. P&P, ADE 11-Dumas No. 206.

ART-219. Palace (International 70) Theatre, 16 East Sixth Street, Cincinnati, Ohio. Opened ca. 1919; 2,616 seats; C. W. & George L. Rapp, architects. Anthony F. Dumas, artist, 1926. P&P, ADE 11-Dumas No. 207.

ART-220. Olympic Theatre, 118 East Seventh Street, Cincinnati, Ohio. Opened September 2, 1906; 1,275 seats. Anthony F. Dumas, artist, 1927. P&P, ADE 11-Dumas No. 208A.

ART-221. Empress (Gayety) Theatre, 814–816 Vine Street, Cincinnati, Ohio. Opened ca. 1911; 1,275 seats. Anthony F. Dumas, artist, 1927. P&P, ADE 11-Dumas No. 208B.

ART-222. Shubert Theatre, Seventh and Walnut Streets, Cincinnati, Ohio. Opened 1921; 2,090 seats; Herbert J. Krapp, architect. Anthony F. Dumas, artist, 1924. P&P, ADE 11-Dumas No. 209.

The Shubert was remodeled from a former YMCA building.

ART-223. Walnut Street Theatre, 622 Walnut Street, Cincinnati, Ohio. Opened September 26, 1892; 2,119 seats; J. B. McElfatrick & Sons, architects. Anthony F. Dumas, artist, 1932. P&P, ADE 11-Dumas No. 210.

ART-224. High Street Theatre, 217 North High Street, Columbus, Ohio. Opened September 3, 1894; 1,835 seats; Anthony F. Dumas, artist, 1939. P&P, ADE 11-Dumas No. 211.

ART-225. Ohio Theatre, 43 East State Street, Columbus, Ohio. Opened March 17, 1928; 2,979 seats; Thomas W. Lamb, architect. Anthony F. Dumas, artist, 1934. P&P, ADE 11-Dumas No. 212.

PENNSYLVANIA

ART-226. Lyric Theatre (Symphony Hall), 23 North Sixth Street, Allentown, Pennsylvania. Opened October 10, 1899; 1,385 seats; J. B. McElfatrick & Sons, architects. Anthony F. Dumas, artist, 1926. P&P, ADE 11-Dumas No. 213.

The Lyric was constructed in 1896 as Central Market Hall. The stone facade was added in 1920.

ART-227. Orpheum (State) Theatre, 35–39 North Sixth Street, Allentown, Pennsylvania. Opened August 27, 1906; 1,421 seats. Anthony F. Dumas, 1928. P&P, ADE 11-Dumas No. 214A.

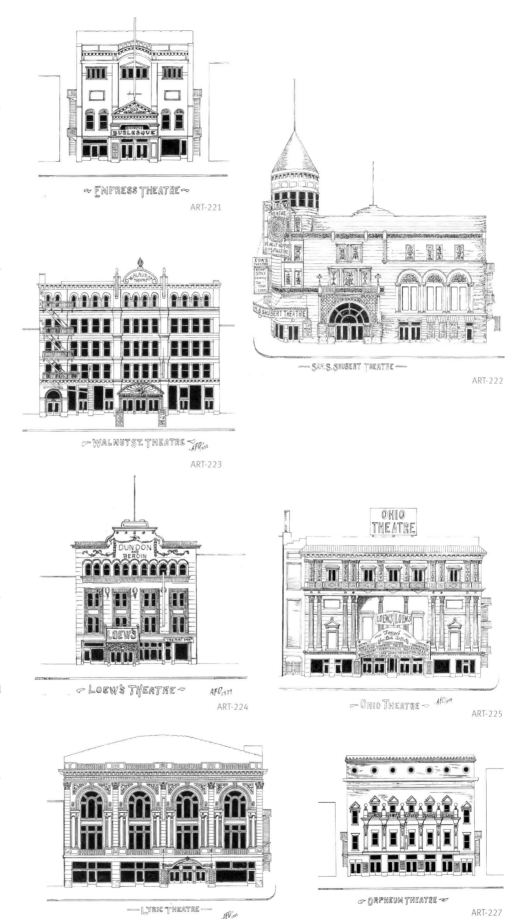

~ EMPRESS THEATRE ~
ART-221

— SAM. S. SHUBERT THEATRE —
ART-222

~ WALNUT ST. THEATRE ~
ART-223

~ LOEW'S THEATRE ~
ART-224

— OHIO THEATRE ~
ART-225

— LYRIC THEATRE —
ART-226

~ ORPHEUM THEATRE ~
ART-227

ART-228
RIALTO THEATRE

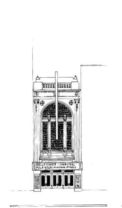

ART-229
WILMER & VINCENTS COLONIAL THEATRE

ART-230
MISHLER'S THEATRE

ART-231
ACADEMY LYCEUM THEATRE

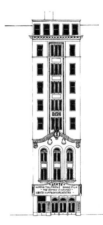

ART-232
DAVIS THEATRE

ART-233
STATE THEATRE

ART-234
GAYETY THEATRE — SHUBERT ALVIN THEATRE

ART-228. Rialto Theatre, 947 Hamilton Street, Allentown, Pennsylvania. 1,679 seats. Anthony F. Dumas, artist, 1928. P&P, ADE 11-Dumas No. 214B.

ART-229. Colonial Theatre, 515 Hamilton Street, Allentown, Pennsylvania. Opened 1920; 1,968 seats; William H. Lee, architect. Anthony F. Dumas, artist, 1928. P&P, ADE 11-Dumas No. 215.

ART-230. Mishler Theatre, 1208–1210 Twelfth Avenue, Altoona, Pennsylvania. Opened February 15, 1906; 910 seats; Albert E. Westover, architect. Anthony F. Dumas, artist, 1932. P&P, ADE 11-Dumas No. 216.

ART-231. Lyceum (Academy, Variety) Theatre, 611 Penn Avenue, Pittsburgh, Pennsylvania. Opened ca. 1912; 2,200 seats. Anthony F. Dumas, artist, 1928. P&P, ADE 11-Dumas No. 217.

ART-232. Davis Theatre, 522 Smithfield Street, Pittsburgh, Pennsylvania. Opened ca. 1915; 2,100 seats. Anthony F. Dumas, artist. P&P, ADE 11-Dumas No. 218A.

ART-233. State Theatre, 335 Fifth Avenue, Pittsburgh, Pennsylvania. 670 seats. Anthony F. Dumas, artist. P&P, ADE 11-Dumas No. 218B.

ART-234. Gaiety (Fulton, Byham) Theatre (left), 101 Sixth Street, 602 Fort Duquesne Boulevard, Pittsburgh, Pennsylvania. Opened October 31, 1905; 2,000 seats; Dodge & Morrison, architects. Alvin (Shubert, Harris, Gateway) Theatre (right), 119 Sixth Street. Opened September 1891. 1,756 seats. Anthony F. Dumas, artist, 1924. P&P, ADE 11-Dumas No. 219A.

ART-235. Grand (Lyric, Warner) Theatre, 332 Fifth Avenue, Pittsburgh, Pennsylvania. Opened March 7, 1918; 2,333 seats; C. Howard Crane and Elmer George Kiehler, architects. Anthony F. Dumas, artist, 1928. P&P, ADE 11-Dumas No. 220.

ART-236. Academy Theatre, Pittsburgh, Pennsylvania. Anthony F. Dumas, artist, 1928. P&P, ADE 11-Dumas No. 221.

ART-237. Victoria (Aldine, Senator, Nixon) Theatre, 956 Liberty Avenue, Pittsburgh, Pennsylvania. Opened ca. 1912; 2,000 seats. Anthony F. Dumas, artist, 1932. P&P, ADE 11-Dumas No. 223.

ART-238. Kenyon Opera House (Pitt, New Penn Avenue, Barry Theatre), 637 Penn Avenue, Pittsburgh, Pennsylvania. Opened ca. 1910; 1,636 seats. Anthony F. Dumas, artist, 1929. P&P, ADE 11-Dumas No. 224.

ART-239. Cross Keys Theatre, 5931 Market Street, Philadelphia, Pennsylvania. Opened December 28, 1914; 1,995 seats; Hoffman & Henon, architects. Anthony F. Dumas, artist. P&P, ADE 11-Dumas No. 225.

ART-240. Embassy Theatre, 745 Penn Street, Reading, Pennsylvania. Opened April 4, 1931; 2,446 seats; William H. Lee, architect. Anthony F. Dumas, artist, 1933. P&P, ADE 11-Dumas No. 227.

ART-241. Astor Theatre, 734 Penn Street, Reading, Pennsylvania. Opened 1928; 2,057 seats; William H. Lee, architect. Anthony F. Dumas, artist, 1938. P&P, ADE 11-Dumas No. 226.

ART-242. Columbia (Majestic, Gayety, Family) Theatre, 230 Penn Avenue, Scranton, Pennsylvania. 900 seats. Anthony F. Dumas, artist. P&P, ADE 11-Dumas No. 228A.

GRAND OPERA HOUSE
ART-235

LIBERTY THEATRE
ART-236

LOEW'S ALDINE THEATRE
ART-237

SHUBERT PITT THEATRE
ART-238

CROSS KEY THEATRE
ART-239

EMBASSY THEATRE
ART-240

ASTOR THEATRE
ART-241

GAIETY THEATRE
ART-242

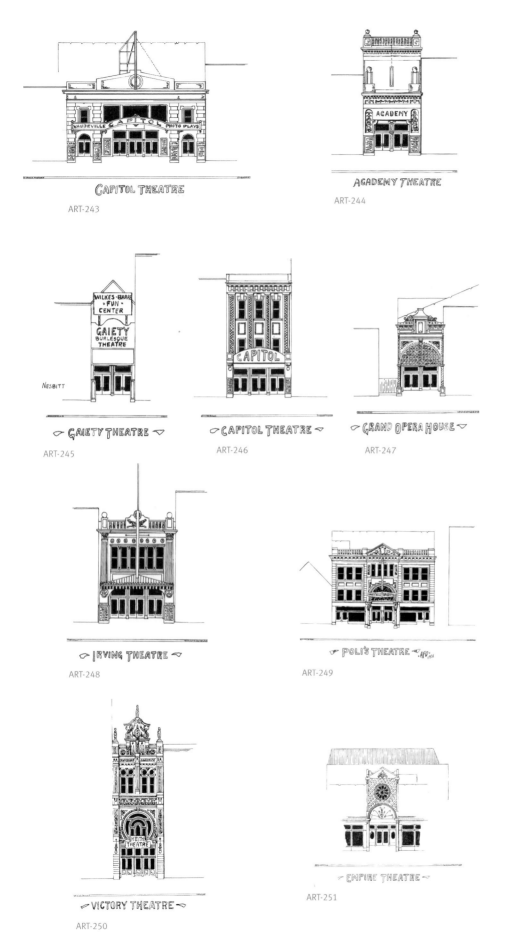

CAPITOL THEATRE
ART-243

ACADEMY THEATRE
ART-244

GAIETY THEATRE
ART-245

CAPITOL THEATRE
ART-246

GRAND OPERA HOUSE
ART-247

IRVING THEATRE
ART-248

POLI'S THEATRE
ART-249

VICTORY THEATRE
ART-250

EMPIRE THEATRE
ART-251

ART-243. Miles (Capitol) Theatre, 208 Pennsyl-vania Avenue, Scranton, Pennsylvania. 1,803 seats. Anthony F. Dumas, artist. P&P, ADE 11-Dumas No. 228B.

ART-244. Academy (Poli's) Theatre, 237 Wyoming Avenue, Scranton, Pennsylvania. 1,857 seats. Anthony F. Dumas, artist. P&P, ADE 11-Dumas No. 228C.

ART-245. Nesbitt (Gaiety) Theatre, 166 South Main Street, Wilkes-Barre, Pennsylvania. Opened October 29, 1897; Anthony F. Dumas, artist, 1928. P&P, ADE 11-Dumas No. 229A.

ART-246. Capitol Theatre, 60 Public Square, Wilkes-Barre, Pennsylvania. 2,009 seats. Anthony F. Dumas, artist, 1928. P&P, ADE 11-Dumas No. 229B.

ART-247. Grand Opera House, 25 South Franklin Street, Wilkes-Barre, Pennsylvania. 1,290 seats; Leon H. Lempert & Son, archi-tects. Anthony F. Dumas, artist, 1928. P&P, ADE 11-Dumas No. 229C.

ART-248. Luzerne (Majestic, Irving) Theatre, 206 South Main Street, Wilkes-Barre, Pennsylvania. Opened February 9, 1908; 1,626 seats; William H. McElfatrick, architect. Anthony F. Dumas, artist, 1928. P&P, ADE 11-Dumas No. 229D.

ART-249. Poli's (Penn) Theatre, 135 South Main Street, Wilkes-Barre, Pennsylvania. Opened October 19, 1908; 2,300 seats; Albert E. Westover, architect. Anthony F. Dumas, artist, 1931. P&P, ADE 11-Dumas No. 230.

RHODE ISLAND

ART-250. Low's Grand Opera House (Gaiety, B. F. Keith's Opera House, B. F. Keith's New, Vic-tory, Empire Theatre), 260 Westminster Street, Providence, Rhode Island. Opened 1878; rebuilt October 24, 1898; 1,801 seats. Anthony F. Dumas, artist, 1936. P&P, ADE 11-Dumas No. 161B.

ART-251. Westminster Musée (Westminster, Empire, Bijou Theatre), 366–368 Westminster Street, Providence, Rhode Island. Opened March 8, 1886; 1,126 seats. Anthony F. Dumas, artist, 1934. P&P, ADE 11-Dumas No. 168B.

TENNESSEE

ART-252. Grand Opera House, 197 South Main Street, Memphis, Tennessee. Opened September 22, 1890; 2,329 seats; J. B. McElfatrick & Sons, architects. Anthony F. Dumas, artist, 1929. P&P, ADE 11-Dumas No. 231.

UTAH

ART-253. Unidentified Orpheum Theatre. Anthony F. Dumas, artist, 1935. P&P, ADE 11-Dumas No. 232A.

ART-254. Orpheum (Casino, Wilkes, Roxy, Salt Lake, Lyric, Promised Valley Playhouse) Theatre, 132 South State Street, Salt Lake City, Utah. Opened December 25, 1905; 1,160 seats; Carl M. Neuhausen, architect. Anthony F. Dumas, artist, 1935. P&P, ADE 11-Dumas No. 232B.

VERMONT

ART-255. Rockingham Town Hall Opera House (Falls Cinema), The Square, Bellows Falls, Vermont. Built 1926; 946 seats. Anthony F. Dumas, artist, 1931. P&P, ADE 11-Dumas No. 233.

ART-256. Strong Theatre, 230 Main Street, Burlington, Vermont. Opened October 24, 1904; 1,450 seats. Anthony F. Dumas, artist. P&P, ADE 11-Dumas No. 234.

WEST VIRGINIA

ART-257. Kearse Theatre, Summers Street, Charleston, West Virginia. Opened 1922; 2,200 seats; Mills & Millspaugh, architects. Anthony F. Dumas, artist, 1934. P&P, ADE 11-Dumas No. 235.

ORPHEUM THEATRE

ART-252

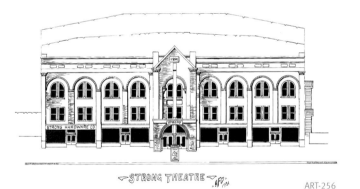

NEW ORPHEUM THEATRE

ART-253

ORPHEUM THEATRE

ART-254

OPERA HOUSE

TOWN HALL

ART-255

STRONG THEATRE

ART-256

KEARSE THEATRE

ART-257

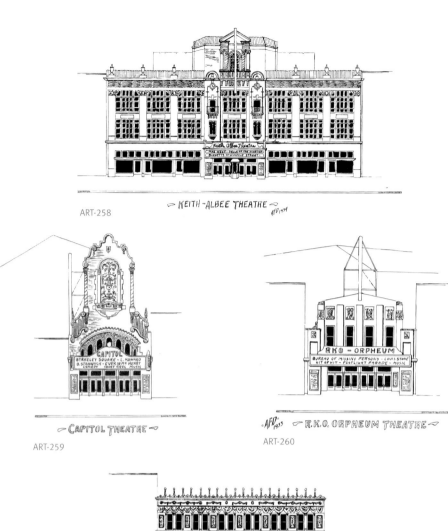

ART-258

⌐ KEITH-ALBEE THEATRE ⌐ AFD 1934

ART-259

⌐ CAPITOL THEATRE ⌐

ART-260

AFD 1933 ⌐ R.K.O. ORPHEUM THEATRE ⌐

ART-261

— DAVIDSON THEATRE — AFD 1926

ART-262

⌐ EMPRESS THEATRE ⌐ AFD 1932

ART-263

⌐ GAYETY THEATRE ⌐ AFD 1934

ART-258. Keith-Albee Theatre, 929 Fourth Avenue, Huntington, West Virginia. Opened May 8, 1928; 2,720 seats; Thomas W. Lamb, architect. Anthony F. Dumas, artist, 1934. P&P, ADE 11-Dumas No. 236.

WISCONSIN

ART-259. Capitol (Oscar Meyer) Theatre, 207–211 State Street, Madison, Wisconsin. Opened January 30, 1928; 2,244 seats; C. W. & George L. Rapp, architects. Anthony F. Dumas, artist, 1933. P&P, ADE 11-Dumas No. 237A.

ART-260. Orpheum Theatre, 216 State Street, Madison, Wisconsin. Opened March 31, 1927; 2,246 seats; C. W. & George L. Rapp, architects. Anthony F. Dumas, artist, 1933. P&P, ADE 11-Dumas No. 237B.

ART-261. Davidson Theatre, 625 North Third Street, Milwaukee, Wisconsin. Opened September 1, 1890; burned and rebuilt, 1894; 1,200 seats; Burnham & Root, architects. Anthony F. Dumas, artist, 1926. P&P, ADE 11-Dumas No. 238.

ART-262. New Star (Saxe, Gayety, Orpheum, Empress) Theatre, 755 North Third Street, Milwaukee, Wisconsin. Opened 1906; 1,500 seats; Kirchoff & Rose, architects. Anthony F. Dumas, artist, 1932. P&P, ADE 11-Dumas No. 239.

ART-263. Gayety Theatre, Milwaukee, Wisconsin. Anthony F. Dumas, artist, 1934. P&P, ADE 11-Dumas No. 240.

ART-264. Merrill Theatre (left), 211 West Wisconsin Avenue, Milwaukee, Wisconsin. Opened 1915; 1,298 seats; Brust & Phillips, architects. Majestic Theatre (center), 219 West Wisconsin Avenue. Opened May 1908; 1,902 seats; Kirchoff & Rose, architects. Garden (Little, Newsreel) Theatre (right), 235 West Wisconsin Avenue; remodeled from Schlitz Palm Garden, 1921; 1,250 seats; Kirchoff & Rose, architects. Anthony F. Dumas, artist, 1924. P&P, ADE 11-Dumas No. 241.

ART-265. Miller (Towne) Theatre, 717–729 North Third Street, Milwaukee, Wisconsin. Opened 1917; 1,200 seats; Wolff & Evans, architects. Anthony F. Dumas, artist, 1928. P&P, ADE 11-Dumas No. 242.

ART-266. Riverside Theatre, 116 West Wisconsin Avenue, Milwaukee, Wisconsin. Opened April 29, 1928; 2,558 seats; Kirchoff & Rose, architects. Anthony F. Dumas, artist, 1934. P&P, ADE 11-Dumas No. 243.

ART-267. Warner (Center, Grand) Theatre, 212 West Wisconsin Avenue, Milwaukee, Wisconsin. Opened May 1, 1931; 2,431 seats; C. W. & George L. Rapp, architects. Anthony F. Dumas, artist, 1933. P&P, ADE 11-Dumas No. 244.

ART-268. Wisconsin Theatre, 528 West Wisconsin Avenue, Milwaukee, Wisconsin. Opened March 24, 1924; 3,275 seats; C. W. & George L. Rapp, architects. Anthony F. Dumas, artist, 1936. P&P, ADE 11-Dumas No. 245.

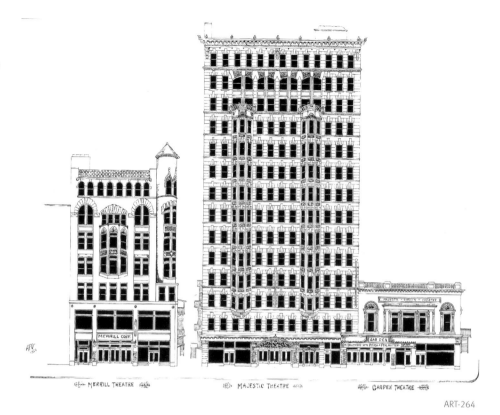

ART-264

ART-265

ART-266

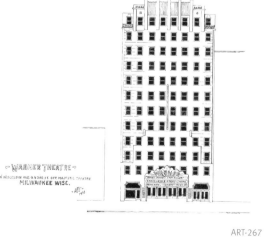

ART-267

ART-268

THEATER BECOMES SHOW BUSINESS

WITH THEIR WIDE WEB OF ROUTES AND SCHEDULES, RAILROADS broke the prairie's isolation. As old towns grew and new towns were born, their residents enjoyed a world of sophistication that had previously existed only in the eastern cities. Theaters and the performers who worked their stages increased exponentially in number. Performers found a new world of fast-paced, nationwide opportunity and the daunting challenge of exploiting it. Theater operators faced their own challenge—to fill the new stages with enough quality talent to draw steady business. Entertainment was set to become an industry.

Independent theatrical agents immersed themselves in the complexities of rail routes and schedules, town populations, theater openings and closings, and seating capacities. Acting as matchmakers, they arranged the calendars of theaters and performers alike. At best, they worked in the interests of both, but in the quest to fill schedules and reduce administrative tasks, theater managers and performers ceded to the agents some of their operational independence. Finding themselves de facto managers of a growing system, a few agents entered into the realm of empire building. Those who succeeded became some of the most feared and hated characters ever to cross the stage of America's theatrical history.

While certain urban theaters continued to focus on drama or opera, most managers found it prudent to cater to everybody all the time. The nationwide common denominator was vaudeville. A vaudeville show was a coordinated series of acts—comedians, song-and-dance teams, animal performers, acrobats, and short dramatic skits. To the audience it offered surprises at every turn, but to an independent manager it was an organizational nightmare. The potential monopolist found it a golden opportunity to establish exclusive, controlling relationships with actors and theaters alike, and to charge outrageously high commissions to both. Those who opted for independence found themselves frozen out of the system.

Since the 1820s American architects had freely borrowed from Europe's historic styles, but only those architects who had emigrated from Europe had actually experienced the buildings that they sought to emulate. Young architects, who learned their trade by apprenticing to older practitioners, acquired their masters' limitations as well as their skills. Pattern books were ubiquitous, but the technology to print photographs remained in the future. The American versions of Greek, Gothic, or Renaissance styles were based upon published line drawings that tended to illustrate details rather than entire buildings.

As rail travel drew the country together, steamships brought Europe closer. Student architects began to venture to Paris in pursuit of advanced professional education and returned with first-hand knowledge of Europe's monuments. Their knowledge and the rapid increase in photographic publications fostered an American Renaissance. The country's best new buildings had a level of scholarship, sophistication, and distinction that could fit as well among their old-world models as in America's growing cities. If the opera houses of the early West had seemed awkward and tentative, underscaled in structure and overscaled in ornament, their newer counterparts looked solid and substantial. Creaky wooden floors and spindly iron posts gave way to plush carpets and hefty columns of genuine, or at least well-imitated, marble. Craftsmanship was superb; designs were literate. Precedent-setting in their appointments and maintenance, the new theaters looked more and more like palaces, fit in every way to represent a theater circuit's corporate identity. In 1927, alongside the site where vaudeville was founded and where B. F. Keith had built the greatest of variety theaters (4-003–4-007), Edward Albee erected the B. F. Keith Memorial, vaudeville's epitome (4-072–4-081).

4-001. The Casino, 1404–1410 Broadway, New York, New York. Opened October 21, 1882; 1,300 seats; Kimball & Wisedell, architects. DPCC, photographer, ca. 1900. P&P, LC-D4-13094.

The Casino bridged two styles of theatrical management. Built to house a resident repertory company in the fashion of Wallack's Theatre, barely visible down the street (see 3-035), it eventually became a presenting house, booking outside shows and performers. Rudolph Aronson, its owner and an adept showman, made his theater into America's leading home of musical comedy. Its most famous show, Florodora, was the forerunner of every dance show from 42nd Street to the Rockettes. To extend his season through the summer, Aronson added an outdoor roof theater, one of the first in the city. Looking like a Moorish fantasy, the Casino was an instant landmark in a growing theatrical district. A year later the Metropolitan Opera House (see 8-039) would open just across the street.

4-002. The Casino, 1404–1410 Broadway, New York, New York. Opened October 21, 1882; 1,300 seats; Kimball & Wisedell, architects. DPCC, photographer, 1900–1910. P&P, LC-D4-36502.

A fashionable audience enters the Casino, perhaps to enjoy the evening breezes in its roof garden.

4-001

4-002

4-003. B. F. Keith's New Theatre, 547 Washington Street and 163 Tremont Street, Boston, Massachusetts. Opened March 26, 1894; 2,700 seats; J. B. McElfatrick & Sons, architects. DPCC, photographer, ca. 1906. P&P, LC-D4-19616.

B. F. Keith's New Theatre set a precedent by bringing the size, elaboration, and elegance of an opera house to a venue intended for working-class audiences. Especially notable were the audience amenities—an array of lobbies, foyers, lounges, promenades, parlors, and smoking rooms. Keith's insistence upon presentability and cleanliness extended even to the boiler room, which was open to public view. The attendants wore white uniforms and the oil cans stood on onyx tables. Despite its internal splendor, the New Theatre had but a modest street presence, an arched entry opening with a stained glass transom on Washington Street.

4-004. B. F. Keith's New Theatre, 547 Washington Street and 163 Tremont Street, Boston, Massachusetts. Opened March 26, 1894; 2,700 seats; J. B. McElfatrick & Sons, architects. DPCC, photographer, ca. 1906. P&P, LC-D4-19610.

In 1897 Keith added a second entrance to his New Theatre. Located on Tremont Street, it faced the Boston Common. To reach the theater, two blocks distant, patrons passed down stairs and through a decorative tunnel under intervening Mason Street.

4-005

4-006

4-007

4-005. B. F. Keith's New Theatre, 547 Washington Street and 163 Tremont Street, Boston, Massachusetts. Opened March 26, 1894; 2,700 seats; J. B. McElfatrick & Sons, architects. Ethel May Stuart Johnson, photographer, 1905. P&P, HABS, MASS,13-BOST,69-21.

4-006. B. F. Keith's New Theatre, 547 Washington Street and 163 Tremont Street, Boston, Massachusetts. Opened March 26, 1894; 2,700 seats; J. B. McElfatrick & Sons, architects. C. John MacFarlane, photographer, 1970. P&P, HABS, MASS,13-BOST,69-3.

The tunnel below Mason Street, shown here in a dilapidated state, was ornamented with richly framed mirrors, an onyx fireplace, and a delicate mural by popular theater decorator Virgilio Tojetti (4-007).

4-007. B. F. Keith's New Theatre, 547 Washington Street and 163 Tremont Street, Boston, Massachusetts. Opened March 26, 1894; 2,700 seats; J. B. McElfatrick & Sons, architects. C. John MacFarlane, photographer, 1970. P&P, HABS, MASS,13-BOST,69-2.

4-008. Low's Opera House (Low's Grand, Gaiety, B. F. Keith's Opera House, B. F. Keith's New Theatre, Victory, Empire Theatre), 260 Westminster Street, Providence, Rhode Island. Opened 1878; 1,801 seats. Unidentified photographer, ca. 1906. P&P, LC-USZ62-79685.

4-009. "Where are you going my pretty maid? I'm going to Keith's Vaudeville, Sir," she said. W. J. Morgan & Company, lithographers, ca. 1905. P&P, LC-USZC4-4959.

B. F. Keith's advertising placed a well-known Mother Goose verse on the tongues of a fashionable young couple to emphasize the polite performances and refined atmosphere that audiences could expect to find in his theaters.

4-010. "Where are you going my pretty maid?" Raymond Oscar Evans, artist. From Baltimore American, October 6, 1916. P&P, Cartoon Drawings Collection, CD 1 - Evans, no. 1 (A size).

Keith's became so well branded, the figures and postures in its advertising so universally known, that they were instantly recognizable to readers of this political cartoon. The figure is Charles Evans Hughes, who ran as a Republican against Woodrow Wilson. The dachshund suggests that Hughes was sympathetic to Germany. "Where are you going . . ." applies Keith's slogan to the Democrats' assertion that the Republicans were going to lead the country into war.

4-011. Hammerstein's Olympia, 1514–
1526 Broadway, New York, New York.
Opened November 25, 1895; J. B. McElfatrick & Sons, architects. DPCC, photographer, 1900–1915. P&P, LC-D4-15640.

Oscar Hammerstein chose a downtrodden
area of carriage repair shops and brothels
for his vast, multifaceted Olympia. An entertainment center, the building included a
1,850-seat theater (later called the Criterion) and a 3,815-seat music hall (later
called the New York Theatre) as well as a
smaller concert hall, a refreshment area,
and a block-long, glass-enclosed roof garden. All were accessible for a single admission. Planned but not built were a
rathskeller, an oriental café, a billiard parlor, a bowling alley, and a Turkish bath. The
overly ambitious Hammerstein was bank-
rupt within a year. He soon built other theaters nearby, but the Olympia had been the
pacesetter. It was the foundation stone of
today's Times Square.

4-012. Hammerstein's Venetian Terrace
(Victoria Roof Garden), 1451–1481 Broadway, New York, New York. Opened June 26,
1899; 1,000 seats; J. B. McElfatrick & Sons,
architects. DPCC, photographer, 1901. P&P,
LC-D4-14750.

Having lost the Olympia to his creditors,
Hammerstein immediately built the Victoria
Theatre at Times Square's southern end.
Gaudy, raffish, but immensely popular, the
Victoria was a roaring success for years. In
its ornamental, deliberately ramshackle roof
theater, summer audiences were able to
catch cool breezes from the nearby Hudson
River.

4-011

4-012

4-013

4-015

4-013. Hammerstein's Paradise Garden, 1451–1481 Broadway, New York, New York. Opened June 26, 1899; 1,000 seats; J. B. McElfatrick & Sons, architects. DPCC, photographer, 1901. P&P, LC-D4-14749.

Behind the Victoria's semi-enclosed roof theater was an open garden atop Hammerstein's adjoining Republic Theatre. Its attractions included a miniature farm, where a cow provided fresh milk and a lascivious trained monkey lifted ladies' skirts.

4-014. Standard (Century, Missouri, Folly) Theatre, 300 West Twelfth Street, Kansas City, Missouri. Opened September 23, 1900; 2,000 seats; Louis S. Curtiss, architect. From *Hughes Annual Views* 1901, Hughes Publishing Co., 1900. P&P, HABS,MO,48-KANCI,14-11.

4-015. Illinois Theatre, 65 East Jackson Boulevard, Chicago, Illinois. Opened October 15, 1900; 1,304 seats; Wilson & Marshall, architects. DPCC, photographer, 1890–1910. P&P, LC-D4-34702.

4-014

4-016. Wonderland Museum & Temple Theatre, 15–19 Monroe Street, Detroit, Michigan. Opened December 23, 1901; 1,573 seats; John Scott (building), James M. Wood (theater), architects. DPCC, photographer, 1901–1905. P&P, LC-D428-45130.

Next door to the Detroit Opera House, shown immediately to its left, stood Wonderland, a commercial museum in the style of P. T. Barnum, and the Temple, Detroit's most popular vaudeville theater.

4-017. Temple Theatre, 15–19 Monroe Street, Detroit, Michigan. Opened December 23, 1901; 1,573 seats; John Scott (building), James M. Wood (theater), architects. DPCC, photographer, 1901–1905. P&P, LC-D428-45123.

The Temple's audiences were met by a narrow but obviously well heated vestibule with the box office at one end. Exposed lamps shed their light upon china cuspidors, then a ubiquitous and important audience amenity.

4-018. Temple Theatre, 15–19 Monroe Street, Detroit, Michigan. Opened December 23, 1901; 1,573 seats; John Scott (building), James M. Wood (theater), architects. DPCC, photographer, 1904. P&P, LC-D428-45125.

The Temple's rear promenade hinted at the theater's spatial complexity. On the right is the orchestra level's curtained standees' rail. Ornamental stairs rose to a narrow mezzanine. Just above was the sloping soffit of the main balcony.

4-019. Temple Theatre, 15–19 Monroe Street, Detroit, Michigan. Opened December 23, 1901; 1,573 seats; John Scott (building), James M. Wood (theater), architects. DPCC, photographer, 1904. P&P, LC-D428-45126.

The architectural style of the Temple's interior looked at once forward and backward. While it displayed the solid classicism of the American Renaissance, the layout retained such features as the parquet circle, whose railing is just visible in the lower right corner.

4-020

4-022

4-021

4-020. Temple Theatre, 15–19 Monroe Street, Detroit, Michigan. Opened December 23, 1901; 1,573 seats; John Scott (building), James M. Wood (theater), architects. DPCC, photographer, 1904. P&P, LC-D428-45122.

The Temple was unusual in having three upper tiers. The first, a mezzanine, provided preferred seating, while the balcony above offered less expensive seats. Still higher, a gallery accommodated the lowest of the low. Floor-level box seats along the sides of the orchestra were characteristic of the vaudeville theater.

4-021. B. F. Keith's New (Chestnut Street, Randolph) Theatre, 1116 Chestnut Street, Philadelphia, Pennsylvania. Opened November 10, 1902; 2,273 seats; Albert E. Westover, architect. DPCC, photographer, 1900–1910. P&P, LC-D4-34743.

Many of B. F. Keith's early theaters were designed by Philadelphia architect Albert E. Westover. His facade for Keith's New Theater combined vast scale with a symphony of curvilinear forms in stone and wrought iron. The curves were echoed and enhanced by the elaborate street lamp. In heavily altered form Keith's New Theatre survived until 1971.

4-022. Orpheum (St. Charles) Theatre, 426 St. Charles Street, New Orleans, Louisiana. Opened 1902; 1,625 seats; Favrot & Livaudais, architects. DPCC, photographer, ca. 1910. P&P, LC-D4-71823.

The Orpheum's site had a long theatrical history. The first St. Charles Theatre (A. Mondelli, architect) opened on November 30, 1835. Burned in 1842, it was rebuilt (Dr. George King Pratt, architect) and reopened the following year. Its rebuilding after another fire, in 1899, looked like its predecessor but bore the Keith-Orpheum banner. When a new Orpheum opened in 1924 in another location, this theater resumed its original name, the St. Charles.

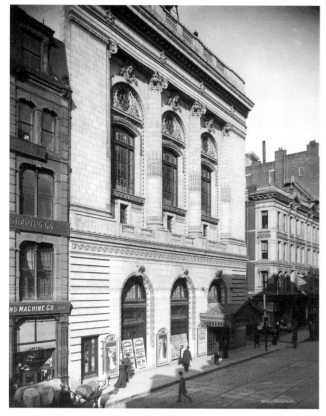

4-023

4-024

4-023. Majestic Theatre, 219 Tremont Street, Boston, Massachusetts. Opened February 16, 1903; 1,897 seats; John Galen Howard (building), James M. Wood (theater), architects. DPCC, photographer, 1903–1906. P&P, LC-D4-17047.

John Galen Howard gave the Majestic a facade of distinction and refinement, but within it was a confection of James M. Wood's molded ornament and glittering light. The auditorium, with its expanse of orchestra seating between balconies and stage, recalls Wood's Temple Theatre in Detroit (4-019 and 4-020).

4-024. Hudson Theatre, 139–141 West Forty-fourth Street, New York, New York. Opened October 19, 1903; 1,048 seats; J. B. McElfatrick & Sons (building), Israels & Harder (auditorium), architects. DPCC, photographer, 1903–1910. P&P, LC-D4-68347.

The Hudson was built to showcase the work of director Henry B. Harris, an affiliate of the Klaw & Erlanger syndicate. J. B. McElfatrick shared with architects Israels & Harder in designing this architectural hybrid.

4-025. Maryland Theatre and Hotel Kernan, 322 West Franklin Street, Baltimore, Maryland. Opened October 19, 1903; 1,972 seats; John D. Allen, architect. DPCC, photographer, ca. 1906. P&P, LC-D4-19127.

Built by promoter James L. Kernan, along with the adjoining hotel and a second theater around the corner, the Maryland opened as a dramatic venue. It became part of the B. F. Keith circuit in 1904 and remained a leading vaudeville and film theater for almost half a century.

4-025

4-026

4-027

4-028

4-026. New Amsterdam Theatre, 214 West Forty-second Street, New York, New York. Opened October 26, 1903; 1,702 seats; Herts & Tallant, architects. DPCC, photographer, ca. 1905. P&P, LC-D4-18607.

Built as the headquarters and flagship theater of Marc Klaw and Abe Erlanger's theatrical syndicate, the New Amsterdam was designed to make a statement. By showcasing several outstanding young artists and decorators, including the architects, Henry B. Herts and Hugh Tallant, its thoroughly rapacious owners might have been trying to say that underneath their rough exteriors, they were true esthetes and genuinely nice guys.

4-027. New Amsterdam Theatre, 214 West Forty-second Street, New York, New York. Opened October 26, 1903; 1,702 seats; Herts & Tallant, architects. Gen. Coll. PN2277.N52 N485 1997.

The New Amsterdam's entry featured an arched cornice supported by yellow marble columns and topped by a statuary group. It was pretty, but there was a problem—it stood illegally on the public sidewalk. This was no mistake. The facade was built on the sly, between Friday evening and Monday morning, while no building inspectors were on duty. When the street was widened a few years later, the finery was removed. Only the elaborate bronze window frames remained to ornament an otherwise blank wall.

4-028. New Amsterdam Theatre, 214 West Forty-second Street, New York, New York. Opened October 26, 1903; 1,702 seats; Herts & Tallant, architects. Gen. Coll. PN2277.N52 N485 1997.

The New Amsterdam's auditorium was an architectural jewel. A rare example of Art Nouveau in American architecture, it was conceived as a flower garden, masterfully integrating form, color, art, and decoration. Appropriately, the opening show was *A Midsummer Night's Dream*. The great stage—a mechanical marvel—later showcased Florenz Ziegfeld's annual *Follies*. After a generation of marginal use and abandonment, the restored New Amsterdam has again become a major Broadway showhouse.

4-029. Iroquois (Hyde & Behman's, Colonial) Theatre, 24 West Randolph Street, Chicago, Illinois. Opened November 23, 1903; 1,724 seats; Benjamin Marshall, architect. Frederick W. Mueller, photographer, December 31, 1903. P&P, LC-USZ62-127744.

It was Christmastime. Children from all around the Midwest had come to visit relatives in Chicago. At the month-old Iroquois, a capacity crowd had gathered to see Eddie Foy in a matinee performance of *Mr. Bluebeard*. On stage, a small electrical fire got out of hand. The asbestos safety curtain jammed halfway through its descent. When the emergency doors opened, a great tongue of flame lashed out over the audience. Within minutes fire and panic had claimed 601 lives. Theaters across the country, even the month-old New Amsterdam in New York (4-028), were closed as municipalities reexamined their fire laws. Repaired and renamed, the Iroquois operated until 1925, when the Oriental Theatre was built on its site. This panorama shows the interior immediately after the fire.

4-030. Entrance elevation, Gaiety (Fulton, Byham) Theatre, 101 Sixth Street, Pittsburgh, Pennsylvania. Opened October 31, 1905; 2,000 seats; Dodge & Morrison, architects. R. Stephenson Guernsey, delineator, 1967. P&P, HABS PA-1180, detail.

4-031. North elevation, Gaiety (Fulton, Byham) Theatre, 101 Sixth Street, Pittsburgh, Pennsylvania. Opened October 31, 1905; 2,000 seats; Dodge & Morrison, architects. Roger S. Gillet, delineator, 1967. P&P, HABS PA-1180.

4-032. Main floor plan, Gaiety (Fulton, Byham) Theatre, 101 Sixth Street, Pittsburgh, Pennsylvania. Opened October 31, 1905; 2,000 seats; Dodge & Morrison, architects. Ralph K. Alster, delineator, 1967. P&P, HABS PA-1180.

By 1905 the parquet circle had pretty much disappeared from theater planning. Here is its last gasp—a slight shift in the curvature of the seating rows about halfway back on the main floor.

4-033. Longitudinal section, Gaiety (Fulton, Byham) Theatre, 101 Sixth Street, Pittsburgh, Pennsylvania. Opened October 31, 1905; 2,000 seats; Dodge & Morrison, architects. Roger S. Gillet, delineator, 1967. P&P, HABS PA-1180.

The Gaiety typified the fully developed vaudeville theater, where an array of box seats, a holdover from the nineteenth-century opera house, was combined with a large single balcony. The former gallery gods may have found a new home at Harry Davis's Nickelodeon a few blocks away (see 6-006).

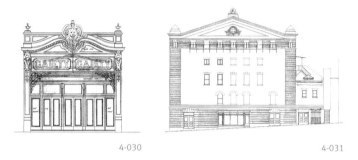

4-030

4-031

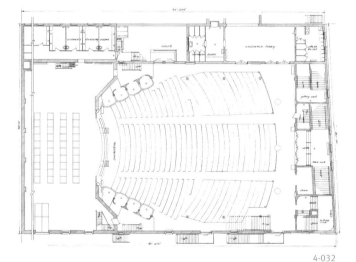

4-032

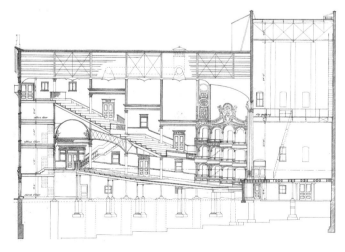

4-033

4-034

4-035

4-036

4-034. Academy of Music, Main and Sixth Streets, Lynchburg, Virginia. Opened February 1, 1905; 1,230 seats; Edward S. Frye & Aubrey Chesterman, architects. Richard Cheek, photographer, October, 1976. P&P, HABS,VA,16-LYNBU,76-1.

4-035. Hippodrome, 456–470 Sixth Avenue, New York, New York. Opened April 12, 1905; 4,678 seats; Frederic Thompson & Jay H. Morgan, architects. DPCC, photographer, ca. 1905. P&P, LC-D4-18531.

Flush with the success of his Luna Park (see 5-008–5-014), architect/promoter Frederic Thompson conceived the Hippodrome, a giant auditorium in central Manhattan. The shows were over-the-top extravaganzas presented on a huge stage, so mechanized that it even could be flooded to present full-scale sea battles. A trademark feature was the magical disappearance of the chorus dancers into a giant water tank from which they escaped unseen through a hidden airlock. Too big and in the wrong place, the Hippodrome never turned a profit, although it limped along for years under Shubert and Keith-Orpheum management.

4.036. New Montauk Theatre, 22–30 Hanover Place, Brooklyn, New York. Opened September 17, 1905; 1,400 seats; Kirby, Petit & Green, architects. DPCC, photographer, ca. 1905. P&P, LC-D4-19291.

William H. Reynolds, a well-known raconteur with a distinct bent for show business and a knack for balancing on the fine edge of propriety, was a state senator only briefly but retained the title throughout his life. A prolific land developer, he built—and ran—Long Beach, Long Island, and Dreamland Park, on Coney Island (see 5-015–5-023). In 1895 the Senator built the Montauk Theater on Brooklyn's Fulton Street. In 1904, when the city acquired the theater's land to extend Flatbush Avenue to the new Manhattan Bridge, Reynolds used the $230,000 payment to build the New Montauk a short distance away. Meanwhile, others purchased the old Montauk for its scrap value, $11,250. Instead of demolishing it as expected, they moved the theater just enough to clear the new roadway and reopened it under a new name, the Crescent. It was alleged, but immediately denied, that Reynolds had profited handsomely through the ruse. The New Montauk was replaced in 1925 by a department store.

4-037. Elkwood Hall (Washington Hall, Amphion, Plainfield, Paramount Theatre), 110–112 West Second Street, Plainfield, New Jersey. Opened 1889; 1,317 seats. John Neagle, photographer, 1906. P&P, LC-USZ62-87216.

Made into a full-scale theater by architect/builder Fuller Claflin, old Elkwood Hall reopened as the Plainfield Theatre on August 24, 1905. As the Paramount it operated until 1957.

4-038. Opening night, unidentified theater, Chicago, Illinois. Opened ca. 1906. George R. Lawrence Co., photographer, ca. 1906. P&P, LC-USZ62-125357.

4-039. Astor Theatre, 1537 Broadway, New York, New York. Opened September 21, 1906; 1,600 seats; George W. Keister, architect. DPCC, photographer, 1906–1915. P&P, LC-D4-39259.

Overshadowed by the giant Astor Hotel, the Astor Theatre borrowed not only the hotel's name, but also the design of its red brick and limestone facades, and even its tiny dome.

4-040

4-041

4-040. Astor Theatre, 1537 Broadway, New York, New York. Opened September 21, 1906; 1,600 seats; George W. Keister, architect. Unidentified photographer, ca. 1906. P&P, U.S. GEOG FILE-New York (State)–New York City–Theaters.

The Astor's interior was a severely interpreted Renaissance design applied to the two-balcony model that had long been the standard for legitimate playhouses. The three lanterns over the proscenium were said to be constructed of bronze and based upon an ancient Athenian prototype. Both assertions are unlikely, but firmly within show business's tradition of illusion and braggadocio.

4-041. Astor Theatre, 1537 Broadway, New York, New York. Opened September 21, 1906; 1,600 seats; George W. Keister, architect. Unidentified photographer, ca. 1906. P&P, U.S. GEOG FILE-New York (State)–New York City–Theaters.

4-042. Alvin (Shubert, Harris, Gateway) Theatre, 119 Sixth Street, Pittsburgh, Pennsylvania. Opened September 1891; 1,756 seats. DPCC, photographer, ca. 1906. P&P, LC-D4-19597.

Harry Davis was a multifaceted entertainment innovator and the mogul of Pittsburgh vaudeville. While his Alvin Theater was a popular showplace, he achieved more lasting recognition from the tiny cinema that he opened in 1905 and called the Nickelodeon (see 6-006). Although it was neither the first cinema nor the first theater to use that name, historians universally credit Davis on both scores.

4-042

4-043

4-044

4-043. Lyric Theatre, 251 Conti Street, Mobile, Alabama. Opened October 22, 1906; 1,200 seats; Stone Brothers, architects. DPCC, photographer, 1906–1920. P&P, LC.D4-71786.

4-044. Mishler Theatre, 1208 Twelfth Avenue, Altoona, Pennsylvania. Opened February 15, 1906; 1,925 seats; Albert E. Westover, architect. David Ames, photographer, July, 1989. P&P, HABS,PA,7-ALTO,110-1.

The Mishler was a scant eight months old when it burned on October 19, 1906. As he designed its rebuilding, architect Westover commented upon the rare opportunity he had to correct his prior design mistakes. Although it has lost its elaborate cornice, the Mishler continues to operate a century later.

4-045. Globe (Lunt-Fontanne) Theatre, 1555 Broadway, 203–217 West Forty-sixth Street, New York, New York. Opened January 10, 1910; 1,416 seats; Carrère & Hastings, architects. American Studio, photographer, ca. 1920. P&P, U.S. GEOG FILE-New York (State)–New York City–Theaters.

Producer Charles Dillingham chose society architects Carrère & Hastings to design his Globe Theatre. Opened just two months after the New Theatre (see 8-070–8-073), by the same architects, it was a Broadwayized version of that elegant theatrical tour de force. The main facade rose just around the corner on Forty-sixth Street, while the Broadway entrance, shown here, served the carriage trade. Long separated from the theater, the Globe's Broadway portal remains, hardly recognizable, as a retail store.

4-045

4-046

4-047

4-048

4-049

4-046. Majestic (Orpheum, Five Flags) Theatre, 405 Main Street, Dubuque, Iowa. Opened November 16, 1910; 1,400 seats; C. W. & George L. Rapp, architects. John Vachon, photographer, April, 1940. P&P, LC-USF34-060474-D.

Brothers in architecture, Cornelius W. and George L. Rapp applied a lush French baroque look to great auditoriums from coast to coast and even in Europe. An early essay, Dubuque's Majestic was a bit less extravagant than the Rapps' later work but almost as Parisian.

4-047. Majestic (Orpheum, Five Flags) Theatre, 405 Main Street, Dubuque, Iowa. Opened November 16, 1910; 1,400 seats; C. W. & George L. Rapp, architects. Jack E. Boucher, photographer, November, 1977. P&P, HABS,IOWA,31-DUBU,8-5.

The Majestic was an architectural hybrid that looked both to the past and the future. The wide main floor, deep, forward-facing balcony, and shallow, underslung mezzanine with its delicately decorated, semiprivate boxes, would become the standard model of movie-palace planning. The two-tiered box seats and the suspended third balcony with its wooden bench seating remained a clear throwback to the opera houses of days gone by.

4-048. Majestic (Orpheum, Five Flags) Theatre, 405 Main Street, Dubuque, Iowa. Opened November 16, 1910; 1,400 seats; C. W. & George L. Rapp, architects. Jack E. Boucher, photographer, November, 1977. P&P, HABS,IOWA,31-DUBU,8-12.

4-049. Majestic (Orpheum, Five Flags) Theatre, 405 Main Street, Dubuque, Iowa. Opened November 16, 1910; 1,400 seats; C. W. & George L. Rapp, architects. Jack E. Boucher, photographer, November, 1977. P&P, HABS,IOWA,31-DUBU,8-4.

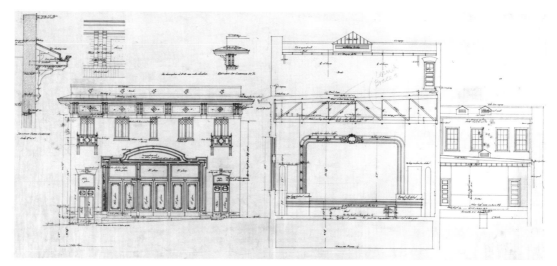

4-050

4-050. New Opera House (Packette Theatre), East Liberty and George Streets, Charles Town, West Virginia. Opened February 11, 1911; 500 seats; Alfred B. Mullett, architect. Photocopy of architect's drawing, 1909. P&P, A. B. Mullett & Co., Archive, ADE - UNIT 3, no. 13 (D size).

As supervising architect of the Treasury, Alfred B. Mullett worked with some of America's greatest public buildings. His later private practice was built around smaller ambitions. This straightforward 500-seat theater could hold 20 percent of Charles Town's population.

4-051. Folies Bergère (Fulton, Helen Hayes) Theatre, 210 West Forty-sixth Street, New York, New York. Opened April 27, 1911; 636 seats; Herts & Tallant, architects. Robert R. Meadows, photographer, December, 1979. P&P, HABS,NY,31-NEYO,84-1.

Architects often have been perplexed by the problem of designing a large, windowless building. Herts & Tallant applied a multicolored, heavily patterned coating of terra cotta topped by a metal cornice of giant comedy masks. The lettering dedicating the theater to Helen Hayes covered a mural panel depicting "Vaudeville paying homage to Les Folies Bergère."

4-052. North elevation, Folies Bergère (Fulton, Helen Hayes) Theatre, 210 West Forty-sixth Street, New York, New York. Opened April 27, 1911; 636 seats; Herts & Tallant, architects. Robert M. Hartman, delineator, 1979. P&P, HABS,NY-5673.

Hartman's delineation of the north facade fully shows the richness and geometric rigor of its composition. This careful documentation accompanied a historic-preservation advocacy campaign to save the Helen Hayes and four other Broadway theaters that were eventually demolished to provide a site for a new Times Square hotel. The furor resulted in granting of landmark protection to several other important buildings in the Broadway theater district.

4-051

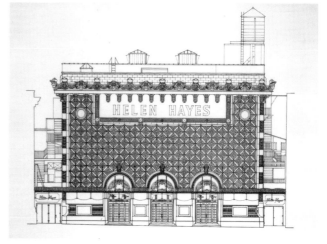

4-052

4-053

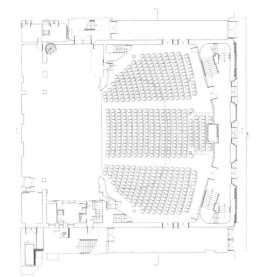

4-054

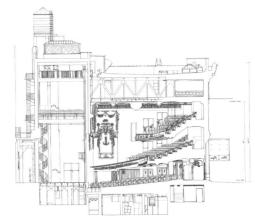

4-055

4-056

4-053. Folies Bergère (Fulton, Helen Hayes) Theatre, 210 West Forty-sixth Street, New York, New York. Opened April 27, 1911; 636 seats; Herts & Tallant, architects. Robert R. Meadows, photographer, December, 1979. P&P, HABS,NY,31-NEYO,84-5.

The Folies opened as a combined cabaret and theater, with tables and chairs on the main floor and conventional theater seating in the two balconies. The ticket price for this combination of theater and elegant dining was far too great to build a faithful audience and within three months the Folies was out of business. Renamed the Fulton and run by the Klaw & Erlanger syndicate, the theater became an elegant Broadway playhouse.

4-054. Orchestra plan, Folies Bergère (Fulton, Helen Hayes) Theatre, 210 West Forty-sixth Street, New York, New York. Opened April 27, 1911; 636 seats; Herts & Tallant, architects. M. Millicent Hall, delineator, 1979. P&P, HABS,NY-5673.

A Broadway theater had to be tightly planned to fit within the 100-foot depth of the building lots created by New York's uniform street grid. That the Folies included almost no lobby space was not atypical—several other theatres had even less!

4-055. Longitudinal section, Folies Bergère (Fulton, Helen Hayes) Theatre, 210 West Forty-sixth Street, New York, New York. Opened April 27, 1911; 636 seats; Herts & Tallant, architects. M. Channing Redford, Robert M. Hartman, Deborah A. Campbell, delineators, 1979. P&P, HABS,NY-5673.

Although a Broadway theater could not be deep, it could be high, and the view from a Broadway second balcony was spectacular, if a bit breathtaking. Never popular, second balconies became passé a few years after the Folies was built.

4-056. Folies Bergère (Fulton, Helen Hayes) Theatre, 210 West Forty-sixth Street, New York, New York. Opened April 27, 1911; 636 seats; Herts & Tallant, architects. Gottscho-Schleisner, Inc., photographer, December 17, 1943. P&P, LC-G612-44562.

Architects Walker & Gillette placed a simplified lambrequin within the Fulton's proscenium. The original proscenium, designed with sloping cornice moldings and an exaggerated flare to give an illusion of great depth, would later be altered to provide a wider stage opening (4-053).

4-057

4-058

4-057. Little (Winthrop Ames, Helen Hayes) Theatre, 238 West Forty-fourth Street, New York, New York. Opened March 12, 1912; 299 seats; Ingalls & Hoffman, architects. Irving Underhill, photographer, ca. 1913; P&P, LC-USZ62-94145.

With only 299 seats, the Little Theatre was just that. Even when a balcony was added to provide 200 more chairs, the theater remained the smallest on Broadway. Perhaps it was a reaction: Winthrop Ames built it just after he left the unworkably gigantic New Theatre (see 8-070–8-073).

4-058. Chase's Polite Vaudeville (B. F. Keith's) Theatre, 619–621 Fifteenth Street NW, Washington, D.C. Opened August 19, 1912; 1,838 seats; J. H. de Sibour, architect. Jet Lowe, photographer, spring, 1979. P&P, HABS,DC,WASH,455-1.

Plimpton B. Chase, Washington's leading vaudeville presenter, commissioned Viscount Jules Henri de Sibour, an architect more accustomed to designing embassies than theaters, to create this elegant marble home for "polite" vaudeville across the street from the Treasury Department and easily visible from the White House. Woodrow Wilson, in his latter days as president, often walked over to catch the afternoon show. Eschewing the presidential box, he preferred to sit anonymously in the back row.

4-059

4-059. Washington Theatre, 1505–1513 Washington Boulevard, Detroit, Michigan. Opened July 21, 1913; 1,862 seats; Arland W. Johnson, architect. DPCC, photographer, P&P, LC-D420-2803.

Washington Boulevard, Detroit's Champs Elysées, was the site of William Fox's first foray into the city. Architect Arland Johnson gave him a festive combination of Palladian windows, terra-cotta reliefs, and tall roof-edge urns. In fifteen years Fox would move his operations to the nearby Fox, the largest movie palace in the nation.

4-060

4-062

4-061

4-060. Spreckels Theatre, 123 Broadway, San Diego, California. Opened August, 1912; 1,133 seats; Harrison Albright, architect. Marvin Rand, photographer, 1971. P&P, HABS,CAL,37-SANDI,24-1

The Spreckels Building provided little external clue to what lay inside. Within, the auditorium was a magnificent volume characterized by two balconies, an impressive arched sounding board, broad arrays of box seats, and a high, dramatic ceiling that was seen through a series of arches that framed its own elaborately framed elliptical dome.

4-061. Spreckels Theatre, 123 Broadway, San Diego, California. Opened August, 1912; 1,133 seats; Harrison Albright, architect. Marvin Rand, photographer, 1971. P&P, HABS,CAL,37-SANDI,24-7.

4-062. Spreckels Theatre, 123 Broadway, San Diego, California. Opened August, 1912; 1,133 seats; Harrison Albright, architect. Marvin Rand, photographer, 1971. P&P, HABS,CAL,37-SANDI,24-5.

4-064

4-065

4-063

4-063. Joy Theatre, 437–439 Ninth Street NW, Washington, D.C. Opened January 10, 1914; 482 seats; W. S. Plager, architect. Imperial (Garden, Central, Gayety) Theatre, 433 Ninth Street NW, Washington, D.C. Opened November 20, 1911; 851 seats; C. W. Somerville, architect. National Photo Company, photographer, ca. 1913. P&P, LC-USZ62-114759.

While B. F. Keith operated nationally, each city had its own theatrical mogul—Balaban & Katz in Chicago, Harry Kunsky in Detroit, Harry Davis in Pittsburgh, and Harry Crandall in Washington, D.C. The Joy, a remodeled haberdashery (foreground), was Crandall's first successful venture into a mogulhood that, for him, would be ill-fated (see 6-077). The Imperial Theatre next door was a bit larger, better equipped, and more attractive theater that later came under the Crandall mantle.

4-064. Victoria Theatre, 235–237 West 125th Street, New York, New York. Opened October 5, 1917; 2,446 seats; Thomas W. Lamb, architect. Rudolph Dupuy, photographer, July, 1985. P&P, HABS,NY,31-NEYO,109-4.

Marcus Loew established this outpost on Harlem's 125th Street, between Oscar Hammerstein's Harlem Opera House and Hurtig & Seamon's New Theatre, later the famed Apollo. Lamb's design was typical of his mature vaudeville form, box seats set within elaborate Palladian arches, delicate decoration borrowed from ancient Rome by way of England's Robert and James Adam, and Lamb's signature curved insets in the upper corners of the proscenium. Loew's Victoria had suffered from age and neglect when it was photographed in 1985.

4-065. Victoria Theatre, 235–237 West 125th Street, New York, New York. Opened October 5, 1917; 2,446 seats; Thomas W. Lamb, architect. Rudolph Dupuy, photographer, July, 1985. P&P, HABS,NY,31-NEYO,109-5.

4-066

4-067

4-068

4-066. Pantages (Orpheum, Roxy) Theatre, 901–909 Broadway, Tacoma, Washington. Opened January, 1918; 1,303 seats; B. Marcus Priteca, architect. Paul Macupia, photographer, August, 1981. P&P, HABS,WASH,27-TACO,5-1.

Alexander Pantages, a prominent manager up and down the Pacific coast, represented the Orpheum circuit, which eventually would merge with B. F. Keith's eastern chain. Pantages' architect, B. Marcus Priteca, was as busy in the West as Thomas Lamb was in the East. In this early design, set on a difficult downhill site, Priteca provided Pantages with a festive wedding cake of terra cotta.

4-067. Pantages (Orpheum, Roxy) Theatre, 901–909 Broadway, Tacoma, Washington. Opened January, 1918; 1,303 seats; B. Marcus Priteca, architect. Paul Macupia, photographer, August, 1981. P&P, HABS,WASH,27-TACO,5-5.

The Pantages' tall, boxy proscenium recalled America's post–Civil War opera houses. A great torch projected out over the audience from the center of its narrow frame (4-068).

4-068. Pantages (Orpheum, Roxy) Theatre, 901–909 Broadway, Tacoma, Washington. Opened January, 1918; 1,303 seats; B. Marcus Priteca, architect. Paul Macupia, photographer, August, 1981. P&P, HABS,WASH,27-TACO,5-7.

4-069

4-069. Hammerstein's (Manhattan, Ed Sullivan) Theatre, 1697–1699 Broadway, New York, New York. Opened November 30, 1927; 1,204 seats; Herbert J. Krapp, architect. Roege, photographer, 1927. P&P, LC-USZ62-116143.

Oscar Hammerstein, theater builder and opera impresario, died on August 1, 1919. As a memorial to the Father of Times Square, his son Arthur built a Times Square theater. Broadway's prolific architect, Herbert J. Krapp, created a rarity—a theater interior in full-fledged Gothic style. The auditorium's murals depicted the operas that the old impresario had premiered in New York. The lobby featured a life-sized statue of Hammerstein. If persevering through difficulty was a Hammerstein trait, this theater exemplified it. Never successful as a showhouse, it became a famous television venue, home of the long-running Ed Sullivan and David Letterman shows.

4-070. Hammerstein's (Manhattan, Ed Sullivan) Theatre, 1697–1699 Broadway, New York, New York. Opened November 30, 1927; 1,204 seats; Herbert J. Krapp, architect. Roege, photographer, ca. 1928. P&P, LC-USZ62-100605.

4-070

4-071

4-071. B. F. Keith Memorial Theatre (Savoy, Boston Opera House, center), 539 Washington Street, 163 Tremont Street, Boston, Massachusetts. Opened October 29, 1928; 2,907 seats; Thomas W. Lamb, architect. Paramount Theatre (left), 549 Washington Street, Boston, Massachusetts. Opened February 24, 1932; 1,797 seats; Arthur Bowditch, architect. Unidentified photographer, 1955. P&P, HABS, MASS,13-BOST,69-23.

American vaudeville culminated almost on the spot where it was born. B. F. Keith's first theatrical venture, a tiny museum, stood just beyond the site of the Paramount Theatre. Keith quickly expanded into the Bijou Theatre, between the Paramount and Keith Memorial sites, and the Boston Theatre, behind the Adams House. In 1893, he built his pacesetting New Theatre (4-003–4-007) behind the Bijou. Upon Keith's death, his partner, Edward F. Albee, demolished the Boston Theatre, replacing it with the lavish B. F. Keith Memorial.

4-072. B. F. Keith Memorial Theatre (Savoy, Boston Opera House), 539 Washington Street, 163 Tremont Street, Boston, Massachusetts. Opened October 29, 1928; 2,907 seats; Thomas W. Lamb, architect. Unidentified photographer, 1938. P&P, HABS, MASS,13-BOST,69-22.

The Tremont Street entry to B. F. Keith's New Theatre (4-004 and 4-005) acquired a new marquee and sign when it became the portal to the B. F. Keith Memorial.

4-072

4-073. B. F. Keith Memorial Theatre (Savoy, Boston Opera House), 539 Washington Street, 163 Tremont Street, Boston, Massachusetts. Opened October 29, 1928; 2,907 seats; Thomas W. Lamb, architect. Unidentified photographer, 1928. P&P, HABS, MASS,13-BOST,69-24.

Entry to the Keith Memorial was indirect. This richly ornamented passage-way, extending from Washington Street to Mason Street, was open freely to the public. Not a commercial arcade, it contained no retail stores, but served solely as a convenience and an introduction to the great theater.

4-074. B. F. Keith Memorial Theatre (Savoy, Boston Opera House), 539 Washington Street, 163 Tremont Street, Boston, Massachusetts. Opened October 29, 1928; 2,907 seats, Thomas W. Lamb, architect. Unidentified photographer, 1928. P&P, HABS, MASS,13-BOST,69-25.

A bronze bust of B. F. Keith (4-075) looked out over the theater's first exclusive space, a richly ornamented lobby called Memorial Hall.

4-075. B. F. Keith Memorial Theatre (Savoy, Boston Opera House), 539 Washington Street, 163 Tremont Street, Boston, Massachusetts. Opened October 29, 1928; 2,907 seats; Thomas W. Lamb, architect. Unidentified photographer, 1928. P&P, HABS, MASS,13-BOST,69-28.

4-076. B. F. Keith Memorial Theatre (Savoy, Boston Opera House), 539 Washington Street, 163 Tremont Street, Boston, Massachusetts. Opened October 29, 1928; 2,907 seats; Thomas W. Lamb, architect. C. John MacFarlane, photographer, 1970. P&P, HABS, MASS,13-BOST, 69-10.

A first glimpse through the rear arcade revealed the auditorium's ornamental richness. At a time when theater designs were becoming increasingly exotic, Thomas Lamb remained true to Keith's vaudeville heritage as he worked within a more conventional French Renaissance design vocabulary.

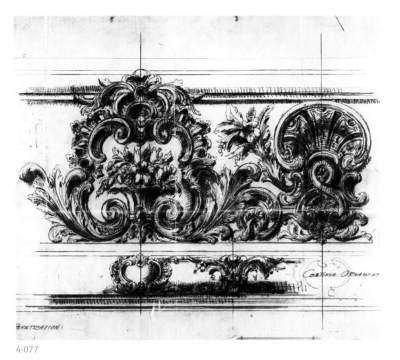

4-077

4-077. B. F. Keith Memorial Theatre (Savoy, Boston Opera House), 539 Washington Street, 163 Tremont Street, Boston, Massachusetts. Opened October 29, 1928; 2,907 seats; Thomas W. Lamb, architect. Architect's drawing, January 6, 1928. P&P, HABS, MASS,13-BOST, 69-39.

4-078. B. F. Keith Memorial Theatre (Savoy, Boston Opera House), 539 Washington Street, 163 Tremont Street, Boston, Massachusetts. Opened October 29, 1928; 2,907 seats; Thomas W. Lamb, architect. C. John MacFarlane, photographer, 1970. P&P, HABS, MASS,13-BOST, 69-16.

The auditorium's expanse was best seen from the rear of the balcony, with its surrounding colonnade and elaborately framed sky dome.

4-078

4-079. B. F. Keith Memorial Theatre (Savoy, Boston Opera House), 539 Washington Street, 163 Tremont Street, Boston, Massachusetts. Opened October 29, 1928; 2,907 seats; Thomas W. Lamb, architect. C. John MacFarlane, photographer, 1970. P&P, HABS, MASS,13-BOST, 69-14.

4-080. B. F. Keith Memorial Theatre (Savoy, Boston Opera House), 539 Washington Street, 163 Tremont Street, Boston, Massachusetts. Opened October 29, 1928; 2,907 seats; Thomas W. Lamb, architect. C. John MacFarlane, photographer, 1970. P&P, HABS, MASS,13-BOST, 69-20.

No matter the luxury of its auditorium, a theater's backstage was starkly utilitarian, even dreary. At the B. F. Keith Memorial, Edward F. Albee, Keith's business partner, broke the mold. The stage door vestibule, shown here during demolition, was carpeted and chandelier lit. The stage doorman occupied an elegant booth of marble and decorative glass.

4-079

4-080

WORLD'S FAIRS & CONEY ISLANDS

AMERICA'S ARCHITECTURAL RENAISSANCE began when Richard Morris

Hunt, the first American architect to study in Paris, at the Ecole des Beaux-Arts,

returned home to New York City. Hunt's mansions for the Vanderbilts, built in the

late 1870s, were eye-openers: they looked as though they had been moved intact

from the Loire Valley to Fifth Avenue. Other young architects followed Hunt to the

Ecole. Young, gifted, and ambitious, these men had the opportunity to recreate in

the heart of an ambitious and expansive America what they had admired abroad.

A great "White City" opened in 1893 on the south side of Chicago. Built to com-

memorate the arrival of Columbus and to exhibit America's progress during its

three hundred years of westernization, the buildings and surroundings of the

World's Columbian Exposition—a sort of stage set, an illusion, an outdoor the-

ater—had a profound and lasting effect on the design of places where Americans

gathered for enlightenment and fun.

The exposition had another side, less sophisticated but equally exotic. Extending from the western edge of the grounds, beyond the expansive formality of the lagoons and promenades, was the Midway (5-003), a mile-long strip of ethnic exhibits, eateries, and theaters that culminated in the original Ferris Wheel. Like a great theater, the exposition's main buildings were magnificently elegant; like a vaudeville performance, the Midway was varied and downright fun.

Attendance at the Chicago Fair was staggering. In its one brief year over twenty-one million people, 10 percent of America's population, passed through its turnstiles. But its theatrical magic survived in America's memory to be recreated in Buffalo (1901) and St. Louis (1904). It also fostered a series of playtime environments in which the fun of the Midway was combined with the thinly clad classicism of the White City.

The most famous of these places grew on the sands of Coney Island, a narrow barrier island that gives Brooklyn, New York, an interface with the Atlantic Ocean. In 1893, George C. Tilyou, a Coney Island native and tireless civic booster, visited the Chicago Fair and was determined to create a great amusement place on his home turf. In 1897 he opened Steeplechase, the first of Coney Island's three great amusement parks. Steeple-chase looked nothing like the White City, but its successors did. Luna Park (1903) and Dreamland (1904) were assemblages of white, classically styled buildings arrayed around tall towers that rose from placid lagoons to be visible from every point on the island.

Steeplechase, Luna, and Dreamland became anchors of a carnival atmosphere that filled Coney Island's streets and alleyways. The entire amusement district was an extended theater, an environment of fantasy, exotic buildings populated by exotic people doing exotic things.

Within a few years, every major city had its variant of Coney Island, a formally planned amusement park, usually developed by a transit company to boost evening and weekend business.

Coney Island, like the world's fairs that inspired them, proved to be ephemeral. Dream-land burned to the ground just seven years after it opened, and when the decaying and tawdry Luna burned in 1944, its passing was little mourned. Across the country, other aging parks replaced their formal esplanades and lagoons with dizzying rides. The old atmosphere was gone, but the parks' effect was profound, bringing theater to the mil-lions as they introduced Americans to the wonders of truly great classical building design. Contemporaries of the moving picture—a new entertainment phenomenon—the parks gave form to its showplaces. Extravagances of thin sheet metal (see 6-012) or sturdy terra cotta (see 6-073), and always lined with light bulbs, movie theaters main-tained the iconography of the Chicago Exposition and Coney Island for a generation.

5-001. Administration Building, World's Columbian Exposition, Chicago, Illinois. Built 1893; Richard Morris Hunt, architect. Francis Benjamin Johnson, photographer, 1893. P&P, LC-USZ62-104794.

Towering above its surroundings, the exposition's headquarters established a visual reference point for the Fair's visitors and a tone of architectural monumentality that prevailed throughout the exhibition grounds.

5-002. North Canal, World's Columbian Exposition, Chicago, Illinois. Built 1893; Daniel H. Burnham, supervising architect, Frederick Law Olmsted, landscape architect. Francis Benjamin Johnson, photographer, 1893. P&P, LC-USZ62-120452.

The Fair's designers set a classical architectural ensemble into an exotically romantic landscape. To a midwestern visitor, a gondola ride through the network of lagoons was transport into a land of dreams.

5-003. Algerian Village Theatre, World's Columbian Exposition, Chicago, Illinois. Built 1893; Alexander Sandier, architect. Allgeier Co., photographer, 1893. P&P, LC-USZ62-101223

To the west of the Fair's formal lagoons was the variegated world of the Midway. Here, where amusement rides mixed with ethnic exhibits, the atmosphere was more one of entertainment than of industrial and artistic display. Near the world's first Ferris wheel, Parisian architect Alexander Sandier's Algerian Village Theatre patched a Saracenic arcade onto a Beaux-Arts block.

5-001

5-002

5-003

5-004

5-005

5-006

5-004. Persian Palace Theatre, California Midwinter Fair, San Francisco, California. Built 1894. I. W. Taber, photographer, 1894. P&P, LC-USZ62-107017.

The California Midwinter Fair was a deliberate offshoot of the Columbian Exposition. Opened in 1894, just as the Chicago fair closed, it provided Chicago's exhibitors a second venue in which to do business. In a setting that was exotic rather than classical, a colorful ensemble of Oriental-, Egyptian-, and Turkish-styled buildings clustered around a central fountain court in San Francisco's Golden Gate Park. The Persian Theatre, a neo–Taj Mahal on the Pacific, was home to the Arabic sword dance and danse du ventre (bellydancing). That social critics found the dance "repulsive" assured its commercial success.

5-005. Temple of Music, Pan-American Exposition, Buffalo, New York. Built 1901; August Esenwein, architect. C. D. Arnold, photographer, 1901. P&P, LC-USZ62-124581.

By night, the Temple of Music and its fountain court were a wonderland of light.

5-006. Temple of Music, Pan-American Exposition, Buffalo, New York. Built 1901; 2,200 seats; August Esenwein, architect. C. D. Arnold, photographer, 1901. P&P, LC-USZ62-96248.

With French émigré John Carrère chairing the Board of Architects, it is not surprising that the Buffalo exposition was a Beaux-Arts environment. The Temple of Music, with its red and gold exterior and blue-green dome and windows, stood out from its surroundings. Throngs could escape to it during the heat of the day as they gathered for orchestral and organ concerts. The Temple achieved a tragic immortality on September 6, 1901, when assassin Leon Czolgosz shot President McKinley. The Horticultural Building, seen behind the Temple of Music, was designed by Peabody & Stearns of Boston.

5-008

5-009

5-007

5-007. Dreamland, on the Midway, Pan-American Exposition, Buffalo, New York. Built 1901; Frederic Thompson, architect. C. D. Arnold, photographer, 1901. P&P, LC-USZ62-78463.

Like its predecessor in Chicago, the Buffalo exposition had a light side. Away from the formal esplanade with a court of fountains and Temple of Music, beside the plaza of restaurants and the Electric Tower, and behind the halls of machinery and electricity, stood Buffalo's Midway. At the Dreamland exhibit, visitors entered through the neck of a dreamy art-nouveau woman into an illusionistic environment of mazes and distorted mirrors designed by the creator of New York's Hippodrome (see 4-035) and Coney Island's Luna Park (5-008–5-014).

5-008. Luna Park, Surf Avenue, Coney Island, Brooklyn, New York. Opened May 1903; Frederic Thompson, architect. DPCC, photographer, 1903–1906. P&P, LC-D4-16699.

Luna and Dreamland, Coney Island's two great outdoor parks, did not pretend to be showplaces of America's arts and industries. Although they adopted the style of international exhibitions, their classically styled white buildings set amid promenades and lagoons were environments designed solely for amusement. Luna Park's monumental entry, with its distinctive heart and pylons, loomed large above its Surf Avenue neighbors.

5-009. Luna Park, Surf Avenue, Coney Island, Brooklyn, New York. Opened May 1903; Frederic Thompson, architect. DPCC, photographer, ca. 1905. P&P, LC-D4-18323.

5-010

5-013

5-011

5-012

5-010. Luna Park, Surf Avenue, Coney Island, Brooklyn, New York. Opened May 1903; Frederic Thompson, architect. DPCC, photographer, ca. 1903. P&P, LC-D4-33798.

The exhibit buildings that flanked Luna's central lagoon cast aside classicism in favor of varied shapes and exotic architectural styles. In such an environment, how could it seem incongruous to encounter parading elephants?

5-011. Luna Park, Surf Avenue, Coney Island, Brooklyn, New York. Opened May 1903; Frederic Thompson, architect. DPCC, photographer, ca. 1905. P&P, LC-D4-18329.

The Old Mill at Luna Park closely resembled the farmyard in Hammerstein's Paradise Garden in central Manhattan (see 4-013).

5-012. Luna Park, Surf Avenue, Coney Island, Brooklyn, New York. Opened May 1903; Frederic Thompson, architect. DPCC, photographer, ca. 1905. P&P, LC-D4-18327.

As the twentieth century progressed, thrill rides replaced fantasy and theatricality as staples of the amusement park environment. At turn-of-the-century Coney Island such devices remained incidental and, by later standards, very tame. Whirl-the-Whirl spun in Luna's version of the Piazza San Marco.

5-013. Luna Park, Surf Avenue, Coney Island, Brooklyn, New York. Opened May 1903; Frederic Thompson, architect. DPCC, photographer, ca. 1905. P&P, LC-D4-18326.

At night Luna became an electrical fantasyland as incandescent lights lined the domes and minarets rose behind the looping arches of the elevated promenades overlooking the lagoon.

5-014

5-015

5-016

5-017

5-014. Luna Park, Surf Avenue, Coney Island, Brooklyn, New York. Opened May 1903; Frederic Thompson, architect. Samuel H. Gottscho, photographer, June 22, 1906. P&P, LC-G612-81772.

The Electric Tower in Luna Park's central lagoon blazed with motion as well as light and made up in exuberance what it lacked in stylistic correctness. The flower-like circular ornaments on the tower's walls appeared to spin in the evening illuminations, as would the lights on thousands of theater marquees in years to come.

5-015. Dreamland Park, Surf Avenue, Coney Island, Brooklyn, New York. Opened May 1904; Kirby, Petit & Green, architects. DPCC, photographer, 1904–1910. P&P, LC-D4-33795.

A few blocks east of Luna Park, the entry to Dreamland made a classical statement that contrasted with the splashy exoticism of Surf Avenue's smaller exhibit buildings (5-024). Dreamland survived only seven years; it was reduced to ashes on May 27, 1911.

5-016. Dreamland Park, Surf Avenue, Coney Island, Brooklyn, New York. Opened May 1904; Kirby, Petit & Green, architects. DPCC, photographer, 1904–1910. P&P, LC-D4-33785.

Dreamland's layout echoed Luna's, but its architecture possessed an elegance approaching that of the Chicago fair. The buildings that surrounded Dreamland's lagoon evoked a formal splendor, while those a bit more distant, as at Luna, reflected the panoply of styles that characterized Chicago's Midway.

5-017. Cafe and outdoor vaudeville, Dreamland Park, Coney Island, Brooklyn, New York. Opened May 1904; Kirby, Petit & Green, architects. DPCC, photographer, ca. 1905. P&P, LC-D4-18321.

5-018

5-020

5-019

5-018. Fighting the Flames, Dreamland Park, Coney Island, Brooklyn, New York. Opened May 1904; Kirby, Petit & Green, architects. DPCC, photographer, ca. 1905. P&P, LC-D4-18319.

Sited along the west side of Dreamland's the central lagoon, Fighting the Flames featured a frieze of electrically lighted lettering and a cornice that incorporated flaming torches into its decorative pattern. The first-floor colonnade supported a row of larger-than-life sculpted firefighters. The concept of providing entertainment and excitement under the guise of education was a formula that remains successful in the theme parks of today.

5-019. Fighting the Flames, Dreamland Park, Coney Island, Brooklyn, New York. Opened May 1904; Kirby, Petit & Green, architects. DPCC, photographer, ca. 1905. P&P, LC-D4-33791.

Inside Fighting the Flames, admission-payers sat in corral-like bleachers that faced a painted backdrop from which a single building facade projected. Suddenly smoke and flame appeared at the windows and horse-drawn pumps arrived noisily at the fire scene. As firefighters hosed the flames, a seemingly endless number of "residents" jumped from the smoking windows into large rescue nets. Quickly leaving the nets so that the next person could jump in, the "rescued" ran back inside in order to be rescued once again!

5-020. Air Ship Building, Dreamland Park, Coney Island, Brooklyn, New York. Opened May 1904; Kirby, Petit & Green, architects. DPCC, photographer, ca. 1905. P&P, LC-D4-33789.

Uncomfortably close to Fighting the Flames, the Air Ship Building's portrayal of a Japanese castle was incongruous.

5-021

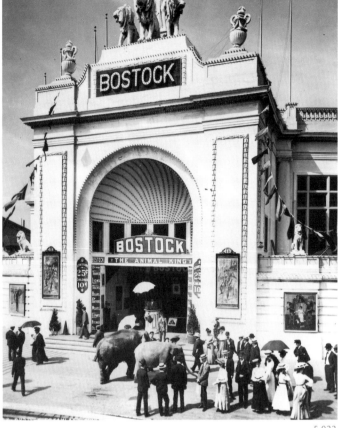

5-022

5-021. Dreamland Park, Surf Avenue, Coney Island, Brooklyn, New York. Opened May 1904; Kirby, Petit & Green, architects. DPCC, photographer, ca. 1905. P&P, LC-D4-18317.

"Meet me tonight in Dreamland, sweet, dreamy Dreamland. There let my dreams come true." The park's brilliant illuminations, and the hopes of many a romantic young visitor, inspired Leo Friedman and Beth Slater Whitson's popular song of 1909.

5-022. Bostock, Dreamland Park, Coney Island, Brooklyn, New York. Opened May 1904; Kirby, Petit & Green, architects. DPCC, photographer, ca. 1905. P&P, LC-D4-18322.

Among Dreamland's theatrical performances were the shows at Bostock's animal ring. The facade was surmounted by a quadriga of elephant-sized lions as some of their smaller cousins perched along the screen walls that flanked the monumental entryway. Outside, a pair of ambling pachyderms enticed visitors to close their parasols and come inside.

5-023

5-023. Ballroom, Dreamland Park, Coney Island, Brooklyn, New York. Opened May 1904; Kirby, Petit & Green, architects. DPCC, photographer, ca. 1905. P&P, LC-D4-18320.

Dreamland's semi-outdoor ballroom bathed dancers, many of whose homes were still gas-lit, in a splendor of electric lights.

5-024

5-025

5-026

5-027

5-024. Surf Avenue, Coney Island, Brooklyn, New York. DPCC, photographer, ca. 1904. P&P, LC-D4-17556.

Between Steeplechase to the west and Dreamland to the east, Surf Avenue was lined with a miscellany of amusement and exhibit buildings. In this exotic setting, where the zoo stood next to the coal mine, outdoor theatrical performances—a horse chase or a display of goat carts—could seem like ordinary, everyday activity.

5-025. The Zoo and The Great Coal Mine, Surf Avenue, Coney Island, Brooklyn, New York. DPCC, photographer, ca. 1904. P&P, LC-D4-17562.

5-026. White World, Surf Avenue, Coney Island, Brooklyn, New York. Opened 1904. DPCC, photographer, 1900–1905. P&P, LC-D4-17559.

Wonders were to be found within the papier-mâché facade of White World. Elsewhere along the avenue more conventional facades fronted recreations of a variety of notably disastrous floods and volcanic eruptions.

5-027. Mount Pelee, Surf Avenue at West Fifth Street, Coney Island, Brooklyn, New York. Opened 1904. DPCC, photographer, 1900–1906. P&P, LC-D4-17561.

5-028

5-029

5-028. Galveston Flood, Surf, Avenue at West Seventh Street, Coney Island, Brooklyn, New York. Opened 1902. DPCC, photographer, 1900–1906. P&P, LC-D4-17558.

5-029. Johnstown Flood, Surf Avenue, Coney Island, Brooklyn, New York. DPCC, photographer, 1900–1906. P&P, LC-D4-17557.

5-030. Loop the Loop, Surf Avenue at West Tenth Street, Coney Island, Brooklyn, New York. Built 1901. DPCC, photographer, 1903–1910. P&P, LC-D4-30858.

5-031. The Flip Flap, Boynton's Sea Lion Park, Surf Avenue, Coney Island, Brooklyn, New York. Introduced July 4, 1895; Lina Beecher, inventor. DPCC, photographer, 1901–1906. P& P, LC-D4-9026.

Although at the beginning of the twentieth century they did not yet dominate the amusement scene, thrill rides were beginning to make their presence felt. The dangerous Flip Flap and the somewhat safer Loop the Loop (5-030) operated as independent Coney Island concessions, while Shoot the Chutes (5-032) dumped giddy participants into a lagoon.

5-030

5-031

5-032

5-035

5-033

5-034

5-032. Shoot the Chutes, Boynton's Sea Lion Park, Surf Avenue, Coney Island, Brooklyn, New York. Introduced July 4, 1895. DPCC, photographer, ca. 1903. P&P, LC-D4-9025.

5-033. The Bowery, Coney Island, Brooklyn, New York. Irving Underhill, photographer, ca. 1912. P&P, LC-USZ62-102216.

Between Surf Avenue and the Atlantic Ocean was Coney Island's version of Manhattan's Bowery, a narrow pedestrian street lined with the interactive theater of game booths and small exhibitions. As colorful as they were raffish, the Bowery's booths and bars provided career-opening opportunities for such entertainers of future fame as Eddie Cantor, Jimmy Durante, and Irving Berlin.

5-034. West end of the Bowery, Coney Island, Brooklyn, New York. DPCC, photographer, ca. 1903. P&P, LC-D401-16697.

5-035. The Bowery, Coney Island, Brooklyn, New York. DPCC, photographer, ca. 1903. P&P, LC-D4-16696.

5-036. Pittsburg's Luna Park, Baum Boulevard at Craig Street, Pittsburgh, Pennsylvania. Opened 1905; Frederick Ingersoll, architect. DPCC, photographer, ca. 1905. P&P, LC-D4-18668.

Luna Park spawned imitators across the country. In 1905 Frederick Ingersoll opened his version in the Oakland section of Pittsburgh. A crescent moon replaced Coney Island's illuminated heart as the identifying symbol, but Pittsburgh's pseudo-classic propylon with its mansard steeples clearly recalls its Brooklyn progenitor (5-008).

5-037. Pittsburg's Luna Park, Baum Boulevard at Craig Street, Pittsburgh, Pennsylvania. Opened 1905; Frederick Ingersoll, architect. DPCC, photographer, ca. 1905. P&P, LC-D4-10925-L.

A bit of Venice at Luna: a steeply arched footbridge crossed the lagoon to the exotic Orient, represented by the Japanese Theatre. Like its forerunner on Coney Island, Pittsburgh's Luna Park was organized around a formal lagoon that doubled as a landing place for Shoot the Chute.

5-038. Luna Park, 2895 Woodland Road, Cleveland, Ohio. Opened May 18, 1905; Frederick Ingersoll, architect. DPCC, photographer, ca. 1905. P&P, LC-D4-33964.

Frederick Ingersoll extended his effort to Cleveland, where his Luna Park followed the Coney Island/Pittsburgh format: a monumental gateway, seen in the distance, a central pool with classical trappings, a bridge, potted ferns on posts, and a Shoot the Chute.

5-039. Luna Park, 2895 Woodland Road, Cleveland, Ohio. Opened May 18, 1905; Frederick Ingersoll, architect. DPCC, photographer, ca. 1905. P&P, LC-D4-18651.

Like its predecessors, Cleveland's Luna Park provided an eclectic environment. Chateau-Alfonse and the Old Shoe stood in contrast to the formal classicism of the central lagoon.

5-040

5-041

5-042

5-043

5-044

5-040. Luna Park, 2895 Woodland Road, Cleveland, Ohio. Opened May 18, 1905; Frederick Ingersoll, architect. DPCC, photographer, ca. 1905. P&P, LC-D4-18650.

A major amusement park provided theatrical performance in a theatrical setting. As a crowd surrounds the circus ring at Cleveland's Luna Park, late afternoon shadows reflect the arches and towers of the Japanese building. The lagoon's Venetian bridge may be seen to the left.

5-041. New Iron Pier, Coney Island, Brooklyn, New York. William B. Holmes, photographer, 1879. P&P, US GEOG FILE - New York–New York City–Boroughs–Brooklyn.

In pre-subway days, when a visit to Coney Island entailed a boat trip from Manhattan, the landing pier became an attraction in its own right. Its exotic profile was a welcoming introduction to the entertainment that lay ahead.

5-042. Heinz Pier, Boardwalk, Atlantic City, New Jersey. Built 1898. DPCC, photographer, 1900–1906. P&P, LC-D4-17266.

Having successfully promoted its products at the World's Columbian Exposition, the H. J. Heinz Company built an exhibition pier on Atlantic City's Boardwalk. Although Atlantic City was more often approached by rail than by boat, this pier was the first of several that would extend its amusement environment out into the Atlantic.

5-043. Steel Pier, 1000 Boardwalk, Atlantic City, New Jersey. Opened 1898. DPCC, photographer, 1910–1920. P&P, LC-D4-500753.

Most famous and longest lasting among Atlantic City's piers, Steel Pier extended 1,790 feet into the ocean. In addition to its amusement booths and outdoor shows, several ballrooms and large theaters hosted prominent entertainers.

5-044. Young's Ocean Pier, Boardwalk, Atlantic City, New Jersey. Opened 1901. DPCC, photographer, ca. 1900. P&P, LC-D4-13709.

Captain John Young opened his Ocean Pier almost next door to the Steel Pier. Its decorative front introduced Boardwalk strollers to an unprepossessing building filled with entertainment venues.

5-045. Young's Million Dollar Pier, 2100 Boardwalk, Atlantic City, New Jersey. Opened 1906; Howard A. Stout, architect. DPCC, photographer, 1905–1920. P&P, LC-D418-36744.

Spurred by the success of Ocean Pier, Young built his Million Dollar Pier near the south end of Atlantic City's amusement district. He resided at the ocean end of the pier in an elaborate Renaissance-style chateau that he called One Atlantic Ocean (5-046).

5-046. Young's Million Dollar Pier, 2100 Boardwalk, Atlantic City, New Jersey. Opened 1906; Howard A. Stout, architect. DPCC, photographer, 1900–1915. P&P, LC-D4-39162.

5-047. Steeplechase Pier, Boardwalk, Atlantic City, New Jersey. Opened 1908. DPCC, photographer, 1900–1915. P&P, LC-D418-35617.

Steeplechase Pier was developed by George C. Tilyou as a clone of his famous enclosed park at Coney Island. Like its Brooklyn relative, the pier was a place of participatory theater, where patrons encountered rolling barrels, whirling floors, unexpected air jets, and other indignities that were as fun to watch as they were thrilling to endure.

5-048. Garden Pier, Boardwalk at New Jersey Avenue, Atlantic City, New Jersey. Opened 1913; Simon & Bassett, architects. P&P, LC-USZ62-73971.

Located uptown from the Boardwalk's frenetic entertainment district, Garden Pier maintained an aura of elegance. Its landscaped esplanade led to a massive ballroom and a B. F. Keith–operated theater, whose presentations rivaled those of Broadway.

THEATERS FOR THE MAGIC SHADOW

IT SEEMS UNLIKELY that live theater, an art form that developed over millennia, could be eclipsed in an instant. Even though it lacked voice, color, and even dimension, the moving picture came from nowhere at the beginning of the twentieth century to displace theater and become the great single force in the history of public entertainment.

The first films, which debuted in New York on April 14, 1894, were short— three minutes or so at most—and were viewed by peering into a machine. On April 23, 1896, at Koster & Bial's Music Hall in New York, a comfortably seated audience was the first to see, projected on a screen, a moving picture. The first movies were perceived simply as novel technological adjuncts to live vaudeville shows, but entrepreneurs quickly made them a stand-alone entertainment force. By 1915 movie houses typically accommodated up to six hundred. Cinema operators worked with a new generation of specialist architects. Together they created halls of unabashed grandeur that played well among young city dwellers who lived modestly but thought expansively.

As movies arrived on the scene in an instant, so, in another instant, they were transformed. Synchronized sound, which premiered in 1927, and accurate color gave the movies a realism that absorbed senses and emotions alike. Like the other newly developing medium—radio—sound pictures engaged their viewers in one-on-one interaction with the characters on screen. In the new intensity of concentration, a fantasy environment became anachronistic. As the 1930s progressed, the stages stood idle and the organs fell silent. The age of the movie palace entered into a long, slow good-bye.

6-001

6-003

6-002

6-004

6-001. The Edison Concert Phonograph. U.S. Printing Company, Cincinnati and New York, ca. 1899. P&P, LC-USZ62-2080.

During the 1890s the public was introduced to the concept that the phonograph could entertain an audience with sequential sound and, with Edison's Vitascope (6-002), an audience could watch a picture move. Advertising posters depicted phonographs and pioneering moving picture shows in typical multitiered vaudeville theaters.

6-002. "Edison's Greatest Marvel, the Vitascope." Metropolitan Print Company, New York, ca. 1896. P&P, LC-USZ62-39741; LC-USZC4-1102 (color).

6-003. "Lyman H. Howe's High Class Moving Pictures." New Magic Pictures. Courier Company, lithographer, ca. 1898. P&P, LC-USZ62-33506; LC-USZC4-5853 (color).

The earliest movie demonstrations were made by independent projectionists who toured with their magic machines. The films were brief and without plots—the effect of movement itself was sufficient to enthrall an audience. Lyman H. Howe broke from the mold to become an early mogul.

6-004. "American Entertainment Co." Donaldson Litho Company, 1898–1900. P&P, LC-USZC4-5941.

6-005. Searchlight Advertising and Amusement Company, Tacoma, Washington. Photograph ca. 1903. P&P, LC-USZ62-21721.

As the century turned, moving pictures were ready to move beyond occasional exhibitions into permanent venues. The Searchlight Company was one of many entrepre- neurial businesses to rent a small space and erect a big sign. To attract nighttime business they hung some bare light bulbs on their double-arched facade. Although they did not call it a theater, they employed exhibition techniques that would remain through the following decade.

6-006. Nickelodeon, 481 Smithfield Street, Pittsburgh, Pennsylvania. Opened June 19, 1905; 200 seats. P&P, LC-USF344-007489-ZB.

Pittsburgh entrepreneur Harry Davis took credit for opening the first permanent screening room and for introducing the term nickelodeon. Although neither claim is true, similar minitheaters opened by the hundreds across the country in 1905 and 1906.

6-007. Hale's Tours. Unidentified photographer, ca. 1905. P&P, LC-USZ62-115729.

On May 28, 1905, at Kansas City's Electric Park, fire-chief-turned-show-man George C. Hale introduced an exhibition gimmick that spread across the country. In a Hale's Tour visitors paid a nickel to a "conductor" to sit in a simulated railroad coach. A movie projected on a small screen at the front of the space gave spectators the impression of moving across the landscape. In some installations the "car" actually rocked and railroad sounds clanged in the background. One film even gave audiences the impression that their "train" was being robbed. The installation pictured in this illustration was operated by Adolph Zukor, who later founded Paramount Pictures.

6-005

6-006

6-007

6-008

6-010

6-009

6-008. Bijou Theatre, 119–121 South Federal Avenue, Mason City, Iowa. Opened 1906; 200 seats. Thomas G. Yanul, photographer, September 19, 1977. P&P, HABS,IOWA,17-MASCIT,9-1.

In their earliest days no one was sure enough of the movies to invest in a purpose-built theater. The typical early cinema was a rented and renovated storefront, as here in the 1896 Zoller Block. The installation could be minimal. Bijou audiences sat on kitchen chairs as they watched Mason City's first movies. Later occupied by a television store, the Bijou was demolished in 1978.

6-009. Mount Vernon Theatre, 918 Ninth Street NW, Washington, D.C. Opened 1910; Alfred B. Mullett & Sons, architects. Ronald S. Comedy, photographer, November 30, 1969. P&P, HABS,DC,WASH-219-2.

From 1906 until World War I, the nickelodeon was a poor man's alternative to vaudeville. The tiny theaters were often found clustered along a downtown street where their showy facades competed for customers' attention. The classic nickelodeon had a pressed metal front incorporating a wide arch. The arch, the building's edges, and, sometimes, integral patterns or lettering were studded with bare light bulbs. The Mount Vernon was designed by the firm founded by Alfred B. Mullett who, as Supervising Architect of the Treasury, had designed some of the country's greatest public buildings. His sons continued his distinguished practice.

6-010. Salem Theatre, Salem, Massachusetts. Unidentified photographer, April 18, 1906. P&P, LC-USZ62-112412.

A nickelodeon district was not unlike an amusement park midway and the theater not unlike a showman's booth. There was a central ticket kiosk with an entry door to one side and an exit to the other. In the recessed entry a clutter of poster easels sought to grab the attention of those who passed by. A barker, a piano, or a phonograph often added sound to the visual cacophony. A nickelodeon presented a twenty-minute assemblage of moving miscellany. As with rides at a carnival, customers typically went from one nickelodeon to another as they enjoyed an evening's entertainment.

6-011

6-012

6-011. Grand Theatre, Niagara Falls, New York. Unidentified photographer, 1911. P&P, LC-USZ62-113364.

An open vestibule, a ticket booth, and twin doors were the nickelodeon's icons. And always there were the light bulbs.

6-012. Leader Theatre, 507–509 Ninth Street NW, Washington, D.C. Opened 1910; 310 seats; Alfred S. Rich & Company, architects. P&P, LC-USZ62-50685.

No nickelodeon was more elaborate than the Leader, a symphony in pressed tin in Washington's Greco-Chinese neighborhood.

6-013. Lyric Theatre, Crisfield Maryland. P&P, LC-USZ62-57864.

6-014. New Theatre, Lopez, Pennsylvania. P&P, LC-USZ62-57862.

In the tiny lumber town of Lopez it was only suitable that the theater's facade be constructed of wood rather than the usual pressed metal. Built by the proprietor of the liquor store next door, the New Theater presented movies three nights a week. After its movie days were over, it existed as a private residence for many more years than it functioned as a theater.

6-013

6-014

6-015

6-016

6-017

6-018

6-015. Unidentified theatre, Chicago, Illinois. Decorators' Supply Corporation, photographer, ca. 1909. P&P, LC-USZ62-83669.

A typical early movie interior was a boxlike room to which decorative elements were applied in as much quantity as the operator could afford. Decorating firms accommodated the burgeoning market through catalog sales. The Decorators' Supply Corporation, a leading Chicago firm since 1883, illustrated both facades and interiors in a publication issued near the end of the nickelodeon age.

6-016. Unidentified theatre, Chicago, Illinois. Decorators' Supply Corporation, photographer, ca. 1909. P&P, LC-USZ62-83670.

6-017. Unidentified theatre, Chicago, Illinois. Decorators' Supply Corporation, photographer, ca. 1909. P&P, LC-USZ62-92101.

6-018. Lyceum Theatre, Chicago, Illinois. Decorators' Supply Corporation, photographer, ca. 1909. P&P, LC-USZ62-92102.

6-019

6-020

6-019. Sheldon Theatre, 1416 West Madison Street, Chicago, Illinois. Decorators' Supply Corporation, photographer, ca. 1909. P&P, LC-USZ62-92105.

6-020. Revelry Theatre, 6342 East Forty-second Street, Chicago, Illinois. Decorators' Supply Corporation, photographer, ca. 1909. P&P, LC-USZ62-92104.

6-021. Normal Theatre, 6850 South Halsted Street, Chicago, Illinois. Decorators' Supply Corporation, photographer, ca. 1909. P&P, LC-USZ62-92107.

6-022. Normal Theatre, 6850 South Halsted Street, Chicago, Illinois. Decorators' Supply Corporation, photographer, ca. 1909. P&P, LC-USZ62-92103.

6-021

6-022

6-023

6-025

6-023. Ashland Theatre, 1656 West Twelfth Street, Chicago, Illinois. Decorators' Supply Corporation, photographer, ca. 1909. P&P, LC-USZ62-92106.

6-024. Crystal (Comique) Theatre, 1249–1251 Broadway, Detroit, Michigan. Opened September 18, 1905; reopened as Comique February 2, 1908; C. Howard Crane, architect. DPCC, photographer, 1910–1920. P&P, LC-D417-306.

The Comique facade was an essay in sheet metal design with swags and tassels that imitated the curtain of a vaudeville theater.

6-025. Princess Theatre, 520–522 Woodward Avenue, Detroit, Michigan. Opened 1908. DPCC, photographer, 1908–1920. P&P, LC-D417-304.

A brightly painted plate of pressed metal sufficed to make a Civil War–era building into an up-to-date movie house. The Princess's sign emphasized popularity, availability, and low price.

6-024

6-026

6-026. Majestic Theatre, 1449 Woodward Avenue, Detroit, Michigan. Opened November 27, 1908; C. Howard Crane, architect. DPCC, photographer, 1908–1913. P&P, LC-D417-305.

Fledgling architect C. Howard Crane applied an oversized nickelodeon front to an old dime museum building on upper Woodward Avenue. Crane went on to become one of America's best known and most prolific theater designers. In 1928 his largest theater, the 5,041-seat Fox, would rise a short distance from the Majestic.

6-027. Nickelodeon (Austin's Palace Theatre, New Palace), 109 Court Street, Boston, Massachusetts. Opened 1889. DPCC, photographer, 1915–1925. P&P, LC-D420-2597.

Alexander Graham Bell carried on his experiments on the top floor of a building in central Boston where, in 1875, he succeeded in transmitting speech by electricity. Within fifteen years the birthplace of the telephone had become the entry to a theater. The Nickelodeon received a new facade in 1911 when it became the New Palace. It closed before Bell's technology could give sound to the films shown within.

6-028. Dixie Theatre, 800–802 H Street NE, Washington, D.C. Opened January 31, 1910; 393 seats; C. Clark Jones & Seward Charles, architects. National Photo Company, photographer. P&P, LC-USZ62-73924.

Inexpensive admissions and daytime operating hours invited youngsters to make the movies a second home. Here an audience of children poses with the Dixie's dapper manager, its beleaguered projectionist, and a couple of local policemen.

6-027

6-028

6-029

6-031

6-029. Dumbarton (Georgetown) Theatre, 1349 Wisconsin Avenue NW, Washington, D.C. Opened August 1913; 460 seats; William Nichols, architect. P&P, LC-USZ62-100051.

The nickelodeon's architectural mannerisms remained even as some theaters sought a more singular identity. A colossal Gothic arch attracted a generation of patrons to the Dumbarton, located in the heart of what would become Washington's most exclusive neighborhood.

6-030. Apollo Theatre, 624 H Street NW, Washington, D.C. Opened September 10, 1913; 894 seats; C. Clark Jones, architect. National Photo Company, photographer, ca. 1920. P&P, LC-USZ62-76694.

Obviously not an exhibit booth but a substantial, permanent building for movies, the Apollo added a showman's flair to the architect's principles of design. Built of masonry, it had the correct Renaissance base, *piano nobile*, cornice, and parapet. Arches and applied panels were carefully proportioned. Festivity was provided by poster panels and rooftop banner poles. The light bulbs that had given glitter to the nickelodeon's front were transposed into a slim steel and glass marquee, the movie theater's new hallmark. Buildings like this graced America's urban neighborhoods and small town Main Streets as the movies settled into a generation of entertainment primacy.

6-031. Casino (Star) Theatre, Main Street, Gunnison, Utah. Opened ca. 1912; 300 seats. P. Kent Fairbanks, photographer, August, 1968. P&P, HABS, UTAH,20-GUNNI,1-1.

By 1912 it was clear that the movies were not a passing fad. As they shed flashy novelty to become a respectable storytelling medium, the places that showed them adopted a new seriousness of design. With a facade that fashioned the nickelodeon's arch into the image of Paris's Opera Garnier, the Casino was clearly out of the nickelodeon class.

6-030

6-032. Gandolfo Theatre, 202 South First Avenue, Yuma, Arizona. Built 1917; 1,500 seats. P&P, LC-USZ62-79082.

6-033. Criterion Theatre, 318 Ninth Street NW, Washington, D.C. Opened 1918; 350 seats; Frank G. Pierson, architect. National Photo Company, photographer, ca. 1920. P&P, LC-USZ62-76696.

6-034. Orpheum Theatre, Nebraska Street, Sioux City, Iowa. Opened ca. 1919; 1,456 seats; George Rapp, architect. P&P, LC-USZ62-16903.

6-035. Manring Theatre, High and Main Streets, Middlesboro, Kentucky. Opened ca. 1921; 985 seats. Unidentified photographer, 1890–1920. P&P, LC-USZ62-121535.

6-036

6-039

6-036. Modern Theatre, Main Street, Harwichport, Massachusetts. 558 seats. P&P, US SUBJECT FILE-Theaters.

6-037. Marshall (Dickinson) Theatre, Manhattan, Kansas. 814 seats. P&P, US SUBJECT FILE-Theaters.

6-038. Barth Theatre, Monroe Street, Carbondale, Illinois. Opened 1919. P&P, US SUBJECT FILE-Theaters.

6-039. National (Mitchell) Theatre, Liberty Street, Barbourville, Kentucky. 500 seats. P&P, US SUBJECT FILE-Theaters.

After the National burned in 1924, it was repaired and the Barbourville Fire Department moved into one of its storefronts. Despite the firefighters' presence, the building burned again, for good, in 1938.

6-037

6-038

6-040

6-041

6-042

6-040. Lyric Theatre, Cambridge, Ohio. P&P, US SUBJECT FILE-Theaters.

6-041. Majestic Theatre, Alto, Texas. P&P, US SUBJECT FILE-Theaters.

6-042. American Theatre, 96 Main Street, Canton, New York. Built 1921; 828 seats. P&P, LC-USZ62-57863.

The emerging movie house style could be seen even in the smallest of cities. In a nod to a short-lived tradition, the American's simple facade incorporated a vestige of the nickelodeon arch. Within, the austere interior was enlivened by a stage set that was painted in perspective to look like theater box seats.

6-043. American Theatre, 96 Main Street, Canton, New York. Built 1921; 828 seats. P&P, SUBJECT FILE-Theaters.

6-043

6-044

6-045

SOUTH ELEVATION
SCALE IN FEET 1/4"=1'-0"   SCALE IN METERS 1:48

6-046

6-044. Powell's Theatre, 4098 Main Street, Chincoteague, Virginia. Built 1923. P&P, US SUBJECT FILE-Theaters.

6-045. Arcadia Theatre, Graham Avenue, Windber, Pennsylvania. Built ca. 1920; 600 seats. Jet Lowe, photographer, 1988. P&P, HABS, PA,56-WIND,1-1.

In name and design the Arcadia gave a touch of elegance to the company-built town of the Berwind-White Coal Mining Company.

6-046. Elevation, Garden Theatre, 10–14 West North Avenue, Pittsburgh, Pennsylvania. Opened 1915; 990 seats; Thomas N. Scott, architect. Craig Morrison, delineator, 1970. P&P, HABS PA-1278.

The Garden, a landmark of Pittsburgh's north side, applied an elaborate white terra-cotta facade to the nickelodeon's simple plan. A small lobby flanked by retail stores, a simple rectangular auditorium that made no provision for live presentation, and second-floor offices were almost universal in theaters of this size and type.

6-047. Garden Theatre, 10–14 West North Avenue, Pittsburgh, Pennsylvania. Opened 1915; 990 seats; Thomas N. Scott, architect. Jack E. Boucher, photographer, 1970. P&P, HABS, PA,2-PITBU,28-1.

As movie attendance was a spur-of-the-moment phenomenon, visibility and ballyhoo were the name of the game in attracting customers. The Garden's carefully proportioned facade was hidden behind a veil of signs as its owners sought an increased street presence.

6-047

6-048

6-048. Garden Theatre, 10–14 West North Avenue, Pittsburgh, Pennsylvania. Opened 1915; 990 seats; Thomas N. Scott, architect. Jack E. Boucher, photographer, 1970. P&P, HABS, PA,2-PITBU,28-3.

As its signs proliferated, the Garden acquired a new ticket kiosk and new lobby fittings from the Libman and Spanjer Company, whose work could be seen throughout the eastern states.

6-050

6-050. Garden Theatre, 10–14 West North Avenue, Pittsburgh, Pennsylvania. Opened 1915; 990 seats; Thomas N. Scott, architect. Jack E. Boucher, photographer, 1970. P&P, HABS, PA,2-PITBU,28-4.

6-049

6-049. Costello Theatre, 23 Fort Washington Avenue, New York, New York. Opened 1914; 585 seats; Louis A. Sheinart, architect. Samuel H. Gottscho, photographer, November 7, 1914. P&P, LC-G622-00815.

6-051

6-051. Saenger (Paramount) Theatre, 301 Desiard Street, Monroe, Louisiana. Opened 1921; 1208 seats. P&P SUBJECT FILE-Theaters.

6-052

6-055

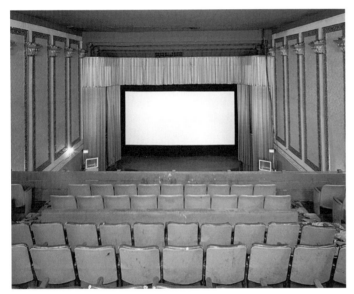

6-053

6-054

6-052. Rivola Theatre (J. H. Green and Company Building), 202 High Avenue West, Oskaloosa, Iowa. Opened April 21, 1921; 600 seats; Vorse, Kraetsch & Kraetsch, architects. David W. Preston, photographer, June, 1984. P&P, HABS,IOWA,62-OSK,2-1.

Inside and out, the Rivola hardly betrays that it was built in 1874 as an agricultural implement store. Despite blocked windows and a newer, inappropriately scaled marquee, the care taken in its design is evident.

6-053. Rivola Theatre (J. H. Green and Company Building), 202 High Avenue West, Oskaloosa, Iowa. Opened April 21, 1921; 600 seats; Vorse, Kraetsch & Kraetsch, architects. David W. Preston, photographer, June, 1984. P&P, HABS,IOWA,62-OSK,2-8.

In a renovation procedure that was applied to theaters across the country, the Rivola's proscenium was concealed by drapes. The intent was twofold—to accommodate a wide screen and to convey an impression of modernity, all at a limited cost. The result seriously diminished both the auditorium's design integrity and the audience's experience.

6-054. Rivola Theatre (J. H. Green and Company Building), 202 High Avenue West, Oskaloosa, Iowa. Opened April 21, 1921; 600 seats; Vorse, Kraetsch & Kraetsch, architects. David W. Preston, photographer, June, 1984. P&P, HABS,IOWA,62-OSK,2-4.

6-055. Rivola Theatre (J. H. Green and Company Building), 202 High Avenue West, Oskaloosa, Iowa. Opened April 21, 1921; 600 seats; Vorse, Kraetsch & Kraetsch, architects. David W. Preston, photographer, June, 1984. P&P, HABS,IOWA,62-OSK,2-3.

The rectilinear simplicity of the Rivola's auditorium was relieved by panels of rich molded ornament and indirect lighting brackets. The proscenium frame integrated exposed light bulbs into its elaborate plaster moldings (6-054).

6-056

6-057

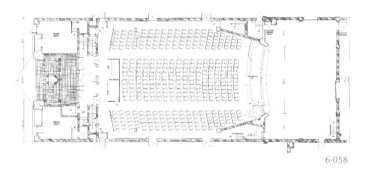

6-058

6-056. Columbia (Paramount) Theatre, 215 Riverside Mall (formerly Third Street), Baton Rouge, Louisiana. Opened September 4, 1920; 1,451 seats; Prather & Stephens, architects. Timothy Allanbrook, delineator, 1978. P&P, HABS, LA-1133, detail.

The Columbia's facade, a Doric variant, verged on the palatial with its rich sculptural ornamentation. In layout the theater was straightforward and plain—a large outdoor vestibule with a free-standing ticket kiosk, flanking storefronts, a tiny lobby, and a rectangular auditorium. Despite its stage and lofty fly tower, there is no spatial complexity—the auditorium remains firmly in the post-nickelodeon, pre-palace era. A small second balcony provided segregated seating for African-American patrons, a fact of life in the South of the 1920s. Painted lettering on the rear stage wall provided grist for a spectacular delineation (6-060).

6-057. Columbia (Paramount) Theatre, 215 Riverside Mall (formerly Third Street), Baton Rouge, Louisiana. Opened September 4, 1920; 1,451 seats; Prather & Stephens, architects. David Kaminsky, photographer, summer, 1978. P&P, HABS,LA,17-BATRO,7-5.

6-058. Plan, Columbia (Paramount) Theatre, 215 Riverside Mall (formerly Third Street), Baton Rouge, Louisiana. Opened September 4, 1920; 1,451 seats; Prather & Stephens, architects. Robert P. Louton, delineator, 1978. P&P HABS, LA-1133.

6-059. Section, Columbia (Paramount) Theatre, 215 Riverside Mall (formerly Third Street), Baton Rouge, Louisiana. Opened September 4, 1920; 1,451 seats; Prather & Stephens, architects. William J. Graham and Kate Johns, delineators, 1978. P&P HABS, LA-1133.

6-060. Columbia (Paramount) Theatre, 215 Riverside Mall (formerly Third Street), Baton Rouge, Louisiana. Opened September 4, 1920; 1,451 seats; Prather & Stephens, architects. George W. Steinrock Jr., delineator, 1978. P&P HABS, LA-1133.

6-059

6-060

6-061

6-062

6-061. Al. Ringling Theatre, 136 Fourth Street, Baraboo, Wisconsin. Opened November 17, 1915; 830 seats; C. W. & George L. Rapp, architects. Douglas C. Green, photographer, 1967. P&P,HABS,WIS, 56-BARAB,1-1.

It was not large, it was out of the way, and its corridors were gas lit, but circus magnate Al. Ringling's gift to his home city was a pivotal monument in American theater design. His architects—two young brothers—had designed a few theaters in other midwestern towns (see 4-046–4-049), but this one was special. Its facade refined the nickelodeon's arch into a French delight. Within, the small lobby was an elegant domed ellipse, the auditorium was a careful adaptation of the Royal Opera at Versailles. Refined decoration and spatial interplay were fused into an architectural ensemble that far outdistanced its contemporaries. With this theater the movie palace was born.

6-062. Al. Ringling Theatre, 136 Fourth Street, Baraboo, Wisconsin. Opened November 17, 1915; 830 seats; C. W. & George L. Rapp, architects. Douglas C. Green, photographer, 1967. P&P, HABS,WIS, 56-BARAB,1-3.

6-063. Al. Ringling Theatre, 136 Fourth Street, Baraboo, Wisconsin. Opened November 17, 1915; 830 seats; C. W. & George L. Rapp, architects. Douglas C. Green, photographer, 1967. P&P, HABS,WIS,56-BARAB,1-4.

6-064. Al. Ringling Theatre, 136 Fourth Street, Baraboo, Wisconsin. Opened November 17, 1915; 830 seats; C. W. & George L. Rapp, architects. Douglas C. Green, photographer, 1967. P&P, HABS,WIS,56-BARAB,1-6.

6-065. Al. Ringling Theatre, 136 Fourth Street, Baraboo, Wisconsin. Opened November 17, 1915; 830 seats; C. W. & George L. Rapp, architects. Douglas C. Green, photographer, 1967. P&P, HABS,WIS,56-BARAB,1-7.

6-063

6-064

6-065

6-066. Tivoli Theatre, 709–713 Broad Street, Chattanooga, Tennessee. Opened March 19, 1921; 1,781 seats; C. W. & George L. Rapp, architects. Jack E. Boucher, photographer, February, 1983. P&P, HABS,TENN,33-CHAT,8-2.

Building upon the success at Baraboo, the Rapp & Rapp office went on to become a defining force in American cinema architecture. The Tivoli was a prototype of the developing building form. Architectonic and without gimmicks, its facade borrowed from northern Italian design, incorporating applied pilasters and a Palladian window. Superimposed on the facade were the exhibitor's requirements, a large vertical sign and a massive marquee, sheet metal, and light bulb extravaganzas that recalled the verve of the nickelodeon facade.

6-067. Tivoli Theatre, 709–713 Broad Street, Chattanooga, Tennessee. Opened March 19, 1921; 1,781 seats; C. W. & George L. Rapp, architects. Jack E. Boucher, photographer, February, 1983. P&P, HABS,TENN,33-CHAT,8-5.

No longer a nickelodeon's cramped vestibule, a movie palace entry was designed to impress. In the Tivoli's outer foyer the facade window was echoed as a spatial transparency that allowed a peek into the main lobby.

6-068. Tivoli Theatre, 709–713 Broad Street, Chattanooga, Tennessee. Opened March 19, 1921; 1,781 seats; C. W. & George L. Rapp, architects. Jack E. Boucher, photographer, February, 1983. P&P, HABS,TENN,33-CHAT,8-4.

6-069

6-070

6-069. Tivoli Theatre, 709–713 Broad Street, Chattanooga, Tennessee. Opened March 19, 1921; 1,781 seats; C. W. & George L. Rapp, architects. Jack E. Boucher, photographer, February, 1983. P&P, HABS,TENN,33-CHAT,8-6.

The main lobby of a great cinema such as the Tivoli was conceived as a civic gathering space and a demonstration of community grandeur. A sweeping stair to the mezzanine was a standard feature.

6-070. Tivoli Theatre, 709–713 Broad Street, Chattanooga, Tennessee. Opened March 19, 1921; 1,781 seats; C. W. & George L. Rapp, architects. Jack E. Boucher, photographer, February, 1983. P&P, HABS,TENN,33-CHAT,8-7.

The movie palace erased the class segregation of the nineteenth-century vaudeville theater. By intent it gave working-class patrons free access to a decidedly upper-class space. The main floor, a sea of seats, was not divided into price categories. Seating in the vast, single, front-facing balcony was also undifferentiated, except in southern states where racial segregation remained in effect. While the auditorium resembled the vaudeville theater sufficiently to be comfortably familiar, its architectural forms were softened. The boxy, square proscenium of the vaudeville house had become wide and gently curved and the sounding board above it was now a compound curve rather than a sloping plane.

6-071

6-071. Tivoli Theatre, 709–713 Broad Street, Chattanooga, Tennessee. Opened March 19, 1921; 1,781 seats; C. W. & George L. Rapp, architects. Jack E. Boucher, photographer, February, 1983. P&P, HABS,TENN,33-CHAT,8-8.

6-072. Tivoli Theatre, 709–713 Broad Street, Chattanooga, Tennessee. Opened March 19, 1921; 1,781 seats; C. W. & George L. Rapp, architects. Jack E. Boucher, photographer, February, 1983. P&P, HABS,TENN,33-CHAT,8-10.

Box seating in a movie palace was impractical and unneeded. Watching a picture screen obliquely was even less desirable than viewing a live presentation from a sharp angle. For a while the familiar boxes remained, eventually to be replaced by lavishly designed grilles that concealed the pipe organs that were standard movie palace accessories.

6-072

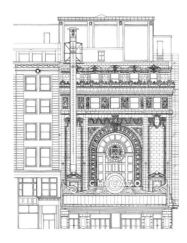

6-073. Chicago Theatre, 175 North State Street, Chicago, Illinois. Opened October 26, 1921; 3,869 seats; C. W. & George L. Rapp, architects. Kaaren R. Dodge, delineator, 1997. P&P, HABS IL-1195, detail

Rapp & Rapp skillfully reworked the nickelodeon's iconic elements into serious architecture in their finest early picture palace. The Chicago's terra-cotta facade was a great glazed arch and its architectural elements were studded with lights. The huge, brilliantly lighted metal sign was visible for blocks along State Street. No longer a tentative gesture toward a new building type, the movie palace had arrived.

6-074. Chicago Theatre, 175 North State Street, Chicago, Illinois. Opened October 26, 1921; 3,869 seats; C. W. & George L. Rapp, architects. Jason A. Aspin, delineator, 1997. P&P, HABS IL-1195, detail.

6-075. Academy of Music (Palladium), 126–148 East Fourteenth Street, New York, New York. Opened 1926; 3,517 seats; Thomas W. Lamb, architect. From *Architecture and Building*, January, 1927. P&P, LC-USZ62-60518.

Exhibition mogul William Fox commissioned Thomas W. Lamb, master of vaudeville theater design, to create a replacement for New York's Academy of Music (see 1-039) on a site immediately across the street from the venerable but doomed hall. Lamb's design vocabulary was a bit cooler than the Rapps' but his product was every bit as impressive. In the lobby, a sweeping marble stair rose to a mezzanine that was concealed by a screen of delicately framed stained glass.

6-076. Academy of Music (Palladium), 126-148 East Fourteenth Street, New York, New York. Opened 1926; 3,517 seats; Thomas W. Lamb, architect. From *Architecture and Building*, January, 1927. P&P, LC-USZ62-60520.

Under the massive balcony, Lamb tucked in a small mezzanine, a provision for smokers.

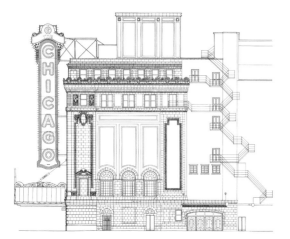

6-073

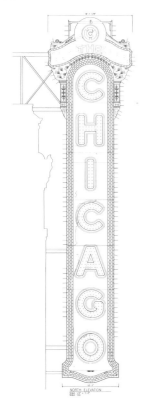

6-074

6-075

6-076

6-077. Ambassador Theatre, 2454 Eighteenth Street NW, Washington, D.C. Opened September 20, 1923; 1,800 seats; Thomas W. Lamb, architect. John P. Wymer, photographer, 1951. P&P, LC-USZ62-113867.

Showman Harry Crandall's Knickerbocker Theatre opened on October 13, 1917. Designed by Reginald W. Geare, Washington's premier theater architect, it was one of the city's finest showplaces, but one destined for a tragic end. On January 28, 1922, its roof collapsed under the weight of a massive snowfall. Ninety-eight people were killed. Crandall commissioned Thomas W. Lamb to design a replacement, the Ambassador, which rose on the Knickerbocker's site.

6-078. Earle (Warner) Theatre, 505 Thirteenth Street NW, Washington, D.C. Opened December 27, 1924; 2,240 seats; C. Howard Crane & Kenneth Franzheim, architects. National Photo Company, photographers, ca. 1924. P&P, LC-USZ62-93740.

Detroit's C. Howard Crane used a French-inspired interior form, lining every inch with rich ornament and elegant drapings. The boxes closest to the stage were vestigial, elaborate shelves that provided a visual base for the plaster organ grilles that rose above.

6-077

6-078

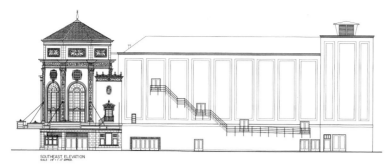

SOUTHEAST ELEVATION
SCALE: 1/8" = 1'-0" APPROX.

6-079

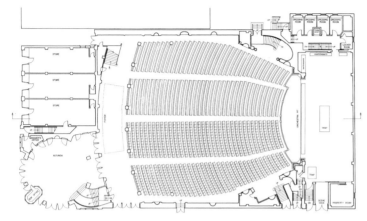

6-080

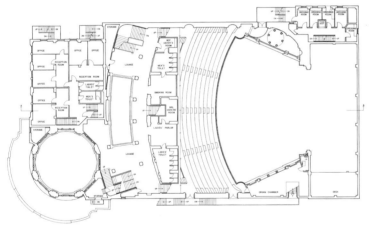

6-081

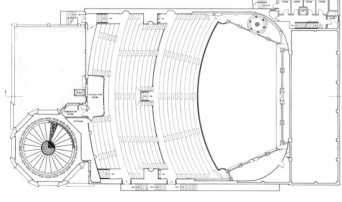

6-082

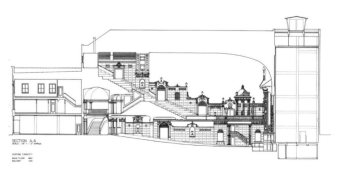

SECTION A-A
SCALE: 1/8" = 1'-0" APPROX.

SEATING CAPACITY:
MAIN FLOOR   1641
BALCONY   1125

6-083

6-079. Grand Riviera Theatre, 9222 Grand River Avenue, Detroit, Michigan. Opened August 24, 1925; 2,766 seats; John Eberson, architect. Craig Morrison, delineator, 1970. P&P, HABS MI-70.

Eberson introduced exoticism into cinema design. The elaborate octagon that marked the entry to the Grand Riviera, a large neighborhood theater in Detroit, gave hardly a hint of what would be found within.

6-080. Grand Riviera Theatre, 9222 Grand River Avenue, Detroit, Michigan. Opened August 24, 1925; 2,766 seats; John Eberson, architect. Craig Morrison, delineator, 1970. P&P, HABS MI-270.

The Grand Riviera superbly illustrates the movie palace plan. Although the rotunda was relatively small, its spectacular height gave spatial excitement to patrons entering the theater (6-085). Interest was enhanced by the curved balcony stair—its asymmetry with the other stair, in the inner foyer, was typically Ebersonian. The seating area was vast, the stage wide but relatively shallow.

6-081. Grand Riviera Theatre, 9222 Grand River Avenue, Detroit, Michigan. Opened August 24, 1925; 2,766 seats; John Eberson, architect. Craig Morrison, delineator, 1970. P&P, HABS MI-270.

6-082. Grand Riviera Theatre, 9222 Grand River Avenue, Detroit, Michigan. Opened August 24, 1925; 2,766 seats; John Eberson, architect. Craig Morrison, delineator, 1970. P&P, HABS MI-270.

6-083. Grand Riviera Theatre, 9222 Grand River Avenue, Detroit, Michigan. Opened August 24, 1925; 2,766 seats; John Eberson, architect. Craig Morrison, delineator, 1970. P&P, HABS MI-270.

The atmospheric interior, Eberson's great innovation, had been introduced a year earlier at the Majestic Theatre in Houston, Texas. In both the Majestic and the Grand Riviera, the effect was that of an urban square surrounded by buildings whose simulated stone facades were verdant with trees, vines, and floral garlands. Stuffed doves were perched about and suspended from the ceiling. Lighting came directly from iron lanterns and luminescent urns and indirectly from decorative windows and coves behind the naturalistic walls. The ceiling, simulating the nighttime sky, was studded with twinkling electric stars and played upon by projected clouds.

6-084

6-085

6-084. Grand Riviera Theatre, 9222 Grand River Avenue, Detroit, Michigan. Opened August 24, 1925; 2,766 seats; John Eberson, architect. Allen Stross, photographer, October, 1970. P&P, HABS, MICH,82-DETRO,16-1.

The Riviera's original marquee was replaced with one that incorporated playful scrolls and a large advertising panel.

6-085. Grand Riviera Theatre, 9222 Grand River Avenue, Detroit, Michigan. Opened August 24, 1925; 2,766 seats; John Eberson, architect. Unidentified photographer, 1925. P&P, HABS, MICH,82-DETRO,16-7.

The mirrored entry rotunda contained Eberson's design specialties: a rich tile floor, banners draped over railings, custom-made lamp brackets, and an unusual iron chandelier that combined traditional crystals with pendant lanterns (6-086).

6-086. Grand Riviera Theatre, 9222 Grand River Avenue, Detroit, Michigan. Opened August 24, 1925; 2,766 seats; John Eberson, architect. Allen Stross, photographer, October, 1970. P&P, HABS, MICH,82-DETRO,16-2.

6-086

6-087

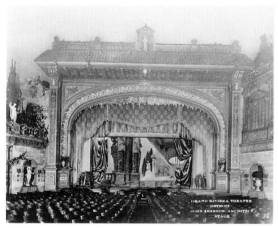

6-088

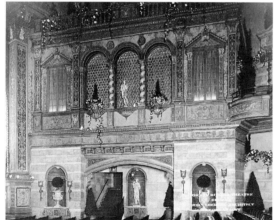

6-089

6-090

6-087. Grand Riviera Theatre, 9222 Grand River Avenue, Detroit, Michigan. Opened August 24, 1925; 2,766 seats; John Eberson, architect. Unidentified photographer, 1925. P&P, HABS, MICH,82-DETRO,16-27.

6-088. Grand Riviera Theatre, 9222 Grand River Avenue, Detroit, Michigan. Opened August 24, 1925; 2,766 seats; John Eberson, architect. Unidentified photographer, 1925. P&P, HABS, MICH,82-DETRO,16-20.

Eberson's auditoriums, playful, colorful, and asymmetrical, were variations on a theme. Common to all were side walls of exterior architectural form, a tiled roof over the proscenium, a working fountain, a domed temple-like pavilion, statues, vines, trees, doves, and a stuffed parrot. At the Riviera, the temple stood to the left, above the fountain, while a windowed pavilion to the right concealed the Robert-Morton pipe organ.

6-089. Grand Riviera Theatre, 9222 Grand River Avenue, Detroit, Michigan. Opened August 24, 1925; 2,766 seats; John Eberson, architect. Unidentified photographer, 1925. P&P, HABS, MICH,82-DETRO,16-23.

6-090. Grand Riviera Theatre, 9222 Grand River Avenue, Detroit, Michigan. Opened August 24, 1925; 2,766 seats; John Eberson, architect. Allen Stross, photographer, October, 1970. P&P, HABS, MICH,82-DETRO,16-3.

The Grand Riviera's inner foyer was a buffer between the entrance and the auditorium. Although not as high as the rotunda, its groin-vaulted ceiling and richly ornamented mezzanine provided spatial variety. The foyer's upper level, elaborately mirrored and richly furnished, provided a place to stroll and gave access to the theater's lounges, whose gated entries were another Eberson trademark.

6-091. Plan, Paramount Theatre, 145 North County Road, Palm Beach, Florida. Opened January 9, 1927; 1,400 seats; Joseph Urban, architect. Richard T. High, delineator, 1971. P&P, HABS FL-230, detail.

Joseph Urban was as renowned for his scenic designs, in which he realized the visions of producer Florenz Ziegfeld, as for his relatively few architectural projects. For the Paramount organization's Palm Beach showplace, he used an appropriately tropical design vocabulary. The Florida climate allowed him to make the entry a virtual outdoor stage set in which visitors passed beneath a great arch and through a private courtyard before entering the theater proper. Urban did not invent the idea of orienting the auditorium diagonally within the building; the concept had been used often in Victorian churches. But in that it enhanced the apparent size of the audience, this orientation worked well, especially where stage space could be limited.

6-092. Paramount Theatre, 145 North County Road, Palm Beach, Florida. Opened January 9, 1927; 1,400 seats; Joseph Urban, architect. Jack E. Boucher, photographer, April, 1972. P&P, HABS,FLA,50-PALM,5-2.

6-093. Paramount Theatre, 145 North County Road, Palm Beach, Florida. Opened January 9, 1927; 1,400 seats; Joseph Urban, architect. Jack E. Boucher, photographer, April, 1972. P&P, HABS,FLA,50-PALM,5-5.

6-094. Paramount Theatre, 145 North County Road, Palm Beach, Florida. Opened January 9, 1927; 1,400 seats; Joseph Urban, architect. Jack E. Boucher, photographer, April, 1972. P&P, HABS,FLA,50-PALM,5-9.

6-092

6-093

6-091

6-094

6-095

6-096

6-097

6-095. Paramount Theatre, 145 North County Road, Palm Beach, Florida. Opened January 9, 1927; 1,400 seats; Joseph Urban, architect. Jack E. Boucher, photographer, April, 1972. P&P, HABS,FLA,50-PALM,5-11.

A precursor to Urban's famous Ziegfeld Theatre in New York the Paramount's auditorium was ornamented with maritime-themed friezes that dematerialized the wall surfaces. The beamed, folded-plate ceiling glowed with subdued light from within and custom-designed chandeliers that resembled fish traps enhanced the exotic atmosphere.

6-096. Paramount Theatre, 145 North County Road, Palm Beach, Florida. Opened January 9, 1927; 1,400 seats; Joseph Urban, architect. Jack E. Boucher, photographer, April, 1972. P&P, HABS,FLA,50-PALM,5-12.

The auditorium's diagonal orientation (6-091) gave the Paramount an extraordinarily wide balcony. Only three rows deep, it was divided into semi-private loges by railings that matched those on the forecourt bridges.

6-097. Missouri Theatre, 713–715 Edmond Street, St. Joseph, Missouri. Opened June 25, 1927; 1,391 seats; Boller Brothers, architects. Jack E. Boucher, photographer, April/May, 1986. P&P, HABS,MO,11-SAJOE,11-1.

By 1927, classicism had waned as a stylistic inspiration for picture palace architects. Following John Eberson's lead, they looked far and wide for exotic sources. The Boller Brothers introduced the glories of Nebuchadnezzar's citadel to the banks of the Mississippi. The brick and terra-cotta facade, now shorn of much of its original ornament, was an Assyrianized Palladian delight. Inside (6-098–6-101), a full population of helmeted charioteers, archers, and winged bulls protected the audience that sat beneath the tent-like ceiling canopy. While some of the ornaments are couched in art deco modernism, others look ancient indeed.

6-098

6-098. Missouri Theatre, 713–715 Edmond Street, St. Joseph, Missouri. Opened June 25, 1927; 1,391 seats; Boller Brothers, architects. Jack E. Boucher, photographer, April/May, 1986. P&P, HABS,MO,11-SAJOE,11-5.

6-100

6-100. Missouri Theatre, 713–715 Edmond Street, St. Joseph, Missouri. Opened June 25, 1927; 1,391 seats; Boller Brothers, architects. Jack E. Boucher, photographer, April/May, 1986. P&P, HABS,MO,11-SAJOE,11-7.

6-099

6-099. Missouri Theatre, 713–715 Edmond Street, St. Joseph, Missouri. Opened June 25, 1927; 1,391 seats; Boller Brothers, architects. Jack E. Boucher, photographer, April/May, 1986. P&P, HABS,MO,11-SAJOE,11-6.

6-101

6-101. Missouri Theatre, 713–715 Edmond Street, St. Joseph, Missouri. Opened June 25, 1927; 1,391 seats; Boller Brothers, architects. Jack E. Boucher, photographer, April/May, 1986. P&P, HABS,MO,11-SAJOE,11-8.

6-102. Indiana Theatre and Indiana Roof Ball-room, 134–140 West Washington Street, Indi-anapolis, Indiana. Opened June 18, 1927; 3,313 seats; Rubush & Hunter, architects. Jack E. Boucher, photographer, August, 1970. P&P, HABS,IND,49-IND,29-2.

Indianapolis residents saw the wonders of Mex-ico's Spanish colonization portrayed in the bril-liant white terra cotta of the Indiana. The facade features full-relief portraits of King Ferdinand and Queen Isabella set in an array of Chur-rigueresque ornament, including probably the only accurate sundial ever placed on the face of an American theater.

6-103. Indiana Theatre, 134 West Washington Street, Indianapolis, Indiana. Opened June 18, 1927; 3,313 seats; Rubush & Hunter, architects. Jack E. Boucher, photographer, August, 1970. P&P, HABS,IND,49-IND,29-8.

The Indiana's interior merged the Mexican style of the facade with patterns derived from classic Indian architecture. Beautifully crafted tin chan-deliers, robust and innovative plasterwork, and a mural of the Taj Mahal lent an eastern character to the main lobby.

6-104. Indiana Theatre and Indiana Roof Ball-room, 134–140 West Washington Street, Indi-anapolis, Indiana. Opened June 18, 1927; 3,313 seats; Rubush & Hunter, architects. Jack E. Boucher, photographer, August, 1970. P&P, HABS,IND,49-IND,29-5.

6-105

6-106

6-107

6-105. Indiana Theatre, 134 West Washington Street, Indianapolis, Indiana. Opened June 18, 1927; 3,313 seats; Rubush & Hunter, architects. Jack E. Boucher, photographer, August, 1970. P&P, HABS,IND,49-IND,29-18.

The Indiana's plasterwork combines intricately ornate modeling with a generous dose of whimsy. The brackets that support the large, urnlike lighting fixture take the form of upended dachshunds; at the peak of the proscenium arch a multibreasted fertility goddess overlooks the audience (6-106).

6-106. Indiana Theatre, 134 West Washington Street, Indianapolis, Indiana. Opened June 18, 1927; 3,313 seats; Rubush & Hunter, architects. Unidentified photographer, 1927. P&P, HABS,IND,49-IND,29-36.

The auditorium's unusual flat ceiling was necessitated by the presence of the large ballroom immediately above (6-115).

6-107. Indiana Theatre, 134 West Washington Street, Indianapolis, Indiana. Opened June 18, 1927; 3,313 seats; Rubush & Hunter, architects. Unidentified photographer, 1927. P&P, HABS,IND,49-IND,29-39.

Wurlitzer organs may have been mighty, but the Indiana's Barton was golden-voiced. Theater organ stop tabs were arranged in semicircular rows to make it easy for the organist to reach them on the fly. The finest consoles were designed to match the instrument's architectural surroundings.

6-108. Indiana Theatre, 134 West Washington Street, Indianapolis, Indiana. Opened June 18, 1927; 3,313 seats; Rubush & Hunter, architects. Unidentified photographer, 1927. P&P, HABS,IND,49-IND,29-28.

In the movie palace experience at its finest, the adventure of freely exploring a large and complex building was as exciting as the movie itself. The Indiana boasted a full complement of corridors, mezzanines, and lounges, diverse but unified within the consistent stylistic amalgam of early Mexico and India (6-109–6-113). The variety and richness of spatial experiences, materials, furnishings, and decorations continued to intrigue even those patrons who visited again and again.

6-108

6-109

6-110

6-111

6-112

6-109. Indiana Theatre, 134 West Washington Street, Indianapolis, Indiana. Opened June 18, 1927; 3,313 seas; Rubush & Hunter, architects. Unidentified photographer, 1927. P&P, HABS,IND,49-IND,29-30.

6-110. Indiana Theatre, 134 West Washington Street, Indianapolis, Indiana. Opened June 18, 1927; 3,313 seats; Rubush & Hunter, architects. Unidentified photographer, 1927. P&P, HABS,IND,49-IND,29-31.

6-111. Indiana Theatre, 134 West Washington Street, Indianapolis, Indiana. Opened June 18, 1927; 3,313 seats; Rubush & Hunter, architects. Unidentified photographer, 1927. P&P, HABS,IND,49-IND,29-32.

6-112. Indiana Theatre, 134 West Washington Street, Indianapolis, Indiana. Opened June 18, 1927; 3,313 seats; Rubush & Hunter, architects. Unidentified photographer, 1927. P&P, HABS,IND,49-IND,29-12.

6-113

6-114

6-113. Indiana Theatre, 134 West Washington Street, Indianapolis, Indiana. Opened June 18, 1927; 3,313 seats; Rubush & Hunter, architects. Unidentified photographer, 1927. P&P, HABS,IND,49-IND,29-34.

6-114. Indiana Theatre, 140 West Washington Street, Indianapolis, Indiana. Opened June 18, 1927; 3,313 seats; Rubush & Hunter, architects; Jack E. Boucher, photographer, August, 1970; P & P, HABS,IND,49-IND,29-10.

6-115. Indiana Roof Ballroom, 140 West Washington Street, Indianapolis, Indiana. Opened September 7, 1927; Rubush & Hunter, architects. Jack E. Boucher, photographer, August, 1970. P&P, HABS,IND,49-IND,29-20.

As moviegoers downstairs in the theater watched their favorite stars on screen, dancers twirled under projected clouds and electrical stars in the plaster sky of the Indiana Roof, the ballroom above the theater's ceiling.

6-115

6-116. Fox (Capitol) Theatre, 1328 F Street NW, Washington, D.C. Opened September 19, 1927; 3,433 seats; C. W. & George L. Rapp, architects. Unidentified photographer, 1937–1940. P&P, LC-USZ62-94696.

As others sought inspiration in exotic lands and cultures, Rapp & Rapp continued to refine and elaborate upon their version of the French Renaissance. The Fox was as grand a space as could be found in the nation's capital. Because of its hillside location, audiences entered at the mezzanine level and walked downstairs to reach the main floor.

6-117. Fox (Capitol) Theatre, 1328 F Street NW, Washington, D.C. Opened September 19, 1927; 3,433 seats; C. W. & George L. Rapp, architects. Theodor Horydczak, photographer, 1927–1937; P&P, LC-H824-T-2187-008.

Executed with the Rapps' customary panache, the Fox's lofty auditorium presented a luxurious medley of curved forms, glittering crystal, and lavish draperies.

6-118

6-119

6-118. Oriental Theatre, 828 Southeast Grand Avenue, Portland, Oregon. Opened December 31, 1927; 2,038 seats; Thomas & Mercier, architects. Angelus Commercial Photographers, 1930. P&P, HABS,ORE,26-PORT,3-26.

The experience of a movie palace began with its marquee, the continuing evocation of the nickelodeon's iconic elements—sheet metal and light bulbs. The great elephant on the marquee was the first of many that the Oriental's patrons would encounter. A later marquee provided more advertising space, easier maintenance, and better visibility to passing cars (6-119).

6-119. Oriental Theatre, 828 Southeast Grand Avenue, Portland, Oregon. Opened December 31, 1927; 2,038 seats; Thomas & Mercier, architects. Lyle E. Winkle, photographer, November 11, 1969. P&P, HABS,ORE,26-PORT,3-2.

It would take a while for sound pictures to effect their influence on theater design. In the meantime, exotic pleasure domes with stages, orchestra facilities, and pipe organs continued to proliferate. The Oriental, which opened just a month after the introduction of sound, brought a touch of Indo-China to America's northwest.

6-120. Oriental Theatre, 828 Southeast Grand Avenue, Portland, Oregon. Opened December 31, 1927; 2,038 seats; Thomas & Mercier, architects. Lyle E. Winkle, photographer, November 11, 1969. P&P, HABS,ORE,26-PORT,3-6.

A seated Buddha and an exotic elephant mask gave visitors an initial greeting; the lobbies and foyers continued the style. Great guardian beasts—lions at the main level, elephants at the balcony—flanked the wide steps to the auditorium.

6-120

6-121

6-124

6-122

6-121. Oriental Theatre, 828 Southeast Grand Avenue, Portland, Oregon. Opened December 31, 1927; 2,038 seats; Thomas & Mercier, architects. Lyle E. Winkle, photographer, November 11, 1969. P&P, HABS,ORE,26-PORT,3-12.

6-122. Oriental Theatre, 828 Southeast Grand Avenue, Portland, Oregon. Opened December 31, 1927; 2,038 seats; Thomas & Mercier, architects. Lyle E. Winkle, photographer, November 11, 1969. P&P, HABS,ORE,26-PORT,3-8.

6-123. Oriental Theatre, 828 Southeast Grand Avenue, Portland, Oregon. Opened December 31, 1927; 2,038 seats; Thomas & Mercier, architects. Lyle E. Winkle, photographer, November 11, 1969. P&P, HABS,ORE,26-PORT,3-11.

6-124. Oriental Theatre, 828 Southeast Grand Avenue, Portland, Oregon. Opened December 31, 1927; 2,038 seats; Thomas & Mercier, architects. From *Pacific Coast Architect*, April, 1928. P&P, HABS,ORE,26-PORT,3-32.

The auditorium showed a kinship to Angkor Wat, with the addition of some chandeliers and drapes.

6-123

6-125

6-126

6-125. Oriental Theatre, 828 Southeast Grand Avenue, Portland, Oregon. Opened December 31, 1927; 2,038 seats; Thomas & Mercier, architects. From *Pacific Coast Architect*, April, 1928. P&P, HABS,ORE,26-PORT,3-30.

6-126. Oriental Theatre, 828 Southeast Grand Avenue, Portland, Oregon. Opened December 31, 1927; 2,038 seats; Thomas & Mercier, architects. From *Pacific Coast Architect*, April, 1928. P&P, HABS,ORE,26-PORT,3-31.

6-127. Oriental Theatre, 828 Southeast Grand Avenue, Portland, Oregon. Opened December 31, 1927; 2,038 seats; Thomas & Mercier, architects. Lyle E. Winkle, photographer, November 11, 1969. P&P, HABS,ORE,26-PORT,3-19.

6-128. Chinese Theatre, 6925 Hollywood Boulevard, Los Angeles, California. Opened May 18, 1927; 2,048 seats; Meyer & Holler, architects. Unidentified photographer, 1927. P&P, LC-USZ62-59632.

Theater owner and producer Sid Grauman is long gone and largely forgotten, but his name remains inextricably connected to his Chinese Theatre, shown here on its opening day. The Chinese followed Grauman's Egyptian Theatre, Million Dollar, and Metropolitan Theatres in spreading grand and exotic cinema design through the home of the movies. Glittering by day and night, the Chinese continues to attract millions to its famous forecourt, where, between 1927 and 1991, 157 film performers left their autographs and footprints.

6-127

6-128

6-129

6-132

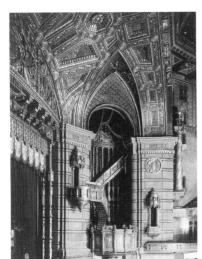

6-130

6-131

6-129. Roxy Theatre, 761 Seventh Avenue, New York, New York. Opened March 11, 1927; 5,886 seats; Walter W. Ahlschlager, architect. T-K Inc., photographers, ca. 1927. P&P, LC-USZ62-98707.

6-130. Roxy Theatre, 761 Seventh Avenue, New York, New York. Opened March 11, 1927; 5,886 seats; Walter W. Ahlschlager, architect. T-K Inc., photographers, ca. 1927. P&P, LC-USZ62-98706.

6-131. Roxy Theatre, 761 Seventh Avenue, New York, New York. Opened March 11, 1927; 5,886 seats; Walter W. Ahlschlager, architect. T-K Inc., photographers, ca. 1927. P&P, LC-USZ62-120169.

6-132. Roxy Theatre, 761 Seventh Avenue, New York, New York. Opened March 11, 1927; 5,886 seats; Walter W. Ahlschlager, architect. T-K Inc., photographers, ca. 1927. P&P, LC-USZ62-98705.

The Roxy, the largest and arguably the most elaborate movie palace ever built, crowned the career of film exhibitor Samuel "Roxy" Rothafel, who was a pioneer in providing cinema patrons with extravagant service in an extravagant architectural setting. Ushers practiced military drill in the Roxy's rotunda lobby and an early cartoon shows a child standing in the space asking her mother, "Does God live here?"

6-133. Ohio Theatre, 39 East State Street, Columbus, Ohio. Opened March 17, 1928; 3,079 seats; Thomas W. Lamb, architect. Unidentified photographer, 1928. P&P, HABS, OHIO,25-COLB,4-1.

As the prosperity of the 1920s spiraled giddily upward, theaters did their best to keep pace, each seeking to outdo its predecessors in size and lavish appointments. Even such staid architectural designers as Thomas W. Lamb turned to the exotic.

6-134. Ohio Theatre, 39 East State Street, Columbus, Ohio. Opened March 17, 1928; 3,079 seats; Thomas W. Lamb, architect. Unidentified photographer, 1928. P&P, HABS, OHIO,25-COLB,4-4.

A movie palace's ticket kiosk was a far cry from the wooden booth of the carnival or nickelodeon. This bronze and marble cabinet made ticket buying an experience to be relished. The low ceiling of the outdoor area around the box office and the first indoor vestibule maintained the height of the marquee. Like the facade, it was a theatrical gesture, preparing patrons for the step beyond.

6-135. Ohio Theatre, 39 East State Street, Columbus, Ohio. Opened March 17, 1928; 3,079 seats; Thomas W. Lamb, architect. Unidentified photographer, 1928. P&P, HABS, OHIO,25-COLB,4-5.

6-136. Ohio Theatre, 39 East State Street, Columbus, Ohio. Opened March 17, 1928; 3,079 seats; Thomas W. Lamb, architect. Unidentified photographer, 1928. P&P, HABS, OHIO,25-COLB,4-6.

The restraint of the facade and vestibule set patrons up for astonishment as they encountered the unabashed richness of the lobby's ornamentation and furnishings. Too shallow to invite forward progression, its volume drew the eye upward as its vaulted ceiling directed attention toward the stairways at the ends.

6-137

6-138

6-139

6-140

6-137. Ohio Theatre, 39 East State Street, Columbus, Ohio. Opened March 17, 1928; 3,079 seats; Thomas W. Lamb, architect. Unidentified photographer, 1928. P&P, HABS, OHIO,25-COLB,4-7.

6-138. Ohio Theatre, 39 East State Street, Columbus, Ohio. Opened March 17, 1928; 3,079 seats; Thomas W. Lamb, architect. Unidentified photographer, 1928. P&P, HABS, OHIO,25-COLB,4-19.

A decorator arranges the lobby mezzanine drapes in preparation for the Ohio's opening.

6-139. Ohio Theatre, 39 East State Street, Columbus, Ohio. Opened March 17, 1928; 3,079 seats; Thomas W. Lamb, architect. Unidentified photographer, 1928. P&P, HABS, OHIO,25-COLB,4-14.

The Ohio's lounges presented a variety of heavily articulated architectural forms and exotic decorations and furnishings. Following a typical movie palace layout, a large lounge below the lobby served orchestra-level patrons.

6-140. Ohio Theatre. 39 East State Street, Columbus, Ohio. Opened March 17, 1928; 3,079 seats; Thomas W. Lamb, architect. Unidentified photographer, 1928. P&P, HABS, OHIO,25-COLB,4-17.

The Ohio's upper reaches provided fertile territory for exploration. Lounges at the mezzanine and balcony levels were smaller than those in the basement, but similar in their variety of styles and their spirit of exotic decoration (6-144–6-147). Even exit passages and stairs were paneled with brocade and lighted by crystal droplets.

6-141

6-142

6-141. Ohio Theatre, 39 East State Street,
Columbus, Ohio. Opened March 17, 1928;
3,079 seats; Thomas W. Lamb, architect.
Unidentified photographer, 1928. P&P,
HABS, OHIO,25-COLB,4-24.

Hardly an inch went undecorated in the
auditorium, a baroque fantasy that incorporated twisted columns, faceted domes, hidden lights of many colors, gold stenciling,
regal draperies, and a great crystal chandelier. Could such an atmosphere ever be
matched? Why, of course! The Stanley Theatre in Utica, New York, was a line-for-line
duplicate.

6-142. Ohio Theatre, 39 East State Street,
Columbus, Ohio. Opened March 17, 1928;
3,079 seats; Thomas W. Lamb, architect.
Unidentified photographer, 1928. P&P,
HABS, OHIO,25-COLB,4-25.

6-143. Elevation, Ohio Theatre, 39 East
State Street, Columbus, Ohio. Opened
March 17, 1928; 3,079 seats; Thomas W.
Lamb, architect. Office of Thomas W. Lamb,
delineators, 1928. P&P, HABS, OHIO,25-
COLB,4-78.

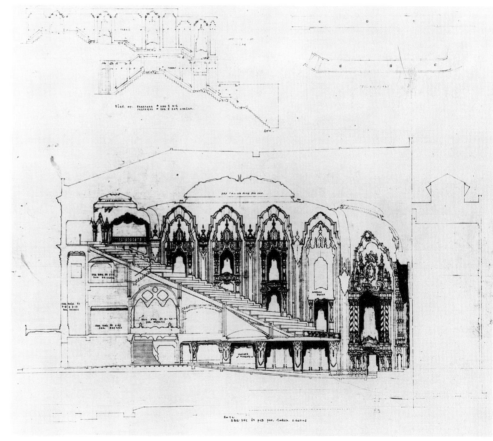

6-143

6-144

6-145

6-146

6-144. Ohio Theatre, 39 East State Street, Columbus, Ohio. Opened March 17, 1928; 3,079 seats; Thomas W. Lamb, architect. Unidentified photographer, 1928. P&P, HABS, OHIO,25-COLB,4-51.

Although it looked like the smoking room of an exclusive club, the mezzanine men's lounge was open for all male patrons to enjoy. The ladies' foyer, with its brocade-lined walls and caged canary, was no less luxurious.

6-145. Ohio Theatre, 39 East State Street, Columbus, Ohio. Opened March 17, 1928; 3,079 seats; Thomas W. Lamb, architect. Unidentified photographer, 1928. P&P, HABS, OHIO,25-COLB,4-57.

The cosmetic room, part of the balcony-level ladies' suite, had a draped silk ceiling; the adjoining lounge appeared to have come straight from Versailles (6-147).

6-146. Ohio Theatre, 39 East State Street, Columbus, Ohio. Opened March 17, 1928; 3,079 seats; Thomas W. Lamb, architect. Unidentified photographer, 1928. P&P, HABS, OHIO,25-COLB,4-13.

The men's lounge, with its globe and animal-skin hangings, was an evocative setting, well suited to vicariously intrepid explorers and mighty hunters of the imagination.

6-147. Ohio Theatre, 39 East State Street, Columbus, Ohio. Opened March 17, 1928; 3,079 seats; Thomas W. Lamb, architect. Unidentified photographer, 1928; P&P, HABS, OHIO,25-COLB,4-60.

6-148. Ohio Theatre, 39 East State Street, Columbus, Ohio. Opened March 17, 1928; 3,079 seats; Thomas W. Lamb, architect. Unidentified photographer, 1928. P&P, HABS, OHIO,25-COLB,4-63.

6-149. Ohio Theatre, 39 East State Street, Columbus, Ohio. Opened March 17, 1928; 3,079 seats; Thomas W. Lamb, architect. Unidentified photographer, 1928. P&P, HABS, OHIO,25-COLB,4-61.

To its patrons a theater's environment was, in a word, all show business. Backstage, the actors may have maintained an aura of haughty elegance, but they prepared for their appearances in the most austere of spaces. Exempted was the show's star, whose dressing room approached the comfort level of a residential living room (6-148).

6-150. Ohio Theatre, 39 East State Street, Columbus, Ohio. Opened March 17, 1928; 3,079 seats; Thomas W. Lamb, architect. Unidentified photographer, 1928. P&P, HABS, OHIO,25-COLB,4-62.

The largest of the movie palaces had private screening rooms like this in which management could preview upcoming availabilities and put together high-quality programming.

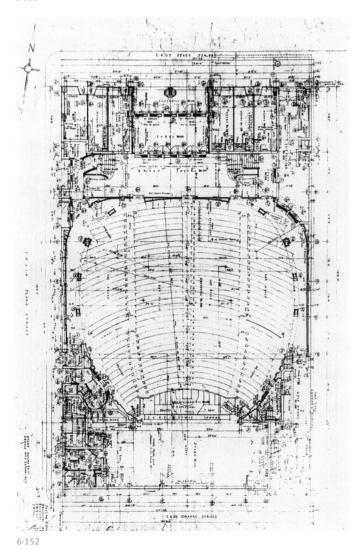

6-153

6-151. Ohio Theatre, 39 East State Street, Columbus, Ohio. Opened March 17, 1928; 3,079 seats; Thomas W. Lamb, architect. Unidentified photographer, 1928. P&P, HABS, OHIO,25-COLB,4-66.

A theater's lighting control board was an ingenious amalgam of electrical and mechanical technologies. Auditorium light controls were located to one side of the board, stage controls to the other. Each horizontal row controlled a color—red, white or blue—coded by the elliptical knobs on the dimmer levers. Twisting a knob locked it into a large color master lever at the center of the board. These levers, in turn, could lock into the central control wheel. As an operator rotated the wheel, one or more master levers would move up as others—and the dimmers linked to them—moved down. The effects of dimming and color blending seemed marvelous to a generation that could not yet dream of the motorized and electronic world that would follow.

6-152. Ohio Theatre, 39 East State Street, Columbus, Ohio. Opened March 17, 1928; 3,079 seats; Thomas W. Lamb, architect. Office of Thomas W. Lamb, delineators, 1928. P&P, HABS, OHIO,25-COLB,4-80.

The Ohio was as straightforward in plan as it was exotic in decoration. The narrow lobby and small stage were subordinated to an auditorium of almost ballooning volume.

6-153. Ohio Theatre, 39 East State Street, Columbus, Ohio. Opened March 17, 1928; 3,079 seats; Thomas W. Lamb, architect. Unidentified photographer, 1928; P & P, HABS, OHIO,25-COLB,4-68.

The Ohio was equipped with three film projectors as well as capabilities for spotlights and slides. Film splicing, rewinding, and sound control were in the purview of the projectionists who inhabited this austere and mysterious aerie.

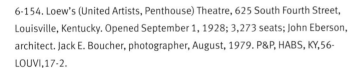

6-155

6-154

6-154. Loew's (United Artists, Penthouse) Theatre, 625 South Fourth Street, Louisville, Kentucky. Opened September 1, 1928; 3,273 seats; John Eberson, architect. Jack E. Boucher, photographer, August, 1979. P&P, HABS, KY,56-LOUVI,17-2.

John Eberson remained true to his trademark "acre of seats in a garden of dreams," returning to that theme in designing a theater for downtown Louisville. The heavily modeled terra-cotta facade incorporated a towering sign capped by a domed pinnacle. Deliberately confining with spindled gril-lages, the vestibule enhanced the dramatic effect of interior spaces.

6-155. Loew's (United Artists, Penthouse) Theatre, 625 South Fourth Street, Louisville, Kentucky. Opened September 1, 1928; 3,273 seats; John Eberson, architect. Unidentified photographer, August, 1928. P&P, HABS, KY,56-LOUVI,17-24.

6-156. Loew's (United Artists, Penthouse) Theatre, 625 South Fourth Street, Louisville, Kentucky. Opened September 1, 1928; 3,273 seats; John Eberson, architect. Jack E. Boucher, photographer, August, 1979. P&P, HABS, KY,56-LOUVI,17-6.

Loew's outer lobby displayed Eberson's distinctive textured plaster walls relieved by blooms of Plateresque ornament. He created spatial variety through asymmetry, placing one balcony staircase in the outer lobby, the other in the main foyer (6-157).

6-156

6-157

6-157. Loew's (United Artists, Penthouse) Theatre, 625 South Fourth Street, Louisville, Kentucky. Opened September 1, 1928; 3,273 seats; John Eberson, architect. Unidentified photographer, August, 1928. P&P, HABS, KY,56-LOUVI,17-27.

6-158. Loew's (United Artists, Penthouse) Theatre, 625 South Fourth Street, Louisville, Kentucky. Opened September 1, 1928; 3,273 seats; John Eberson, architect. Jack E. Boucher, photographer, August, 1979. P&P, HABS, KY,56-LOUVI,17-7.

6-159. Loew's (United Artists, Penthouse) Theatre, 625 South Fourth Street, Louisville, Kentucky. Opened September 1, 1928; 3,273 seats; John Eberson, architect. Jack E. Boucher, photographer, August, 1979. P&P, HABS, KY,56-LOUVI,17-8.

6-158

6-159

6-161

6-162

6-160

6-160. Loew's (United Artists, Penthouse) Theatre, 625 South Fourth Street, Louisville, Kentucky. Opened September 1, 1928; 3,273 seats; John Eberson, architect. Jack E. Boucher, photographer, August, 1979. P&P, HABS, KY,56-LOUVI,17-10.

Loew's spectacular inner foyer was crowned with a ceiling whose reticulated banding framed a gallery of portrait heads. Most of the portraits represented classical writers and composers, but Eberson's own face could be found in a roundel near one end (6-162). The stairway that culminated the procession through the lobby was a spatial and ornamental highlight (6-161).

6-161. Loew's (United Artists, Penthouse) Theatre, 625 South Fourth Street, Louisville, Kentucky. Opened September 1, 1928; 3,273 seats; John Eberson, architect. Unidentified photographer, August, 1928. P&P, HABS,KY,56-LOUVI,17-34.

6-162. Loew's (United Artists, Penthouse) Theatre, 625 South Fourth Street, Louisville, Kentucky. Opened September 1, 1928; 3,273 seats; John Eberson, architect. Jack E. Boucher, photographer, August, 1979. P&P, HABS, KY,56-LOUVI,17-11.

6-163. Loew's (United Artists, Penthouse) Theatre, 625 South Fourth Street, Louisville, Kentucky. Opened September 1, 1928; 3,273 seats; John Eberson, architect. Unidentified photographer, August, 1928. P&P, HABS,KY,56-LOUVI,17-32.

6-163

6-164

6-165

6-166

6-167

6-164. Loew's (United Artists, Penthouse) Theatre, 625 South Fourth Street, Louisville, Kentucky. Opened September 1, 1928; 3,273 seats; John Eberson, architect. Unidentified photographer, August, 1928. P&P, HABS, KY,56-LOUVI,17-47.

6-165. Loew's (United Artists, Penthouse) Theatre, 625 South Fourth Street, Louisville, Kentucky. Opened September 1, 1928; 3,273 seats; John Eberson, architect. Unidentified photographer, August, 1928. P&P, HABS, KY,56-LOUVI,17-46.

The asymmetry of Loew's auditorium was more subtle than many of Eberson's others. Here the artificial trees, flowers, birds, and trickling fountain reached their full state of refinement. The idiosyncrasy of the freeform curves that ornamented the under-balcony walls were a hallmark of the puckish Eberson (6-166).

6-166. Loew's (United Artists, Penthouse) Theatre, 625 South Fourth Street, Louisville, Kentucky. Opened September 1, 1928; 3,273 seats; John Eberson, architect. Unidentified photographer, August, 1928. P&P, HABS, KY,56-LOUVI,17-51.

6-167. Loew's (United Artists, Penthouse) Theatre, 625 South Fourth Street, Louisville, Kentucky. Opened September 1, 1928; 3,273 seats; John Eberson, architect. Jack E. Boucher, photographer, August, 1979. P&P, HABS, KY,56-LOUVI,17-17.

6-168. Pantages (Warnor's) Theatre, 1400–1430 Fulton Street, Fresno, California. Opened October 28, 1928; 2,000 seats; B. Marcus Priteca, architect. L. Beuthel, photographer, ca. 1929. P&P, LC-USZ62-101145.

B. Marcus Priteca designed many of Alexander Pantages's theaters. In this one he dematerialized the theater's usually solid facades with arcades that enhanced the building's sense of welcome to those who passed by its doors.

6-169. Fox (Music Hall, Emerald Palace) Theatre, 702–710 Olive Way, Seattle, Washington. Opened April 19, 1929; 2,282 seats; Sherwood D. Ford, architect. John Stamets, photographer, September, 1991. P&P, HABS, WASH,17-SEAT,11-3.

Generally, theater architects needed to ornament only the main facade; the rest of the building could remain a windowless box. At the Seattle Fox, architect Ford pulled out all the stops, clothing the entire building in a carefully composed Spanish style that evoked Seattle's western heritage. His lobbies and lounges juxtaposed smooth, undecorated walls with elaborate architectural highlights. The effects of light and shadow in the Fox's gracefully curved archways were particularly striking (6-172–6-174).

6-170

6-171

6-172

6-173

6-170. Fox (Music Hall, Emerald Palace) Theatre, 702–710 Olive Way, Seattle, Washington. Opened April 19, 1929; 2,282 seats; Sherwood D. Ford, architect. John Stamets, photographer, September, 1991. P&P, HABS, WASH,17-SEAT,11-4.

6-171. Fox (Music Hall, Emerald Palace) Theatre, 702–710 Olive Way, Seattle, Washington. Opened April 19, 1929; 2,282 seats; Sherwood D. Ford, architect. John Stamets, photographer, September, 1991. P&P, HABS, WASH,17-SEAT,11-6.

6-172. Fox (Music Hall, Emerald Palace) Theatre, 702–710 Olive Way, Seattle, Washington. Opened April 19, 1929; 2,282 seats; Sherwood D. Ford, architect. John Stamets, photographer, September, 1991; P & P, HABS, WASH,17-SEAT,11-17.

6-173. Fox (Music Hall, Emerald Palace) Theatre, 702–710 Olive Way, Seattle, Washington. Opened April 19, 1929; 2,282 seats; Sherwood D. Ford, architect. John Stamets, photographer, September, 1991. P&P, HABS, WASH,17-SEAT,11-16.

6-174

6-175

6-174. Fox (Music Hall, Emerald Palace) Theatre, 702–710 Olive Way, Seattle, Washington. Opened April 19, 1929; 2,282 seats; Sherwood D. Ford, architect. John Stamets, photographer, September, 1991. P&P, HABS, WASH,17-SEAT,11-20.

6-175. Fox (Music Hall, Emerald Palace) Theatre, 702–710 Olive Way, Seattle, Washington. Opened April 19, 1929; 2,282 seats; Sherwood D. Ford, architect. John Stamets, photographer, September, 1991. P&P, HABS, WASH,17-SEAT,11-27.

6-176. Fox (Music Hall, Emerald Palace) Theatre, 702–710 Olive Way, Seattle, Washington. Opened April 19, 1929; 2,282 seats; Sherwood D. Ford, architect. John Stamets, photographer, September, 1991. P&P, HABS, WASH,17-SEAT,11-31.

6-176

6-177

6-179

6-178

6-177. Fox (Music Hall, Emerald Palace) Theatre, 702–710 Olive Way, Seattle, Washington. Opened April 19, 1929; 2,282 seats; Sherwood D. Ford, architect. John Stamets, photographer, September, 1991. P&P, HABS, WASH,17-SEAT,11-34.

6-178. Fox Theatre, 20 Flatbush Avenue, Brooklyn, New York. Opened August 31, 1928; 4,305 seas; C. Howard Crane & Kenneth Franzheim, architects. Jack E. Boucher, photographer, October, 1970. P&P, HABS, NY,24-BROK,41-3.

6-179. Fox Theatre, 20 Flatbush Avenue, Brooklyn, New York. Opened August 31, 1928; 4,305 seats; C. Howard Crane & Kenneth Franzheim, architects. Jack E. Boucher, photographer, October, 1970. P&P, HABS, NY,24-BROK,41-2.

As the 1920s neared their end, movie palaces reached an apogee of size and exotic elaboration. As a display of sheer fantasy, it would be difficult to top the Brooklyn Fox. The entrance was unassuming, but within, a story unfolded. The lobby (6-178), a derivation of Southeast Asian styles, incorporated fountain-like art deco newel lights on its grand stair (6-180).

6-180. Fox Theatre, 20 Flatbush Avenue, Brooklyn, New York. Opened August 31, 1928; 4,305 seats; C. Howard Crane & Kenneth Franzheim, architects. Jack E. Boucher, photographer, October, 1970. P&P, HABS, NY,24-BROK,41-12.

The auditorium's elaborate organ grilles featured fountains that operated until the day the building was demolished. Like a skilled puppet master, C. Howard Crane manipulated the theme of water, using it as a unifying element in telling the tale of Marco Polo's voyages to the exotic Far East.

6-181. Fox Theatre, 20 Flatbush Avenue, Brooklyn, New York. Opened August 31, 1928; 4,305 seats; C. Howard Crane & Kenneth Franzheim, architects. Jack E. Boucher, photographer, October, 1970. P&P, HABS, NY,24-BROK,41-15.

THEATERS IN A PHOTOGRAPHER'S LENS

THE STOCK MARKET CRASH OF 1929 signaled an end to the building spree of the Roaring Twenties. In response to the lingering Depression, President Franklin D. Roosevelt established a series of programs to employ idled professionals. The Historic American Buildings Survey put architects to work documenting America's historic buildings; the Works Progress Administration hired artists to decorate new public buildings, and the Farm Security Administration's photographers recorded the Administration's relief work in America's farmlands. Working unobtrusively, using small-format Leica cameras, Walker Evans, Ben Shahn, Dorothea Lange, Marion Post Wolcott, Gordon Parks, and others whose work appears in this book applied their discerning eyes to capture the spirit of rural America. That so many of their images include theaters is testimony to the importance of movies in Depression-era America. These photographs, grouped by photographer, are "people" pictures that show a nation's relationship with its favorite entertainment medium.

LENS-001

LENS-001. Circus, Roswell, New Mexico. Arthur Rothstein, photographer, April, 1936. P&P, LC-USF34-002942-E.

LENS-002. Empire Theatre, Zeigler, Illinois. 863 seats. Arthur Rothstein, photographer, January, 1939. P&P, LC-USF34-026901-D.

LENS-003. Park Theatre, 32 East Park Street, Butte, Montana. 877 seats. Arthur Rothstein, photographer, summer, 1939. P&P, LC-USF33-003128-M3.

LENS-002

LENS-003

LENS-004

LENS-004. Rialto Theatre, 26 East Park Street, Butte, Montana. Opened ca. 1916; 1,311 seats. Arthur Rothstein, photographer, summer, 1939. P&P, LC-USF33-003128-M2.

LENS-005. Lyric Theatre, 314 Oak Street, Farmington, Minnesota. 300 seats. Arthur Rothstein, photographer, September, 1939. P&P, LC-USF34-028161-D.

LENS-006. Grundy Theatre, Grundy Center, Iowa. Arthur Rothstein, photographer, September, 1939. P&P, LC-USF34-028298-D.

LENS-007. Palace Theatre, 45 South Loudon Street, Winchester, Virginia. Opened October 15, 1931; 738 seats; Mr. Howell, architect. 738 seats. Arthur Rothstein, photographer, February, 1940. P&P, LC-USF33-003464-M2.

LENS-008. Capitol Theatre, 48 Rouss Avenue, Winchester, Virginia. 966 seats. Arthur Rothstein, photographer, February, 1940. P&P, LC-USF33-003464-M4.

LENS-006   LENS-007

LENS-008

LENS-009

LENS-010

LENS-009. Masonic Opera House (Majestic Theatre), 45 East Second Street, Chillicothe, Ohio. Opened December, 1876; building constructed 1853 as Masonic Hall; 638 seats; John W. Cook, architect. Arthur Rothstein, photographer, February, 1940. P&P, LC-USF33-003472-M2.

LENS-010. Greenbelt Theatre, 129 Centerway, Greenbelt, Maryland. Opened September 21, 1938; 590 seats; Reginald S. Wadsworth and Douglas D. Ellington, architects. Arthur Rothstein, photographer, December, 1941. P&P, LC-USF34-024488-D.

A product of the New Deal, Greenbelt was a pioneering venture in town planning. It was planned as an ideal community, self-contained, attractively designed and landscaped, and surrounded by green space. Intended as a Washington, D.C. suburb, it had no major businesses. Its commercial center was limited to convenience stores for the residents and, of course, a cinema.

LENS-011. Liberty Theater, 420 St. Charles Street, New Orleans, Louisiana. 1,333 seats. Walker Evans, photographer, 1935–1936. P&P, LC-USF342-T01-001285-A.

LENS-012. Arcadia Theatre, Geneva, Alabama. 332 seats. Walker Evans, photographer, August, 1936. P&P, LC-USF342-008235-A.

LENS-011

LENS-012

LENS-013. Pastime Theatre (converted from a church), Woodville, Mississippi. Ben Shahn, photographer, October, 1935. P&P, LC-USF33-006097-M5.

LENS-014. Dixie Theatre, Pursglove, Scotts Run, West Virginia. 315 seats. Ben Shahn, photographer, October, 1935. P&P, LC-USF33-006120-M2.

Black Fury, the movie advertised in the tattered posters, was about a coal strike, a subject that hit home in this Depression-ridden mining town.

LENS-015. Unidentified theater, Main Street, Lancaster, Ohio. Ben Shahn, photographer, August, 1938. P&P, LC-USF33-006389-M3.

LENS-016

LENS-017

LENS-018

LENS-016. Star Theatre, Main Street, Escalante, Utah. Dorothea Lange, photographer, April, 1936. P&P, LC-USF34-001335-C.

LENS-017. Rex (Harlem) Theatre, Leland, Mississippi. Dorothea Lange, photographer, June, 1937. P&P, LC-USF34-017417-E.

For another view see 8-017.

LENS-018. Unidentified theater, Oklahoma City, Oklahoma. Dorothea Lange, photographer, June, 1937. P&P, LC-USF34-017049-E.

LENS-019. Star Theatre, Stanley, North Dakota. 200 seats. Russell Lee, photographer, October, 1937. P&P, LC-USF34-030872-E.

LENS-020. Texas Theatre, Pharr, Texas. 480 seats. Russell Lee, photographer, February, 1939. P&P, LC-USF33-011978-M4.

LENS-021. Unidentified theater, Quemado, Texas. Russell Lee, photographer, March, 1939. P&P, LC-USF34-032590-D.

LENS-022. Unidentified theater, Quemado, Texas. Russell Lee, photographer, March, 1939. P&P, LC-USF34-032591-D.

The wooden front of the theater in Quemado was studded with used bottle caps. Whether this was intended as decorative treatment or as a primitive lath to which stucco was never applied is not known.

LENS-023

LENS-026

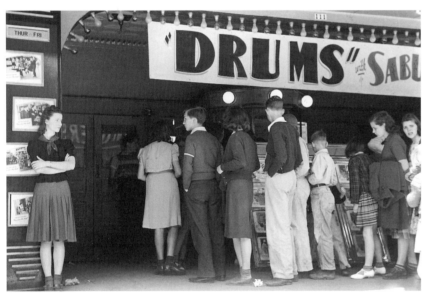

LENS-024

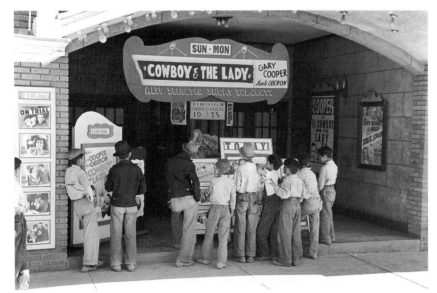

LENS-025

LENS-023. Teatro Nacional, 819 West Commerce Street, San Antonio, Texas. 1,680 seats. Russell Lee, photographer, March, 1939. P&P, LC-USF33-012059-M5.

LENS-024. Augus Theatre, San Augustine, Texas. 410 seats. Russell Lee, photographer, April, 1939. P&P, LC-USF33-012141-M3.

LENS-025. Granada Theatre, Alpine, Texas. 1,000 seats. Russell Lee, photographer, May, 1939. P&P, LC-USF33-012208-M1.

Russell Lee made an editorial statement about truancy as he photographed these schoolchildren going to the-movies.

LENS-026. Unidentified theater, New Iberia, Louisiana. Russell Lee, photographer, November, 1938. P&P, LC-USF33-011877-M1.

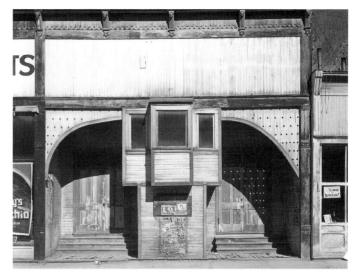

LENS-027. Fox Theatre, 27 South Cascade Avenue, Montrose, Colorado. 789 seats. Russell Lee, photographer, September, 1940. P&P, LC-USF34-037630-D.

LENS-028. Star (Gem, Lode) Theatre, 1309 Greene Street, Silverton, Colorado. Opened 1919; building constructed 1909; 296 seats. Russell Lee, photographer, September, 1940. P&P, LC-USF34-037751-D.

LENS-029. Shasta Theatre, 303 Central Valley Street, Shasta Lake City, California. 377 seats. Russell Lee, photographer, November, 1940. P&P, LC-USF34-038090-D.

LENS-030. Earl Carroll Theatre, Sunset Boulevard, Hollywood, California. Opened 1938. Russell Lee, photographer, April, 1942. P&P, LC-USW3-022818-E.

LENS-031

LENS-032

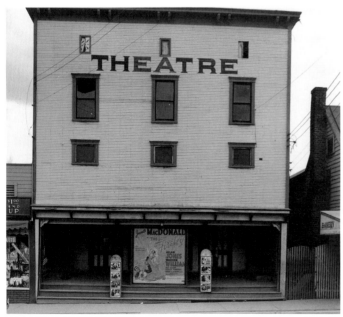

LENS-033

LENS-034

LENS-031. Unidentified theater, Washington, D.C. John Vachon, photographer, April, 1937. P&P, LC-USF33-001063-M3.

LENS-032. Unidentified theater, Washington, D.C. John Vachon, photographer, April, 1937. P&P, LC-USF33-001065-M5.

LENS-033. Ideal Theatre, Romney, West Virginia. 300 seats. John Vachon, photographer, March, 1938. P&P, LC-USF34-008306-E.

LENS-034. Lincoln Music Hall (Ninth Street Opera House, Academy of Music, Orpheum, Strand Theatre), 401 Ninth Street NW, Washington, D.C. Opened 1889; 1,148 seats; Appleton P. Clark Jr., architect. John Vachon, photographer, June, 1938. P&P, LC-USF33-001010-M1.

LENS-035. Lincoln Music Hall (Ninth Street Opera House, Academy of Music, Orpheum, Strand Theatre), 401 Ninth Street NW, Washington, D.C. Opened 1889; 1,148 seats; Appleton P. Clark Jr., architect. John Vachon, photographer, June, 1938. P&P, LC-USF33-001010-M5.

The night crew works to change posters at the venerable Strand.

LENS-036. Bijou Theatre, 30 East Fifth Street, Cincinnati, Ohio. Opened July 1908. 290 seats. John Vachon, photographer, October, 1938. P&P, LC-USF33-T01-001218-M5.

LENS-037. Unidentified theatre, Hillsborough, North Carolina. John Vachon, photographer, April, 1938. P&P, LC-USF33-001086-M4.

LENS-038

LENS-039

LENS-040

LENS-038. Paramount Theatre, 222 East Fifth Street, North Platte, Nebraska. 1,192 seats. John Vachon, photographer, October, 1938. P&P, LC-USF33-001327-M1.

LENS-039. Manos Theatre, Davis Avenue, Elkins, West Virginia. 1,008 seats. John Vachon, photographer, June, 1939. P&P, LC-USF33-001390-M3.

LENS-040. Hippodrome Theatre, 201 Davis Avenue, Elkins, West Virginia. 648 seats. John Vachon, photographer, June, 1939. P&P, LC-USF33-001390-M5.

LENS-041. Greendale Theatre, 5639 Broad Street, Greendale, Wisconsin. Opened ca. 1936; 600 seats. John Vachon, photographer, September, 1939. P&P, LC-USF34-060121-D.

LENS-042. Royal Theatre, 709 Vine Street, Cincinnati, Ohio. Opened ca. 1910; 281 seats. John Vachon, photographer, September, 1939. P&P, LC-USF33-001631-M2.

LENS-043. World Playhouse, 410 South Michigan Avenue, Chicago, Illinois. 400 seats. John Vachon, photographer, July, 1940. P&P, LC-USF33-001907-M1.

LENS-041

LENS-042

LENS-043

LENS-044

LENS-046

LENS-045

LENS-044. Greenbelt Theatre, 129 Centerway, Greenbelt, Maryland. Opened September 21, 1938; 590 seats; Reginald S. Wadsworth and Douglas D. Ellington, architects. John Vachon, photographer, September, 1940. P&P, LC-USF34-065871-D.

LENS-045. Monroe Theatre, 59 West Monroe Street, Chicago, Illinois. Opened 1900; 950 seats; W. Carbys Zimmerman, architect. John Vachon, photographer, July, 1940. P&P, LC-USF33-001965-M3.

LENS-046. Temple Theatre, 203 North Washington Street, Saginaw, Michigan. Opened 1927; 2,239 seats. John Vachon, photographer, August, 1941. P&P, LC-USF34-063871-D.

LENS-047

LENS-048

LENS-047. Glades Theatre, Moore Haven, Florida. 200 seats. Marion Post Wolcott, photographer, January, 1939. P&P, LC-USF34-050671-E.

LENS-048. Scottish Rite Auditorium (Federal Theatre), 417 NW Third Street, Miami, Florida. Opened March 12, 1924; 1,100 seats; Kiehael & Elliott, architects. Marion Post Wolcott, photographer, January, 1939. P&P, LC-USF34-050774-E.

LENS-049. Palace Theatre, Beale Street, Memphis, Tennessee. 1,200 seats. Marion Post Wolcott, photographer, October, 1939. P&P, LC-USF33-030639-M3.

LENS-050. Ritz Theatre, Starke, Florida. 280 seats. Marion Post Wolcott, photographer, December, 1940. P&P, LC-USF34-056721-D.

An Army transport vehicle parks in front of the newly remodeled theater in Starke, a boomtown near Camp Blanding.

LENS-049

LENS-050

LENS-051

LENS-052

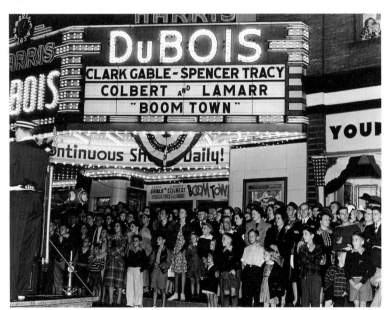

LENS-053

LENS-054

LENS-051. State Theatre, 320 South Salisbury Street, Raleigh, North Carolina. 1,199 seats. Jack Delano, photographer, May, 1940. P&P, LC-USF33-020504-M4.

LENS-052. Hollywood Theatre, Carrboro, North Carolina. Jack Delano, photographer, May, 1940. P&P, LC-USF34-040676-D.

Carrboro became desolate when its only industry—textiles—went dormant.

LENS-053. DuBois (Harris) Theatre, 8 North Brady Street; DuBois, Pennsylvania. 581 seats. Jack Delano, photographer, September, 1940. P&P, LC-USF34-041221-D.

Spectators at a Labor Day parade.

LENS-054. Unidentified theater, Beaver Falls, Pennsylvania. Jack Delano, photographer, January, 1941. P&P, LC-USF34-043157-D.

LENS-055. Hazelwood Theatre, 4921 Second Avenue, Pittsburgh, Pennsylvania. 600 seats. Jack Delano, photographer, January, 1941. P&P, LC-USF34-043164-D.

LENS-056. Greenland Theatre, Main Street, Greensboro, Georgia. 750 seats. Jack Delano, photographer, June, 1941. P&P, LC-USF33-020956-M3.

LENS-057. Unidentified theater, Western Avenue, Blue Island, Illinois. Jack Delano, photographer, February, 1943. P&P, LC-USW3-017010-E.

LENS-058

4-059

LENS-060

LENS-061

LENS-058. Coosa Theatre, 20 North Seventeenth Avenue, Childersburg, Alabama. 943 seats. Jack Delano, photographer, 1941. P&P, LC-USF34-044400-D.

Workers construct the first permanent movie theater in Childersburg, a war-time boomtown near a DuPont gunpowder plant.

4-059. Orpheum (Lafayette, Shubert) Theatre, 153 West Lafayette Street, Detroit, Michigan. Opened September 7, 1914; 1,489 seats; Smith, Hinchman & Grylls, architects. Arthur S. Siegel, photographer, July, 1942. P&P, LC-USF34-110172-C.

LENS-060. Mid-City Theatre, 1223 Ninth Street NW, Washington, D.C. Opened 1913; 250 seats; Samuel R. Turner, architect. Gordon Parks, photographer, January, 1943. P&P, LC-USW3-013836-C.

LENS-061. Terminal Theatre, Market Street, Upper Darby, Pennsylvania. Simon & Simon, architects. Paul Vanderbilt, photographer, summer, 1936. P&P, LC-USW3-056177-E.

LENS-062

LENS-063

LENS-062. State Theatre (Cine I, Cine II), 1118 Elm Street, Manchester, New Hampshire. Opened 1929; 2,130 seats. Edwin Locke, photographer, September, 1937. P&P, LC-USF33-004250-M3.

LENS-063. State Theatre (Cine I, Cine II), 1118 Elm Street, Manchester, New Hampshire. Opened 1929; 2,130 seats. Edwin Locke, photographer, September, 1937. P&P, LC-USF33-004250-M1.

LENS-064. Empress Theatre, 416 Ninth Street NW, Washington, D.C. Opened March 20, 1910; 382 seats; B. Frank Meyers, architect. David Myers, photographer, July, 1939. P&P, LC-USF34-015943-C.

LENS-064

LENS-065

LENS-066

LENS-067

LENS-068

LENS-065. Bijou Theatre, 318 Main Street, Holyoke, Massachusetts. 1,255 seats. John Collier Jr., photographer, October, 1941. P&P, LC-USF34-080990-E.

LENS-066. Unidentified theater, Middle River, Maryland. John Collier Jr., photographer, August, 1943. P&P, LC-USW3-036085-C.

Middle River was a community built by the Farm Security Administration for wartime workers at the Glen L. Martin aircraft plant near Baltimore.

LENS-067. Greenbelt Theatre, 129 Centerway, Greenbelt, Maryland. Opened September 21, 1938; 590 seats; Reginald S. Wadsworth and Douglas D. Ellington, architects. Marjory Collins, photographer, May/June, 1942. P&P, LC-USW3-003454-C.

LENS-068. Paramount Theatre, 1501 Broadway, New York, New York. Opened November 19, 1926; 3,364 seats; C. W. & George L. Rapp, architects. Marjory Collins, photographer, September, 1942. P&P, LC-USW3-007679-D.

LENS-069

LENS-071

LENS-070

LENS-069. New Theatre, 210 West Lexington Street, Baltimore, Maryland. Opened December 17, 1910; 1,400 seats; A. Lowther Forrest, architect. Marjory Collins, photographer, April, 1943. P&P, LC-USW3-022132-D.

LENS-070. Varieties (Variety) Theatre, 110–112 Third Avenue, New York, New York. Opened 1914; 594 seats; Louis A. Sheinart, architect. Marjory Collins, photographer, September, 1942. P&P, LC-USW3-007684-D.

LENS-071. Circle Theatre (Annapolis Theatre of Magic), Annapolis, Maryland. 824 seats; Henry P. Hopkins, architect. Lieutenant Whitman, photographer, July, 1942. P&P, LC-USW3-005100-E.

LENS-072. Bundy Theatre, 3414 Pico Boulevard, Santa Monica, California. 912 seats. Ann Rosener, photographer, February, 1943. P&P, LC-USW3-035297-D.

The Bundy remained open all night to attract workers from large aircraft plants nearby.

LENS-072

THEATERS FOR THE MODERN ERA

A PALATIAL ENVIRONMENT, once symbolic of a prosperity that seemed within reach, became a bitter reminder of need during the Depression. In this climate a new architectural movement began to achieve acceptance: Modernism. The architectural modernist eschewed fantasy and historical recall, seeking, rather, to create minimalist buildings. To a modernist designer, a building was seen less as a decorative object than as a means of containing and manipulating space. The enclosure should neither intrude upon nor distract from the building's function. Light should be abundant, but it should come surreptitiously, from tiny apertures in the ceiling. Glass was the material of choice. When solid, walls might be finished in the rarest of materials, but had to remain smooth, without applied decoration. Indeed, an early theorist of Modernism likened ornament to crime!

Modernism did not square well with theater architecture. Both designers and patrons were accustomed to environments profuse with eclectic ornamentation, extensions of the fantasy presented on stage or screen. To accommodate the new style, theater designers initially retained the overall movie palace form, but compromised the decoration, replacing historic recall with smoothly modeled forms and surfaces. The modernist era opened with theatrical monuments on America's coasts. Both the Paramount in California (7-001–7-015) and Radio City Music Hall in New York (7-016–7-023) were in every way movie palaces, but evoked no historical style. These two theaters served as models for the many new cinemas that settled into America's towns and city neighborhoods. Porcelain enamel facades with integral neon lettering and sleek, suavely curved interior forms became the design signatures of the smaller movie houses. Stages and pipe organs were things of the past as the theater environment moved from grandeur to simplicity. To maintain continuity with tradition, designers abstracted the stage curtain, extending it beyond the proscenium to fully surround the auditorium.

When New York's Beekman Theatre (7-061–7-064) opened in 1952, New York Times film critic Bosley Crowther praised it as "tastefully planned and decorated in sleek but not ostentatious style, with plenty of room for lounging, having coffee, and stretching the legs, as well as for freedom of passage in and out of the widely spaced rows." He contrasted it with the "older downtown and neighborhood 'barns,'" which he considered "architecturally passé and dull." In the new order patrons would come to see the show, not the showplace.

7-001. Paramount Theatre, 2025 Broadway, Oakland, California. Opened December 16, 1931; 3,408 seats; J. R. Miller and Timothy Pflueger, architects. Gabriel Moulin Studios, photographer, 1932. P&P, HABS,CAL,1-OAK,9-17.

The colorful tile facade and sleek stainless steel signage stood out in eye-opening contrast against downtown Oakland's stock of period-inspired buildings and street fixtures.

7-002. Paramount Theatre, 2025 Broadway, Oakland, California. Opened December 16, 1931; 3,408 seats; J. R. Miller and Timothy Pflueger, architects. Jack E. Boucher, photographer, 1975. P&P, HABS,CAL,1-OAK,9-5.

On the Paramount's facade, the spirit of cinema, a giant puppeteer, controls a varied troupe of performers. The colorful tile mosaic was designed jointly by architect Timothy Pflueger and artist Gerald Fitzgerald.

7-003. Paramount Theatre, 2025 Broadway, Oakland, California. Opened December 16, 1931; 3,408 seats; J. R. Miller and Timothy Pflueger, architects. Gabriel Moulin Studios, photographer, 1932. P&P, HABS,CAL,1-OAK,9-19.

The black and silver outdoor vestibule was lighted with some 2,860 glittering bulbs.

7-004. Paramount Theatre, 2025 Broadway, Oakland, California. Opened December 16, 1931; 3,408 seats; J. R. Miller and Timothy Pflueger, architects. Jack E. Boucher, photographer, 1975. P&P, HABS,CAL,1-OAK,9-9.

If the entry was severely toned, the lobby was anything but. Above a high dado of polished black granite, glass panels in the side walls glowed with golden light while the complex grillage of the ceiling was backlighted in green. Over the entry doors a great glass sculpture, the Fountain of Light, shone in brilliant gold (7-005). The architects claimed that the resemblance to Buddha was totally accidental.

7-005

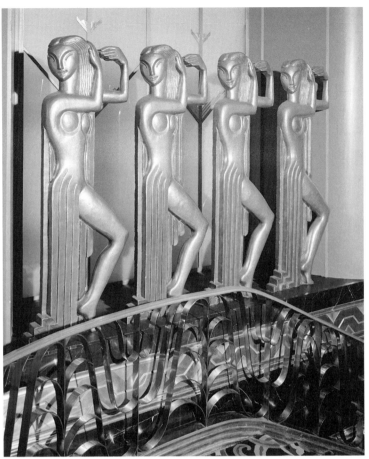

7-007

7-005. Paramount Theatre, 2025 Broadway, Oakland, California. Opened December 16, 1931; 3,408 seats; J. R. Miller and Timothy Pflueger, architects. Jack E. Boucher, photographer, 1975. P&P, HABS,CAL,1-OAK,9-10.

7-006. Paramount Theatre, 2025 Broadway, Oakland, California. Opened December 16, 1931; 3,408 seats; J. R. Miller and Timothy Pflueger, architects. Gabriel Moulin Studios, photographer, 1932. P&P, HABS,CAL,1-OAK,9-21.

The Paramount's auditorium combined gilded wall panels in elaborate relief, a shiny, backlit ceiling filigree, and a richly embroidered tomato-red main curtain.

7-007. Paramount Theatre, 2025 Broadway, Oakland, California. Opened December 16, 1931; 3,408 seats; J. R. Miller and Timothy Pflueger, architects. Jack E. Boucher, photographer, 1975. P&P, HABS,CAL,1-OAK,9-11.

7-006

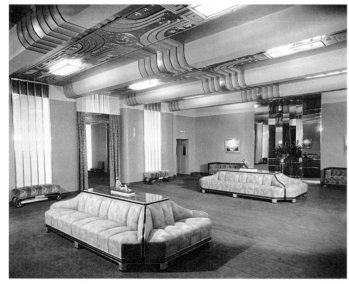

7-008

7-009

7-008. Paramount Theatre, 2025 Broadway, Oakland, California. Opened December 16, 1931; 3,408 seats; J. R. Miller and Timothy Pflueger, architects. Gabriel Moulin Studios, photographer, 1932. P&P, HABS,CAL,1-OAK,9-24.

The Paramount's complement of lounges and audience comfort spaces displayed great visual variety. In place of historically inspired forms, the rooms were ornamented with smooth panels of rare woods and layered gilding that played against colored walls.

7-009. Women's lounge, lower level, Paramount Theatre, 2025 Broadway, Oakland, California. Opened December 16, 1931; 3,408 seats; J. R. Miller and Timothy Pflueger, architects. Gabriel Moulin Studios, photographer, 1932. P&P, HABS,CAL,1-OAK,9-25.

7-010

7-010. Women's smoking room, lower level, Paramount Theatre, 2025 Broadway, Oakland, California. Opened December 16, 1931; 3,408 seats; J. R. Miller and Timothy Pflueger, architects. Gabriel Moulin Studios, photographer, 1932. P&P, HABS,CAL,1-OAK,9-26.

In the ladies' smoking room a mural by Charles Stafford Duncan depicted a group of handsomely dressed women picnicking under a seaside tree.

7-011. Lounge, mezzanine, Paramount Theatre, 2025 Broadway, Oakland, California. Opened December 16, 1931; 3,408 seats; J. R. Miller and Timothy Pflueger, architects. Gabriel Moulin Studios, photographer, 1932. P&P, HABS,CAL,1-OAK,9-28.

7-011

7-012

7-013

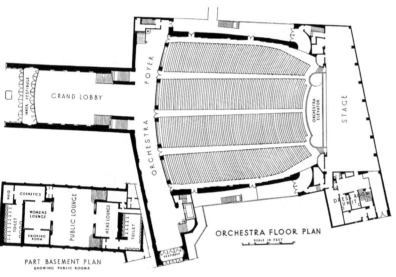

GRAND LOBBY

ORCHESTRA FOYER

STAGE

ORCHESTRA ELEVATOR

COSMETICS

WOMENS LOUNGE

PUBLIC LOUNGE

MENS LOUNGE

SMOKING ROOM

TOILET

TOILET

DRESSING ROOM

ORCHESTRA FLOOR PLAN
SCALE IN FEET

PART BASEMENT PLAN
SHOWING PUBLIC ROOMS

7-014

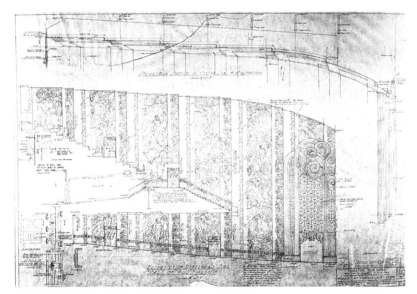

7-015

7-012. Women's cosmetic room, mezzanine, Paramount Theatre, 2025 Broadway, Oakland, California. Opened December 16, 1931; 3,408 seats; J. R. Miller and Timothy Pflueger, architects. Gabriel Moulin Studios, photographer, 1932. P&P, HABS,CAL,1-OAK,9-29.

7-013. Men's lounge, mezzanine, Paramount Theatre, 2025 Broadway, Oakland, California. Opened December 16, 1931; 3,408 seats; J. R. Miller and Timothy Pflueger, architects. Gabriel Moulin Studios, photographer, 1932. P&P, HABS,CAL,1-OAK,9-30.

7-014. Paramount Theatre, 2025 Broadway, Oakland, California. Opened December 16, 1931; 3,408 seats; J. R. Miller and Timothy Pflueger, architects; from *Motion Picture Herald*, March 12, 1932. P&P, HABS,CAL,1-OAK,9-31.

Adapted to an unusual and irregular site, the Paramount's plan provided for incoming audiences to wait in the grand lobby while the previous audience exited on the side street. As might be expected in a cinema of this date, the stage was less than commodious.

7-015. Paramount Theatre, 2025 Broadway, Oakland, California. Opened December 16, 1931; 3,408 seats; J. R. Miller and Timothy Pflueger, architects. P&P, HABS,CAL,1-OAK,9-38.

The Miller & Pflueger office carefully detailed the elaborate relief work of the auditorium walls and the suspended ceiling grillage whose concealed lighting filled the auditorium with a variety of rich colors.

7-016

7-017

7-016. International (Radio City) Music Hall, 1260 Sixth Avenue, New York, New York. Opened December 27, 1932; 5,901 seats; Associated Architects (Reinhard & Hofmeister; Corbett, Harrison & MacMurray; Raymond Hood, Godley & Fouilhoux), architects; Edward Durrell Stone, design architect; Donald Deskey, interiors coordinator. Metropolitan Photo Service, photographer, April 11, 1939. P&P, NYWTS-SUBJ/GEOG–Theatrical–Theatres–Radio City Music Hall–Exteriors.

Radio City Music Hall's restrained exterior was marked only by three great circular plaques by sculptor Leo Friedlander. Inside, the theater's lobbies and lounges provided a showcase for such prominent art deco artists as Ezra Winter, Stuart Davis, Georgia O'Keeffe, Ruth Reeves, Yasuo Kuniyoshi, William Zorach, and Robert Laurent.

7-017. International (Radio City) Music Hall, 1260 Sixth Avenue, New York, New York. Opened December 27, 1932; 5,901 seats. Associated Architects (Reinhard & Hofmeister; Corbett, Harrison & MacMurray; Raymond Hood, Godley & Fouilhoux), architects; Edward Durrell Stone, design architect; Donald Deskey, interiors coordinator. Samuel H. Gottscho, photographer, December 9, 1932. P&P, LC-G612-T-19439.

The main lobby is characterized by smoothly curved balconies, a sweeping stair, gilded mirrors in tomato-red walls, and spectacularly long chandeliers. The stairway wall features Ezra Winter's 40-foot-high mural variously titled *The Fountain of Youth* and *The Author of Life* (7-018).

7-018. International (Radio City) Music Hall, 1260 Sixth Avenue, New York, New York. Opened December 27, 1932; 5,901 seats. Associated Architects (Reinhard & Hofmeister; Corbett, Harrison & MacMurray; Raymond Hood, Godley & Fouilhoux), architects; Edward Durrell Stone, design architect; Donald Deskey, interiors coordinator. Samuel H. Gottscho, photographer, December 9, 1932. P&P, LC-G612-T-19439.

7-018

7-019

7-019. International (Radio City) Music Hall, 1260 Sixth Avenue, New York, New York. Opened December 27, 1932; 5,901 seats; Associated Architects (Reinhard & Hofmeister; Corbett, Harrison & MacMurray; Raymond Hood, Godley & Fouilhoux), architects; Edward Durrell Stone, design architect; Donald Deskey, interiors coordinator. Samuel H. Gottscho, photographer, December 24, 1932. P&P, LC-G612-T-19491.

Sculptor Robert Laurent's *Goose Girl* highlights the first mezzanine.

7-020. International (Radio City) Music Hall, 1260 Sixth Avenue, New York, New York. Opened December 27, 1932; 5,901 seats; Associated Architects (Reinhard & Hofmeister; Corbett, Harrison & MacMurray; Raymond Hood, Godley & Fouilhoux), architects; Edward Durrell Stone, design architect; Donald Deskey, interiors coordinator. Samuel H. Gottscho, photographer, December 7, 1932. P&P, LC-G612-T-19401.

The Music Hall's auditorium is said to have been conceived as a tropical sunrise. Painted in a neutral beige, the arches that radiate from the great stage take on the variable colors of the concealed lighting. The curtain rises in independently controlled swagged lifts. Twin Wurlitzer organ consoles slide out from openings on either side of the stage.

7-020

7-021. International (Radio City) Music Hall, 1260 Sixth Avenue, New York, New York. Opened December 27, 1932; 5,901 seats; Associated Architects (Reinhard & Hofmeister; Corbett, Harrison & MacMurray; Raymond Hood, Godley & Fouilhoux), architects; Edward Durrell Stone, design architect; Donald Deskey, interiors coordinator. Samuel H. Gottscho, photographer, December 17, 1932. P&P, LC-G612-T-19459.

Grille-like openings in the ceiling may be independently backlighted to match or contrast with the tone of the main ceiling. The stepped side stages act as alternative performance platforms that facilitate processional entry to the main stage (7-022).

7-022. International (Radio City) Music Hall, 1260 Sixth Avenue, New York, New York. Opened December 27, 1932; 5,901 seats; Associated Architects (Reinhard & Hofmeister; Corbett, Harrison & MacMurray; Raymond Hood, Godley & Fouilhoux), architects; Edward Durrell Stone, design architect; Donald Deskey, interiors coordinator. Samuel H. Gottscho, photographer, December 17, 1932. P&P, LC-G612-T-19455.

7-023. International (Radio City) Music Hall, 1260 Sixth Avenue, New York, New York. Opened December 27, 1932; 5,901 seats; Associated Architects (Reinhard & Hofmeister; Corbett, Harrison & MacMurray; Raymond Hood, Godley & Fouilhoux), architects; Edward Durrell Stone, design architect; Donald Deskey, interiors coordinator. Kenneth Russell Chamberlain, artist, ca. 1935. P&P, unprocessed item PR 13 CN 1993:004.7.

Artist Kenneth Russell Chamberlain captured a view of the Rockettes that ordinarily would be seen only from the theater's lofty spotlight gallery.

7-024

7-025

7-026

7-024. Leimert Park (Leimert, Vision) Theatre, 3314 West Forty-third Place, Los Angeles, California. Opened 1931; 1,185 seats; Morgan, Walls & Clements, architects. Marvin Rand, photographer, ca. 1975. P&P, HABS,CAL,19-LOSAN,38-1.

The Leimert Park's needle-like tower sign represented a distinctive Californian style.

7-025. Academy Theatre, 3141 West Manchester Boulevard, Inglewood, California. Opened 1939; 1,156 seats; S. Charles Lee, architect. Marvin Rand, photographer, ca. 1975. P&P, HABS,CAL,19-INGWO,2-2.

7-026. Puck Theatre (project). Winold Reiss, artist, ca. 1935. P&P, unprocessed item PR 13 CN 1990:038 (folder 28); LC-USZC4-7832 (color).

Winold Reiss's proposals for an unbuilt theater clearly show the way in which smooth, carefully proportioned planes in bold and interesting textures and colors supplanted period-derived sculptural forms in theater decoration.

7-027. Puck Theatre (project). Winold Reiss, artist, ca. 1935. P&P, unprocessed item PR 13 CN 1990:038 (folder 28); LC-USZC4-4842 (color).

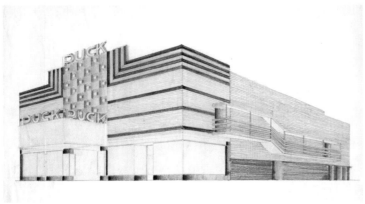

7-027

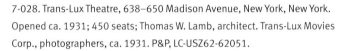

7-028

7-028. Trans-Lux Theatre, 638–650 Madison Avenue, New York, New York. Opened ca. 1931; 450 seats; Thomas W. Lamb, architect. Trans-Lux Movies Corp., photographers, ca. 1931. P&P, LC-USZ62-62051.

A Trans-Lux Theater was less a destination for an evening's entertainment than a comfortable place in which to pass an hour or so between downtown errands and appointments. Admission was cheap and the show was brief—no feature picture, only a newsreel and a travelogue or two. The theater's sleek design—even its sign—proclaimed the new age of modernity. Its projection technique was as radical as its shining surfaces. To achieve a glare-free image, the projector was located behind the screen. The light passing through the screen gave the theater the Trans-Lux name. The turnstile entry (7-031) was as mechanical, impersonal, and up-to-date as the automat down the street.

7-029. Trans-Lux Theatre, 638–650 Madison Avenue, New York, New York. Opened ca. 1931; 450 seats; Thomas W. Lamb, architect. Trans-Lux Movies Corp., photographers, ca. 1931. P&P, LC-USZ62-116406.

7-030. Trans-Lux Theatre, 638–650 Madison Avenue, New York, New York. Opened ca. 1931; 450 seats; Thomas W. Lamb, architect. Trans-Lux Movies Corp., photographers, ca. 1931. P&P, LC-USZ62-98374.

7-031. Trans-Lux Theatre, 638–650 Madison Avenue, New York, New York. Opened ca. 1931; 450 seats; Thomas W. Lamb, architect. Trans-Lux Movies Corp., photographers, ca. 1931. P&P, LC-USZ62-90297.

7-031

7-032

7-032. New Grand (Roxy) Theatre, 106 South Main Street, Brigham City, Utah. Opened December 25, 1932; 485 seats. John Enlow, photographer, November 6, 1980. P&P, HABS, UTAH,2-BRICI,4-2.

The New Grand was built on the site of nineteenth-century Rosenbaum Hall. Its late-art-deco facade was added in 1949.

7-033. Kamoi Theatre, Ala Malama Avenue and Kamoi Streets, Kaunakakai (Molokai), Hawaii. Opened July 25, 1939. Jim Kolva, photographer, March, 1988. P&P, HABS,HI,5-KAUKA,1-4.

Theater design in America's Pacific island territory came from different cultural sources and accommodated vastly different climate conditions than the eurocentric buildings of the mainland. The Kamoi was a simply built wooden structure without basement or ornamentation. Its interior, shown just before the theater's demolition (7-035), was as simple as the outside.

7-034. Kamoi Theatre, Ala Malama Avenue and Kamoi Streets, Kaunakakai (Molokai), Hawaii. Opened July 25, 1939. Jim Kolva, photographer, March, 1988. P&P, HABS,HI,5-KAUKA,1-6.

7-035. Kamoi Theatre, Ala Malama Avenue and Kamoi Streets, Kaunakakai (Molokai), Hawaii. Opened July 25, 1939. Jim Kolva, photographer, March, 1988. P&P, HABS,HI,5-KAUKA,1-11.

7-033

7-034

7-035

7-036. Beach Theatre, 430 Lincoln Road, Miami Beach, Florida. Opened 1941; 1,800 seats; Weed & Reeder, architects; Pereira & Pereira, design consultants. Gottscho-Schleisner, Inc., photographers, March 8, 1941. P&P, LC-G612-T-39560.

In a time before even a single Miami Beach hotel room contained a television set, a stroll along Lincoln Road might take a visitor to the movies. The Beach Theatre's multiscalloped marquee and sidewalk plantings provided a festive and enticing invitation. Visible through the wide glass doorway, the polished, marble-clad vestibule hinted at the posh surroundings within.

7-037. Beach Theatre, 430 Lincoln Road, Miami Beach, Florida. Opened 1941; 1,800 seats; Weed & Reeder, architects; Pereira & Pereira, design consultants. Gottscho-Schleisner, Inc., photographers, March 8, 1941. P&P, LC-G612-T-39572.

7-038. Beach Theatre, 430 Lincoln Road, Miami Beach, Florida. Opened 1941; 1,800 seats; Weed & Reeder, architects; Pereira & Pereira, design consultants. Gottscho-Schleisner, Inc., photographers, March 8, 1941. P&P, LC-G612-T-39564.

Not unlike the lobbies of nearby hotels, the Beach's entry was a place of luxurious spaciousness. Its stairway swept gently and dramatically upward past mirrored walls and screens of tropical foliage.

7-039

7-041

7-040

7-039. Beach Theatre, 430 Lincoln Road, Miami Beach, Florida. Opened 1941; 1,800 seats; Weed & Reeder, architects; Pereira & Pereira, design consultants. Gottscho-Schleisner, Inc., photographers, March 8, 1941. P&P, LC-G612-T-39568.

7-040. Beach Theatre, 430 Lincoln Road, Miami Beach, Florida. Opened 1941; 1,800 seats; Weed & Reeder, architects; Pereira & Pereira, design consultants. Gottscho-Schleisner, Inc., photographers, March 8, 1941. P&P, LC-G612-T-39562.

The lobby's theatricality was but a prelude to the auditorium, where the audience sat within textured walls, swirling plaster ornament, and dramatic hidden lighting.

7-041. Beach Theatre, 430 Lincoln Road, Miami Beach, Florida. Opened 1941; 1,800 seats; Weed & Reeder, architects; Pereira & Pereira, design consultants. Gottscho-Schleisner, Inc., photographers, March 8, 1941. P&P, LC-G612-T-39574.

A shell-like drinking fountain topped by an aquarium provided a touch of novelty and elegance in the upstairs lounge.

7-042

7-043

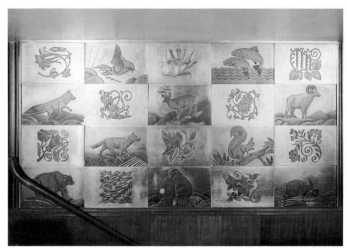

7-044

7-042. Fourth Avenue Theatre (Lathrop's Showhouse), 630 West Fourth Avenue, Anchorage, Alaska. Opened May 31, 1947; 750 seats; B. Marcus Priteca, architect. Jet Lowe, photographer, July, 1985. P&P, HABS,AK,2-ANCH,1-7; P&P, HABS, AK, 2-ANCH, 1-8 (color).

Six years in the building, this highly developed and sophisticated theater brought to Anchorage a monument of permanence that stood in marked contrast to its frontier town surroundings. The facade's yellow and orange panels imparted a warm glow to the streetscape, while the interior, with its South American walnut woodwork, murals of Mt. McKinley and native wildlife, and relief panels depicting Alaskan commerce and industry, was a showplace of community pride.

7-043. Fourth Avenue Theatre (Lathrop's Showhouse), 630 West Fourth Avenue, Anchorage, Alaska. Opened May 31, 1947; 750 seats; B. Marcus Priteca, architect. Jet Lowe, photographer, July, 1985. P&P, HABS,AK,2-ANCH,1-3.

7-044. Fourth Avenue Theatre (Lathrop's Showhouse), 630 West Fourth Avenue, Anchorage, Alaska. Opened May 31, 1947; 750 seats; B. Marcus Priteca, architect. Jet Lowe, photographer, July, 1985. P&P, HABS,AK,2-ANCH,1-4.

The theater's founder, August Lathrop, called this "the children's mural." Its depictions of Alaskan wildlife are formed of layered Masonite with a gilded and glazed finish.

7-045. Fourth Avenue Theatre (Lathrop's Showhouse), 630 West Fourth Avenue, Anchorage, Alaska. Opened May 31, 1947; 750 seats; B. Marcus Priteca, architect. Jet Lowe, photographer, July, 1985. P&P, HABS,AK,2-ANCH,1-5.

Graceful architectural forms and extraordinary height give a sense of monumentality to this midsized auditorium. Features include a sky-blue ceiling with painted stars and an illuminated Big Dipper, Lucite chandeliers, and large murals representing old and new Alaska that flank the stage.

7-045

7-046

7-047

7-048

7-049

7-046 Cheverly Theatre (Publick Playhouse), 5445 Landover Road, Cheverly, Maryland. Opened 1947; 940 seats; John Eberson, architect. Theodor Horydczak, photographer, ca. 1950. P&P, LC-H814-0725-036.

With the passing of the fantasy palaces, John Eberson and his son Drew began to work in a new style, a suavely cursive version of art deco. Subtly contrasting tones of red brick and integrated illuminated lettering distinguished the Cheverly's boldly geometrical exterior.

7-047. Amenia Theatre, Amenia, New York. 250 seats. P&P, US SUBJECT FILE-THEATERS.

This designer borrowed heavily from history to evoke the Dutch history of the tiny Hudson River Valley town of Amenia.

7-048. Community Theatre, Hudson, New York. 1,500 seats; William I. Hohauser, Inc., architect. Gottscho-Schleisner, Inc., photographers, October 12, 1939. P&P, LC-G612-T-36240.

The modern era did not always evoke modernist architecture. Hudson's Community Theatre borrowed the portico design from Mount Vernon to create an eighteenth-century image in this historic river town.

7-049. Koster's (Niobrara) Theatre, Elm Street, Niobrara, Nebraska. Opened July 1930; 240 seats. Sam Amato, photographer, October, 1977. P&P, HABS,NEB,54-NIOB,6-2.

Far removed from the dream palaces or even the sleekly sophisticated neighborhood cinemas of the great cities, residents of small-town America found amusement in simple surroundings. Koster's Theatre so closely resembles the rest of its storefront block that its purpose is hard to identify. Its interior is entirely straightforward: straight rows of seats, tiny lobby, no stage, no restrooms, no ornamentation. It was well equipped, wired for sound, and air cooled. Remarkably, when it opened, its 240 seats could hold fully a third of Niobrara's population.

7-050. Poinciana Plaza Playhouse, 70 Royal Poinciana Plaza, Palm Beach, Florida. Opened 1958; 878 seats; John L. Volk, architect. Gottscho-Schleisner, Inc., photographers, January 9, 1959. P&P, LC-G613-73291.

In 1893 Henry Flagler's sprawling Royal Poinciana Hotel established Palm Beach as a premier resort and Poinciana Plaza, built on the hotel's site, was designed to continue its spirit of gilt-edged elegance.

7-051. Poinciana Plaza Playhouse, 70 Royal Poinciana Plaza, Palm Beach, Florida. Opened 1958; 878 seats; John L. Volk, architect. Gottscho-Schleisner, Inc., photographers, January 9, 1959. P&P, LC-G613-73297.

7-052. Poinciana Plaza Playhouse, 70 Royal Poinciana Plaza, Palm Beach, Florida. Opened 1958; 878 seats; John L. Volk, architect. Gottscho-Schleisner, Inc., photographers, January 9, 1959. P&P, LC-G613-73299.

Colonnades along the sidewalls lend a touch of classical decoration to the Plaza's otherwise smooth-surfaced auditorium.

7-053. Poinciana Plaza Playhouse, 70 Royal Poinciana Plaza, Palm Beach, Florida. Opened 1958; 878 seats; John L. Volk, architect. Gottscho-Schleisner, Inc., photographers, January 9, 1959. P&P, LC-G613-73300.

A generously formed stage apron extends the performers' area into the audience. The curtain, with its dramatic double curve and swagged operation, is an ornament in its own right.

7-050

7-051

7-052

7-053

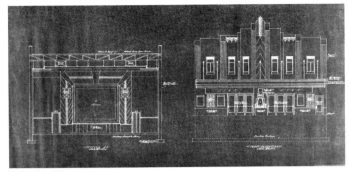

7-054

7-055

7-056

7-057

7-054. Circle Theatre, 2103 Pennsylvania Avenue NW, Washington, D.C. Opened March 1910; 479 seats; Alfred B. Mullett, architect; alterations 1935; 670 seats; Luther R. Ray, architect. Architect's blueprint, 1935. P&P, ADE-UNIT 2750, no. 8.

Built as an undistinguished neighborhood cinema, the Circle was enlarged and reconfigured into a respectable piece of late-art-deco design, a story shared by numerous theaters in urban neighborhoods across America.

7-055. Rainbo Theatre, 9217 Grand River Avenue, Detroit, Michigan. Opened 1938; 282 seats; C. Howard Crane, architect. Joe Clark, photographer, 1951. P&P, SSF - Motion picture theaters–Michigan–Detroit.

A modest endeavor by an architect who had designed some of America's greatest movie palaces (see 6-078 and 6-183), the Rainbo, with its multicolored sign, typified the small neighborhood theater type. The unconventional spelling of the theater's name reflects a desire for streamlining that was common during the early modernist decades.

7-056. Reality Theatre, South Main Street, Robertsdale, Pennsylvania. Opened December 23, 1948. Jet Lowe, photographer, fall, 1989. P&P, HABS,PA,31-RODA,10-1.

The Reality was the second theater to serve the company town of Robertsdale. In 1918, the Rockhill Iron & Coal Company opened the 425-seat Liberty Theatre, which burned in 1936. Its replacement was built over a decade later by developer Gene Yanni, a former company employee who had been paralyzed in a mine accident. Yanni explained that the theater's unusual name reflected that he had turned the town's seemingly impossible dream of a new theater into a reality. The vending machine in front of the box office reflected an updated reality in which ticket revenues were insufficient to operate the theater. The building later became a museum.

7-057. Viers Mill Theatre, 12202 Viers Mill Road, Silver Spring, Maryland. Opened August 3, 1950; 900 seats; Richard L. Parli, architect. Theodor Horydczak, photographer, ca. 1950. P&P, LC-H814-2631-001.

7-058. Arcade (Comedy, Studio) Theatre, 1931 Broadway, New York, New York. Opened 1948; 560 seats. Gottscho-Schleisner, Inc., photographers, September 28, 1948. P&P, LC-G612-53906.

The Arcade Theatre existed as early as 1903, when it was remodeled from an existing office building and music hall. Its last remodeling—in 1948, when it was renamed the Studio—made it into an intimate screening room for the exhibition of art films. The simply designed interior was given sophistication by the use of a stepped ceiling and angled panels that contrasted against printed wall surfaces. The austere atmosphere, devoid of ornament, lighting effects, curtain, or any other visual distraction, allowed filmgoers to devote their attention solely to the picture on the screen. Located in the down-at-heel neighborhood depicted in Leonard Bernstein and Stephen Sondheim's West Side Story, the Studio stood on the site later occupied by Avery Fisher Hall, in the Lincoln Center for the Performing Arts.

7-059. Arcade (Comedy, Studio) Theatre, 1931 Broadway, New York, New York. Opened 1948; 560 seats. Gottscho-Schleisner, Inc., photographers, September 28, 1948. P&P, LC-G612-53907.

7-060. Beekman Theatre, 1254 Second Avenue, New York, New York. Opened April 1952; Fellheimer & Wagner, architects, John J. McNamara, associate. Gottscho-Schleisner, Inc., photographers, April 30, 1952. P&P, LC-G613-61208.

From the outside, the Beekman, designed by John J. McNamara, a close associate of Thomas W. Lamb, was a work of well-proportioned simplicity. The brightly lit marquee and tall facade window recalled the cinema palaces of an earlier generation, as did the domed ceiling, exotic marble walls, and polished metal doors in the ticket vestibule. But within, the theater was a studied response to the evolving role of the cinema in the age of television. Built as a component of a large apartment development, it embodied a simple and informal elegance that positioned it as a communal living room. As at home, food and beverages were integral to entertainment. The theater's comfortable lounge seated up to seventy-five occupants, who were able to view the movie as they sipped their coffee.

7-058

7-059

7-060

7-061

7-062. Beekman Theatre, 1254 Second Avenue, New York, New York. Opened April 1952; Fellheimer & Wagner, architects, John J. McNamara, associate. Gottscho-Schleisner, Inc., photographers, April 25, 1952. P&P, LC-G613-61156.

At the Beekman tickets were purchased in a sleek foyer rather than a sidewalk booth.

7-062. Beekman Theatre, 1254 Second Avenue, New York, New York. Opened April 1952; Fellheimer & Wagner, architects, John J. McNamara, associate. Gottscho-Schleisner, Inc., photographers, April 25, 1952. P&P, LC-G613-61153.

The Beekman's auditorium achieved elegance through fine proportions and detailing. Elements of theatrical grandeur were abstracted. Curtains were skillfully combined with undulating wall panels and hidden lighting to recall the grand era of the movies. There even was a tiny stage apron.

7-063. Beekman Theatre, 1254 Second Avenue, New York, New York. Opened April 1952; Fellheimer & Wagner, architects, John J. McNamara, associate. Gottscho-Schleisner, Inc., photographers, April 25, 1952. P&P, LC-G613-61149.

Beekman patrons could enjoy coffee service in an elegantly informal gathering space. The lounge was situated under the elevated rear portion of auditorium seats. An observation window, just visible in the right wall, coincided with the auditorium's center aisle. Through it patrons were able to enjoy an unobstructed view of the screen.

7-062

7-063

7-064. Loew's Tower East (Seventy-second Street East) Theatre, 1230 Third Avenue, New York, New York. Opened 1962; 500 seats; Emery Roth & Sons, architects. Samuel H. Gottscho, photographer, October 14, 1962. P&P, LC-G613-78800.

7-065. Loew's Tower East (Seventy-second Street East) Theatre, 1230 Third Avenue, New York, New York. Opened 1962; 500 seats; Emery Roth & Sons, architects. Samuel H. Gottscho, photographer, October 14, 1962. P&P, LC-G613-78803.

7-066. Loew's Tower East (Seventy-second Street East) Theatre, 1230 Third Avenue, New York, New York. Opened 1962; 500 seats; Emery Roth & Sons, architects. Samuel H. Gottscho, photographer, October 14, 1962. P&P, LC-G613-78805.

7-064

7-065

7-066

SPECIAL-PURPOSE THEATERS

THEATERS AND AFRICAN-AMERICANS

As a nation of immigrants, America has had a rich heritage of ethnic theaters. New York City alone supported French, Italian, Chinese, and Yiddish playhouses, as well as numerous German, Bohemian, and other quasi-theatrical gathering halls. Attended primarily by homesick immigrants, each offered welcome to all who were conversant in their common tongue.

Even though almost every American came from someplace else, ethnicity never became fully transparent in American culture. Echoing sentiments heard on the street, performers in mainstream and ethnic theaters alike commonly poked fun at immigrants' dress, accents, or behavior, even though many of the performers themselves were still close to their own foreign roots. Making no effort to conceal their Jewishness, Joe Weber and Lew Fields based their famous act upon characterizing non-Jewish Germans. The Marx Brothers later did their turn with regard to Italians and Jews, and Minnie Pearl lampooned America's homegrown ethnics—rural people as seen by city-dwellers. Generally accepted in the spirit of fun, at least by those who were not being mocked, the characterizations ended as each group became assimilated into mainstream American life.

For Americans of African descent, the journey was far more difficult. Because their heritage and personal appearance were one, they could not assimilate simply by donning non-ethnic clothing and losing an accent. They were held apart from a mainstream society that shunned them as participants even as it found them suitable as comedic subjects, leading to the crafting of an entire dramatic genre that caricatured African-Americans.

From the earliest days Africans participated in America's theatrical life. In eighteenth-century New York, the African Gardens, an outdoor theater, was owned and operated by blacks for a black audience. But there were very few such venues, and most blacks had to find their entertainment in white-operated theaters. Consistent with the long-standing pattern of class separation, African-Americans usually were provided with a separate box office and an entry route that bypassed the main lobby and generally included a steep, narrow stair to an upper balcony where they faced uncomfortable seats and a generally inferior level of amenity. As movie theaters proliferated, every city came to have distinct "colored" theaters. Architecturally indistinguishable from other theaters, these served to keep black patrons in the neighborhoods where they lived. The resistance met by blacks who attempted to attend traditionally white theaters made them flashpoints of community protest in the growing civil rights movement of the mid-twentieth century.

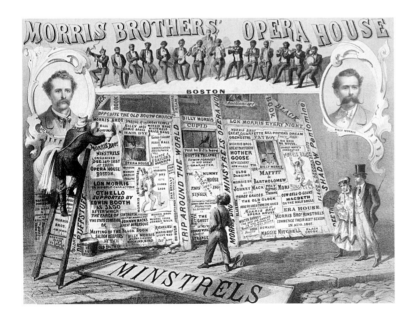

8-001. Morris Brothers' Opera House, Boston, Massachusetts. Opened ca. 1858. A. Trochsler & Co., lithographer, ca. 1867. P&P, LC-USZ62-114520.

The black billposter, the young boy, and the chorus line of minstrels—white actors performing with blackened faces and countrified costumes—identify the genre, the lettering describes the acts, and portraits of Lon and Billy Morris reassure the fashionable white couple that this is their brand of entertainment. The theater operated only for six years; it burned in October 1864.

8-002

8-003

8-002. Cartee's Lyceum (New American Opera House, Sanford's Opera House, Dumont's Opera House, Eleventh Street Opera House), Eleventh Street at Ranstead Street, Philadelphia, Pennsylvania. Opened December 4, 1854; 850 seats. William H. Rau, photographer, ca. 1911. P&P, LC-USZ62-113365.

Firebrand preacher Henry Ward Beecher predicted that in time every theater would be turned into a church. The opposite more often was the case. Originally a Reformed Presbyterian Church, this building spent most of its existence as a popular minstrel hall, where white audiences reveled at "black" genre acts. In later years its management sought to draw attention by outlining the classical facade with dozens of electric lights. In 1911 the old opera house was replaced by a newer popular phenomenon, a Horn & Hardart automat.

8-003. Buckley's Hall (New Olympic Theatre, Metropolitan Music Hall, Academy of the Drama, Hooley & Campbell's Minstrel Hall, German Theatre, Canterbury Hall, Palace of Mirrors, Broadway Theatre, St. Nicholas Hall, Heller's Salon Diabolique, San Francisco Minstrel Hall, Charles T. White's Athenaeum, Metropolitan, Grand Central, Comedy, Herrmann's Theatre), 585 Broadway, New York, New York. Opened August 25, 1856; 700 seats. Wood, engraver; from *Frank Leslie's Illustrated Newspaper*, September 20, 1856. P&P, LC-USZ62-2520.

Located in the heart of New York's growing Broadway theater district, across the street from Niblo's Garden (see 1-031), this small theater was best known as a minstrel hall. Its auditorium was simply built but elaborately decorated with trompe l'oeil painted paneling. The single balcony indicated an audience with minimal class stratification. Best known as the home of Buckley's Serenaders, it was renamed eighteen times in its thirty-five-year life span.

8-004. Primrose & Dockstader's Great American Minstrels. H. C. Miner Lithographing Company, lithographers, ca. 1898. P&P, LC-USZ62-24431.

Said Lew Dockstader, "Minstrelsy in silk stockings, set in square cuts and bag wigs, is about as palatable an amusement as a salad of pine shavings and sawdust with a little salmon, lobster, or chicken . . . What is really good is killed by the surroundings." Here "the man who makes millions laugh" livens an upscale audience with minstrel humor.

8-004

8-005

8-006

8-007

8-005. Grand Theatre, 133 South Twelfth Street, Baton Rouge, Louisiana. Built 1891–1895; 475 seats. David J. Kaminsky, photographer, 1978. P&P, HABS,LA,17-BATRO,3-1.

Opened in the early 1890s as a "Negro opera house and dance hall" with lodge rooms on the second floor, the Grand later became a movie theatre. In the 1950s, it was made into a nightclub and motel that closed in 1969. By 1978 it remained the only theater building of African-American heritage in Baton Rouge.

8-006. Regal Theatre, 4710 South Martin Luther King Drive, Chicago, Illinois. Opened 1928; 2,797 seats; Levy & Klein, architects. Russell Lee, photographer, April, 1941. P&P, LC-USF34-038807-D.

The Regal was Chicago's most famous historically African-American movie palace. Its architects had designed some of Chicago's finest theaters and the Regal ranked with the best of them. Long after its demolition its name, still strong in local memory, was transferred to the former Avalon Theatre, a John Eberson palace in the Persian mode, even deeper in Chicago's South Side.

8-007. Regal Theatre, 4710 South Martin Luther King Drive, Chicago, Illinois. Opened 1928; 2,797 seats; Levy & Klein, architects. Russell Lee, photographer, April, 1941. P&P, LC-USF34-038553-D.

8-008

8-009

8-008. Regal Theatre, 4710 South Martin Luther King Drive, Chicago, Illinois. Opened 1928; 2,797 seats; Levy & Klein, architects. Russell Lee, photographer, April, 1941. P&P, LC-USF34-038824-D.

8-009. Regal Theatre, 4710 South Martin Luther King Drive, Chicago, Illinois. Opened 1928; 2,797 seats; Levy & Klein, architects. Russell Lee, photographer, April, 1941. P&P, LC-USF34-038566-D.

8-010. Regal Theatre, 4710 South Martin Luther King Drive, Chicago, Illinois. Opened 1928; 2,797 seats; Levy & Klein, architects. Russell Lee, photographer, April, 1941. P&P, LC-USF34-038552-D.

8-011. Unidentified theater, Beale Street, Memphis, Tennessee. Marion Post Wolcott, photographer, October, 1939. P&P, LC-USF33-030638-M2.

Songwriter W. C. Handy lived on Beale Street, just around the corner from Memphis's Grand Opera House. By 1909, when he wrote "The Memphis Blues," the street had become not only home to a new music genre, but a landmark of African-American culture. Within two decades six theaters on the street's central block catered to black audiences and occasional white visitors. Rufus Thomas would later say, "If you were black one night on Beale Street, you would never want to be white again."

8-010

8-011

8-012

8-015

8-013

8-014

8-012. Daisy Theatre, 329–331 Beale Street, Memphis, Tennessee. Jack E. Boucher, photographer, March, 1974. P&P, HABS,TENN,79-MEMPH,6-5.

The Daisy, now a museum of Memphis jazz, was the most ornamental of Beale Street's theatres.

8-013. Lyceum Theatre, Mount Bayou, Mississippi. Russell Lee, photographer, January, 1939. P&P, LC-USF34-032007-D.

The Lyceum flourished between 1921 and 1934. When it closed, it found new life as a restaurant. Mount Bayou was an all-black town founded and subsidized by the Yazoo Mississippi Valley Railroad.

8-014. Lyceum Theatre, Mount Bayou, Mississippi. Russell Lee, photographer, January, 1939. P&P, LC-USF33-011969-M2.

8-015. Unidentified theater, Belzoni, Mississippi. Marion Post Wolcott, photographer, October, 1939. P&P, LC-USF33-030577-M2.

It often took a long climb for an African-American to enjoy a Saturday afternoon movie. The "colored balcony" remained a fact of life through the first half of the twentieth century.

8-017

8-018

8-016

8-016. Unidentified theater, Birmingham, Alabama. Arthur Rothstein, photographer, 1940; from Look Magazine, December 3, 1940. P&P, LC-USZ62-112456.

8-017. Rex (Harlem) Theatre, Leland, Mississippi. 176 seats. Marion Post Wolcott, photographer, November, 1939. P&P, LC-USF34-052508-D.

Of Leland's two theaters it was clear who was welcome at the Rex. Its appearance was meager—an erratic row of light bulbs stood in place of a marquee—as two young men contemplated their options for an afternoon's entertainment (see LENS-017).

8-018. Gem Theatre, 206 South Side Street, Waco, Texas. 558 seats. Russell Lee, photographer, November, 1939. P&P, LC-USF34-038808-D.

At Waco's Gem Theatre a standard advertising sign sufficed as a marquee to identify it as a theater that welcomed black patronage.

8-019. Sunset Theatre & Café, North Carolina. Billy E. Barnes, photographer, 1964–1968. P&P, LC-USZ62-108292.

As late as the mid-1960s this nondescript showplace maintained separate entrances for "white" and "colored" customers.

8-019

Wherever itinerant salesmen stayed in dreary commercial hotels in unfamiliar locales, whenever unsophisticated farmers forayed into the big city, there were burlesque theaters. They were right downtown, generally among the bars and novelty stores of a faded commercial district. Some had once been prominent legitimate stages, others were converted storefronts—appearances mattered little to an undemanding male audience. Burlesque probably never had an era of true greatness, but it was a long-lived theatrical subculture, unique in its history and architectural impact.

By the 1860s, devastated by tragic fires and waning attendance, the great museums of P. T. Barnum's era (see 1-023–1-026) were gone. The display of sensational oddities and human "freaks" had found a new home in small, seedy storefronts (8-021). These disreputable halls abounded in multilayered theatrical districts where they stood cheek-by-jowl with other venues that ranged from dramatic theaters to concert saloons. The concert saloon was a unique theatrical type that combined variety entertainment with alcohol. The acts were second-rate. The halls were modest in size and shabby in character. The customers, who sat at tables, consumed quantities of beer served by attentive "pretty waiter girls."

In 1866, when a revolutionary new show, *The Black Crook*, incorporated chorus dancing into a play, American musical theater was born. Scantily clad by the standards of the day, the dancers played to upscale audiences of mixed gender at Niblo's Garden, one of New York's most respected variety theaters (see 1-031). Others modified *The Black Crook*'s model, making their performances deliberately risqué. In these early burlesque companies, all-woman casts performed such traditionally male roles as soldiers, Indians, or Amazons (8-026). By the twentieth century, women of burlesque portrayed their own gender (8-024). At first attractive and winsome, the portrayals moved toward caricature. Such hardly-dainty performers as Sophie Tucker, Mae West, and Gypsy Rose Lee presented themselves in roles of worldly experience and tough sexuality (8-025). Their double entendre material excluded them from the sanitized big-time vaudeville, but interspersed between bawdy comedians and scanty choruses, they wriggled and cajoled their way to resounding success.

Eventually business travelers took to the air and farmers lost their naïveté. As urban renewal eradicated the seedy quarters of downtown, the old burlesque theaters disappeared. Burlesque, itself, had moved out of the theater and away from downtown. Its successor entertainment was found in the bars of the roadside strip.

8-020

8-020. The Bowery Burlesquers. Ca. 1898. P&P, POS-T-BUR .B69.

Two theatrical districts, coincident but contrasting, developed in late nineteenth-century New York. As Broadway became lined with elegant theaters that catered to the carriage trade, the Bowery took on a low-grade cast.

8-021. A night scene in the Bowery, New York, New York. Henry Muhrman, artist; from *Harper's Weekly*, February 26, 1881, p. 140. Gen. Coll., AP2 .H32.

That P. T. Barnum became renowned as an unsavory pitchman was not entirely justi-fied. Others in his business took the concept of unsavory to new depths. New York's Bowery became populated with low-level entertainment as portrayed in this maga-zine illustration, where a Dickensian barker hawks the enticements of his establish-ment—a tawdry and eerily gaudy dime museum—to children of the nighttime street.

8-022. Unidentified concert saloon, New York, New York. From Kenneth T. Jackson, ed., *Encyclopedia of New York City*, p. 271. Gen. Coll., F128.3.E75.

Entertainment places for the working-class, concert saloons sprang up in quantity in the Bowery theater district.

8-021

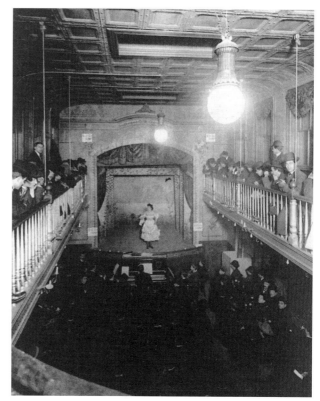

8-022

8-023

8-027

8-024

8-025

8-026

8-023. McGurk's Suicide Hall, 295 Bowery, New York, New York. Opened 1895. Bain News Service, photographer, January 26, 1914. P&P, LC-USZ62-93754.

Notorious among the concert saloons was John McGurk's Bowery establishment, the building with the awning, where a sailor clientele was served alcohol, music, and back-room sex. Even the prostitutes who worked there recognized that McGurk's represented the bottom rung of the social ladder. In 1899 alone at least six committed suicide, and another seven made unsuccessful attempts. While the management ostensibly tried to prevent the practice, it was not averse to the sensationalism that drew its clients. McGurk's became a restaurant in 1902. Its neighbor to the south (right) was another entertainment establishment, a German beer hall known as the Volks Garten, whose period of activity corresponded with that of its unsavory neighbor.

8-024. Canary Cottage burlesque dancers. Hartsook, photographer, ca. 1916. P&P, LC-USZ62-113672.

8-025. Star Burlesque. Reginald Marsh, artist, 1933. P&P, LC-USZC4-6588.

8-026. Imperial Burlesquers, "As Good As the Best." Courier Company, lithographers, ca. 1906. P&P, LC-USZC4-1715.

8-027. Pillars of the Stage. Ray Rohn, artist. P&P, DLC/PP-1980:81.249.

The multiple tiers of ornamental box seats are typical of the burlesque theater and the show on stage certainly is a burlesque chorus line of the militaristic genre. In his depiction of the proscenium columns and the skirt-like valance, the artist gives surrealistic form to the dictum that in the theater, it is sex that sells.

8-029

8-030

8-028

8-028. Gayety (Sam S. Shubert) Theatre, 513 Ninth Street NW, Washington, D.C. Opened August 26, 1907; 2,150 seats, William H. McElfatrick, architect. Unidentified photographer, August 4, 1907. P&P, LC-USZ62-107032.

For over forty years, the Gayety was Washington's setting for Eastern Wheel Burlesque presentations. When burlesque lost audiences nationwide, its closing was not unexpected. What *was* unexpected was the theater's second life. To avoid admitting African-American patrons, Washington's National Theatre closed in 1948. Left without a theater, its lessees, the Shubert Organization, acquired the old Gayety. It opened on March 6, 1950 as the Shubert, and for almost a decade remained Washington's premier legitimate stage. It closed permanently after a fire in 1959.

8-029. Gayety (Sam S. Shubert) Theatre, 513 Ninth Street NW, Washington, D.C. Opened August 26, 1907; 2,150 seats; William H. McElfatrick, architect. John Vachon, photographer, April, 1937. P&P, LC-USF33- 001063-M1.

8-030. Gayety (Sam S. Shubert) Theatre, 513 Ninth Street NW, Washington, D.C. Opened August 26, 1907; 2,150 seats; William H. McElfatrick, architect. John Vachon, photographer, April, 1937. P&P, LC-USF33- 001063-M2.

8-031. Gayety (Sam S. Shubert) Theatre, 513 Ninth Street NW, Washington, D.C. Opened August 26, 1907; 2,150 seats; William H. McElfatrick, architect. John Ferrell, photographer, March, 1942. P&P, LC-USF34-011455-D.

As the Gayety entered its last decade of burlesque presentation, nighttime customers clustered around the gaudy display front that had been patched over its once-elegant entry.

8-031

In the half-century after the Civil War, it seemed that every theater was an opera house. But in most, opera was only an occasional visitor, as were Shakespeare, Beethoven, or any other presentations of more serious intent than variety and melodrama. Throughout the period, though, there were theaters that actually *did* devote themselves to drama, opera, and fine music. Found in major cities, these usually were not commercial ventures but were built by and for the community's upper crust. They were large and highly decorated, with lavish foyers and numerous box seats. Today's counterparts of such places are civic institutions, publicly subsidized homes to symphony orchestras and opera companies. In earlier days the fare was more varied. Most large auditorium floors could be leveled to accommodate dancing. Political conventions were frequent, and circuses and sporting events (8-153) often shared the stage with serious music.

The twentieth century brought specialized auditoriums. Symphony halls combined superb acoustics with open orchestra platforms, often backed by large pipe organs. New York led the nation in building theaters designed specifically for opera. An attempt was even made to build a monumental theater devoted to fine drama (8-070–8-073). The experiment failed but the theater was among the most lavish ever built.

The grand and haughty theaters of this section are special in that they tried to rise above mere entertainment to a higher plane of artistic endeavor. To the extent that they succeeded, they became some of America's greatest theatrical monuments.

8-032. West Battery (Castle Clinton, Castle Garden), Battery Park, New York, New York. Built 1808; Lt. Col. Jonathan Williams and John McComb Jr., architects. Nathaniel Currier, lithographer, 1848. P&P, LC-USZ62-2060; LC-USZC2-1758 (color).

In 1824, an old defensive fortification on an artificial island at Manhattan's southern tip was deeded to the City of New York to become an outdoor concert venue called Castle Garden. In 1845, when its central courtyard was roofed over, it became a permanent theater, most famously the site where P. T. Barnum presented Jenny Lind, the "Swedish Nightingale." After ten years as New York's principal opera house, the old castle became a pre–Ellis Island immigrant reception station. It later served as the city's aquarium and as a museum and embarkation point for the Statue of Liberty. In the twenty-first century, a new theatrical use is proposed for this great old structure.

8-032

8-033. Boston Music Hall (Orpheum Theatre), 413 Washington Street, Boston, Massachusetts. Opened 1852; 2,585 seats; George Snell, architect; from *Frank Leslie's Illustrated Newspaper*, March 15, 1856, p. 216. P&P, LC-USZ62-60914.

Boston's first concert hall, with its combined Gothic and Renaissance detailing, was not built to accommodate theatrical scenery. Two wall-hugging balconies framed its open concert stage, here shown at the 1856 Beethoven Festival.

8-034. Boston Music Hall (Orpheum Theatre), 413 Washington Street, Boston, Massachusetts. Opened 1852; 2,585 seats; George Snell, architect; from *Frank Leslie's Illustrated Newspaper*, June 5, 1869, p. 216. P&P, LC-USZ62-95677.

On November 2, 1863, the Music Hall gained a new look when its pipe organ, the first major concert organ in America, was dedicated. The instrument was built by E. F. Walcker, of Ludwigsburg, Germany. Its case was designed by Boston architect Hammatt Billings and built by the Herter Brothers of New York. In 1881 the newly founded Boston Symphony made the Music Hall its first home. When the orchestra moved to Symphony Hall in 1900 (8-063), the Music Hall slipped from its lofty cultural pedestal. It was gutted and rebuilt to designs of architect Thomas W. Lamb, opening as the Orpheum Theatre on January 20, 1916. The organ found its own new home in the delightful Music Hall in nearby Methuen.

8-035. French Opera House, Bourbon and Toulouse Streets, New Orleans, Louisiana. Opened May, 1859; 1,600 seats; Gallier & Esterbrook, architects. DPCC, photographer, ca. 1910. P&P, LC-D4-39617.

New Orleans' unique ethnic heritage gave it one of the era's finest theaters, where audiences of fashion and elegance gathered in an extraordinary multitiered auditorium to hear French-language programs. The Opera House was consumed by fire on December 4, 1919.

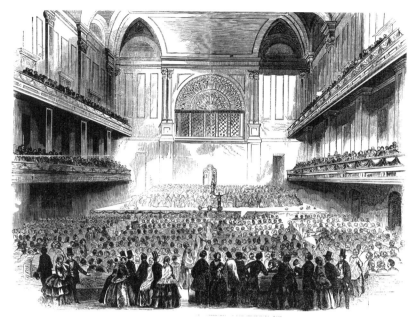

8-033

8-034

8-035

8-036

8-037

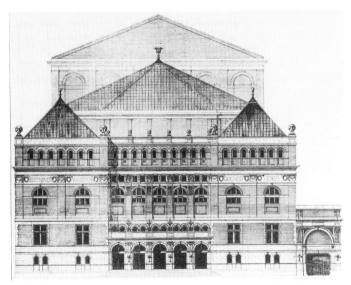

8-038

8-036. Steinway Hall, 71–73 East Fourteenth Street, New York, New York. Opened October 31, 1866; 1,800 seats; Heinrich Beck, architect. C. E. Bolles, photographer, ca. 1890. P&P, LC-USZ62-95749.

Some music-related businesses maintained significant concert halls. Steinway Hall, an adjunct to the piano company's Manhattan showroom, had neither proscenium nor curtain but an open platform flanked by a concert organ. An ample seating capacity and a location in the heart of the Union Square theater district made the hall a sought-after concert and lecture venue. This view shows Theodore Thomas's orchestra, forerunner of both the New York Philharmonic and the Chicago Symphony. Overshadowed by Andrew Carnegie's new music hall far uptown, Steinway Hall closed in 1890.

8-037. Chickering Hall, 130 Fifth Avenue, New York, New York. Opened November 1875; 1,450 seats; George B. Post, architect; from *Frank Leslie's Illustrated Newspaper*, April 2, 1887. P&P, LC-USZ62-120369.

Responding to its competitor on Fourteenth Street, the Chickering piano company opened its own hall a few blocks uptown. More imposing in external appearance, Chickering Hall was a worthy rival that never attained Steinway Hall's musical stature. Here the hall is seen in multipurpose mode, hosting an art auction.

8-038. Metropolitan Opera House (project), Forty-third Street at Vanderbilt Avenue, New York, New York. Projected 1880; Potter & Robertson, architects; from *American Architect & Building News*, November 13, 1880. P&P, LC-USZ62-79566, detail.

Since 1854, Col. James H. Mapleson's Academy of Music (see 1-039) had been New York's society showplace. But as the century progressed, instant fortunes created a new elite. Shunned as upstarts by the Academy's old-money crowd, a group of rising industrialists with names like Vanderbilt, Goelet, and Whitney determined to build an opera house of their own. Constrained by a small site, the new opera house would forever lack the great lobbies, grand stairs, and huge stages of its European counterparts, but its resident company, the Metropolitan Opera, would become second to none in musical renown. Neither the site nor the design illustrated here was ultimately selected for the new building.

8-039. Metropolitan Opera House, 1413–1425 Broadway, New York, New York. Opened October 22, 1883; 3,045 seats; Josiah Cleveland Cady, architect. DPCC, photographer, ca. 1905. P&P, LC-D4-18310.

Col. Mapleson denounced it as a "yellow brewery," even as the Metropolitan Opera quickly eclipsed his Academy of Music. Within ten years the new house would be the hub of its own theater district: the Casino (see 4-001), Empire, Broadway, and Knickerbocker Theatres all opened within a block of its doors. By the end of another decade Times Square, marked by the tower in the distance, would begin to generate an even stronger theatrical energy.

8-040. Metropolitan Opera House, 1413–1425 Broadway, New York, New York. Opened October 22, 1883; 3,045 seats; Josiah Cleveland Cady, architect. Jack E. Boucher, photographer, May, 1966. P&P, HABS,NY,31-NEYO,79-5.

Under the Metropolitan's Broadway marquee, every Saturday around noon a line of people began to form to purchase standing-room tickets for the evening's performance. Many brought along portable radios to listen to the live broadcast of the ongoing matinee.

8-041. Metropolitan Opera House, 1413–1425 Broadway, New York, New York. Opened October 22, 1883; 3,045 seats; Josiah Cleveland Cady, architect. Jack E. Boucher, photographer, May, 1966. P&P, HABS,NY,31-NEYO,79-3.

After a severe fire in 1893, the Met called upon architect J. B. McElfatrick to rebuild its stage and interior, but no amount of alteration could make its cramped production facilities truly adequate. During performances, scenery had to be shuttled from a nearby warehouse and stored on the Seventh Avenue sidewalk, as seen in this photograph of the stage facade. A canvas drape attached to the rear wall provided protection from the rain.

8-039

8-040

8-041

8-042

8-044

8-043

8-042. Metropolitan Opera House, 1413–1425 Broadway, New York, New York. Opened October 22, 1883; 3,045 seats; Josiah Cleveland Cady, architect. Jack E. Boucher, photographer, May, 1966. P&P, HABS,NY,31-NEYO,79-20.

8-043. Metropolitan Opera House, 1413–1425 Broadway, New York, New York. Opened October 22, 1883; 3,045 seats; Josiah Cleveland Cady, architect. Jack E. Boucher, photographer, May, 1966. P&P, HABS,NY,31-NEYO,79-23.

8-044. Metropolitan Opera House, 1413–1425 Broadway, New York, New York. Opened October 22, 1883; 3,045 seats; Josiah Cleveland Cady, architect. Jack E. Boucher, photographer, May, 1966. P&P, HABS,NY,31-NEYO,79-19.

Although relatively small, the Metropolitan's lobbies were not without elegance. This upper stair hall remained unchanged from 1883 until the building closed in 1966. Within the auditorium, elegant elliptical stairs provided access to the upper levels (8-042). Nearby drinking fountains presented a refreshing scene of cherubs in an idyllic garden (8-043).

8-046

8-045. Metropolitan Opera House, 1413–1425 Broadway, New York, New York. Opened October 22, 1883; 3,045 seats; Josiah Cleveland Cady, architect. Jack E. Boucher, photographer, May, 1966. P&P, HABS,NY,31-NEYO,79-13.

The Metropolitan's elaborate proscenium bore the names of leading opera composers. Its sides terminated in elaborate sculptural displays of music, cherubs, and garlands over truncated columns.

8-046. Metropolitan Opera House, 1413–1425 Broadway, New York, New York. Opened October 22, 1883; 3,045 seats; Josiah Cleveland Cady, architect. Jack E. Boucher, photographer, May, 1966. P&P, HABS,NY,31-NEYO,79-11.

In 1903, the Metropolitan's auditorium was given its third incarnation as architects Carrère & Hastings, favorites of New York society, provided an interior that was as grand as any in the world. Although its gilt and ornament rivaled the opera houses of Europe, its open balconies were as American as apple pie. Here an asbestos safety screen hides the Met's famous gold curtain.

8-047. Metropolitan Opera House, 1413–1425 Broadway, New York, New York. Opened October 22, 1883; 3,045 seats; Josiah Cleveland Cady, architect. Jack E. Boucher, photographer, May, 1966. P&P, HABS,NY,31-NEYO,79-12.

8-047

8-048

8-048. Metropolitan Opera House, 1413–1425 Broadway, New York, New York. Opened October 22, 1883; 3,045 seats; Josiah Cleveland Cady, architect. Jack E. Boucher, photographer, May, 1966. P&P, HABS,NY,31-NEYO,79-15.

The multitiered form of the auditorium was derived from European precedent. Here, from bottom up, are the orchestra, parterre boxes, grand tier, dress circle, balcony, and family circle.

8-049. Metropolitan Opera House, 1413–1425 Broadway, New York, New York. Opened October 22, 1883; 3,045 seats; Josiah Cleveland Cady, architect. Jack E. Boucher, photographer, May, 1966. P&P, HABS,NY,31-NEYO,79-17.

The Metropolitan's topmost level provided a good view of the elaborate ceiling, but a distant one of the stage below.

8-049

8-050. Chicago Auditorium, 58 East Congress Street, Chicago, Illinois. Opened December 9, 1889; 3,747 seats; Adler & Sullivan, architects. J. N. Taylor, photographer, 1890. P&P, HABS,ILL,16-CHIG,39-75.

A great hotel was built on Chicago's lakefront in anticipation of the World's Columbian Exposition. Within its massive bulk, which included offices as well as lodging space, was a remarkable auditorium, consciously a rival to the Metropolitan Opera. Its entrance was marked by the tallest tower in the city. The powerful exterior incorporated the heavy masonry textures that had been introduced into American architectural practice by H. H. Richardson. The interiors combined Dankmar Adler's planning genius with Louis Sullivan's distinctive ornament. Extraordinary in size, mechanical provisions, acoustics, production flexibility, and beauty, the Auditorium came to be revered as one of America's greatest theater buildings.

8-051. Chicago Auditorium, 58 East Congress Street, Chicago, Illinois. Opened December 9, 1889; 3,747 seats; Adler & Sullivan, architects. Cervin Robinson, photographer, July 23, 1963. P&P, HABS,ILL,16-CHIG,39-2

8-052. Main floor plan, Chicago Auditorium, 58 East Congress Street, Chicago, Illinois. Opened December 9, 1889; 3,747 seats; Adler & Sullivan, architects. Robert C. Giebner, delineator, 1965. P&P, HABS IL-1007.

The Auditorium filled the central area of the U-shaped hotel and office block. The relative size of its stage and lobbies, exceptional in American practice, approached that of major European halls.

8-053. Section, Chicago Auditorium, 58 East Congress Street, Chicago, Illinois. Opened December 9, 1889; 3,747 seats; Adler & Sullivan, architects. Robert C. Giebner, delineator, 1965. P&P, HABS IL-1007.

The Auditorium's complexity was unprecedented. Dwarfed by the huge stage, the auditorium was steeply raked in accordance with developing acoustical theories. Above its large main balcony, two smaller upper tiers could be closed when unneeded by hinged ceiling panels. A small recital hall was tucked in above and behind the topmost balcony. Over the arches of the main ceiling, a bridgelike structure bore the hotel's banquet hall.

8-050

8-051

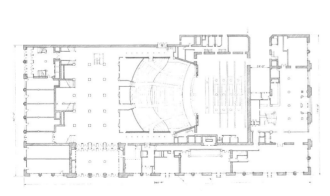

8-052

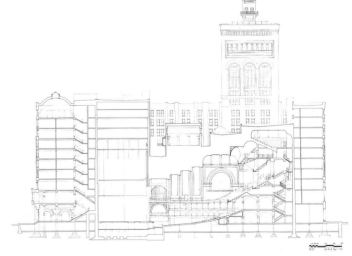

8-053

8-054

8-055

8-056

8-057

8-054. Chicago Auditorium, 58 East Congress Street, Chicago, Illinois. Opened December 9, 1889; 3,747 seats; Adler & Sullivan, architects. J. N. Taylor, photographer, 1890. P&P, HABS,ILL,16-CHIG,39-83.

The broad lobbies provided ample room for crowds to mingle and secluded spots for a quiet pause. That the Auditorium provided elegance and comfort without ostentation was looked upon as a forceful expression of America's democratic spirit.

8-055. Chicago Auditorium, 58 East Congress Street, Chicago, Illinois. Opened December 9, 1889; 3,747 seats; Adler & Sullivan, architects. J. N. Taylor, photographer, 1890. P&P, HABS,ILL,16-CHIG,39-86.

8-056. Chicago Auditorium, 58 East Congress Street, Chicago, Illinois. Opened December 9, 1889; 3,747 seats; Adler & Sullivan, architects. J. N. Taylor, photographer, 1890. P&P, HABS,ILL,16-CHIG,39-88.

In a nineteenth-century theater, audience amenities usually were sparse. The Auditorium's were extraordinary. The ladies' parlor incorporated elegant detail and comfortable seating into its ample space.

8-057. Chicago Auditorium, 58 East Congress Street, Chicago, Illinois. Opened December 9, 1889; 3,747 seats; Adler & Sullivan, architects. J. N. Taylor, photographer, 1890. P&P, HABS,ILL,16-CHIG,39-76.

Grand in scale but restrained in detailing, the Auditorium's entry vestibule featured richly patterned Numidian marble walls, mosaic floors, and delicate plaster moldings. Radiators wrapped around its massive columns.

8-058. Chicago Auditorium, 58 East Congress Street, Chicago, Illinois. Opened December 9, 1889; 3,747 seats; Adler & Sullivan, architects. J. N. Taylor, photographer, 1890. P&P, HABS,ILL,16-CHIG,39-89.

The Auditorium was a vessel of cream and gold, its elliptical arches lined with thousands of warmly glowing carbon-filament lamps. Decorations included a stained glass skylight and large murals on the balcony walls and above the stage. The proscenium was a double construction. In conventional use it appeared as a delicately modeled, gilded wall around a rectangular opening. The wall was actually a heavily constructed reducing curtain. It could be fully raised, opening the stage from wall to wall and to the lower rim of Charles Holloway's arching mural.

8-059. Chicago Auditorium, 58 East Congress Street, Chicago, Illinois. Opened December 9, 1889; 3,747 seats; Adler & Sullivan, architects. J. N. Taylor, photographer, 1890. P&P, HABS,ILL,16-CHIG,39-91.

Part of the Auditorium's unique flexibility was the ability to adjust its size. Here, the ceiling panels that conceal the two upper balconies are shown in their closed position. The mural, *Spring Song*, was executed by Albert Fleury.

8-060. Chicago Auditorium, 58 East Congress Street, Chicago, Illinois. Opened December 9, 1889; 3,747 seats; Adler & Sullivan, architects. J. N. Taylor, photographer, 1890. P&P, HABS,ILL,16-CHIG,39-94.

With the reducing curtain in lowered position, the stage is set for a performance of Wagner's *Lohengrin*.

8-058

8-059

8-060

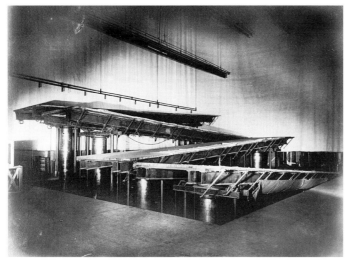

8-061

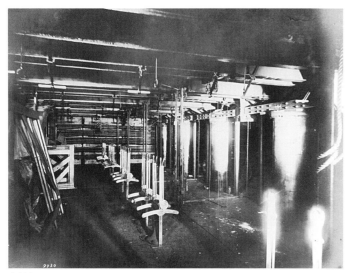

8-062

8-063

8-061. Chicago Auditorium, 58 East Congress Street, Chicago, Illinois. Opened December 9, 1889; 3,747 seats; Adler & Sullivan, architects. J. N. Taylor, photographer, 1890. P&P, HABS,ILL,16-CHIG,39-92.

Architect/engineer Dankmar Adler toured European opera houses as he designed the Auditorium's operating equipment. The stage floor was modeled on the Asphaleia system, used in the Budapest Opera House. Powered by hydraulic rams, it could rise as a unit or as four separate elevators, each of which could tilt independently from side to side. In its era this capability was repeated only in New York's New Amsterdam Theatre (see 4-026–4-028).

8-062. Chicago Auditorium, 58 East Congress Street, Chicago, Illinois. Opened December 9, 1889; 3,747 seats; Adler & Sullivan, architects. J. N. Taylor, photographer, 1890. P&P, HABS,ILL,16-CHIG,39-95.

Below the floor, complex power and control systems operated the mechanical stage.

8-063. Symphony Hall, Massachusetts and Huntington Avenues, Boston, Massachusetts. Opened October 15, 1900; 2,631 seats; McKim, Mead & White, architects. DPCC, photographer, ca. 1904. P&P, LC-D4-17045.

In 1900 the Boston Symphony left the Music Hall (8-033 and 8-034) for a new home far from the congestion of the city center. Symphony Hall was reminiscent of a northern Italian basilica. Its nave was a delicately detailed concert hall of rectilinear form with a large main floor and two shallow balconies hugging the rear and sides. Designed by consulting acoustician Wallace Sabine, the hall was one of the world's finest musical performance environments.

8-064. Orchestra Hall, 220 South Michigan Avenue, Chicago, Illinois. Opened December 14, 1904; 2,582 seats; D. H. Burnham and Co., architects. George R. Lawrence Co., photographer, February 18, 1907. P&P, PAN SUBJECT - Groups, no. 293.

Having initiated the New York Philharmonic, Theodore Thomas moved to Chicago, where he established the Chicago Symphony Orchestra. Architect Daniel Burnham, an orchestra trustee, donated his services to design Orchestra Hall. Like other specialized orchestra facilities, the hall had an open platform surrounded by choral risers and a concert organ. Then, as now, its acoustics were considered superlative. Theodore Thomas had little chance to enjoy his new hall. He died three weeks after it opened.

8-065. Orchestra Hall, 220 South Michigan Ave., Chicago, Illinois. Opened December 14, 1904; 2,582 seats; D. H. Burnham and Co., architects. George R. Lawrence Co., photographer, March, 1908. P&P, PAN SUBJECT - Sports, no. 37.

Chicago was home not only to a fine orchestra, but also to America's leading manufacturer of billiard supplies. Although it had been purpose-built as a concert hall, Orchestra Hall's stage was adaptable enough to accommodate a billiard table. The Brunswick-Balke-Collender Company's 1908 tournament prompted a fine photograph of Orchestra Hall's interior. Brunswick and Orchestra Hall are still important Chicago institutions.

8-066. Manhattan Opera House (Manhattan Center, Hammerstein Ballroom), 311 West Thirty-fourth Street, New York, New York. Opened December 3, 1906; 3,000 seats; William E. Mowbray and William H. McElfatrick, architects. DPCC, photographer, ca. 1906. P&P, LC-D4-36514.

Operatic impresario and entrepreneur Oscar Hammerstein opened his Manhattan Opera House as a rival to the Metropolitan Opera. Unattractive to the city's elite, the venture never was financially successful, although it was so artistically strong that the Metropolitan bought out Hammerstein's rights to produce opera in New York. With the money, Hammerstein immediately built an opera house in London. The London house is gone, but behind a new facade, the Manhattan Opera House continues to be a popular concert venue.

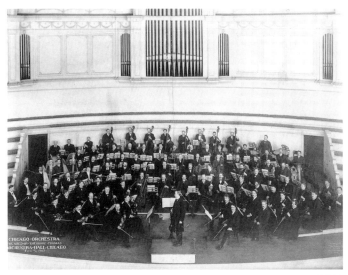

8-064

8-065

8-066

8-067

8-069

8-068

8-067. Boston Opera House, 343 Huntington Avenue, Boston, Massachusetts. Opened November 8, 1908; 3,944 seats; Wheelwright & Haven, architects. DPCC, photographer, 1909–1910. P&P, LC-D4-71536.

The Boston Symphony was the first of several cultural institutions to establish
themselves on Boston's broad Huntington Avenue. In the Fenway district, just
west of Symphony Hall, a new Museum of Fine Arts and the Boston Opera
House rose simultaneously. Architect Parkman B. Haven's facade monumentally echoed the form of Symphony Hall, while the multitiered, horseshoe-
shaped interior sought to outdo the most lavish of European opera halls. The
Opera House was demolished in 1957.

8-068. Philadelphia (Metropolitan, Met) Opera House, 1400–1418 Poplar
Street, Philadelphia, Pennsylvania. Opened November 17, 1908; 3,482
seats; William H. McElfatrick, architect. Jack E. Boucher, photographer, 1974.
P&P, HABS,PA,51-PHILA,540-4.

8-069. Philadelphia (Metropolitan, Met) Opera House, 1400–1418 Poplar
Street, Philadelphia, Pennsylvania. Opened November 17, 1908; 3,482
seats; William H. McElfatrick, architect. Unidentified photographer, ca. 1925.
P&P, HABS,PA,51-PHILA,540-1.

Forced to curtail his operatic endeavors in New York, Oscar Hammerstein
opened a massive opera house in Philadelphia. After squelching Hammerstein's effort as an opera producer, the Metropolitan Opera used the Philadelphia building for many years. When the opera left in favor of the Academy of
Music, the old hall become a moving picture house called the Met. Later used
as a church, also called the Met, the hall's superb acoustics made it a favorite
recording site for the Philadelphia Orchestra.

8-070. New (Century) Theatre, 21–29 Central Park West, New York, New York. Opened November 6, 1909; 2,000 seats; Carrère & Hastings, architects. Irving Underhill, photographer, November 13, 1909. P&P, LC-USZ62-74647.

Having made the Metropolitan Opera an ongoing artistic and financial success, New York's elite sought to establish America's version of a national theater. Its architects, trained at the Ecole des Beaux-Arts, produced a building that bore a noticeable resemblance to New Orleans' French Opera House (8-035).

8-071. New (Century) Theatre, 21–29 Central Park West, New York, New York. Opened November 6, 1909; 2,000 seats; Carrère & Hastings, architects. Irving Underhill, photographer, November 13, 1909; P & P, LC-USZ62-98711.

From the lobbies to the auditorium, size and ostentation were the New Theatre's glory and its curse. The auditorium more resembled an opera house than a dramatic theater. Its deep main floor was surrounded by a ring of private boxes surmounted by two large balconies. Easily America's grandest theatrical interior, it totally lacked the intimate scale necessary for successful dramatic presentation.

8-072. New (Century) Theatre, 21–29 Central Park West, New York, New York. Opened November 6, 1909; 2,000 seats; Carrère & Hastings, architects. Unidentified photographer, ca. 1910. P&P, LC-USZ62-100606.

Immediately after its opening, the New Theatre retained experienced theater architect William H. McElfatrick to remedy its disastrous sight lines and acoustics. For the theater's second season the parquet boxes were replaced with open seating and the always-obstructed side seats at all levels were removed. This heavily retouched photograph indicates that new private boxes were to occupy the second tier. To calm the hall's echoes and excessive reverberation, a fringed fabric canopy was suspended from the ceiling. Still unsuitably large for dramatic use, the theater, now called the Century, came under the management of the Shubert brothers, who used it for large-scale musicals. It was through this auditorium that Irving Berlin and the soldier cast of *Yip! Yip! Yaphank!* marched off to overseas service. The Century was demolished in 1930.

8-070

8-071

8-072

8-073

8-074

8-075

8-073. New (Century) Theatre, 21–29 Central Park West, New York, New York. Opened November 6, 1909; 2,000 seats; Carrère & Hastings, architects. Irving Underhill, photographer, November 13, 1909. P&P, LC-USZ62-98710.

8-074. Orchestra Hall (Town, Paradise Theatre), 3711 Woodward Avenue, Detroit, Michigan. Opened October 23, 1919; 2,286 seats; C. Howard Crane, architect. Architect's rendering, 1919. P&P, HABS,MICH,82-DETRO,17-12.

Early in 1919 the four-year-old Detroit Symphony sought noted pianist Ossip Gabrilowitsch as its music director. Dissatisfied with the orchestra's home, the Arcadia Ballroom, Gabrilowitsch agreed to the appointment only if a new hall were provided for the season's opening. It is said that a bride and groom were walking down the aisle of Westminster Presbyterian Church as wreckers began to demolish it in late April. Orchestra Hall opened on the site just six months later.

8-075. Orchestra Hall (Town, Paradise Theatre), 3711 Woodward Avenue, Detroit, Michigan. Opened October 23, 1919; 2,286 seats; C. Howard Crane, architect. Manning Brothers, photographers, ca. 1920. P&P, HABS,MICH,82-DETRO,17-13.

Despite a constricted schedule, Detroit architect C. Howard Crane, already a nationally known theater designer, created a hall of distinction and refined elegance. Its plaster walls resembled finely laid stone and its restrained ornament befitted a hall dedicated to culture.

8-076. Section, Orchestra Hall (Town, Paradise Theatre), 3711 Woodward Avenue, Detroit, Michigan. Opened October 23, 1919; 2,286 seats; C. Howard Crane, architect. Architect's drawing, July 26, 1919. P&P, HABS,MICH,82-DETRO,17-25.

Orchestra Hall proved to be an acoustical masterpiece. Its three-tiered flat ceiling imparted the sonic qualities of a classic rectilinear concert hall to a seating plan that provided the comfort and unobstructed sight lines of a large movie theater.

8-077. First-floor plan, Orchestra Hall (Town, Paradise Theatre), 3711 Woodward Avenue, Detroit, Michigan. Opened October 23, 1919; 2,286 seats; C. Howard Crane, architect. Architect's drawing, July 20, 1919. P&P,HABS,MICH, 82-DETRO,17-16.

Challenged to provide a large auditorium on a limited site, Crane had to limit the space allocated to the lobbies and the stage, which was far from commodious.

8-078. Mezzanine plan, Orchestra Hall (Town, Paradise Theatre), 3711 Woodward Avenue, Detroit, Michigan. Opened October 23, 1919; 2,286 seats; C. Howard Crane, architect. Architect's drawing, July 26, 1919. P&P,HABS,MICH, 82-DETRO,17-17.

Following the social divisions of the opera house, Orchestra Hall's mezzanine, composed entirely of box seats for the city's elite, had an exclusive entry and lobby system. The large mezzanine foyer, part of the main stair to the balcony, was not connected to the mezzanine box circle.

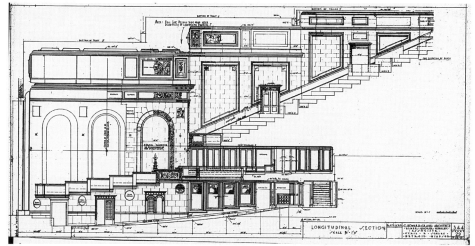

8-076

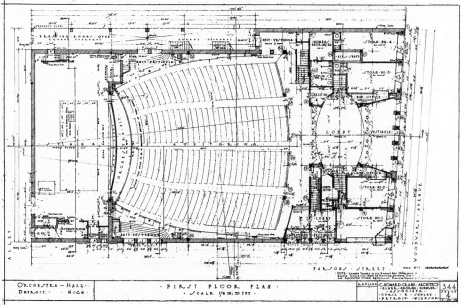

8-077

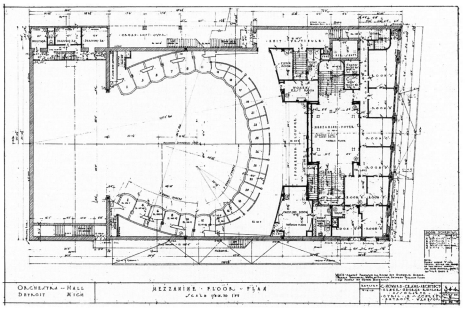

8-078

8-079

8-079. Orchestra Hall (Town, Paradise Theatre), 3711 Woodward Avenue, Detroit, Michigan. Opened October 23, 1919; 2,286 seats; C. Howard Crane, architect. Allen Stross, photographer, October, 1970. P&P, HABS,MICH,82-DETRO,17-5.

When the Detroit Symphony relocated in 1939, its former hall took on new life, first as the Town Theatre, then as the Paradise, an African-American jazz theater. After the Paradise closed in 1951, the building remained shuttered. But the spattering of generations of birds, the ravages of leaking rainwater, even fires that left the chandelier hanging low among the burned seats, failed to erase the hall's elegance. Eventually its superb acoustics drew the attention of local musicians and the public alike. In 1989, after a fourteen-year campaign, the Detroit Symphony returned to an impeccably restored Orchestra Hall.

8-080. War Memorial Opera House, 401 Van Ness Avenue, San Francisco, California. Opened October 15, 1932; 3,252 seats; Arthur Brown and G. Albert Lansburgh, architects. Jet Lowe, photographer, September, 1981. P&P, HABS,CAL,38-SANFRA,71-B-1.

Newest of America's classically styled opera houses, San Francisco's War Memorial combined the efforts of the finest architectural specialists. Arthur Brown, designer of nearby City Hall, was one of the country's leading classical designers, while G. Albert Lansburgh was one of its leading theater architects.

8-080

Time spent at sea, with little distraction from wind and waves, provides a setup for the-atrical activity to which mariners from time immemorial have responded by improvising leisure-time entertainments.

Large passenger steamships shortened and popularized the ocean journey. From about 1860 until trans-Atlantic flights became the norm, the ocean liner provided luxuri-ously for its well-heeled passengers. Among the accommodations were theaters whose elegance fully equaled—and in some cases surpassed—any small neighborhood movie house on land.

On an ocean liner, entertainment was incidental to a journey. On the floating theaters that plied America's internal waterways from the 1830s until the Great Depression, there was no journey—entertainment was the entire experience. The showboats floated down America's great rivers—the Ohio, the Mississippi, and the Missouri—stopping each after-noon at a convenient landing. Each boat was equipped with a steam calliope whose sound carried far inland through the noiseless air. Rural folk, as eager for a rare bit of contact with the outside world as for the show itself, flocked to the landing. Part of a showboat's success was its ability to move deep into the hinterlands. Its very shallow draft allowed it to penetrate into the most remote reaches of the tidewater bayous. Unpowered, the boats depended upon a companion towboat that, contrary to its name, actu-ally *pushed* the awkward showboat along its course.

A watergate in a capital city is a bit of romantic fancy that conjures up visions of kings and premiers arriving in state yachts or royal barges. At the turn of the twentieth century, behind the Lincoln Memorial in Washington, D.C., a broad flight of steps leading into the Potomac River was built so that such vessels could dock in elegance. Although royal yachts were scarce, the Watergate has been a popular site for riverside concerts since 1935. The National Park Service once proposed a grand barge, suitable to accommodate a large orchestra whose spectators could sit on the broad marble steps (8-090).

8-081

8-081. *U.S.S. New York*. Launched Decem-ber 2, 1891. Edward H. Hart, photographer, 1893–1901. P&P, LC-D4-20781.

The cruiser *New York* saw heavy-duty fight-ing in Cuba during the Spanish-American War. As the *Saratoga* and, later the *Rochester*, she served until the dawn of World War II, when she was scuttled to pre-vent her reuse by Japanese forces. Here, some crewmembers share musical revelry below decks.

8-082

SPALDING & ROGERS'S FLOATING CIRCUS PALACE.

8-082. Spalding & Rogers's Floating Circus Palace. Built 1851; 3,400 seats; from *Gleason's Pictorial Drawing-Room Companion*, February 19, 1853. P&P, LC-USZ62-2643.

The Floating Circus Palace was a waterborne colossus whose seating capacity doubled that of the St. Charles Theatre in New Orleans, the largest auditorium in the early Southwest (see 1-017). Its construction was typical. Atop a shallow barge was a full-scale conventional theater with a dress circle, family circle, and a second gallery that was assigned to African-Americans. There was a large pipe organ to which, in 1858, a calliope was added, the first on the river. The Floating Circus Palace also included a sideshow, a museum, a print shop in which the boat's daily newspaper, the *Palace Journal*, was published, dressing and sleeping rooms for a crew and cast of over one hundred, and accommodations for a contingent of performing animals. A concert saloon, the "Ridotto," was located on the towboat. The Floating Circus Palace operated until 1862 when it was commandeered by the Confederate army for use as a hospital ship.

8-083

8-083. Showboat *Goldenrod*, St. Louis, Missouri. Launched September, 1909; 1,400 (later 980) seats. Arthur Rothstein, photographer, January, 1939. P&P, LC-USF33-003027-M1.

The *Goldenrod* was another floating palace; its austere exterior concealed the most ornate theater on the river. The stage was elaborately equipped, and the gilt-decorated auditorium featured a balcony, twenty-two boxes, red velour drapery, and 2,500 electric lights arranged in ornamental patterns on the walls and ceiling. After twenty-eight years on the Mississippi and Ohio, the *Goldenrod* was permanently docked in St. Louis, where she continued to present shows to a reduced audience capacity.

8-084. *Bryant's New Showboat III*, Point Pleasant, West Virginia. Built 1918; 880 seats. Arthur S. Siegel, photographer, June, 1943. P&P, LC-USW3-030401-D.

The three versions of Billy Bryant's *New Showboat* that plied the Mississippi and Ohio Rivers operated long enough to see the showboat era's poignant end. In 1929, Bryant tied up at Cincinnati but failed to find customers for *Ten Nights in a Bar Room*. The audience that eventually did come was not the usual working-class folk, who were familiar with the play and accepted it as legitimate drama, but a crowd of high society sophisticates who knew it only from the movies. Rejecting Bryant's serious treatment, they demanded that the play be presented as the parody that they had seen in *Show Boat*. The vessel became a freight barge during World War II.

8-085. Showboat *Majestic*, Point Pleasant, West Virginia. Built 1923; 450 seats. Arthur S. Siegel, photographer, June, 1943. P&P, LC-USW3-030423-D.

Captain Tom Reynolds's *Majestic* spent its early summers exploring the southern tributaries of the Ohio and Monongahela Rivers. In winter it docked at Point Pleasant, where Reynolds's children attended school. Relatively small, and with a draft of only twelve inches, the *Majestic* could round the narrowest of bends and reach the shallowest of bayous. The crew was small. Reynolds was captain, pilot, carpenter, director, and actor. His wife kept the books and sold tickets and candy. The children worked the towboat, *Attaboy* (8-086), acted, and played in the band. The *Majestic*'s days ended in the late 1940s.

8-086. Towboat *Attaboy*, Point Pleasant, West Virginia. Arthur S. Siegel, photographer, June 1943. P&P, LC-USW3-030432-D.

Kerosene-powered so it did not need a full crew, the *Attaboy* pushed the *Majestic* and provided the floating theater's light and heat.

8-087

8-088

8-089

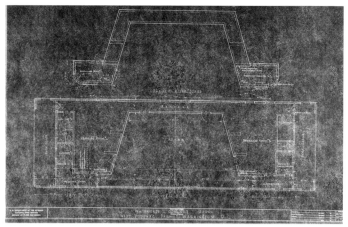

8-090

8-087. *S. S. Independence*. Launched June 3, 1950; 144 seats; Henry Drey-fuss, architect. Gottscho-Schleisner, Inc., photographer, January 29, 1951. P&P, LC-G613-58617.

The *Independence* set upon her maiden voyage on February 1, 1951, carrying a thousand passengers on a Mediterranean cruise prior to a career on the New York–Genoa route. A welcome pastime during the fifty-three-day cruise was a movie in the liner's suavely designed cinema.

8-088. *S. S. Brasil*, Moore McCormack Line. Launched September 4, 1958; 160 seats. Gottscho-Schleisner, Inc., photographer, October 15, 1958. P&P, LC-G613-73075.

The 737-passenger *Brasil* and her sister ship the *Argentina*, the last ocean lin-ers built in the United States, sailed from New York on fourteen-day South American cruises. Sold in 1971, she was renamed the *Universe Explorer*.

8-089. *S. S. Victoria*. Launched July, 1936; 250 seats; Gustavo Pulitzer, designer. Gottscho-Schleisner, Inc., photographer, February 10, 1960. P&P, LC-G613-75037.

Built in 1938 as the *Dunnottar Castle*, the ship carried 508 passengers on the New York–Liverpool route. After service as a troop ship during World War II, she was refitted in 1958 as the *Victoria*. As the *Princesa Victoria*, this elegant survivor became the oldest liner in active passenger service. Her theater, among the largest afloat, remained intact through the vessel's several mod-ernizations.

8-090. Proposed Watergate Concert Barge, West Potomac Park, Washington, D.C. U.S. National Park Service, Branch of Plans & Design, June 1938. P&P, Thomas Tileston Waterman Archive, ADE - UNIT 1726.

MILITARY THEATERS

While military life may entail brief moments of heroism and danger, a soldier's days are primarily spent in the tedium of lengthy cantonment. Recreation always has been important as a way to build morale and pass the days. Indeed, it may have won America's independence. When George Washington's forces sneaked across the Delaware River to Trenton, the British were caught unawares, noisily celebrating Christmas Eve. The Trenton Christmas party probably did not take place in a theater, but many military outposts, temporary and permanent, contained places of entertainment. Theaters were prominent components of the huge camps where troops trained for the First World War. The more permanent bases built during the Second World War and the Cold War decades were even greater in size and in the number of theaters on their grounds. Spartan in appearance, post theaters doubled as training auditoriums and as places that provided moments of respite to millions of young service people distanced from home and family.

America's ultimate military theater arose in an entirely different spirit. In 1861 the federal government seized Robert E. Lee's estate, Arlington, and established on its extensive grounds a national cemetery for American servicemen and women. To accommodate memorial functions, Arlington maintains two amphitheaters (8-103–8-110).

8-091

8-091. Soldiers' Theatre (Fourteenth Brooklyn), Culpeper Court House, Virginia. Edwin Forbes, artist, January, 1864. P&P, LC-USZC4-4204.

During an extended encampment at Culpeper, the soldiers of the Fourteenth Brooklyn Regiment converted an old warehouse into a creditable theater complete with extended stage and trompe-l'oeil box seats.

8-092

8-093

8-094

8-095

8-092. War Department Theater, U.S. Army Cantonment, Camp Upton, Yaphank, New York. Thompson Illustragraph Co., photographer, ca. 1919. P&P, PAN US MILITARY-Camps no. 119.

The First World War created a need to temporarily house great numbers of recruits being trained for overseas combat. The resulting bases were vast, with resources equal to many a small town. Camp Upton, near New York City, centered on a large theater with a commodious stage and an interesting history. In 1918 it became home to *Yip! Yip! Yaphank*, a homegrown musical show about army life, presented by a cast of soldiers. Written by a trainee from New York, the young Irving Berlin, the show featured such song classics-to-be as "Mandy" and the soldier's lament, "Oh! How I Hate to Get Up in the Morning." In August the show moved from Camp Upton to the Century Theater in Manhattan (8-070–8-073), where it enjoyed a thirty-two-performance run.

8-093. Subase Theatre, Moore Street at Nimitz Street, U.S. Naval Base, Pearl Harbor, Hawaii. Opened 1931. William Lindsey, photographer, March 3, 1994. P&P, HABS,HI,2-PEHA,44-2.

The post–World War I United States established major military bases across the contiguous states and in far-flung territories. Centers of combat support and training, these were less battlefield way-stations than long-term temporary homes for the soldiers assigned to them. Although military culture required that their buildings maintain a Spartan aesthetic, each base had a main theater that was equipped for good quality film presentation and occasional live shows.

8-094. Theater, Sturgis, Butner, and Martin Roads, Fort Sherman, Colon Vic., Canal Zone. P&P, HABS,CZ,1-COLON.V,2A-3.

8-095. Theater, Sturgis, Butner, and Martin Roads, Fort Sherman, Colon Vic., Canal Zone. P&P, HABS,CZ,1-COLON.V,2A-14.

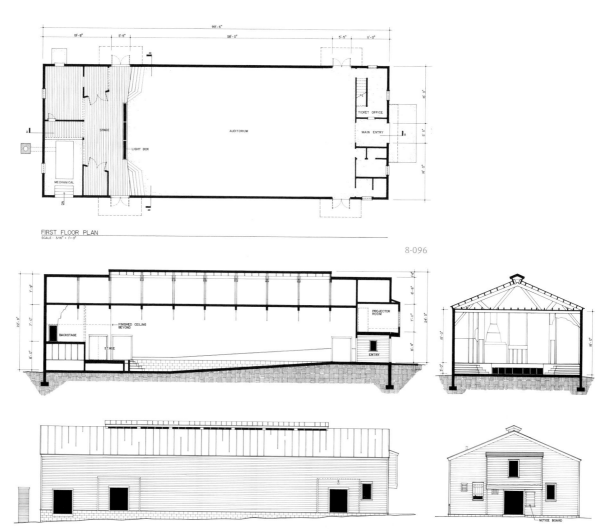

FIRST FLOOR PLAN
SCALE : 3/16" = 1'-0"

8-096

8-097

8-096. Plans, Margaret Bay Cantonment Theater, Naval Operating Base
Dutch Harbor and Fort Mears, Unalaska, Alaska. Opened 1941. Carey P.
Feierabend, delineator, 1985. P&P, HABS AK-34-Q, detail.

Military theater designs conformed strictly to regulated standards. In outlying areas of the great bases, identical barnlike wooden buildings provided
the soldier population with entertainment environments that assiduously
avoided attractiveness. This Alaskan facility served until 1987.

8-097. Elevations and sections, Margaret Bay Cantonment Theater, Naval
Operating Base Dutch Harbor and Fort Mears, Unalaska, Alaska. Opened
1941. Carey P. Feierabend, delineator, 1985. P&P, HABS AK-34-Q.

8-098. Gymnasium-Cafeteria-Theater, East K Street between Eleventh and
Twelfth Streets, Oakland Naval Supply Center, Oakland, California. Built
1944. Bruce D. Judd, photographer, December 1994–April 1995. P&P,
HABS,CAL,1-OAK,16G-22.

Occasionally, a theater at a permanent military facility was given a degree of
internal nicety comparable to that of a small-town or suburban cinema.

8-098

8-099

8-102

8-100

8-101

8-099. Building 946 (Theatre), Fort Barry, Rosenstock Road, Sausalito Vic., California. Opened April 22, 1941; 1,038 seats; Col. Charles D. Hartman, architect. Dewey Livingston, photographer, April 25, 1995. P&P,HABS,CAL, 21-SAUS.V,1A-5.

8-100. Building 946 (Theatre), Fort Barry, Rosenstock Road, Sausalito Vic., California. Opened April 22, 1941; 1,038 seats; Col. Charles D. Hartman, architect. Dewey Livingston, photographer, May 2, 1995. P&P, HABS,CAL,21-SAUS.V,1A-10.

Audience amenities in a 1940s cantonment theater consisted of a tiny lobby, unadorned ticket windows, a candy stand, and a spartan men's toilet.

8-101. Theater, Fort Randall, California Boulevard north of Jackson Lake, Cold Bay, Alaska. Built 1942. James Stuhler, photographer, November, 1984. P&P, HABS,AK,1-COLBA,1-C-1.

Occasionally Quonset construction was used in place of the more common wooden box form. Fort Randall's theater was the last of its type when it was demolished in 1985.

8-102. Stage Door Canteen, New York, New York. Marjory Collins, photographer, August, 1942. P&P, LC-USW3-006816-D.

The Stage Door Canteen, operated by the American Theater Wing, was not located on a military base, but under the stage of Loew's State Theatre in Times Square (see 9-040–9-044). Catering to servicemen on leave in the great city, the Canteen provided a free respite from military duty, with Broadway performers volunteering as waiters and entertainers. The place inspired the story of a lonely soldier and a girl named Eileen in Irving Berlin's ballad, "I Left My Heart at the Stage Door Canteen."

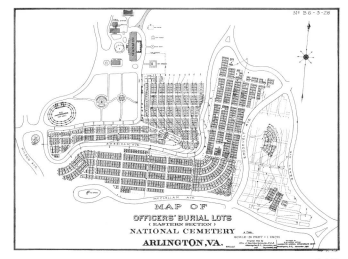

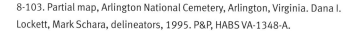

8-103

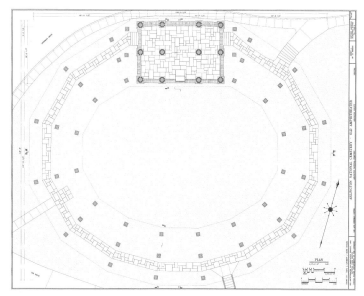

8-104

8-103. Partial map, Arlington National Cemetery, Arlington, Virginia. Dana I. Lockett, Mark Schara, delineators, 1995. P&P, HABS VA-1348-A.

Decoration Day, now Memorial Day, was initiated on May 30, 1868 and Arlington National Cemetery's first amphitheater was dedicated five years later as a place to conduct its annual celebration. An Ionic triple colonnade in a setting of verdant beauty, it was located near the great mansion for which the cemetery is named. In this adaptation of an early quartermaster's map, the amphitheater is shown at the left, Arlington Mansion at the top.

8-104. Plan, Old Amphitheater, Arlington National Cemetery, Arlington, Virginia. Opened May 30, 1873, Gen. Montgomery C. Meigs, architect. Dana I. Lockett, Mark Schara, delineators, 1995. P&P, HABS VA-1348-A.

8-105. Old Amphitheater, Arlington National Cemetery, Arlington, Virginia. Opened May 30, 1873, Gen. Montgomery C. Meigs, architect. DPCC, photographer, ca. 1900. P&P, LC-D4-13040.

8-106. Old Amphitheater, Arlington National Cemetery, Arlington, Virginia. Opened May 30, 1873, Gen. Montgomery C. Meigs, architect. Mark Schara, photographer, August, 1995. P&P, HABS,VA,7-ARL,11A-14.

In 1880 a marble reading desk was placed in the amphitheater's rostrum. Its architect, John L. Smithmeyer, later was co-designer of the Library of Congress.

8-105

8-106

8-107

8-108

8-110

8-109

8-107. Memorial Amphitheater, Arlington National Cemetery, Arlington, Virginia. Dedicated May 30, 1920; 4,000 seats; Carrère & Hastings, architects. Theodor Horydczak, photographer, 1920–1950. P&P, LC-H814-A05-040.

8-108. Memorial Amphitheater, Arlington National Cemetery, Arlington, Virginia. Dedicated May 30, 1920; 4,000 seats; Carrère & Hastings, architects. Theodor Horydczak, photographer, 1920–1950. P&P, LC-H814-A05-035-A.

8-109. View of Unknown Soldier's Tomb, Memorial Amphitheater, Arlington National Cemetery, Arlington, Virginia. Dedicated May 30, 1920; 4,000 seats; Carrère & Hastings, architects. Theodor Horydczak, photographer, 1931–1950. P&P, LC-H824-1933-009.

8-110. Memorial Amphitheater, Arlington National Cemetery, Arlington, Virginia. Dedicated May 30, 1920; 4,000 seats; Carrère & Hastings, architects. Theodor Horydczak, photographer, 1920–1950. P&P, LC-H814-A05-023.

In the aftermath of World War I, attendance at Memorial Day celebrations so increased that the old amphitheater became inadequate and was supplanted by an elegant new facility. The nation's sacred gathering place, the Memorial Amphitheatre is a monument to all who have been lost in the country's wars. On its steps are the tombs of America's Unknown Soldiers.

SHAKESPEAREAN THEATERS

William Shakespeare's stature is unmatched in theater history. During the nineteenth century some of the most noted actors in England and America devoted their careers to his works. Almost every new theater of the day opened with a performance of Hamlet or Macbeth, for patrons who were sufficiently familiar with the plays to detect the slightest misstep and point it out vociferously. A rivalry between two Shakespearean actors was at the heart of America's only true theater riot (see 1-027).

Although it was a mainstay of their programming, the grand opera houses that dotted America's prairie towns were not architecturally adapted to Shakespearean repertory. In the twentieth century, however, several buildings were erected specifically for it, including scholarly reconstructions of the Globe. Other theaters, like the Shakespeare Festival Theatre in Stratford, Connecticut, were designed for those who view Shakespeare as timeless and enjoy his works in modern presentations.

8-111

8-111. Park (Empire) Theatre, North Broad Street at Fairmount Avenue, Philadelphia, Pennsylvania. Opened September 16, 1889; 1,694 seats; J. B. McElfatrick & Sons, architects. U.S. Printing Company, lithographers, ca. 1898. P&P, POS-TH-1898.S52 No. 1.

8-112. Folger Shakespeare Library, 201 East Capitol Street SE, Washington, D.C. Opened April 23, 1932; Paul Philippe Cret, architect; Alexander B. Trowbridge, consulting architect. Theodor Horydczak, photographer, ca. 1932. P&P, LC-H824-L04-022-B.

8-112

8-113

8-116

8-113. Folger Shakespeare Library, 201 East Capitol Street SE, Washington, D.C. Opened April 23, 1932; Paul Philippe Cret, architect; Alexander B. Trowbridge, consulting architect. Samuel H. Gottscho, photographer, June 22, 1932. P&P, LC-G612-18402.

8-114. Folger Shakespeare Library Theatre, 201 East Capitol Street SE, Washington, D.C. Opened April 23, 1932; 300 seats; Paul Philippe Cret, architect; Alexander B. Trowbridge, consulting architect. Theodor Horydczak, photographer, ca. 1932. P&P, LC-H814-L04-105.

The building contains a theater that evokes the courtyard of an English Renaissance inn, where Shakespeare's plays are presented in a style and setting that their author would find familiar.

8-115. Folger Shakespeare Library Theatre, 201 East Capitol Street SE, Washington, D.C. Opened April 23, 1932; 300 seats; Paul Philippe Cret, architect; Alexander B. Trowbridge, consulting architect. Theodor Horydczak, photographer, ca. 1932. P&P, LC-H814-L04-103.

8-116. Folger Shakespeare Library Theatre, 201 East Capitol Street SE, Washington, D.C. Opened April 23, 1932; 300 seats; Paul Philippe Cret, architect; Alexander B. Trowbridge, consulting architect. Samuel H. Gottscho, photographer, June 22, 1932. P&P, LC-G612-18408.

8-114

8-115

8-117. American Shakespeare Festival Theatre (Stratford Festival Theater), Stratford, Connecticut. Opened July 12, 1955; 1,500 seats; Edwin L. Howard, architect. Gottscho-Schleisner, Inc., photographer, December 6, 1955. P&P, LC-G613-68466.

It seems natural that a town called Stratford should celebrate Shakespeare with a theater devoted to his works. From a distance, the Festival Theatre recalls the Royal Shakespeare Theatre at Stratford-upon-Avon, in England. Inside it is thoroughly non-historicist, a place where Shakespeare can be presented comfortably in a nontraditional fashion. The auditorium takes the form of a university theater, evoking the historical Shakespearean theater form only in its angular balcony rail and its somewhat rough-hewn box seats.

8-118. Lobby, American Shakespeare Festival Theatre (Stratford Festival Theater), Stratford, Connecticut. Opened July 12, 1955; 1,500 seats; Edwin L. Howard, architect. Gottscho-Schleisner, Inc., photographer, December 6, 1955. P&P, LC-G613-68473.

8-119. American Shakespeare Festival Theatre (Stratford Festival Theater), Stratford, Connecticut. Opened July 12, 1955; 1,500 seats; Edwin L. Howard, architect. Gottscho-Schleisner, Inc., photographer, December 6, 1955. P&P, LC-G613-68472.

8-117

8-118

8-119

Ah, summer! With the coming of the warm season people throughout history have sought outdoor recreation. The great amusement parks (see Section Five) that were direct fore-runners of the movie palace (see Section Six) drew thousands of patrons, but summer-time offered other theatrical experiences.

America's earliest summer theaters had direct or indirect religious associations. From Martha's Vineyard, Massachusetts, to Ocean Grove, New Jersey, Methodists established summer communities where small cottages or tents clustered around giant auditoriums that presented secular entertainments as well as religious services. Akin to these camp meetings were chautauquas. Originating in western New York State, these programs found a nationwide audience for lectures and entertainments.

Less serious in intent were summer concerts in the park. Almost every American city had a rustic park with some sort of auditorium. When the topography permitted, there might even be an outdoor bowl where music could be enjoyed in a spectacular setting. These concerts' popularity led great symphony orchestras and opera companies to pres-ent summer series in settings outside of their urban concert halls.

Summer informality was epitomized by come-as-you-are theater in converted barns. While they usually presented revivals of popular musicals and comedies, some barn theaters featured works of emerging dramatists in presentations that transcended those to be found in the city's commercial theaters.

Finally, there was the drive-in. Small children make theater-going a challenge. Responding to the post–World War II baby boom, moving picture exhibitors devised a theater type uniquely suited to young families. The requirements were simple—a parking lot fitted with a billboard-like screen, a projection booth, and an ample refreshment stand. Admission was cheap, and once inside there was dinner for the family, play equip-ment for the children, and a place for them to sleep away the evening—the back seat. And as they grew toward adulthood, the baby boomers' own babies discovered that the drive-in afforded a privacy level that rivaled their parents' favorite dating spot: the back of the movie house balcony.

8-120. The Great Auditorium, Pilgrim Pathway at Ocean Pathway, Ocean Grove, New Jersey. Opened August 9, 1894; 10,000 seats; Frederick T. Camp, architect. David Ames, photographer, August, 1991. P&P, HABS,NJ,13-OCEG,1A-1.

The Ocean Grove Camp Meeting was founded in 1869 as a place where Methodists could gather during the summer in a setting that was strong in spirit and free of sin. For over a century, alcoholic beverages were prohibited in its year-round community. Every Sunday businesses were shuttered and gates were drawn across the town's entries, as automobiles were banned from view and operation. Over six hundred tiny tents clustered around the Great Auditorium where summer worship and entertainment activities took place.

8-121. The Great Auditorium, Pilgrim Pathway at Ocean Pathway, Ocean Grove, New Jersey. Opened August 9, 1894; 10,000 seats; Frederick T. Camp, architect. DPCC, photographer, 1900–1908. P&P, LC-D4-33232.

Since its opening, every president of the United States has spoken from the Great Auditorium's platform and major entertainers from Mark Twain to Enrico Caruso to Victor Borge have performed there.

8-120

8-121

8-122

8-0123

8-122. Amphitheatre, Chautauqua, New York. Opened 1893; 5,600 seats; Paul Pelz, architect. William Henry Jackson, photographer, 1893–1897. P&P, LC-D4-4427.

Contemporary in date and spirit with the Great Auditorium was the Chautauqua Amphitheatre in western New York. Founded as a Methodist summer camp, the Chautauqua Institution provided an edifying and educational place of summer retreat in a lovely lakeside setting. Its success became the foundation of a movement. In the latter part of the nineteenth century chautauquas were founded in such far-flung places as Florida and California.

8-0123. Amphitheatre, Chautauqua, New York. Opened 1893; 5,600 seats; Paul Pelz, architect. William Henry Jackson, photographer, 1880–1897. P&P, LC-D4-4472.

8-124. Chautauqua Assembly, Clarinda, Iowa. Opened August 5, 1908. F. J. Bandholtz, photographer, August 12, 1908. P&P, LC-USZ62-24372.

The chautauqua movement reached Iowa in 1904, when a touring company made presentations in fifteen towns. Soon after, several permanent facilities were built. Clarinda's assembly hall, built in 1908, is the oldest remaining chautauqua building in the state.

8-124

8-125. Pain's Great War Spectacle, Manhattan Beach, Brooklyn, New York. Sackett & Wilhelms Lithography Co., lithographers, ca. 1890. P&P, POS-TH-SPE, no. 34 (color).

This poster promised fiery excitement for summer audiences in Manhattan Beach, but its presenters were as interesting as the show. Peter Pain's family manufactured and sold gunpowder in England as early as 1593 and shifted its attention to fireworks in the eighteenth century. In 1879 James Pain Jr. conceived the pyrospectacular, a show in which actors and musicians performed while re-created historical disasters exploded behind them. For over thirty years, the Mexican War, the Siege of Vicksburg, the Last Days of Pompeii, the Siege of Vera Cruz, and other Pain spectacles toured America's major cities. After over five hundred years, the Pain Company continues in business.

8-126. Pain's Pyro Spectacle, Manhattan Beach, Brooklyn, New York. Pain's Pyro Spectacle Company, photographers, ca. 1895. P&P, Panoramic Photographs Collection, PAN SUBJECT - Events, no. 66 (E size).

When Pain presented his pyrospectacle of Japan and China at Coney Island's easternmost outpost, a sea of temporary seats faced a wide stage on the shore of the Atlantic.

8-127. Pain's Spectacle, Manhattan Beach, Brooklyn, New York. B. J. Falk, photographer, ca. 1903. P&P, LC-USZ62-114523.

At evening's end the elaborate recreation of Pompeii would erupt in explosive flames. In preparation for the mayhem, performers presented a kick-line dance that would have seemed familiar to audiences at Radio City Music Hall (see 7-016–7-023) a generation later.

8-125

8-126

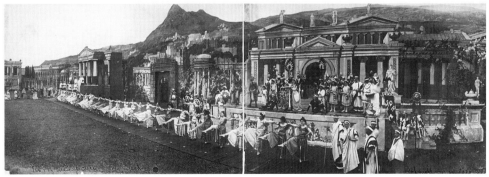

8-127

8-128

8-129

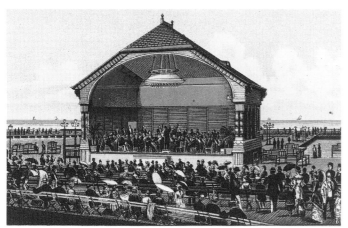

8-130

8-131

8-128. Amphitheater and Catalina Island Incline, Avalon, Catalina Island, California. Opened ca. 1904. DPCC, photographer, 1900–1915. P&P, LC-D418-31433.

A funicular railway built in 1904 connected the hotels of Avalon City with Pebble Beach, at Lover's Cove, on the opposite side of the mountain. Along the route were a mountaintop inn, a restaurant, and the Amphitheater, which provided concertgoers a spectacular view not only of the stage, but of the Bay and the picturesque town of Avalon. The resort's palmy days ended in 1915, when most of its buildings burned.

8-129. Amphitheater, Avalon, Catalina Island, California. Opened ca. 1904. DPCC, photographer, 1900–1915. P&P, LC-D418-31432.

8-130. Long Beach Music Pavilion, Long Beach, New York. Opened July 17, 1880. Unidentified artist, ca. 1883. P&P, LC-USZ62-80388.

8-131. Outdoor Theatre, Fairmount Park, Highway 24 at Willow Street, Kansas City, Missouri. Opened 1887. George R. Lawrence, photographer, ca. 1907. P&P, Panoramic Photographs Collection, PAN SUBJECT - Events, no. 68.

Before the advent of the active amusement parks of the 1890s, urbanites enjoyed picnicking in the large summer gardens built by local transit companies. Fairmount Park was situated along the Air Line, an interurban trolley that connected Kansas City with Independence, Missouri. It included athletic and horse-racing facilities as well as the popular outdoor theater.

8-132. Rustic Theatre, Riverton Park, Route 302, Portland, Maine. Opened ca. 1896. DPCC, photographer, 1900–1915. P&P, LC-D4-39320.

Portland's trolley park, Riverton, was established in 1896 as a place of rural retreat on the banks of the Presumpscot River. Set within extensive picnic grounds were a bandstand, croquet facilities, a dancing casino, and a petting zoo as well as the rustic theater. Riverton became an amusement park in 1923 and closed six years later.

8-133. Euclid Avenue Garden Theatre, 4505 Euclid Avenue, Cleveland, Ohio. Opened March, 1904. DPCC, photographer, 1900–1910. P&P, LC-D4-36527.

8-134. Hippodrome, Euclid Beach Park, Cleveland, Ohio. Opened ca. 1895. DPCC, photographer, ca. 1905. P&P, LC-D4-33960.

Euclid Beach, a trolley park on Cleveland's east side, began as a bucolic summer resort, became an amusement park in 1901, and operated for seventy-five years. The elaborate Hippodrome, added in 1907, claimed incorrectly to be the first theater in the country to be exclusively devoted to motion pictures.

8-135. Theatre, Olentangy Park, Columbus, Ohio. Opened ca. 1899. DPCC, photographer, 1900–1915. P&P, LC-D4-39062.

The Villa, built in 1893 by the Columbus Street and Railway Company, had been in operation for six years when it was revamped as the still elegant, but more amusement-oriented Olentangy Park. The impressive theater, added as part of the conversion, was advertised as the largest in America.

8-136

8-139

8-137

8-138

8-136. Theatre, Forest Park, Little Rock, Arkansas. DPCC, photographer, 1900–1915. P&P, LC-D4-39507.

8-137. Wharf Theatre, Provincetown, Massachusetts. Opened 1923; 350 seats. Carl Van Vechten, photographer, July 31, 1936. P&P, Carl Van Vechten Photograph Collection, LOT 12736, no. 1332.

The Wharf was one of two theaters that descended from the seminal Provincetown Playhouse. Founded in 1915, the Playhouse defined the theatrical vanguard as the first to present the work of budding playwright Eugene O'Neill. Within two seasons the company moved to Broadway, returning to its old home to entertain summer visitors. The Wharf was inauspicious, lacking a lobby and most amenities, but it was popular with townspeople, as it often used local talent in its casts. Destroyed in a windstorm on February 14, 1940, the theater was not rebuilt.

8-138. Barn Theatre, 6750 West Loomis Road, Greendale, Wisconsin. John Vachon, photographer, September, 1939. P&P, LC-USF34-060124-D.

One of three "greenbelt" communities built during the Great Depression, Greendale provided 572 housing units in an attractive community on the outskirts of Milwaukee. At the end of its main street vista was the theater, a dairy barn built in 1923 that had lost its supporting fields as the town rose around it. By 1955 the barn had found yet another use as a youth hostel.

8-139. Gem Theatre, Peaks Island, Portland, Maine. Opened ca. 1880. DPCC, photographer, ca. 1904. P&P, LC-D4-17739.

The cylindrical profile of the Gem Theatre dominated Peaks Island. Converted from an old roller-skating rink, the Gem was Maine's first summer stock theater, entertaining visitors who had made the boat trip from nearby Portland. Opening night was a New England–wide social event. After the Gem burned, the island, once briefly known as the Coney Island of the East, reverted to life as a picturesque community of resident artists and Portland commuters.

8-141

8-142

8-143

8-140

8-140. Theatre, Berkshire (Tanglewood). Opened ca. 1943, Saarinen & Swanson, architects. Gottscho-Schleisner, Inc., photographer, June 25, 1946. P&P, LC-G612-49241.

8-141. Theatre, Berkshire (Tanglewood) Music Center, Lenox, Massachusetts. Opened ca. 1943; Saarinen & Swanson, architects. Gottscho-Schleisner, Inc., photographer, June 25, 1946. P&P, LC-G612-49234.

Summertime musical presentations in the tranquility of the countryside have become traditional among America's major orchestras. When Tanglewood, the Tappan family estate, was given to the Boston Symphony in 1936, concerts were presented in the partial shelter of a tent. After a rainout, the tent was replaced by the 5,100-seat Koussevitsky Music Shed, followed by the Theatre, with its innovative roof suspended from exposed bowed beams.

8-142. Theatre, Berkshire (Tanglewood) Music Center, Lenox, Massachusetts. Opened ca. 1943; Saarinen & Swanson, architects. Gottscho-Schleisner, Inc., photographer, June 25, 1946. P&P, LC-G612-49240.

8-143. Theatre, Berkshire (Tanglewood) Music Center, Lenox, Massachusetts. Opened ca. 1943; Saarinen & Swanson, architects. Gottscho-Schleisner, Inc., photographer, November 27, 1943. P&P, LC-G612-44437.

8-144

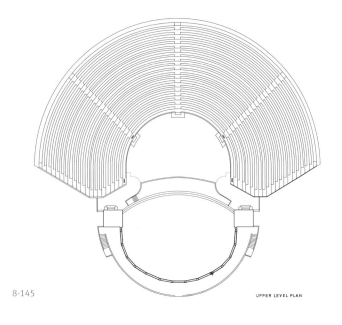

8-145

UPPER LEVEL PLAN

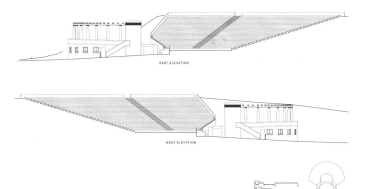

EAST ELEVATION

WEST ELEVATION

8-146

8-144. Outdoor Theatre, Caramoor, Katonah, New York. Opened 1958, Frederick Keisler, architect. Gottscho-Schleisner, Inc., photographer, June 18, 1958. P&P, LC-G613-72521.

Walter and Lucie Rosen's estate, Caramoor, a traditionally styled great house near Katonah, was built for music. Mrs. Rosen was sufficiently proficient in playing the theremin that she had performed with the Philadelphia Orchestra in Carnegie Hall and the couple regularly held musical evenings at their summer home. In 1945 the Rosens established a foundation to maintain the house as a museum and home to an annual international music festival. This outdoor stage, designed by Austrian-American modernist Frederick Keisler, served the 1958 season.

8-145. Plan, Chi Omega Greek Theatre, Dickson Street, Fayetteville, Arkansas. Opened June 28, 1930; 2,750 seats; Jamieson & Spearl, architects. Steve Armstrong and Earnest Duckery, delineators. P&P, HABS AR-44.

As specialized as—and even rarer than—Shakespearean theaters are outdoor bowls that recall the theaters of ancient Greece. The Greek Theater at the University of Arkansas retains the classical spirit but modifies the Grecian form by truncating the circular orchestra space and curving the proscenium colonnade to accommodate a large ellipsoidal stage.

8-146. East and west elevations, Chi Omega Greek Theatre, Dickson Street, Fayetteville, Arkansas. Opened June 28, 1930; 2,750 seats; Jamieson & Spearl, architects. Steve Armstrong and Earnest Duckery, delineators. P&P, HABS AR-44.

8-147. Star Drive-in Theatre, U.S. Highway 59 at Minnesota Highway 200, Mahnomen, Minnesota. 130 spaces. Jet Lowe, photographer, May, 1990. P&P, HABS,MINN,44-MAHN,1-1.

At its heart, a drive-in was a parking lot supplied with a screen, a sign, and a projection booth. The Star displayed these elements in their most basic form.

8-148. Westbury Drive-in, Brush Hollow Road, Westbury, New York. Unidentified photographer, 1954. P&P, LC-USZ62-122332.

8-149. Drive-in theater, Hollywood, California. United Press International, photographer, 1957. P&P, LC-USZ62-119370.

Sound quality never was the drive-in's strong suit. In the earliest theaters, large speakers atop the screen broadcast the sound to the patrons and the surrounding community alike. In-car speakers were a marked improvement: the sound was better for the patrons, silent for the neighbors. People who drove off without removing the speaker from their window remained a problem until the end. Here actress Natalie Wood demonstrates the latest model.

8-147

8-148

8-149

8-150

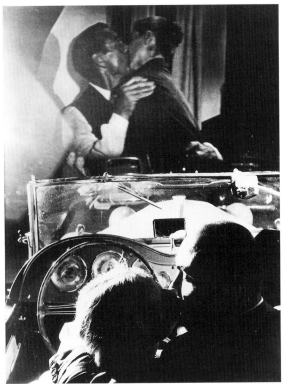

8-151

8-152

8-150. All-weather Drive-in Theatre, Sunrise Highway, Copiague, New York. 2,500 spaces; 1,200 seats; John & Drew Eberson, architects. Joseph R. Burstin, photographer, 1957. P&P, LC-USZ62-122331.

The All-weather Drive-in was one of the largest ever built. In addition to space for 2,500 cars, it had a 1,200-seat indoor theater, a playground, cafeteria, and a full-service restaurant. A four-car trackless train shuttled people from their cars to the various facilities on the 28-acre property.

8-151. Drive-in theater. United Press International, photographer, 1957. P&P, LC-USZ62-122330.

Inspired by Gary Cooper and Audrey Hepburn, and unperturbed by the photographer, two drive-in customers share the tenderness of their own romance.

8-152. Airway Drive-in Theatre, St. Charles Rock Road, Meadville, Pennsylvania. 400 spaces. United Press International, photographer, 1961. P&P, LC-USZ62-119379.

Some drive-ins provided in-car heaters, but in Meadville, with the snow piled high, it was "too cold for kissin'."

ARENAS: WHEN A STAGE JUST WON'T DO

From the gladiatorial contests of ancient Rome to Ringling Bros. and Barnum & Bailey, from Buffalo Bill's Wild West to the Beatles, there have always been performances for which a conventional stage is too small. Such presentations have moved from the theater's confining box into performance facilities that are as big and informal as an outdoor stadium but provide audiences the comfort of a protected indoor environment. Some arenas have been as highly ornamented as conventional theaters; others have been as utilitarian as factories. Their common element, other than size, is a configuration of steeply raked seating encircling a large flat floor that may be used as an open performance area or fitted with additional seats to accommodate an even larger audience.

Although they are usually perceived as places to view athletic events, most arenas accommodate a wide variety of presentations, and can readily interchange trade shows and large conventions with sports events. Some have fully equipped stages as well as traditional arena floors.

Arenas have had a wide and varied history. Some of these huge structures were permanent landmarks in their communities; others were built of canvas, designed to present their show and then move on. All have been integral to the richness and variety of America's theatrical heritage.

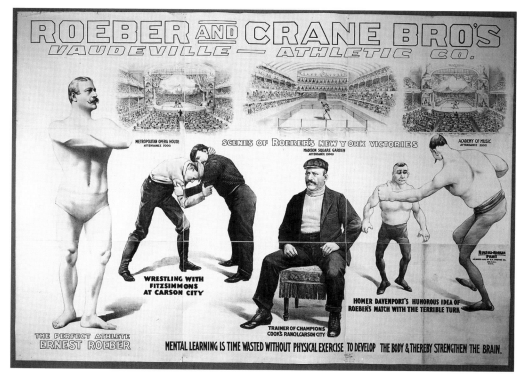

8-153

8-153. Roeber and Crane Bro's Vaudeville–Athletic Co. U.S. Printing Company, lithographers, ca. 1898. P&P, LC-USZ62-21438.

Despite their lofty artistic ambitions, even the most elite nineteenth-century theaters were used as general-purpose auditoriums. According to their poster, Roeber and Crane presented professional wrestling to an audience of 5,500 at the Academy of Music in Philadelphia, to 7,000 at the Metropolitan Opera House in New York, and to 15,000 at Madison Square Garden.

8-154

8-154. Barnum's Grand Roman Hippodrome (Gilmore's Garden, Madison Square Garden), Madison and Park Avenues, Twenty-fifth and Twenty-sixth Streets, New York, New York. Opened April 30, 1874; 10,000 seats. Unidentified delineator, 1889. P&P, LC-USZ62-2503.

Trains once rolled down the surface of New York City's Park Avenue to Madison Square. When the first Grand Central Terminal opened in 1871, the railroad leased its old downtown station to an entertainment consortium led by P. T. Barnum. Outside, the building was a plain-walled affair with diminutive corner towers. Within, it was only partially enclosed. The oval arena, in the location of former train platforms, remained open to the sky, but could be shielded by canvas in bad weather. On April 9, 1882, in this first building to be called Madison Square Garden, Barnum introduced to the world an elephant named Jumbo. In 1889 the former Hippodrome was replaced by a much superior Madison Square Garden (8-155).

8-155. Madison Square Garden, Madison and Park Avenues, Twenty-fifth and Twenty-sixth Streets, New York, New York. Opened June 16, 1890; 10,704 permanent seats, 2,242 floor seats in main hall, 1,038 seats in Garden Theatre; McKim, Mead & White, architects. DPCC, photographer, 1900–1910. P&P, LC-D4-33775.

The Madison Square Garden that rose on the site of Barnum's Hippodrome became a major New York landmark whose name was passed along to two successor buildings elsewhere in the city. In addition to a massive amphitheater with an equally massive stage, it housed a moderate-sized conventional theater, an extensive roof garden (opened May 30, 1891), a concert hall (opened October 23, 1891), a restaurant, and America's highest observation tower at the time, all topped by Augustus Saint-Gaudens's gilded Diana weathervane. The popular venue was the masterpiece and evening haunt of architect Stanford White, who was murdered there in 1906 by the jealous husband of Evelyn Nesbitt, rumored to be White's paramour.

8-155

8-156. Madison Square Garden, Madison and Park Avenues, Twenty-fifth and Twenty-sixth Streets, New York, New York. Opened June 16, 1890; 10,704 permanent seats, 2,242 floor seats in main hall, 1,038 seats in Garden Theatre; McKim, Mead & White, architects. Poster, 1891. P&P, LC-USZ62-19692.

Madison Square Garden opened with a performance by Eduard Strauss's Famous Imperial Court Orchestra, advertised in this massive poster.

8-156

8-157. Northern Liberty Market (Convention Hall Center Market), Fifth and K Streets NW, Washington, D.C. Opened January 1875; 5,000 seats; James H. McGill, architect. Unidentified photographer, ca. 1925. P&P, LC-USZ62-96461.

The Northern Liberty Market, a monumental structure that boasted the largest unsupported roof span in Washington at the time, opened in 1875. It was only modestly successful and by 1891 was converted into Convention Hall, for which a second floor was inserted into its volume.

8-158. Olympia, 5920 Grand River Avenue, Detroit, Michigan. Opened October 17, 1927; 17,000 seats; C. Howard Crane, architect. Carla Anderson, photographer, May, 1986. P&P, HABS,MICH,82-DETRO,25-2.

A majestic presence on Grand River Avenue, Olympia's 17,000 seats made it one of America's great arenas. Although best known as home to the city's professional hockey team, Olympia hosted a wide variety of large events. It once even presented a fully staged opera.

8-159. Olympia, 5920 Grand River Avenue, Detroit, Michigan. Opened October 17, 1927; 17,000 seats; C. Howard Crane, architect. Architect's plan drawing, November 13, 1927. P&P, HABS,MICH,82-DETRO,25-7.

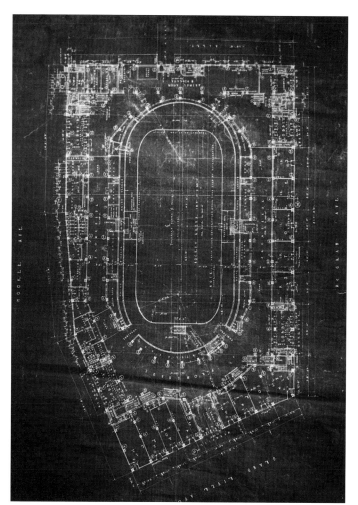

8-160

8-161

8-162

8-160. Olympia, 5920 Grand River Avenue, Detroit, Michigan. Opened October 17, 1927; 17,000 seats; C. Howard Crane, architect. Unidentified photographer, 1969. P&P, HABS,MICH,82-DETRO,25-15.

8-161. Chicago Stadium, 1800 West Madison Street, Chicago, Illinois. Opened March 28, 1929; 17,317 seats; Hall, Lawrence & Ratcliffe, architects. Unidentified photographer, 1929. P&P, U.S. GEOG FILE - Illinois - Chicago - Stadiums.

Chicago Stadium, the "Madhouse on Madison," was considered to be the largest indoor arena in the world when it opened. Especially notable was its Barton pipe organ, the largest theater-type instrument ever built, which was suspended in a vast chamber above the arena floor and controlled by a huge six-manual console. Unable to compete with newer venues, the stadium was demolished in 1995.

8-162. Pan-Pacific Auditorium, 7600 West Beverly Boulevard, Los Angeles, California. Opened 1935; 6,000 seats; Wurdeman & Becket, architects. Marvin Rand, photographer, 1972-1977. P&P, HABS,CAL.19-LOSAN,41-2.

A modernist showpiece, the Auditorium hosted sports, political events, circuses, trade shows, and concerts. Notable performers ranged from Elvis Presley to Leopold Stokowski, Dwight Eisenhower to the Ice Capades. Although long considered a historic landmark, the building fell into disuse. It was destroyed by a spectacular fire in May 24, 1989.

8-163. The Grand Lay-out. Gibson & Company, lithographer, ca. 1874. P&P, LC-USZ62-1028; LC-USZC4-6048 (color).

Upon its arrival, as roustabouts erected the tents, circus performers paraded through town with their calliope, gaudy wagons, and caged animals. Having made the community aware of its presence, the entourage headed for the circus grounds with, the managers hoped, a following of eager customers. Here, a circus parade circles the array of its variformed tents. In the background at least six trains converge on the site.

8-164. Unidentified circus. Calvert Lithographing Company, lithographer, ca. 1891. P&P, LC-USZ62-24532; LC-USZC4-5117 (color).

The centerpiece of every traveling circus was the enormous big top. Smaller tents were located nearby to house sideshows. Here, a parade of elephants and caged big cats circles through the circus grounds.

8-165. Primrose & Dockstader's Huge Minstrel Company. Flourished ca. 1900; 3,000 seats. Strobridge Lithographing Company, lithographers, ca. 1900. P&P, POS-MIN-.P753, no. 5.

The circus held no exclusive rights to massive tents. Primrose and Dockstader's Company, premier minstrel performers, were proud of their "great canvas theatre." Inside, it was a theater in every way, with a proscenium stage, a parquet circle, rows of upholstered seats, and carpeted aisles.

8-166. Primrose & Dockstader's Huge Minstrel Company. Flourished ca. 1900; 3,000 seats. Strobridge Lithographing Company, lithographers, ca. 1900. P&P, LC-USZ62-2650.

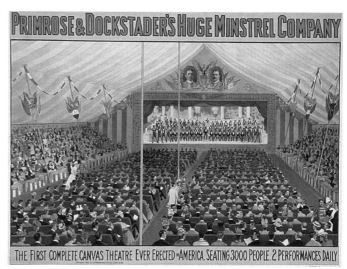

8-167

8-168

8-169

8-167. Adam Forepaugh & Sells Brothers Consolidated Shows. Courier Lithographing Company, lithographers, ca. 1900. P&P, LC-USZ62-24530; LC-USZC4-5120 (color).

If a minstrel show could use a tent, a circus certainly could find accommodation in a permanent arena. Kilpatrick made his famous downstairs run in a large wooden-roofed hall with parquet circle and balcony, said to be Madison Square Garden (see 8-156), while "the frolics and amusing antics of twenty funny felt-crowned fools" were seen in a more expected big-top setting (8-168).

8-168. Adam Forepaugh & Sells Brothers Consolidated Shows. Strobridge Lithographing Company, lithographers, ca. 1899. P&P, LC-USZ62-24107; LC-USZC4-2986 (color).

8-169. Unidentified circus. Exhibit Supply Company, photographer, ca. 1923. P&P, LC-USZ62-109396.

8-170

8-171

8-172

8-170. South Louisiana State Fair, Donaldsonville, Louisiana. Russell Lee, photographer, October, 1938. P&P, LC-USF33-011752-M1.

In a side tent, a visitor to the fair peers into a Mutoscope.

8-171. South Louisiana State Fair, Donaldsonville, Louisiana. Russell Lee, photographer, October, 1938. P&P, LC-USF34-031678-D.

Later, at the same Mutoscope, a group of boys explores a girlie flick while the Laurel & Hardy machine next to it remains idle.

8-172. Traveling carnival, Old Trap, North Carolina. Jack Delano, photographer, July, 1940. P&P, LC-USF33-020568-M1.

Never the size of a circus big top, a carnival tent generally had a canvas entry vestibule on one of its long sides. Next to it, a portable wooden box office welcomed customers. Inside was a stage with a canvas proscenium, a film screen, and conventional vaudeville scenery. This troupe followed the movements of migrant workers, stopping wherever there was a large settlement. The show included a band concert, a movie, and vaudeville.

8-173. Traveling carnival, Old Trap, North Carolina. Jack Delano, photographer, July, 1940. P&P, LC-USF33-020567-M3.

8-173

8-174

8-175

8-176

8-177

8-174. Lasses White All Star Minstrels, Sikeston, Missouri. Russell Lee, photographer, May, 1938. P&P, LC-USF34-031256-D.

In his earliest performing days, Le Roy "Lasses" White toured with Lee David "Honey" Wilds, presenting blackface minstrel tent shows in rural communities. Later he performed with the Grand Old Opry before turning to Hollywood, where he appeared in some sixty-four movies, generally as a comic sidekick to cowboy star Jimmy Wakely. Photographer Russell Lee carefully chronicled the process of erecting the tent that would hold the week's performances.

8-175. Lasses White All Star Minstrels, Sikeston, Missouri. Russell Lee, photographer, May, 1938. P&P, LC-USF34-031254-D.

With the main poles in place, the large canvas tent was positioned around them.

8-176. Lasses White All Star Minstrels, Sikeston, Missouri. Russell Lee, photographer, May, 1938. P&P, LC-USF34-031253-D.

8-177. Lasses White All Star Minstrels, Sikeston, Missouri. Russell Lee, photographer, May, 1938. P&P, LC-USF34-031260-D.

The perimeter of the tent is elevated into position. Roll-down sides will be installed later.

8-178

8-179

8-180

8-178. Lasses White All Star Minstrels, Sikeston, Missouri. Russell Lee, photographer, May, 1938. P&P, LC-USF34-031268-D.

The peak of the tent is hoisted onto the main poles.

8-179. Lasses White All Star Minstrels, Sikeston, Missouri. Russell Lee, photographer, May, 1938. P&P, LC-USF34-031269-D.

With a heave, the intermediate supports are put into position.

8-180. Lasses White All Star Minstrels, Sikeston, Missouri. Russell Lee, photographer, May, 1938. P&P, LC-USF34-031243-D.

The tent's sides are put into place as chairs are installed within.

8-181. Lasses White All Star Minstrels, Sikeston, Missouri. Russell Lee, photographer, May, 1938. P&P, LC-USF34-031272-D.

The tent in place, a roustabout takes a much-deserved rest on a hammock suspended beneath the truck.

8-181

8-182

8-185

8-183

8-184

8-182. Strickland's Place, Starke, Florida. Marion Post Wolcott, photographer, December, 1940. P&P, LC-USF34- 056685-D.

In rural areas, a sudden population boom could prompt the establishment of tent movies. Strickland's Place served workers and soldiers at nearby Camp Blanding. In addition to movies, Strickland's accommodated church picnics and provided fishermen with a private landing.

8-183. Federal Theatre, San Bernardino, California. Dorothea Lange, photographer, February, 1937. P&P, LC-USF34-016228-D.

Under government sponsorship, the Depression-era Federal Theatre Project presented fine drama at a modest price. In San Bernardino, the shows took place under canvas.

8-184. Rutland Fair, Rutland, Vermont. Jack Delano, photographer, September, 1941. P&P, LC-USF34-045499-D.

Located next to the circus big top or the state fair midway was the sideshow, a row of nondescript booths made seductive by large, colorful banners. The shows within were marketed in the same way as early movies. A barker rasped into a microphone to draw a crowd as one of the entertainers appeared briefly outside as a lure. That the show was a letdown came as no surprise, but maybe it was worth the dime to recognize the scam.

8-185. Movie tent, Kymulga, Alabama. Jack Delano, photographer, 1941. P&P, LC-USF34-044351-D.

The photographer noted that although it opened with great expectations, this movie tent operation closed down after three days due to lack of attendance. Kymulga was the closest village to a DuPont gunpowder plant in nearby Childersburg.

8-186

8-187

8-186. Rutland Fair, Rutland, Vermont. Jack Delano, photographer, September, 1941. P&P, LC-USF34-045490-D.

Sideshow performers were not necessarily human. The booths frequently displayed as freaks genetically malformed animals—two-headed calves, six-legged sheep. Others, often reptiles, were presented as monstrously dangerous even though they were normal and benign. The "live monster" may well have been a small garden lizard. Step in if you dare!

8-187. Rutland Fair, Rutland, Vermont. Jack Delano, photographer, September, 1941. P&P, LC-USF34-045502-D.

"It's real; it's alive!" A pitchman points out the wonders that credulous spectators would find at a modest admission price. "Step right up!"

8-188. Rutland Fair, Rutland, Vermont. Jack Delano, photographer, September, 1941. P&P, LC-USF34-045504-D.

8-188

The flashy banners hid the nitty-gritty of traveling show business. Windowless trailers functioned as dressing rooms for the exotic dancers of the fair's girlie show.

8-189. Hagenbeck & Wallace Circus sideshow. Theodor Horydczak, photographer, ca. 1920–1950. P&P, LC-H822-1729.

The sideshow tent presented a genuinely spectacular wall of art to spectators heading for the big top to the left.

8-189

It's Hot   HOT POP CORN

ENCORE: WHAT PEOPLE DO TO THEATERS!

THEATERS OCCUPY A UNIQUE PLACE in the heart of an affectionate public. Historically, they have been old at thirty-five, obsolete at fifty. Yet, they seem to have been around forever. The memories that they hold make them beloved; we are alarmed when one is threatened and deeply saddened when one disappears. Unfortunately, many have.

Theaters have suffered from loss of fashion and functional change. Some were left high and dry when new entertainment districts grew in other areas of the city. The horseshoe balconies of early legitimate theaters imposed sight lines that were ill-suited to film presentation and many early cinemas proved to be uncomfortably cavernous and reverberant when sound-film technology arrived. The movie palaces that had brought crowds downtown became obsolete in the post–World War II era when television revealed its superior efficiency in delivering entertainment to mass audiences. Some theater owners tried to survive by making their buildings look modern, but their efforts, generally partial and under-budgeted, rarely were successful. Others cut staff and reduced services, entering a downward spiral of deterioration. Many theaters closed.

Some remained alive by becoming other things—a challenging accomplishment. Compared with other building types, theaters are notoriously hard to make into anything else. Their windowless envelopes, sloping floors, stepped balconies, and the specialized construction of their stages get in the way of most non-theater uses. The most frequent occupants of former theaters are supermarkets, large drugstores, which take advantage of the unencumbered volumes, and churches, which find them ready-made assembly places.

Theaters taken for granted by one generation became historic monuments in the next. While many of America's greatest theaters have been lost, others are finding new life. The means, in most cases, has been to transfer the buildings from the private sector to the community. Not-for-profit organizations have restored the buildings and shifted their programming from inexpensive mass-market entertainment to cultural presentations that serve a higher-ticket clientele. Their success has demonstrated that historic theater reuse is both culturally sound and an act of economic common sense. As the age of the Victorian opera house once yielded to the movie palace, the age of the movie palace is becoming the age of the performing arts center; across the country, old and historic theaters large and small, grand and homespun, are again becoming glittering showplaces of entertainment, culture, and community pride.

9-001. Musical Fund Hall, 808 Locust Street, Philadelphia, Pennsylvania. Opened December 1824; William Strickland, architect. P&P, SUBJ FILE-THEATERS.

One of Philadelphia's early concert and meeting facilities, Musical Fund Hall was the site of the Republican Party's first nominating convention, in 1856.

9-002. Musical Fund Hall, 808 Locust Street, Philadelphia, Pennsylvania. Opened 1824; William Strickland, architect; new facade 1893; Addison Hutton, architect. George A. Eisenman, photographer, April, 1976. P&P, HABS,PA,51-PHILA,494-1.

In 1893 the present facade transformed the building's street presence. In 1981, when the hall was reconfigured as an apartment building, every vestige of the original interior was removed.

9-001

9-002

9-003. Capitol Theatre, Frankfort, Kentucky. Built 1883. John Vachon, photographer, November, 1940. P&P, LC-USF34-061812-D.

People make theaters into other things and they make other things into theaters. In Kentucky, the colorful marquee of the Capitol, whose 19-cent movies made it Frankfort's bargain house, upstaged the Gothic lines of the venerable city hall. Public assembly places or windowless commercial buildings are naturals for conversion.

9-004. Detroit Opera House, 5–15 Campus Martius, Detroit, Michigan. Opened September 12, 1898; 1,757 seats; Mason & Rice, architects. Arthur S. Siegel, photographer, July, 1942. P&P, LC-USF34-110158-C.

Once the city's pride, the Detroit Opera House fell on hard times during the Great Depression. From 1936 until 1966 it functioned as Sam's Cut Rate, Michigan's largest discount store. Proprietor Sam Osnos had an affinity for old theaters. He converted Detroit's former Grand Opera House (see 3-039 and 3-040) into a store like this and had similar intentions for the city's Orchestra Hall (see 8-074–8-079).

9-005. Studio Theatre, P Street at Fourteenth Street NW, Washington, D.C. National Photo Company, photographer, ca. 1920. P&P, LC-USZ62-117636.

The Trew Motor Company's combined showroom, warehouse, and service garage became a popular playhouse.

9-003

9-004

9-005

9-006

9-007

9-008

9-006. Roxbury Gas Light Company Gasholder, 7 Gerard Street, Boston, Massachusetts. Jet Lowe, photographer, 1982. P&P, HAER,MASS,13-BOST,85-1.

Specialized buildings are less likely candidates for conversion, but in Boston, a cylindrical brick building built to enclose a natural gas storage tank, served as a moving picture theater in the 1920s.

9-007. Victor Theatre, 119 West Church Street, Anderson, South Carolina. Opened 1922. P&P, HABS,SC,4-AND,9-2.

A building's theatrical life often was brief and disappeared leaving hardly a trace. The building in the center of this image had other uses before and after it housed the Victor, but its unassuming interior (9-008) was filled with mirth and merriment for three brief years in the 1920s. The Victor's history is not unique. A search for America's remaining theatrical venues will turn up many buildings just like this one.

9-008. Victor Theatre, 119 West Church Street, Anderson, South Carolina. Opened 1922. P&P, HABS,SC,4-AND,9-4.

9-009

9-010

9-009. G. F. Andrae Opera House (Fox Theatre), 1124 Main Street, Stevens Point, Wisconsin. Opened 1893; 771 seats; Oscar Cobb & Sons, architects. Edward J. Purcell, photographer, November, 1984. P&P, HABS,WIS,49-STEPO,1-1.

When the Opera House became the Fox, its facade remained relatively intact, as did the unused stage and dressing rooms. The auditorium, though, acquired a look of streamlined simplicity. Only the curve of the balcony remained as a reminder of the opera house's Victorian origin.

9-010. G. F. Andrae Opera House (Fox Theatre), 1124 Main Street, Stevens Point, Wisconsin. Built 1893; 771 seats; Oscar Cobb & Sons, architects. Edward J. Purcell, photographer, November, 1984. P&P, HABS,WIS,49-STEPO,1-15.

9-011. G. F. Andrae Opera House (Fox Theatre), 1124 Main Street, Stevens Point, Wisconsin. Opened 1893; 771 seats; Oscar Cobb & Sons, architects. Edward J. Purcell, photographer, November, 1984. P&P, HABS,WIS,49-STEPO,1-12.

9-011

9-012

9-013

9-014

9-015

9-012. Pabst Theatre, 144 East Wells Street, Milwaukee, Wisconsin. Opened November 9, 1895; 1,820 seats; Otto Strack, architect. P&P, HABS,WIS,40-MILWA,33-5.

The Pabst Theatre exhibited the post–Civil War spirit of civic beneficence. Frederick Pabst, a transplanted German, had worked as a steamboat captain before marrying into a wealthy Milwaukee brewing family. When the Nunnemacher Grand Opera House (Stadt Theatre) burned, Frederick and his son Gustave financed this replacement. Their architect, German-born Otto Strack, had previously designed the family's brewery. Although more experienced with breweries than theaters, he turned himself with dexterity to the design of this hall, whose technologies were heavily based upon the Chicago Auditorium (see 8-050–8-062).

9-013. Pabst Theatre, 144 East Wells Street, Milwaukee, Wisconsin. Opened November 9, 1895; 1,820 seats; Otto Strack, architect. George R. Lawrence Co., photographer, 1901. P&P, PAN SUBJECT–Groups, no. 283 (E size).

Like other great urban theaters, the Pabst saw occasional use for non-theatrical events. This photograph of an American Bankers Association's Convention shows the original box seats, delightful in their laciness and distinguished by the powerful geometry of the surmounting ornamental disk.

9-014. Pabst Theatre, 144 East Wells Street, Milwaukee, Wisconsin. Opened November 9, 1895; 1,820 seats; Otto Strack, architect. George R. Lawrence Co., photographer, November 23, 1906. P&P, LC-USZ62-52876.

The Pabst's original proscenium, shown here during a 1906 concert by the Arion Musical Club, featured the straight upper edge and elaborately painted canvas curtain that typified the nineteenth-century theater.

9-015. Pabst Theatre, 144 East Wells Street, Milwaukee, Wisconsin. Opened November 9, 1895; 1,820 seats; Otto Strack, architect. P&P, HABS,WIS,40-MILWA,33-8.

In 1928 the Pabst was fitted with new box seats and proscenium, giving the venerable hall the look of an up-to-date movie palace, the architectural forté of the renovators, Milwaukee architects Dick & Bauer.

9-016

9-017

9-016. Unidentified RKO Theater, New York, New York. Sales counter by Weiss & Bassner, designers. Gottscho-Schleisner, Inc., photographer, December 12, 1949. P&P, LC-G612-56304.

As the Great Depression forced admission prices down, exhibitors sought supplemental revenue sources. Popcorn and candy became integral to the movie-going experience, but their sales counters were uncomfortably shoehorned into older theaters. Curvaceous, brightly lit modern counters stand uneasily in the classical interiors of two New York movie palace lobbies, while a scalloped canopy gamely attempts to fit into the exotic surroundings of a third (9-018).

9-017. Unidentified RKO Theater, New York, New York. Sales counter by Weiss & Bassner, designers. Gottscho-Schleisner, Inc., photographer, December 12, 1949. P&P, LC-G612-56303.

9-018. Unidentified RKO Theater, New York, New York. Gottscho-Schleisner, Inc., photographer, December 12, 1949. P&P, LC-G612-56306.

9-018

9-019. Palace Theatre, 1306 F Street NW, Washington, D.C. Opened November 4, 1918; 2,463 seats; Thomas W. Lamb, architect. National Photo Company, photographer, 1924. P&P, LOT 12359-6-C.

Loew's showcase in America's capital had a large and magnificent interior but little street presence—at first just a gently curved marquee topped by an illuminated sign. In 1938 a high, curved parapet was built as a modern backdrop to a taller sign (9-020). The original facade, with its cornice and low parapet, remained untouched.

9-020. Palace Theatre, 1306 F Street NW, Washington, D.C. Opened November 4, 1918; 2,463 seats; Thomas W. Lamb, architect. Jeffery Wolf, photographer, December, 1979. P&P, HABS, DC, WASH,249-2.

9-019

9-020

9-021   9-022   9-023

9-024

9-025

9-021. Capitol Theatre, 1639 Broadway, New York, New York. Opened October 24, 1919; 4,448 seats; Thomas W. Lamb, architect. American Studio, photographer, ca. 1920. P&P, U.S. GEOG FILE - New York–New York City–Theatres.

The Capitol was Marcus Loew's first mega-showplace and his successors kept this Times Square landmark up to date. Their careful documentation allows us to see the morphology of its internal and external changes (9-021– 9-039). To draw patrons to its location at the northern reaches of the Square, the Capitol's original arched canopy was supplemented by large illuminated signs, one on the facade and two on the roof. By 1959 one roof sign was gone, a new facade sign was so tall that the building's cornice had to be notched to clear it, and a bulky marquee so overspanned the facade that it wrapped around the corner. In 1960 the clean, modern look arrived. The marquee became a slim slab of polished stainless steel and only the cutout in the cornice remained as a reminder of the tall sign. Radial lighting strips and a curved ceiling welcomed customers into a newly modernized vestibule (9-026 and 9-027).

9-022. Capitol Theatre, 1639 Broadway, New York, New York. Opened October 24, 1919; 4,448 seats; Thomas W. Lamb, architect. Gottscho-Schleisner, Inc., photographer, August 30, 1959. P&P, LC-G613-74439.

9-023. Capitol Theatre, 1639 Broadway, New York, New York. Opened October 24, 1919; 4,448 seats; Thomas W. Lamb, architect. Gottscho-Schleisner, Inc., photographer, January 12, 1960. P&P, LC-G613-74962.

9-024. Capitol Theatre, 1639 Broadway, New York, New York. Opened October 24, 1919; 4,448 seats; Thomas W. Lamb, architect. Gottscho-Schleisner, Inc., photographer, August 30, 1959. P&P, LC-G613-74440.

9-025. Capitol Theatre, 1639 Broadway, New York, New York. Opened October 24, 1919; 4,448 seats; Thomas W. Lamb, architect. Gottscho-Schleisner, Inc., photographer, January 12, 1960. P&P, LC-G613-74963.

9-026

9-027

9-026. Capitol Theatre, 1639 Broadway, New York, New York. Opened October 24, 1919; 4,448 seats; Thomas W. Lamb, architect. Gottscho-Schleisner, Inc., photographer, January 12, 1960. P&P, LC-G613-74951.

9-027. Capitol Theatre, 1639 Broadway, New York, New York. Opened October 24, 1919; 4,448 seats; Thomas W. Lamb, architect. Gottscho-Schleisner, Inc., photographer, January 12, 1960. P&P, LC-G613-74957.

9-028. Capitol Theatre, 1639 Broadway, New York, New York. Opened October 24, 1919; 4,448 seats; Thomas W. Lamb, architect. Gottscho-Schleisner, Inc., photographer, August 30, 1959. P&P, LC-G613-74441.

The Capitol's inner lobby was one of the most elegant to be found in any of New York's early cinema palaces. Its central feature was the broad, graceful marble stairway leading to a long upper promenade that served the theater's huge balcony. To some the stair was daunting. In the fall of 1959 it was bisected by a shiny, new, and less-than-elegant escalator (9-029).

9-029. Capitol Theatre, 1639 Broadway, New York, New York. Opened October 24, 1919; 4,448 seats; Thomas W. Lamb, architect. Gottscho-Schleisner, Inc., photographer, January 12, 1960. P&P, LC-G613-74956.

9-028

9-029

9-030

9-031

9-032

9-030. Capitol Theatre, 1639 Broadway, New York, New York. Opened October 24, 1919; 4,448 seats; Thomas W. Lamb, architect. Gottscho-Schleisner, Inc., photographer, January 12, 1960. P&P, LC-G613-74950.

At the head of the stairs, the balcony promenade's spectacular length remained untouched by modernization, as did the main floor foyer, which it overlooked. The area immediately under the promenade originally held the auditorium's rear rows. To reduce the theater's capacity, the under-promenade area was reworked as an incongruously sleek, tunnel-like passage (9-032).

9-031. Capitol Theatre, 1639 Broadway, New York, New York. Opened October 24, 1919; 4,448 seats; Thomas W. Lamb, architect. Gottscho-Schleisner, Inc., photographer, January 12, 1960. P&P, LC-G613-74949.

9-032. Capitol Theatre, 1639 Broadway, New York, New York. Opened October 24, 1919; 4,448 seats; Thomas W. Lamb, architect. Gottscho-Schleisner, Inc., photographer, January 12, 1960. P&P, LC-G613-74948.

9-033

9-034

9-035

9-033. Capitol Theatre, 1639 Broadway, New York, New York. Opened October 24, 1919; 4,448 seats; Thomas W. Lamb, architect. Gottscho-Schleisner, Inc., photographer, January 12, 1960. P&P, LC-G613-74955.

The Capitol's auditorium saw a sequence of changes to remove seating capacity that was no longer needed. Besides replacing the rear orchestra rows with the new tunnel foyer, Loew's architects installed a curtain to close and conceal the rear section of the balcony but allow it to be opened for a large audience. Figures 9-033 and 9-034 show the curtain pulled up to the ceiling and lowered across the seats. Figure 9-035 shows an additional curtain, perhaps a mock-up, which covers a significant part of the balcony's midsection. In all configurations, the curtains are open at the center to avoid obstructing the projection beam.

9-034. Capitol Theatre, 1639 Broadway, New York, New York. Opened October 24, 1919; 4,448 seats; Thomas W. Lamb, architect. Gottscho-Schleisner, Inc., photographer, January 12, 1960. P&P, LC-G613-74954.

9-035. Capitol Theatre, 1639 Broadway, New York, New York. Opened October 24, 1919; 4,448 seats; Thomas W. Lamb, architect. Gottscho-Schleisner, Inc., photographer, January 12, 1960. P&P, LC-G613-74953.

9-036. Capitol Theatre, 1639 Broadway, New York, New York. Opened October 24, 1919; 4,448 seats; Thomas W. Lamb, architect. Gottscho-Schleisner, Inc., photographer, January 12, 1960. P&P, LC-G613-74960.

9-036

9-037

9-037. Capitol Theatre, 1639 Broadway, New York, New York. Opened October 24, 1919; 4,448 seats; Thomas W. Lamb, architect. Gottscho-Schleisner, Inc., photographer, August 30, 1959. P&P, LC-G613-74442.

Loew's first attempt to modernize the Capitol's auditorium was tentative. By 1959 the sides of the proscenium had been covered with draperies and the original grand drape had given way to a lambrequin that recalled a streamlined automobile radiator or an early radio set. In 1960 the box seats were removed and the entire frontal area was swathed in folds of gold drapery (9-036–9-038).

9-038. Capitol Theatre, 1639 Broadway, New York, New York. Opened October 24, 1919; 4,448 seats; Thomas W. Lamb, architect. Gottscho-Schleisner, Inc., photographer, January 12, 1960. P&P, LC-G613-74961.

9-039. Capitol Theatre, 1639 Broadway, New York, New York. Opened October 24, 1919; 4,448 seats; Thomas W. Lamb, architect. Gottscho-Schleisner, Inc., photographer, August 8, 1962. P&P, LC-G613-78510.

As a final effort to bring the Capitol into the modern age, Loew's installed a wide, curved screen along with a suspended ceiling and straight curtains that enveloped the auditorium and greatly reduced its size. So that the audience could once again see a stage presentation in the Capitol's original ornate magnificence, the screen, ceiling, and drapes were removed for a single night in 1965—the night the theater closed.

9-038

9-039

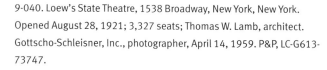

9-040. Loew's State Theatre, 1538 Broadway, New York, New York. Opened August 28, 1921; 3,327 seats; Thomas W. Lamb, architect. Gottscho-Schleisner, Inc., photographer, April 14, 1959. P&P, LC-G613-73747.

Loew's flagship theater in the heart of Times Square was built just two years after the Capitol, which it equaled in elaboration, if not in size. In 1959 the State, like its larger neighbor, was given a new look. The sleek metal and glass marquee led into a lobby that was clearly of the modern era.

9-041. Loew's State Theatre, 1538 Broadway, New York, New York. Opened August 29, 1921; 3,327 seats; Thomas W. Lamb, architect. Gottscho-Schleisner, Inc., photographer, April 14, 1959. P&P, LC-G613-73736.

9-042. Loew's State Theatre, 1538 Broadway, New York, New York. Opened August 29, 1921; 3,327 seats; Thomas W. Lamb, architect. Gottscho-Schleisner, Inc., photographer, April 14, 1959. P&P, LC-G613-73738.

9-043

9-043. Loew's State Theatre, 1538 Broadway, New York, New York. Opened August 29, 1921; 3,327 seats; Thomas W. Lamb, architect. Gottscho-Schleisner, Inc., photographer, April 14, 1959. P&P, LC-G613-73734.

While the State's auditorium retained its most of its Adamesque decoration, the organ grilles and ornate box seats succumbed to clean-lined modernity. As the boxes were removed and the proscenium cut away to accommodate a new wide screen, the entire proscenium area was bandaged with drapery arranged to rise in elegant swags.

9-044. Loew's State Theatre, 1538 Broadway, New York, New York. Opened August 29, 1921; 3,327 seats; Thomas W. Lamb, architect. Gottscho-Schleisner, Inc., photographer, April 14, 1959. P&P, LC-G613-73726.

To place the projectors level with the screen, a new booth was constructed within the volume of the balcony, where its ports were set in a wide, deep, and smoothly curvaceous notch.

9-044

9-045. Indiana Theatre, 134 West Washington Street, Indianapolis, Indiana. Opened June 18, 1927; 3,313 seats; Rubush & Hunter, architects. Jack E. Boucher, photographer, August, 1970. P&P, HABS,IND,49-IND,29-15.

As cinema matured, the monochromatic, silent image projected on a small, flat screen evolved to incorporate sound, color, and a size that wrapped around the audience and filled its senses. When the proscenium openings of older theaters were scaled and proportioned to the old, nearly square image, the new wide screens could not fit within their confines. Cinerama, the widest of several screen types, could be shown in the Indiana only by masking the theater's robustly ornamented proscenium and organ grilles (see 6-106). Although Cinerama was installed in only one theater in each major city, universal adoption of its smaller counterpart, CinemaScope, required that hundreds of cinemas across the country be similarly modified (9-044).

9-046. Forrest (Coronet, Eugene O'Neill) Theatre, 230–238 West Forty-eighth Street, New York, New York. Opened November 24, 1925; 1,075 seats; Herbert J. Krapp, architect; alterations 1945, Walker & Gillette, architects. Gottscho-Schleisner, Inc., photographer, December 14, 1945. P&P, LC-G612-48326

In 1945, at the age of twenty, Broadway's Forrest Theatre needed a facelift. Renamed the Coronet, its marquee was extended horizontally and its exterior balcony was extended upward to give the theater a French Quarter look.

9-047. Forrest (Coronet, Eugene O'Neill) Theatre, 230–238 West Forty-eighth Street, New York, New York. Opened November 24, 1925; 1,075 seats; Herbert J. Krapp, architect; alterations 1945, Walker & Gillette, architects. Gottscho-Schleisner, Inc., photographer, December 14, 1945. P&P, LC-G612-48303

Inside, renovation was confined to the front of the auditorium, where it would show the most. The forward wall areas were wrapped in velour tied into an elaborate swag over the now-hidden proscenium (9-048), while toward the rear the original surfaces remained exposed (9-050). The domed ceiling was changed only by forcing brash round air diffusers into the delicate scrolls of its Adamesque ornament (9-049). The promenade at the rear of the house was left untouched (9-047). This cavalier attitude toward design integrity gave the theaters of Broadway a reputation for presenting timeless shows in tarnished, time-worn surroundings. This has since been corrected. As the Eugene O'Neill, this house, along with most of its Broadway neighbors, now appears much as it did on opening night.

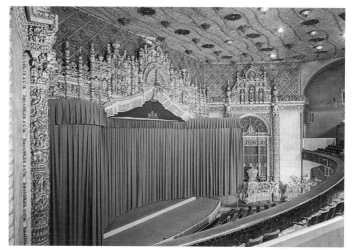

9-045

9-046

9-047

9-048

9-049

9-050

9-051

9-048. Forrest (Coronet, Eugene O'Neill) Theatre, 230–238 West Forty-eighth Street, New York, New York. Opened November 24, 1925; 1,075 seats; Herbert J. Krapp, architect; alterations 1945, Walker & Gillette, architects. Gottscho-Schleisner, Inc., photographer, December 14, 1945. P&P, LC-G612-48304.

9-049. Forrest (Coronet, Eugene O'Neill) Theatre, 230–238 West Forty-eighth Street, New York, New York. Opened November 24, 1925; 1,075 seats; Herbert J. Krapp, architect; alterations 1945, Walker & Gillette, architects. Gottscho-Schleisner, Inc., photographer, December 14, 1945. P&P, LC-G612-48306.

9-050. Forrest (Coronet, Eugene O'Neill) Theatre, 230–238 West Forty-eighth Street, New York, New York. Opened November 24, 1925; 1,075 seats; Herbert J. Krapp, architect; alterations 1945, Walker & Gillette, architects. Gottscho-Schleisner, Inc., photographer, December 14, 1945. P&P, LC-G612-48307.

9-051. Wallack's (Germania Star) Theatre, 842–846 Broadway, New York, New York. Opened September 25, 1861; Thomas R. Jackson, architect; altered December 23, 1884, J. B. McElfatrick & Sons, architects. F. S. Armitage, American Mutoscope and Biograph Company, photographer, April 18, 1902. Motion Picture, Broadcasting and Recorded Sound Division, LC 1874.

The ultimate blow to a theater is, of course, to tear it down. After forty years of service, New York's entertainment district had moved so far uptown from Wallack's famous Broadway theater (see 1-037) that the old house had to make way for a new commercial building. In Frederick S. Armitage's extraordinary, pioneering stop-motion film, the Star melts away.

9-052

9-052. Knickerbocker (Empress, Gayety) Theatre, 246–254 South High Street, Columbus, Ohio. Opened 1916. Steven M. Elbert, photographer, 1980. P&P, HABS,OHIO,25-COLB,35-1.

As a last resort theaters sometimes become other things. As a theater, Columbus's Knickerbocker ran the gamut from top-quality movie presentation to burlesque. In 1960, shorn of its auditorium, it became the local bus terminal. The building was demolished in 1980.

9-053. Granada Theatre, 6425–6441 North Sheridan Road, Chicago, Illinois. Opened September 18, 1926; 3,422 seats; Levy & Klein, architects. Unidentified photographer ca. 1933. P&P, HABS,ILL,16-CHIG,109-30.

Among Chicago's great showplaces, none glittered more than the Granada, which presided over a neighborhood far north of the city's center. By 1989 its audiences had found other pastimes in other places, and the theater's time had come. The facade was hollow-eyed and the interior, impressive to the end, was about to become dust. Contrast the Granada's lavishly sumptuous beginning with its poignantly sumptuous end (9-055–9-059).

9-054. Granada Theatre, 6425–6441 North Sheridan Road, Chicago, Illinois. Opened September 18, 1926; 3,422 seats; Levy & Klein, architects. Thomas G. Yanul, photographer, September/October, 1989. P&P, HABS, ILL,16-CHIG,109-1.

9-053

9-054

9-055

9-057

9-056

9-055. Granada Theatre, 6425–6441 North Sheridan Road, Chicago, Illinois. Opened September 18, 1926; 3,422 seats; Levy & Klein, architects. Thomas G. Yanul, photographer, September/October, 1989. P&P, HABS,ILL,16-CHIG,109-17.

9-056. Granada Theatre, 6425–6441 North Sheridan Road, Chicago, Illinois. Opened September 18, 1926; 3,422 seats; Levy & Klein, architects. Architect's rendering, ca. 1925. P&P, HABS,ILL,16-CHIG,109-31.

9-057. Granada Theatre, 6425–6441 North Sheridan Road, Chicago, Illinois. Opened September 18, 1926; 3,422 seats; Levy & Klein, architects. Thomas G. Yanul, photographer, September/October, 1989. P&P, HABS,ILL,16-CHIG,109-15.

9-058. Granada Theatre, 6425–6441 North Sheridan Road, Chicago, Illinois. Opened September 18, 1926; 3,422 seats; Levy & Klein, architects. Thomas G. Yanul, photographer, September/October, 1989. P&P, HABS, ILL,16-CHIG,109-13.

9-059. Granada Theatre, 6425–6441 North Sheridan Road, Chicago, Illinois. Opened September 18, 1926; 3,422 seats; Levy & Klein, architects. Thomas G. Yanul, photographer, September/October, 1989. P&P, HABS, ILL,16-CHIG,109-8.

9-060. Fox Theatre, 20 Flatbush Avenue, Brooklyn, New York. Opened August 31, 1928; 4,305 seats; C. Howard Crane & Kenneth Franzheim, architects. Herbert G. Frank Jr., photographer, January, 1971. P&P, HABS, NY,24-BROK,41-23.

The end of a great theater always brings a tear. It was once a monument, a place of pride and warm memories, a truly spectacular environment. Here, the Fox's fountains, which remained operable until the end, stand tall amidst the rubble of the once-grand auditorium.

BIBLIOGRAPHY

CULTURAL HISTORY

Eremberg, Lewis A. *Steppin' Out*. Westport, Conn.: Greenwood Press, 1981.

Nasaw, David. *Going Out: The Rise and Fall of Public Amusements*. New York: Basic Books, 1993.

Peiss, Kathy. *Cheap Amusements*. Philadelphia: Temple University Press, 1985.

Rosenzweig, Roy. *Eight Hours for What We Will: Workers and Leisure in an Industrial City, 1870–1920*. Cambridge: Cambridge University Press, 1983.

Sante, Luc. *Low Life: Lures and Snares of Old New York*. New York: Vintage Books, 1992.

THEATER ARCHITECTURE, DESIGN, AND EQUIPMENT

Beranek, Leo L. *Music, Acoustics and Architecture*. New York: John Wiley & Sons, 1962.

Birkmire, William L. *The Planning and Construction of American Theatres*. New York: John Wiley & Sons, 1901.

Burris-Meyer, Harold, and Edward C. Cole. *Theatres and Auditoriums*. Huntington, N.Y.: Robert E. Krieger, 1964.

Carlson, Marvin. *Places of Performance: the semiotics of theater architecture*. Ithaca, N.Y.: Cornell University Press, 1989.

Forsyth, Michael. *Buildings for Music*. Cambridge. Mass.: MIT Press, 1985.

_____. *Auditoria: Designing for the Performing Arts*. New York: Van Nostrand Reinhold, 1987.

Gregersen, Charles E. *Dankmar Adler: His Theatres and Auditoriums*. Athens, Ohio: Swallow Press, 1989.

Gurr, Andrew, with John Orrell. *Rebuilding Shakespeare's Globe*. New York: Routledge, 1989.

Hodges, C. Walter. *The Globe Restored: A Study of the Elizabethan Theatre*. New York: W. W. Norton, 1973.

_____. *The Third Globe, Symposium for the Reconstruction of the Globe Playhouse*. Detroit: Wayne State University Press, 1981.

Izenour, George C. *Theater Design*. New York: McGraw-Hill, 1977.

_____. *Theatre Technology*. New York: McGraw-Hill, 1988.

Leacroft, Richard, and Helen Leacroft. *Theatre and Playhouse*. London: Methuen, 1984.

_____. *The Development of the English Playhouse*. Ithaca, N.Y.: Cornell University Press, 1973.

Mackintosh, Iain. *Architecture, Actor & Audience*. London: Routledge, 1993.

Meloy, Arthur S. *Theatres and Motion Picture Houses*. New York: Architects' Supply & Publishing, 1916.

Mullin, Donald C. *The Development of the Playhouse.* Berkeley: University of California Press, 1970.

Mulryne, J. R., and Margaret Shewring. *Shakespeare's Globe Rebuilt.* Cambridge: Cambridge University Press, 1997.

Orrell, John. *The Theatres of Inigo Jones and John Webb.* Cambridge: Cambridge University Press, 1985.

Penzel, Frederick. *Theatre Lighting Before Electricity.* Middletown, Conn.: Wesleyan University Press, 1978.

Rees, Terence. *Theatre Lighting in the Age of Gas.* London: Society for Theatre Research, 1978.

Sexton, Randolph Williams, and B. F. Betts. *American Theatres of Today.* New York: Architectural Book Publishing, 1927.

Smith, Irwin. *Shakespeare's Globe Playhouse: A Modern Reconstruction in Text and Scale Drawings.* New York: Charles Scribner's Sons, 1956.

Tidworth, Simon. *Theatres: An Architectural and Cultural History.* New York: Praeger, 1973.

Valentine, Maggie. *The Show Starts on the Sidewalk: An Architectural History of the Movie Theatre Starring S. Charles Lee.* New Haven: Yale University Press, 1994.

THEATER HISTORY

Allen, Robert C. *Horrible Prettiness: burlesque and american culture.* Chapel Hill: University of North Carolina Press, 1991.

Bank, Rosemarie K. *Theatre Culture in America, 1825–1860.* Cambridge: Cambridge University Press, 1997.

Blumenthal, George. *My Sixty Years in Show Business: A Chronicle of the American Theater, 1874–1934.* New York: Olympia, 1936.

Bryant, Betty. *Here Comes the Showboat!* Lexington: University Press of Kentucky, 1994.

Butch, Richard. *The Making of American Audiences: From Stage to Television, 1750–1990.* Cambridge: Cambridge University Press, 2000.

Chach, Maryann, et al. *The Shuberts Present: 100 Years of American Theatre.* New York: Harry N. Abrams, 2001.

Click, Patricia C. *The Spirit of the Times: amusements in nineteenth-century Baltimore, Norfolk and Richmond.* Charlottesville, Va.: University Press of Virginia, 1989.

Dudden, Faye E. *Women in the American Theatre: Actresses and Audiences 1790–1870.* New Haven: Yale University Press, 1994.

Engle, Roy, and Tice L. Miller, eds. *The American Stage: Social and Economic Issues from the Colonial Period to the Present.* Cambridge: Cambridge University Press, 1993.

Frick, John W. and Carlton Ward. *Directory of Historic American Theatres.* Westport, Conn.: Greenwood Press, 1987.

Gillespie, C. Richard. *The James Adams Floating Theatre.* Centreville, Md.: Tidewater, 1991.

Graham, Philip. *Showboats: The History of an American Institution.* Austin: University of Texas Press, 1951.

Grimsted, David. *Melodrama Unveiled: American Theater and Culture 1800–1850.* Chicago: University of Chicago Press, 1968.

Hill, West T., Jr. *The Theatre in Early Kentucky, 1790–1820*. Lexington: University Press of Kentucky, 1971.

Hirsch, Foster. *The Boys from Syracuse: The Shuberts' Theatrical Empire*. Carbondale, Ill.: Southern Illinois University Press, 1998.

Lewis, Philip C. *Trouping: How the Show Came to Town*. New York: Harper & Row, 1973.

McConachie, Bruce A. *Melodramatic Formations: American Theatre and Society, 1820–1870*. Iowa City: University of Iowa Press, 1992.

McNamara, Brooks. *The American Playhouse in the Eighteenth Century*. Cambridge, Mass.: Harvard University Press, 1969.

_____. *The Shuberts of Broadway*. New York: Oxford University Press, 1990.

Marston, William Moulton, and John Henry Feller. *Proctor: Vaudeville Pioneer*. New York: Richard R. Smith, 1943.

Mason, Jeffrey D. *Melodrama and the Myth of America*. Bloomington: Indiana University Press, 1993.

Nagler, A. M. *The Medieval Religious Stage: Shapes and Phantoms*. New Haven: Yale University Press, 1976.

Naylor, David, and Joan Dillon. *American Theatres: Performance Halls of the Nineteenth Century*. New York: John Wiley & Sons, 1997.

Nicoll, Allardyce. *The Development of the Theatre: a study of theatrical art from the beginnings to the present day*. New York: Harcourt Brace Jovanovich, 1966.

Rankin, Hugh F. *The Theater in Colonial America*. Chapel Hill: University of North Carolina Press, 1960.

Shattuck, Charles H. *Shakespeare on the American Stage: from Booth and Barrett to Sothern and Marlowe*. Washington, D.C.: Folger Shakespeare Library, 1987.

Slout, William L., ed. *Popular Amusement in Horse and Buggy America*. San Bernardino, Cal.: Borgo Press, 1995.

_____. *Broadway Below the Sidewalk: Concert Saloons of Old New York*. San Bernardino, Cal.: Borgo Press, 1994.

Snyder, Robert W. *The Voice of the City: Vaudeville and Popular Culture in New York*. New York: Oxford University Press, 1989.

Stagg, Jerry. *The Brothers Shubert*. New York: Random House, 1968.

Stein, Charles W., ed. *American Vaudeville as Seen by its Contemporaries*. New York: Da Capo Press, 1984.

Taylor, William R., ed. *Inventing Times Square: Commerce and Culture at the Crossroads of the World, 1880–1939*. New York: Russell Sage Foundation, 1991.

Young, William C. *Famous American Playhouses 1716–1899*. Chicago: American Library Association, 1973.

_____. *Famous American Playhouses 1900–1971*. Chicago: American Library Association, 1973.

Zellers, Parker. *Tony Pastor: Dean of the Vaudeville Stage*. Ypsilanti, Mich.: Eastern Michigan University Press, 1971.

Zietz, Karyl Lynn. *The National Trust Guide to Great Opera Houses in America*. New York: John Wiley & Sons, 1996.

AMUSEMENT PARKS AND CIRCUSES

Bogdan, Robert. *Freak Show.* Chicago: University of Chicago Press, 1988.

Dennett, Andrea Stulman. *Weird and Wonderful: The Dime Museum in America.* New York: New York University Press, 1997.

Denson, Charles. *Coney Island Lost and Found.* Berkeley, Cal.: Ten Speed Press, 2002.

Kuhnhardt, Philip B. *P. T. Barnum: America's Greatest Showman.* New York: Alfred A. Knopf, 1995.

McCullough, Edo. *Good Old Coney Island.* New York: Fordham University Press, 2000.

McNamara, Brooks. *Step Right Up.* Jackson: University Press of Mississippi, 1995.

Register, Woody. *The Kid of Coney Island: Fred Thompson and the Rise of American Amusements.* Oxford: Oxford University Press, 2001.

Saxon, A. H. *P. T. Barnum: The Legend and the Man.* New York: Columbia University Press, 1989

MOVIE PRODUCTION AND EXHIBITION

Balio, Tino, ed. *The American Film Industry.* Madison: University of Wisconsin Press, 1985.

Belton, John. *Widescreen Cinema.* Cambridge, Mass.: Harvard University Press, 1992.

Bowser, Eileen. *The Transformation of Cinema 1907–1915.* New York: Charles Scribner's Sons, 1990.

Fernett, Gene. *American Film Studios: An Historical Encyclopedia.* Jefferson, N.C.: McFarland & Company, 1988

Fuller, Kathryn H. *At the Picture Show: Small Town Audiences and the Creation of Movie Fan Culture.* Washington, D.C.: Smithsonian Institution Press, 1996.

Gabler, Neal. *An Empire of Their Own: How the Jews Invented Hollywood.* New York: Crown Publishers, 1988.

Gomery, Douglas. *Shared Pleasures: A History of Movie Presentation in the United States.* Madison: University of Wisconsin Press, 1992.

Hall, Ben M. *The Best Remaining Seats.* New York: Bramhall House, 1961.

Jones, Janna. *The Southern Movie Palace: Rise, Fall and Resurrection.* Gainesville: University Press of Florida, 2003.

Koszarski, Richard. *An Evening's Entertainment: The Age of the Silent Feature Picture, 1915–1928.* New York: Charles Scribner's Sons, 1990.

Melnick, Ross, and Andreas Fuchs. *Cinema Treasures: A New Look at Classic Movie Theaters.* St. Paul, Minn., MBI Publishing Company, 2004.

Musser, Charles. *The Emergence of Cinema: The American Screen to 1907.* New York: Charles Scribner's Sons, 1990.

_____. *High-Class Moving Pictures: Lyman H. Howe and the Forgotten Era of Traveling Exhibition, 1880–1920.* Princeton, N.J.: Princeton University Press, 1991.

_____. *Before the Nickelodeon: Edwin S. Porter and the Edison Manufacturing Company.* Berkeley: University of California Press, 1991.

Naylor, David. *American Picture Palaces: The Architecture of Fantasy.* New York: Van Nostrand Reinhold, 1981.

_____. *Great American Movie Theaters.* Washington, D.C.: Preservation Press, 1987.

Phillips, Ray. *Edison's Kinetoscope and Its Films: A History to 1896.* Westport, Conn.: Greenwood Press, 1997.

Putnam, Michael. *Silent Screens: The Decline and Transformation of the American Movie Theater.* Baltimore: Johns Hopkins University Press, 2000.

Sanders, Don and Susan. *The American Drive-In Movie Theatre.* Osceola, Wisc.: Motorbooks International, 1997.

Segrave, Kerry. *Drive-In Theaters: A History from Their Inception in 1933.* Jefferson, N.C.: McFarland & Company, 1992.

Stones, Barbara. *America Goes to the Movies: 100 Years of Motion Picture Exhibition.* North Hollywood, Cal.: National Association of Theatre Owners, 1993.

THEATER ORGANS

Junchen, David L. *Encyclopedia of the American Theatre Organ.* Vols. 1–3. Pasadena, Cal.: Showcase Publications, 1985–89.

_____. *The Wurlitzer Pipe Organ: An Illustrated History.* American Theatre Organ Society, 2005.

Kaufman, Preston J. *Encyclopedia of the American Theater Organ.* Vol. 3. Pasadena, Cal.: Showcase Publications, 1995.

Landon, John W. *Behold the Mighty Wurlitzer: The History of the Theatre Pipe Organ.* Westport, Conn.: Greenwood Press, 1983.

Smith, Stephen D. *The Atlantic City Convention Hall Organ.* Atlantic City, N.J.: Atlantic City Convention Hall Organ Society, 2001.

THEATERS AND COMMUNITIES

Bagley, Mary. *The Front Row: Missouri's grand theatres.* St. Louis, Mo.: Gateway Publishing, 1984.

Balk, Alfred W., ed. *Movie Palace Masterpiece: Saving Syracuse's Loew's State/Landmark Theatre.* Syracuse, N.Y.: Landmark Theatre Foundation, 1998.

Berger, Robert, and Anne Conser. *The Last Remaining Seats: Movie Palaces of Tinseltown.* Los Angeles: Balcony Press, 1997.

Besse, Kirk J. *Show Houses Twin Cities Style.* Minneapolis: Victoria Publications, 1997.

Boston Symphony Orchestra. *Symphony Hall: The First 100 Years.* Boston: Boston Symphony Orchestra, 2000.

Botto, Louis. *At This Theatre: 100 Years of Broadway Shows, Stories and Stars.* New York: Applause Books, 2002.

Brandt, Nat. *Chicago Death Trap: the Iroquois theatre fire of 1903.* Carbondale, Ill.: Southern Illinois University Press, 2003.

Brown, T. Allston. *A History of the New York Stage.* New York: Benjamin Blom, 1964; reprint of 1903 work.

Casto, Marilyn. *Actors, Audiences and Historic Theaters of Kentucky.* Lexington: University Press of Kentucky, 2000.

Cone, John Frederick. *First Rival of the Metropolitan Opera*. New York: Columbia University Press, 1983.

Cron, Theodore O., and Burt Goldblatt. *Portrait of Carnegie Hall*. New York: Macmillan, 1966.

Cropsey, Eugene H. *Crosby's Opera House: Symbol of Chicago's Awakening*. Madison, N.J.: Fairleigh Dickinson University Press, 1999.

Cruise, Boyd, and Merle Harton. *Signor Faranta's Iron Theatre*. New Orleans: Historic New Orleans Collection, 1982.

Dalton, Curt. *When Dayton Went to the Movies*. Dayton, Ohio: Curt Dalton, 1999.

Dimmick, Ruth Crosby. *Our Theatres To-Day and Yesterday*. New York: H. K. Fly, 1913.

Doyle, Michael V. *Michigan Movie Theatres*. Haslett, Mich.: Boreal Press, 2003.

Eiland, William U. *Nashville's Mother Church: The History of the Ryman Auditorium*. Nashville: Opryland USA, 1992.

Frick, John W. *New York's First Theatrical Center: The Rialto at Union Square*. Ann Arbor: UMI Research Press, 1984.

Fuller-Seeley, Kathryn. *Celebrate Richmond Theater*. Richmond, Va.: Dietz Press, 2002.

Glazer, Irvin R. *Philadelphia Theatres, A–Z*. Westport, Conn.: Greenwood Press, 1986.

_____. *Philadelphia Theaters: A Pictorial Architectural History*. Philadelphia: Athenaeum of Philadelphia, 1994.

Glenn, George D., and Richard L. Poole. *The Opera Houses of Iowa*. Ames: Iowa State University Press, 1993.

Hall, Joan Upton, and Stacey Hasbrook. *Grand Old Texas Theaters That Won't Quit*. Plano: Republic of Texas Press, 2002.

Halloran, Pat. *the Orpheum! Where Broadway Meets Beale*. Memphis, Tenn.: Lithograph Publishing, 1997.

Hatch, Anthony P. *Tinder Box: the Iroquois Theatre Disaster 1903*. Chicago: Academy Chicago, 2003.

Headley, Robert Kirk, Jr. *Exit: A History of Movies in Baltimore*. University Park, Md.: Robert K. Headley, 1974.

_____. *Motion Picture Exhibition in Washington, D. C.: An Illustrated History of Parlors, Palaces and Multiplexes in the Metropolitan area, 1894–1997*. Jefferson, N.C.: McFarland & Company, 1999

Henderson, Mary C. *The City and the Theatre: A history of New York Playhouses A 250-year Journey from Bowling Green to Times Square*. New York: Back Stage Books, 2004.

_____. *The New Amsterdam: The Biography of a Broadway Theatre*. New York: Hyperion, 1997.

Johnson, Stephen Burge. *The Roof Gardens of Broadway Theatres, 1883–1942*. Ann Arbor: UMI Research Press 1985.

Kaufman, Preston J. *Fox–The Last Word*. Pasadena, Cal.: Showcase Publications, 1979.

Livingston Furman, Evelyn E. *The Tabor Opera House: A Captivating History*. Leadville, Colo.: Evelyn E. Livingston Furman, 1972.

Marion, John Francis. *Within These Walls: a history of the Academy of Music in Philadelphia*. Philadelphia: Academy of Music, 1984.

Merkling, Frank, et. al., eds. *The Golden Horseshoe: The Life and Times of the Metropolitan Opera House.* New York: Viking Press, 1965.

Miller, Zane L. and George F. Roth. *Cincinnati's Music Hall.* Virginia Beach, Va.: Jordan & Company, 1978.

Moody, Richard. *The Astor Place Riot.* Bloomington: Indiana University Press, 1958.

Morrison, Andrew Craig. *Opera House, Nickel Show and Palace.* Dearborn, Mich.: Greenfield Village and Henry Ford Museum, 1974.

Morrison, William. *Broadway Theatres History and Architecture.* Mineola, N.Y.: Dover Publications, 1999.

Schroeder, Richard. *Lone Star Picture Shows.* College Station: Texas A&M University Press, 2001.

Siry, Joseph M. *The Chicago Auditorium Building: Adler and Sullivan's Architecture and the City.* Chicago: University of Chicago Press, 2002.

Stone, Susannah Harris. *The Oakland Paramount.* Berkeley, Cal.: Lancaster-Miller, 1982.

Tompkins, Eugene. *The History of the Boston Theatre, 1954–1901.* Boston: Houghton Mifflin, 1908.

Vacha, John. *Showtime in Cleveland: The Rise of a Regional Theater Center.* Kent, Ohio: Kent State University Press, 2001.

Van Hoogstraten, Nicholas. *Lost Broadway Theatres.* Princeton: Princeton Architectural Press, 1997.

Waller, Gregory A. *Main Street Amusements: movies and commercial entertainment in a southern city 1896–1930.* Washington, D.C.: Smithsonian Institution Press, 1995.

Widen, Larry, and Judi Anderson. *Milwaukee Movie Palaces.* Milwaukee: Milwaukee County Historical Society, 1986.

Young, Toni. *The Grand Experience: A History of the Grand Opera House.* Watkins Glen, N.Y.: American Life Foundation, 1976.

GLOSSARY

ACT CURTAIN. A stage curtain, traditionally of green baize fabric, that closes the proscenium between a performance's acts or scenes. Also called an act drop.

ACTING AREA. The central portion of a stage, open and visible to the audience, in which acting takes place.

AISLE. A clear linear walkway between seating areas of an auditorium.

AMPHITHEATER. In Greco-Roman antiquity, a theater form in which steep seating risers surround a level performance area of circular or elliptical form. The best-known example is the Flavian amphitheatre, or Coliseum, in Rome. In American practice, one of several alternative names for the topmost seating tier, especially in a theater where there are three or more upper tiers. For a minimal admission, patrons were provided with seating on unupholstered wooden benches; this area and its access stairs and passages often were designed to entirely separate its patrons from those in other levels of the auditorium. Conventionally called the "gallery," this level might also be called the "top balcony," the "family circle," or even the "pit."

APRON. The portion of the stage floor that projects beyond the proscenium line into the audience area.

ASBESTOS CURTAIN. A framed, semi-rigid curtain, traditionally made of asbestos, rigged to completely fill the proscenium opening and to move into place automatically as a barrier between stage and auditorium in the event of an on-stage fire. Although no longer constructed of toxic material, these curtains often still are called by their traditional name.

ATMOSPHERIC THEATER. A theater in which the auditorium resembles an exterior environment, with an unornamented ceiling painted to resemble the nighttime sky set with electrically lighted stars and animated with projected images of clouds, airplanes, or the moon. The design technique is closely associated with architect John Eberson, although it predated his practice and was imitated by many others.

AUDITORIUM. The space within a theater in which the audience gathers to view a performance.

BACKDROP. The rear curtain of a stage setting, often of flat canvas painted to define the setting of the action.

BALCONY. An overhanging upper seating tier in an auditorium. In nineteenth-century theaters this usually was the second tier of a three-tier auditorium or the third tier of a four-tier auditorium. In twentieth-century theaters it was the single upper tier.

BORDER LIGHT. A linear lighting fixture spanning the stage from above, generally a long metal trough fitted with white, red, and blue incandescent lamps to provide varied lighting effects.

BOWLED FLOOR. An auditorium floor that is dished so that all seats in each curved row are at the same level. In a tilted flat floor the central seats of a curved row are higher than the end seats giving the seating a humpbacked appearance.

BOX SEAT. Seating in semi-enclosed compartments generally occupied by those who can afford the high cost of admission. The term often applies to the enclosures themselves, which often are highly ornamental architectural features.

BOX SET. A stage setting defined with flat rear and sidewalls and ceiling, often realistically painted to resemble a room or an outdoor scene.

BURLESQUE. A form of entertainment featuring slapstick comedy, scantily clad chorus and/or striptease performers, generally appealing to a predominantly male, working-class audience.

CANTILEVERED BALCONY. A balcony supported by internal trusses rather than by visible columns that obstruct audience sight lines. Introduced about 1903, this balcony type characterizes the twentieth-century auditorium form.

CINEMA. A theater designed and equipped for the exhibition of moving pictures. When provided, a cinema stage usually is shallow by comparison with the stage in a legitimate theater.

CONCERT HALL. A theater designed for the presentation of orchestral music. Often in place of a full stage there is an open platform backed by the display facade of a large pipe organ.

CONCERT SALOON. An assembly space that combined variety performances with alcoholic beverage service. The presence of servers billed as "pretty waiter-girls" attracted a predominantly male, working-class audience.

CROSS AISLE. An walkway passing laterally across an auditorium, generally leading to exit doors at the sides.

CROSSOVER. A space behind or below the acting area that connects the wings, allowing a performer to move quickly and, to the audience, invisibly from one side of the stage to the other.

CYCLORAMA. A curtain that extends across the rear of the stage to enclose the acting area, usually giving the illusion of spatial depth. Also called "cyc."

DIME MUSEUM. A showplace in which curiosities such as preserved biological specimens or live, usually deformed, animals or people were exhibited on a commercial basis.

DOWNSTAGE. The area of the stage located toward the audience; the lower level of a raked stage.

DRESS CIRCLE. In a multi-tiered theater, the level immediately above the main floor. Often compartmented, this is considered the most elite area in an auditorium.

DRESSING ROOM. A room in which performers dress and apply makeup in preparation for their performance.

DROP. A curtain or scenic piece lowered into view from above.

ENCORE DOOR. A narrow opening to one or both sides of a nineteenth-century theater proscenium that allowed a performer to pass from the stage to the stage apron when the proscenium was closed by the rigid main curtain.

FAMILY CIRCLE. An upper tier of a nineteenth-century theater, generally below the balcony in a four-tier auditorium or the gallery in a three-tier auditorium. Often used interchangeably with balcony.

FLAT. A two-dimensional scenic piece constructed of painted cloth stretched over a light wooden frame and set vertically on the stage. Flats may be hinged to create a three-dimensional form. They generally are rectangular but may contain one or more openings or be shaped to a specialized outline, like a tree or an urban skyline.

FLIES. The space above a stage used for suspending scenic pieces out of audience view and housing the machinery and equipment associated with the movement of these pieces.

FLY GALLERY. An elevated platform at the side of a stage from which stage personnel operate the mechanical components of the fly system.

FLY LOFT. The internal volume above a stage in which scenic pieces are suspended out of audience view.

FLY TOWER. The upward projecting exterior volume of a theater within which the fly loft is contained.

FOOTLIGHTS. A row of exposed or recessed lights at the front edge of the stage apron.

FOYER. A space through which the audience passes as it enters or leaves a theater. The term is imprecise and may be applied to the promenade or the principal lobby space, although it more generally refers to a subsidiary space within a multiroom lobby area.

GALLERY. The topmost tier of a nineteenth-century three-tier theater, typically fitted with wooden bench seating available at a minimal admission price.

GALLERY GODS. Those patrons seated in the gallery of a nineteenth-century theater who were notorious for disrupting the performance by catcalling to performers and throwing objects onto the stage.

GRAND DRAPE. The heavy swagged and ornamented valance at the top of the proscenium, typically of a movie palace.

GREEN ROOM. A room adjoining the stage in which performers assemble to await their call to appear or greet visitors after a performance.

GRIDIRON. A working platform of wooden or steel slats at the top of a fly loft.

GROOVES. A system of wooden channels in the floor and extending from the walls above the sides of the acting area, through which rigid scenic pieces could slide in and out of audience view.

HEMP HOUSE. A theater in which the stage rigging is composed of fiber ropes and flown scenery is counterweighted with free-hanging sandbags. Although many of these systems remain in use, stages now generally are rigged with steel cables and modular iron counterweights arranged in carriers that slide in steel tracks.

HORSESHOE BALCONY. An upper tier that extends around the rear and sides of an auditorium with a continuously curved front railing.

KINETOSCOPE. A moving picture device, invented by Thomas Edison, consisting of a tall case in which a continuous loop of film was passed in front of a light and seen by a single viewer peering through an eyepiece.

LEGITIMATE THEATER. A theater designed, equipped, and operated for the presentation of spoken or musical drama rather than vaudeville, burlesque, variety, or moving pictures.

LOBBY. A space, often large and elaborate, through which the audience passes while entering or leaving a theater.

LOGE. The front section of a theater's first upper tier, generally separated from the upper portion of the tier by a railing and often further divided by railings into compartments available at a premium admission price.

MAIN CURTAIN. The stage curtain that closes the proscenium before and after a performance. In nineteenth-century practice this generally was a smooth canvas sheet, painted with scenes and simulated cloth draping, often incorporating advertising. In twentieth- and twenty-first-century practice it is generally fabricated of heavy velour, often elaborately decorated and fringed.

MARQUEE. A canopy projecting over the entrance to a theater to protect arriving patrons from inclement weather. Early marquees generally were of glass framed with metal and containing perimeter lighting. Cinema marquees often were boxlike constructions bearing the theater's name, with changeable lettering to advertise the bill and ornamental lighting, usually arranged to provide the illusion of movement.

MEZZANINE. In an American movie theater, a shallow, curving intermediate tier tucked in between the orchestra floor and a large single balcony. The mezzanine sometimes was furnished with upholstered loveseats rather than conventional theater seating, and often was a place where smoking was allowed.

MIGHTY WURLITZER. A theater pipe organ manufactured by the Wurlitzer Company of North Tonawanda, New York, often applied generically to any theater organ.

MOVIE PALACE. A cinema of extraordinary size (generally over 2,000 seats) and elaboration. Also called picture palace.

MUSIC HALL. A theater designed, equipped, and operated for the presentation of musical, variety, or vaudeville entertainment.

MUTOSCOPE. An early moving picture device in which a single viewer, peering through an eyepiece, could see a series of photographs attached to a rotating cylinder and rapidly flipped by means of a crank to provide the illusion of motion.

NICKELODEON. An early cinema, generally small in size, which presented brief programs of novelty films for an admission fee of five or ten cents. First appearing in 1905, these tiny halls flourished for half a dozen years and disappeared with the introduction of feature-length films.

OPERA CHAIR. An audience seat type generally based on a cast-iron frame fitted with a wooden or upholstered back and seat, usually operable to fold out of the way when not in use.

OPERA HOUSE. A theater designed, equipped, and operated for the presentation of opera. Also often applied in nineteenth-century America to any theater whose owners wanted it to be considered upscale and grand. The present-day equivalent of this usage is "performing arts center," which may range in scope from a multi-auditorium facility to a converted neighborhood movie theater.

ORCHESTRA. The main-floor seating area of a theater, previously called the parquet and, before that, the pit.

ORCHESTRA PIT. A recessed area immediately in front of, and sometimes extending under, the stage, in which the orchestra is seated while accompanying a stage presentation. The space is provided to minimize audience distraction from the players and their instruments. Some orchestra pits are designed as elevating platforms that may be raised to stage level or lowered to the theater's basement.

ORGAN CHAMBER. A concealed space containing the pipes and mechanisms of an organ and arranged to provide unimpeded sound transfer into the auditorium. Sound volume is modulated by operable wooden louvers, or swell shades, generally behind decorative grillework.

ORGAN GRILLE. The decorative wood or plaster screen that conceals the swell shades of a pipe organ.

PAINT BRIDGE. An elevated walkway spanning the rear of a stage at approximately the height of the proscenium and separated slightly from the rear wall. A canvas may be raised and lowered through the gap to provide scene painters with access to its entire surface.

PARQUET. The main-floor seating area of a nineteenth-century theater. Earlier called the pit, this later was called the orchestra level.

PARQUET CIRCLE. An area encircling the rear and sides of a parquet, divided from the main seating area by railings or a low parapet and often further divided by railings into compartments available at a premium price. Seating within this area generally followed the tight horseshoe-shaped curve of the balconies above

PIT. In eighteenth- and early nineteenth-century theaters, the main-floor seating area, generally provided with undivided wooden bench seating available at a minimal admission price. The pit was later upgraded in comfort and called the parquet or orchestra.

PLATFORM. An elevated performance area that is not enclosed by a proscenium nor provided with a fly loft or others means of setting and changing scenery.

PROMENADE. A passageway spanning the rear of an auditorium behind the seating area, connecting the lobby with the several auditorium aisles and often used to accommodate standees.

PROSCENIUM. The large opening, often arched and capable of closure by curtains, that separates the stage from the auditorium.

RAKED STAGE. A stage or platform in which the floor slopes downward from the rear (upstage) toward the audience (downstage). Almost universal in nineteenth-century scenic design, this feature is rarely seen in later construction.

RIGGING. The mechanisms, generally ropes, pulleys, sandbags, and counterweights, that control the movement of scenic pieces.

SIGHT LINES. The view of the stage to members of the audience.

SMOKE VENT. An opening in the roof of a stage provided with hinged panels that open automatically in the event of a fire. This feature allows the fire to create an updraft and vent itself through the stage roof rather than through the proscenium into the auditorium.

SOUNDING BOARD. The angled or flaring portion of an auditorium ceiling immediately above the proscenium, formed to enhance the acoustical properties by reflecting sound downward toward the audience.

STADIUM SEATING. An auditorium configuration in which seating is arranged on steep, ascending risers to provide a view of the stage or screen that is totally unobstructed, even by the heads of other patrons.

STAGE. The volume of a theater separated from the auditorium by the proscenium wall and provided with the means of manipulating scenery above and to the sides of the acting area.

STAGE RIGHT/STAGE LEFT. Directions on a stage as perceived by a performer facing the audience. Stage right is to the audience's left, stage left to the audience's right.

STANDEES' RAIL. A railing or parapet behind the last rows of seats, separating the auditorium from the promenade. The area above the parapet often contains glass panels or curtains to further separate the two areas.

THEATER ORGAN. A pipe organ specifically designed for theater use, generally as an accompaniment to silent film. A theater organ is characterized by voices that imitate orchestral instruments, wind pressures that produce high sound volumes, and a unified wiring system that permits a great deal of versatility in a relatively small number of stops.

TRAP. A removal panel in the floor of a stage. Traps vary in size and mechanization. They may be large and passive to admit the passage of scenery, or equipped with elevators or even a counterweighted catapult that can project a performer upward through the floor with startling speed.

UPSTAGE. Toward the rear of the stage. On a steeply raked stage, a performer at the rear is elevated and able to distract attention from one lower down, a practice that has come to be called "upstaging."

VARIETY. A show type consisting of several unrelated presentations by performers of varied talents, typically singers, dancers, standalone comedians, animal trainers, contortionists, and other circus-type specialties.

VAUDEVILLE. A show type consisting of several segments, generally unrelated, combining short comedic or dramatic sketches with variety performers.

VESTIBULE. A small space between two doors set in sequence, generally the space between the exterior doors and the first lobby of a theater. Sometimes used imprecisely for any small space in the lobby sequence.

VOMITORY. An entry into a theater balcony in which steps or a ramp from below lead upward to a cross aisle. Of ancient Roman derivation, the name recalls the similarity of crowds passing through such an exit to water surging through an aperture.

WINGS. The areas of a stage located to each side of the acting area and concealed from audience view by proscenium, curtains, or a box set.

INDEX

ABOUT THE CD-ROM

The CD-ROM includes direct links to four of the most useful online catalogs and sites, which you may choose to consult in locating and downloading images included on it or related items. Searching directions, help, and search examples (by text or keywords, titles, authors or creators, subject or location, and catalog and reproduction numbers, etc.) are provided online, in addition to information on rights and restrictions, how to order reproductions, and how to consult the materials in person.

1. The Prints & Photographs Online Catalog (PPOC) (http://www.loc.gov/rr/print/catalogabt.html) contains over one million catalog records and digital images representing a rich cross-section of graphic documents held by the Prints & Photographs Division and other units of the Library. It includes a majority of the images on this CD-ROM and many related images, such as those in the HABS and HAER collections cited below. At this writing the catalog provides access through group or item records to about 50 percent of the Division's holdings.

SCOPE OF THE PRINTS AND PHOTOGRAPHS ONLINE CATALOG

Although the catalog is added to on a regular basis, it is not a complete listing of the holdings of the Prints & Photographs Division, and does not include all the items on this CD-ROM. It also overlaps with some other Library of Congress search systems. Some of the records in the PPOC are also found in the LC Online Catalog, mentioned below, but the P&P Online Catalog includes additional records, direct display of digital images, and links to rights, ordering, and background information about the collections represented in the catalog. In many cases, only "thumbnail" images (GIF images) will display to those searching outside the Library of Congress because of potential rights considerations, while onsite searchers have access to larger JPEG and TIFF images as well. There are no digital images for some collections, such as the Look Magazine Photograph Collection. In some collections, only a portion of the images have been digitized so far. For further information about the scope of the Prints & Photographs online catalog and how to use it, consult the Prints & Photographs Online Catalog *HELP* document.

WHAT TO DO WHEN DESIRED IMAGES ARE NOT FOUND IN THE CATALOG

For further information about how to search for Prints & Photographs Division holdings not represented in the online catalog or in the lists of selected images, submit an email using the "Ask a Librarian" link on the Prints & Photographs Reading Room home page or contact: Prints & Photographs Reading Room, Library of Congress, 101 Independence Ave., SE, Washington, D.C. 20540-4730 (telephone: 202-707-6394).

2. The American Memory site (http://memory.loc.gov), a gateway to rich primary source materials relating to the history and culture of the United States. The site offers more than seven million digital items from more than 100 historical collections.

3. The Library of Congress Online Catalog (http://catalog.loc.gov/) contains approximately 13.6 million records representing books, serials, computer files, manuscripts, cartographic materials, music, sound recordings, and visual materials. It is especially useful for finding items identified as being from the Manuscript Division and the Geography and Map Division of the Library of Congress.

4. Built in America: Historic American Buildings Survey/Historic American Engineering Record, 1933–Present (http://memory.loc.gov/ammem/hhhtml/hhhome.html) describes and links to the catalog of the Historic American Buildings Survey (HABS) and the Historic American Engineering Record (HAER), among the most heavily represented collections on the CD-ROM.